STUDY GUIDE FOR KALAT'S

Introduction to Psychology

5TH EDITION

RUTH H. MAKI AND WILLIAM S. MAKI
Texas Tech University

with a Guide for Nonnative Speakers by
SALLY C. GEARHART
Santa Rosa Junior College

Brooks/Cole • Wadsworth
I(T)P® An International Thomson Publishing Company

Belmont • Albany • Bonn • Boston • Cincinnati • Detroit • Johannesburg • London • Madrid • Melbourne
Mexico City • New York • Pacific Grove • Paris • Singapore • Tokyo • Toronto• Washington

Senior Assistant Editor: *Faith Stoddard*
Editorial Assistant: *Stephanie M. Andersen*
Production Editor: *Mary Vezilich*
Cover Design: *E. Kelly Shoemaker*
Printing and Binding: *Mazer Corporation*

For more information, contact:

WADSWORTH PUBLISHING COMPANY
10 Davis Drive
Belmont, CA 94002
USA
http://www.thomson.com/wadsworth.html

International Thomson Editores
Seneca 53
Col. Polanco
11560 México, D. F., México

International Thomson Publishing Europe
Berkshire House 168-173
High Holborn
London WC1V 7AA
England

International Thomson Publishing Japan
Hirakawacho Kyowa Building, 3F
2-2-1 Hirakawacho
Chiyoda-ku, Tokyo 102
Japan

Thomas Nelson Australia
102 Dodds Street
South Melbourne, 3205
Victoria, Australia

International Thomson Publishing Asia
60 Albert Street
#15-01 Albert Complex
Singapore 189969

Nelson Canada
1120 Birchmount Road
Scarborough, Ontario
Canada M1K 5G4

International Thomson Publishing GmbH
Königswinterer Strasse
53227 Bonn
Germany

5   4   3   2   1

ISBN 0-534-35910-8

Acknowledgment
Our sincere thanks to Michele Patterson and Cara Warzynski who supplied the page references to the text and cross-referenced the objectives and the various types of test questions in the Study Guide.

CONTENTS

GETTING THE MOST OUT OF YOUR PSYCHOLOGY COURSE (AND COLLEGE)

You are about to begin to study a fascinating subject--psychology. In some ways, you have been studying psychology for years. You have always been observing, predicting, and trying to control human behavior. Now, however, you are going to learn about how psychologists study behavior using scientific methods. Psychology is inherently an interesting topic, so you should be motivated to learn more about it. This introduction is designed to help you get the most out of your psychology course and out of your college experience.

BEFORE THE COURSE BEGINS

Start with a Positive Attitude

What you believe can influence how well you do. In your text, you will read about an experiment by Greenwald, Spangenberg, Pratkanis, and Eskanazi (1991) in which students listened to tapes that were supposed to have subliminal (below threshold for perception) messages. The messages were about losing weight or about increasing self-esteem. The subliminal messages themselves had no effect, but students' expectancies did produce changes. Those students who thought that the tape should increase self-esteem did increase in self-esteem (even when the tapes contained no messages). So, thinking that they would be more self-confident made the students feel more self-confident.

Set Difficult, but Realistic, Goals

Expecting that you will do well in a course is the first step to doing well. But, thinking about doing well isn't enough. You need to produce a good study plan and stick to it to actually do well. Make a pronouncement at the beginning of the term that you will work as hard as possible to succeed in your courses. But, that's not enough. Set specific, difficult, but realistic, goals for each of your courses (getting all A's, a B average, or a C average--whatever is reasonable for you). In addition, set up a specific short-term goal for each test and assignment that you do for each course. Such goals will both help to increase your self-confidence and your performance (Locke and Latham, 1990). College instructors tend to give lower grades than high-school instructors, and the competition is much tougher. And yes, college instructors give Fs to students, even those who take all the tests (if, of course, they fail most of them). So, don't take success for granted. On the other hand, don't become discouraged. Set up realistic goals and work to meet them. Plan to reward yourself at the end of the term if you achieve your goal. The reward could be something like going on a camping trip to a favorite place, buying new clothes, or whatever might work to motivate you. Then, stick to your contingency plan. That is, give yourself the reward only if you meet your goal. Setting up smaller rewards for your short-term goals, such as getting a B on a test, is also a good idea.

Look Through Your Textbook.

You have already purchased your book, so you have accomplished the first step to succeeding in your introductory psychology course. Take a look at your text. Although you may think that you already know what psychology is, you probably don't have a good idea of what this course will be about (even if you took a course in high school). In college, psychology is generally taught as a scientific discipline. So, you will observe as you look through your text that there is a chapter on research methodology early in the book. That chapter is critical for you to understand how psychological research is done and why it is important to do research in psychology. Start with an open mind; you are about to study behavior in a way that you never have before. Look at the various chapters in your book so that you can see the range of topics that it covers. Yes, there is biology in psychology; understanding the biological underpinnings of behavior is an important component of the area of psychology known as psychobiology. Other psychologists study learning, memory, development, and language. As you look at your text, you will discover that personality and mental disorders are covered toward the end of the book. You can understand those topics much better after you understand the biology of behavior, the principles of learning, and the development of behavior. So, read through the chapter objectives in your book to prepare yourself for the topics that you will study in the course. Knowing what is coming will make you better able to integrate and understand the topics.

Find Some Friends (or Make Some) Who Are Taking the Course

One of the best ways to study is with a study group. Learning in a small group is a very effective way to learn. (Druckman & Bjork, 1994, Chapter 7). Such a group can force you to read the material and to understand it well enough to be able to present it to others. Four people is about the right number for your study group. Contact three other students and find a time once a week when you can meet for about 2 hours. Put this time into your schedule for the term and stick to it; plan to meet with your study group every week at the prearranged time. Make sure that you have serious students who are willing to spend the time both in and out of the study group to prepare for the course. Don't let anyone have a free ride. Everyone in the study group must be committed to learning as much as possible in the course.

Make a Practical Schedule

At most universities, you are expected to spend about 2-3 hours a week studying for every 1 hour a week that you are in class. This means that you should study about 6-9 hours a week for a course that meets 3 hours a week. If you are taking five such courses, this translates into a "workweek" of 35-45 hours. Think of studying as your job. (If you have another job, think of studying as a second job.) Be sure that you are able to schedule enough hours to do the "job" that you are actually paying to do. Yes, college is different from other types of jobs in that you are paying to do it (or someone else is, if you are fortunate enough to have financial assistance). The fact that you are paying to be in college makes it doubly important that you take it seriously and do your studying "job" competently.

So before classes begin, set up a schedule that you are likely to be able to follow. Put in all the things that you must do at specific times--classes, the times when your study groups for various classes have agreed to meet, your other job for which you are paid (if you have one), meetings that you must attend, time for family obligations, social activities, and so on. Then, see where you can schedule blocks of time for study. Unlike high school, you will probably have lots of free time between classes during the day. USE IT! Don't look at those 2 hours between classes and assume that it is time to waste, or time to sit around and talk with friends. Assume that your psychology class meets 2 hours after another class 3 days a week. Schedule those 2 hours to go to the library and study for psychology on those 3 days. If you use those 2 hours to study for psychology 3 times a week, you have arranged for almost all the time that you need to study for the course. Add 2 hours for a study group for psychology, plus an hour to review one night a week, and you have provided enough study time for one of your courses, psychology. Set up a similar schedule for your other courses. It is important that you set up a studying schedule **that will work for you**. If you always get hungry and eat lunch, don't put study time in the library from 11 to 1. You simply won't stick to it. Also, if you cannot sit still very long, don't schedule a block of 4 hours straight for study. Put a study place in your schedule and stick to it. For most students, going to your Union's dining center and planning to study will not work. Friends will join you, and soon you will be talking and not studying. So, before classes even begin, work up a schedule that fits your life-style, including both specific times for study and also places where you will study. Try your schedule for a while; if some part of it is not working, rearrange it and try the new schedule for a while. The important aspect of setting up such a schedule is that you end up studying at a constant rate. You will be "up" on the readings and you will not need to cram for tests.

If you've tried to set up a schedule based on 3 hours of studying per course and you simply could not fit in enough hours because of your other commitments, you should think about changing your course schedule. Don't take more courses than you have time for. It is better to take longer to get through college with good grades than either to fail your courses or to squeak through with a minimal GPA. Too easy a schedule can be a mistake also. So, before the term begins, you need to assess your situation accurately and decide whether you will have the time to handle the course schedule that you have set for yourself.

WHAT TO DO DURING CLASS

Go to Class

In most college courses, your instructor won't take attendance, and he or she may not even know whether you're there or not. Still, it is important to attend every class. One reason is that many instructors present material in class that is not in the textbook, and that material is often included on tests. If you miss classes, you miss important material, and you will miss more test questions. (And no, don't tell your instructor that you missed the last class, and ask her whether she "covered anything important." Of course she did; instructors always cover topics that they, at least, deem important.) Even if your instructor does not ask test questions that are directly related to lecture, but not covered in the book, he or she still probably uses the lecture to emphasize certain topics. There is a huge amount of material covered in your introductory psychology textbook. No one could possibly learn it all in one, or even two, academic terms. Thus, students can use the lecture to determine which topics the instructor finds most important (and probably most interesting). Those topics are likely to be overrepresented on tests relative to topics that your instructor did not discuss in class. You cannot know which specific topics will be emphasized on the test unless you attend every class and listen to what is being covered.

What to Do (and Not to Do) in the Classroom

You should attend class in order to learn. Hearing material, as well as reading it, will help you to understand and remember it better. If this is why you are attending class, why sit in the back of the room where both hearing and seeing will be more difficult? The backs of large classrooms are often noisy with students talking and otherwise disrupting the class. So, avoid the back. You have taken the time to come to class (and you have paid for it!), so sit in the front and make the most of it. Most of the best students sit in the front and they interact with the instructor. Sitting in front and being an active learner will both help you to learn better and help make the class more interesting to you. Even in very large classes, instructors usually get to know a few students who sit near the front and who interact with them.

Don't sit with your friends if you will end up talking with them during class. You should have "talk with friends" time in your schedule, and the middle of class isn't the time. Talking in class distracts the instructor, distracts your fellow students (who have also paid to attend the course), and means that you get less out of the course. If sitting with your friends means talking with them, sit somewhere else. And don't go to class either to read the newspaper or to study for tests in other classes. If those are your goals, go somewhere else where the lecturer won't distract you, and you won't distract the lecturer.

So, you are in class, and you have chosen a seat near the front where you can both see and hear well. You are all ready to pay attention and learn all you can. What do you do in class?

Listen, and *Understand* What Is Being Said

Listen carefully and ask questions if you do not understand what is being presented. If you are embarrassed to raise your hand in class, ask your instructor before or after class or during office hours. Or if you have a teaching assistant, find him or her during office hours. Another alternative is to write out your question and hand it to the instructor or leave it on the podium before the next class. Most instructors will make every effort to answer students' questions. Don't let material that is unclear go by--make every effort to understand it.

Take Notes

Taking notes improves class performance, and taking notes and reviewing those notes helps even more. Students take better notes with more experience in college. Notes become more organized, more selective, and more accurate (Van Meter, Yokoi, & Pressley, 1994). Your notes should differ depending upon what you will need to know for tests. If your instructor will want you to know definitions on a multiple-choice or a matching test, then you need to take down more verbatim facts. If, however, concepts will be stressed either on multiple-choice or essay tests, then you will need to write more general concepts in your notes (Van Meter et al., 1994). Whatever the final purpose of your notes, never try to write down everything verbatim without thinking about it. Try to pick out important points. After you understand a point, write it in your own words (unless it's a definition and you will need to know it verbatim for the test). Go back over your notes soon after class and put comments on them. While the lecture is still fresh in your mind, fill in gaps that you missed and clarify points that are fuzzy in your notes. Try to add some other examples or apply the concepts to other situations, and jot those down in your comments. Later, your notes, plus comments written very soon after the lecture, will make a great source to review for your tests.

An example of a good set of notes with comments written on them is shown on p. x. The student put the line down the left side before class. The class notes were written on the right side. The purpose of the left column is to add comments after class. The printed comments in the left column were added after the lecture to clarify the notes.

Make Up Missed Classes

If you have to miss class, get the notes from someone who takes good notes. (But do not miss class unless missing it is really necessary.) Don't assume that the material you missed won't be on the test; it surely will! Make an agreement in your study group that you will share notes with each other (but only when one member has a good reason for missing class). Even getting notes from someone won't be as good as being there yourself. Notes are personalized with material that the notetaker thought was important and material that the notetaker did not know before (Van Meter et al., 1994). Therefore, looking at two sets of notes would be a good idea. Go through one set of notes and write out your own notes in your own words. Then look at the other set of notes and fill in things that were missing from the first set and write in clarifications for the first set. Put in question marks where you don't understand something and be sure to have that clarified either in your study group or by your instructor or your teaching assistant.

GET THE MOST OUT OF YOUR STUDY TIME

The goal of studying is to understand and remember information so that it can be used at some later time: first, for tests in your course; later, as knowledge to help you better understand your experiences and solve real-world problems. If this broader goal is to be met, you need to understand material; simply memorizing terms and definitions is not enough. Most instructors will try to tap your understanding of material on tests. Understanding and applying material takes time, but the methods described below will make your studying more efficient and more effective than simply reading the textbook several times. As a student, your main job is to learn and apply information, so you should have already planned your time so that this can be accomplished on a regular basis, several times a week. Learning the material presented in your courses is a matter of getting information into memory and later getting it out. Chapter 7 of your textbook contains an entire chapter on memory processes, but those aspects that are specifically relevant to studying will be described below.

Sample Notes for Improving Memory Lecture

Date: *Wednesday, Oct. 17*	*Improving Memory by Using Mnemonic Devices* Text: Chap. 7
Mnemonic means memory in Greek	1. *Useful mnemonics*
Also called peg system	A. *Pegword*
	How does it work?
Need to be able to imagine thing you want to remember	*Uses words that rhyme with numbers (1 is a bun, 2 is a shoe)*
Imagery plus verbal code puts it into memory twice	*Make interacting image of rhyme and thing to be remembered*
	Go through rhyme at retrieval, pulling out images
	Useful for remembering imageable things in order (up to 10)
Originated by Greek speech-givers	B. *Method of loci (locations)*
	How does it work?
Can use rooms in home	*Uses well-learned locations along a route*
So, imagine what you want to buy in each place	*Make interacting image of location and thing to be remembered*
This is the retrieval plan	*Imagine walking though locations at retrieval, pulling out images*
	Useful for remembering imageable things in order (many)
	C. *First-letter mnemonic*
	How does it work?
Like "Every good boy does fine"	*Take first letter of words to form a sentence or story*
	Use the sentence or story to retrieve the first letters
	Useful for memorizing in order (many things)
Need to watch that you don't remember rhyme, but not real items	*May be difficult to get from first letter to term*
	D. *Keyword mnemonic*
	How does it work?
Need to be able to imagine keyword	*Turn unfamiliar term into English keyword that sounds similar*
	Make an image of keyword and meaning of term
	Unfamiliar term should result in retrieval of keyword plus image
	When can it be used?
Think of Russian word delo as jello	*Foreign language vocabulary*
Imagine a "cap race" with the leader changing often, for capricious	*English vocabulary*
Use for plant species in hierarchy- imagine angel for angiosperm	*Biological taxonomies*
	2. *Why do mnemonics work?*
A. and B. are the two main points about memory	A. *They promote a deep level of processing*
To remember well, you need to 1) get it in (encode) well	1. *Many use visual images which forces one to think of meaning*
2) get it out (retrieve)	2. *Most tie new material to already known material*
	B. *They give a good retrieval scheme to pull memory out*

Memory is Dependent Upon a High Level of Learning and Good Retrieval Cues

Research on memory has shown that the amount of time that information can be retained in memory is directly related to the level of learning. *Information that is overlearned* (learned perfectly and then studied beyond that point) *is remembered longer* than information that is just barely learned (Krueger, 1929). One way to ensure that material is learned well is to *process the information to a deep or meaningful level* (Craik & Tulving, 1975). Material that you thought of only in terms of surface structure (e.g., what do the words sound like?) is not as well remembered as information that you thought of in terms of its meaning (how is this concept similar to one that I already know?). Students often repeat a definition over and over to themselves with the idea that this will strengthen the concept in memory. Memorizing a definition word for word is unimportant; being able to use the word is much more important. Furthermore, experimental studies have shown that mere repetition does not increase the likelihood that the material will be recalled later. Craik and Watkins (1973) showed that words that had been repeated over and over for 12 seconds or more were not remembered any better than words that had been repeated for only 1 second. On the other hand, *repetition that involves thinking about the meaning of material and connecting it with information that is already known is effective in increasing memory.*

Effective Ways of Producing High Levels of Learning

Material that is understood is remembered better than material that is not understood (Bransford & Johnson, 1973). Understanding material means that you have tied it into concepts that you already know, and this is one of the ways to produce a meaningful memory. If you do not understand material, don't simply try to memorize it by repetition. This is not effective. It is almost certain that the material you do not understand will appear on the test, so spend the time to ask someone to help you understand it. A good test of understanding is to try to apply the material to real-life situations or to come up with some examples of your own.

Making images of concepts can help memory. Images may help because they result in both a visual and a verbal memory code (Paivio, Walsh, & Bons, 1994). Try to visualize concepts whenever possible! Making bizarre images can also help. Use bizarreness sparingly, however, because bizarre images are only remembered better when they are mixed in with common images (McDaniel, Einstein, DeLosh, May, & Brady, 1995) and when you will have to remember without many cues on your test (Riefer & LaMay, 1998).

Generating information can increase memory. Jacoby (1978) showed that generating answers, even if they were simple, led to better memory for the answers than simply reading them. Foos, Mora, and Tkacz (1994) found that generating outlines, questions, and answers led to better test performance than reading instructor-prepared materials. However, make sure your questions and outlines hit most of the main points because generating helps only on test questions directly related to what you generate. Anything that you can do to produce material rather than being a passive reader should help (Linden & Wittrock, 1981).

Repetitions of material should be distributed, not massed. Many experiments, using many different types of materials, have shown that repeating material immediately after the first presentation (massed presentation) does little to help memory. *Repeating material after other material has been presented* (distributed presentation) *does help memory* (e.g., Melton, 1970). Studying once a day for a week will lead to better memory later than studying the same material seven times during a single day (Bahrick Bahrick, Bahrick, & Bahrick, 1993). For example, reading your text twice with 24 hours between the first reading and the rereading will produce better memory than reading it twice with no time between the readings (Krug, Davis, & Glover, 1990). So, a good plan would be to read a chapter before your instructor is going to lecture on it and then to reread it 2-3 days later, after hearing the lecture. Plan your study time so that you can take advantage of the effects of distributed study. Don't put off studying until the last minute so that all you can do is massed study (otherwise known as cramming). It won't be very effective in the long run.

Retrieval Cues are Important to Get Information Out of Memory

Practice retrieving rather than spending all your time trying to input material into memory. Material that has been tested is remembered longer than material that wasn't tested (Runquist, 1983). Furthermore, testing yourself in a distributed way is also helpful. Gradually increasing the intervals at which you test yourself is better than always testing yourself after the same amount of time. For example, you might study material and then test yourself on it after one hour, then after three more hours, and then after a day has passed (Cull, Shaughnessy, & Zechmeister, 1996).

Retrieval is best when the conditions of testing match the conditions of learning (Tulving & Thomson, 1973). No matter how well you know material, you must ultimately show your knowledge by pulling the material out of memory. Simply getting it into memory is not enough; retrieval is also necessary. Many experiments have shown that if you think of a concept in one way while learning it, you will need to think of it in the same way when your memory is tested. Otherwise, you may not be able to remember it. If you are going to have essay tests, plan how you would answer a question. Learn a series of key words that will help you to recall each point. You might find that a mnemonic system, such as the method of loci described in Chapter 7, could be helpful. If you are going to take a multiple-choice test, try to think of the concept in as many different ways as possible. *The more ways that you store a concept in memory, the more likely that your understanding will match one of the alternatives on the test.* Nitsch (1977/1979) has shown that people can better recognize a concept that is tested in a new way if they have learned with varied examples. So, try to think of as many different examples and ways of understanding a concept as you can.

Similar physical conditions at encoding and retrieval help. The match between study and test is also true for environmental conditions. There is some evidence that studying and being tested in the same room might help (Smith, Glenberg, & Bjork, 1978). However, don't worry if your tests are in a different place from your lectures. Saufley, Otaka, and Bavaresco (1985) found that students who took tests in rooms that were different from their classrooms did not do any worse than students who took tests in their classrooms. If you learn material well and in several different environments, you will probably be able to remember the material in any setting. However, there is some interesting recent evidence that suggests that the music you listen to may affect your ability to learn and remember on tests. Balch, Bowman, and Mohler (1992) found that students who read text material while listening to music that had words remembered less of what they read than students who either listened to no music or who listened to music without words. They also found that students who listened to either classical music or jazz while studying did better on tests when listening to that same music during the tests. Your instructor probably won't want you to listen to tape recorded music during your tests (he or she may become suspicious about what you're listening to if you have an ear phone in your ear). So, your best bet is to study without music. This is particularly true if you are introverted. Music is distracting to introverts and listening while reading results in poorer memory for material (Furnham & Bradley, 1997). Instead of listening to music while studying, use music as a reward. After you have studied for an hour with no music, take a 15- minute music and refreshment break and listen to your favorite music, undisturbed by studying.

Using Your Study Group

Each week your study group should meet for about 2 hours; that time should be used for studying, not visiting. (You may plan to all go out afterward for an hour to visit, but visiting should be avoided during the study-group time itself.) Groups will need to work out their own study procedures, but here is a schedule that will make the group efficient in studying.

Last Week's Material

1. Each member should have written questions over a part of the material as assigned at the last meeting. During the week, group members should write answers to all question. The study session should begin by trading the written answers to questions and having everyone "grade" someone else's questions. The textbook and notes should be used to ensure accurate grading.

2. A discussion about any difficult concepts or frequently missed questions should follow until everyone understands each answer.

This Week's Material

3. Each group member will have been assigned a topic to "teach" (perhaps a section from the chapter, or from a recent lecture). How you break up the material may depend upon how much the instructor takes out of the book on tests and how much he or she takes out of lecture.

4. Each group member should "teach" the other members his or her assigned material. All group members should feel free both to ask questions and to clarify concepts as each person teaches.

Next Week's Assignments

5. Everyone should have looked at what is coming next week and have an idea about what topic he or she would like to teach next. Part of the assignment will be to write about five questions on the topic; the other part of the assignment will be to prepare to teach it. Study groups may find other procedures that work for them. However, using the group to provide tests for each other is an essential aspect of the study plan. Use of the study group is incorporated into the SPAR system described below

SPAR: A Method of Studying

The SPAR method is a study method that should help you to incorporate the guidelines described above. It was developed by Rusche (1984) and is similar to the SQ3R method (presented in Chapter 7), but it is easier to remember the key words that go with SPAR than with SQ3R (people forget the three Rs). **SPAR** stands for **S**urvey, **P**rocess meaningfully, **A**sk questions, and **R**eview and self-test. Application of this method, with your textbook and study guide, lecture material, and study group, will be described.

Survey

The main goal here is to ask "What am I to learn?" Having a general idea of the topics will help you to tie the material in with concepts that you already know.

Textbook and Study Guide

First, look at the Outline of the chapter in your book. This gives you an overview of the contents of the chapter. Next, read through the introductory material in the chapter to give you some idea about how the ideas presented in the chapter are relevant in everyday life. At the beginning of each section, there are questions that will be answered in the section. Think about how you would answer them before reading the chapter. There is a Summary at the end of each section. Read each point in the summary and think about what type of information would be needed to understand that point. The last part of each section in the text contains *The message*. These are good summaries of the main points of a chapter. Finally, read the Objectives in the study guide for a more detailed idea about the specific concepts to be learned.

Lecture

Look at your course outline or syllabus so you know what your instructor will cover each day. Read the relevant material in your textbook before going to class so that you will have the background for the topic.

Study Group

At the end of each weekly meeting, assignments of topics should be made for the next week. Looking over the upcoming material in order to agree on topic assignments will also serve the Survey function in SPAR. Each member should be assigned a specific topic to teach the next week and also to emphasize in writing questions.

Process Meaningfully

The main goal here is to understand the material in a meaningful way, that is, to process it deeply and produce a high level of learning.

Textbook and Study Guide

Read the chapter carefully. Do your first reading of the chapter before your instructor lectures on the topic. Stop and think about what you have read at the end of each section. Don't just try to recite what is in each section-- understanding is critical. Try to relate material to what you already know. Think of other examples of the concepts. If you can form visual images of the concepts, do so. Answer the questions that are asked in the Concept Check sections of each chapter. Try to answer the questions in the Something to Think About sections. Remember, it is better to generate answers than simply to read. If your instructor has assigned more than one section, it would probably be better to work with only one section at a time.

Lecture

Go back over your notes soon after class and put comments in the left column. While the lecture is still fresh in your mind, fill in gaps that you missed and clarify points that are fuzzy in your notes. Try to add some other examples or apply the concepts to other situations, and jot those down in your comments. See the sample notes given earlier.

Study Group

One of the best ways to learn is to teach others. Presenting material to other individuals forces one to process it meaningfully. Each member of the study group will need to process some of the material very meaningfully in order to "teach" the other members. "Knowing" something requires far less processing than "teaching" something. However, everyone should read all of the material and process it meaningfully as described above.

Ask Questions

The goal here is to anticipate the types of questions that you will be asked later, so you will have practice in picking out the main concepts.

Textbook and Study Guide

The study guide will make this portion of SPAR easy because the questions are provided. Complete the Comprehension Check portion of the study guide soon after reading the relevant section. The questions are similar to those that are likely to appear on a multiple-choice test. The questions, alternatives, and explanations include the terms that are described at the back of each textbook chapter in the Terms to Remember section. Circle the answer to each question without looking at your text.

Check your answer. If your answer is wrong, write the correct answer in the blank beneath the question. Look up the concept on the page in your text indicated beside the correct answer. Write why your answer was wrong. Check your reason against that given in the study guide. If you want to remember the concept better, it is important that you generate the reason rather than simply reading it in the study guide. Also, look at why the other alternatives are wrong to be sure that you understand the concepts tested in the question. If you still do not understand, reread the section of text that is associated with the objective tested in the question. If that does not help, ask your instructor or teaching assistant to explain the concept to you.

Lecture

Go back over your lecture notes. Write questions of the type given under the Short-Answer Essay section of your study guide. Try to write one question for each main point discussed in lecture. It is important that you write the questions, so you can use them later. Be sure that your questions are relevant to the material and that they are not too general, but also not too specific. Examples of good questions over the notes on memory are given below.

Sample Questions from Memory Improvement Lecture

1. *How does the pegword system work? How is it similar to and different from the Method of Loci ?*

2. *Describe how the keyword system can be used to remember definitions for abstract words?*

3. *How do all mnemonic systems encourage a deep level of processing?*

4. *In what ways do mnemonic systems work as effective retrieval schemes?*

Study Group

Here's where the study group really comes in. You can answer not only your own questions, but those written by the other members of your group. Each member of the group should be responsible for a specific topic. Part of the responsibility should be to write at least five questions on that topic that could be answered by the other group members. Short-answer questions are probably best. Because you have the study guide with questions covering text material, you should mostly write questions that focus on lecture material. After each group member has "taught" his or her topic, the questions prepared by group members should be passed out. Actually, simply preparing the written questions is a great way to learn.

Review and Self-Test

The main goal here is to test your memory and understanding of the material by answering questions of the type that will appear on a test.

Textbook and Study Guide

Presumably you have already read all of the assigned sections in a chapter and completed the comprehension check in the study guide. Wait at least 24 hours before going on. This will allow you to forget material that was not processed meaningfully enough. It is important that you find out which material was not well learned before the actual test in your course. Now, return to the study guide. Write out answers to the short-answer essay questions for the chapter. The questions require retrieval from memory with few cues, so that your level of learning can be tested. If you can write answers under these conditions, you know the material well enough to do well on any kind of test. The study guide provides answers to these questions so you can check yourself. It also provides the page in the textbook where the answer appears. Don't simply read the answers. You know by now that generating answers is important for later memory. Once you have checked your answer, keep trying to answer the questions yourself until you can produce a correct answer from memory without the textbook or your notes. Now take the posttest and check your answers using the page references to look up errors.

Lecture

Write answers to the questions that you wrote over lecture material. Check your answers against your notes. If you cannot produce a good answer to a question, get some help. Once you have a good answer to each question, keep trying to produce that answer from memory without using your notes or text.

Study Group

During the week, each group member should write answers to the questions prepared by other group members, as well as those he or she wrote, without looking at the book or notes. This should be done during the week between your meetings. At the beginning of the next meeting, you can exchange your answers, and everyone can "grade" someone else's. The group should discuss errors and make sure that everyone understands the concepts, especially those that were missed on the "test."

PREPARING FOR TESTS

If you have followed all of the above advice, you will be almost ready for the test when it comes. There should be no need to do massive cramming on the night before the test. However, you should add an extra hour or two to review the material. Use the materials produced in your study group. Take out those short-answer questions that the members of your group wrote and write answers again. Write the answers to the short-answer questions in the study guide again. Spend some time scoring your answers and also look back at your original answers. What have you forgotten this time that you knew before? Have you corrected earlier mistakes, as judged by the answers that were "graded" by your study group? Look over your notes, paying specific attention to your comments. Did you get the answers to issues that you had questions about? Look at the chapter outlines in the study guide and in the textbook. Can you give a sentence or two explaining each topic? When you know all of the answers well, take the posttest without using your book or notes. Score the test. If you made an error, look up the correct answer on the page given. The study guide also provides numbers of questions that test the same concept in the Comprehension Check and the Short-Answer Essay sections. Look back and see if you understood those questions and why the alternatives on the Comprehension Check were wrong. If would be a good idea to review the posttest questions, the objectives in the study guide, and the summary in the text just before you take the test in your course.

Watch Out for Overconfidence

There are many studies in psychology (e.g., Fischhoff, Slovic, & Lichtenstein, 1977) that show that college students tend to be overconfident. This is particularly true when tests are difficult (Schraw & Roedel, 1994). This means that you may go into a test thinking that you know more than you do. One of the best ways to combat overconfidence is to take a practice test that is as similar as possible to the actual test (Glover, 1989). However, make sure that the practice test is very similar; just answering a few questions may not predict how well you will do on an actual test (Maki & Serra, 1992). Probably, the best way to ensure against overconfidence is to take a test that is more demanding than the actual test. For example, if your test will be multiple-choice and you practice with short-answer essays, you probably won't be overconfident because essay tests demand more knowledge than multiple-choice tests. If your actual test will be short-answer essay, then using multiple-choice practice tests to gauge your level of knowledge would not be a good idea. Multiple-choice tests would be fine to use as part of your study, but do not assume that if you get everything correct on a multiple-choice practice test that you will be able to do well on a short-answer essay test. Write some essay questions for yourself or use essay questions produced by your study group, and use your performance on those to judge how well you will do on the actual test. Try to make your practice-test experience as similar as you can to the actual test, and better yet, make your practice-test experience more demanding than the actual test is likely to be.

TAKING TESTS

General Advice for All Types of Tests

Be Prepared and Arrive Early at the Test Site

Have everything that you need for the test. If you are to use a special ID number, make sure that you have found that before the test. If you need to use a special pencil or test booklet, make sure to have those with you. Arrive a few minutes early for the test. If you are allowed to select a seat, find a seat where distractions will be minimal. If students turn in their tests when they are finished, sit in a place where they will not be walking around you. In an auditorium, the best seats are in the middle of a row where students will not step over you. Don't sit near the place where the tests are to be turned in and don't sit near the door. If other students do begin to leave and you are not finished yet, don't panic. You will be allowed the full test time and if you do the test carefully and check your answers, you will probably need most of the time. Assume that those "early birds" did not know the material and guessed at most of the answers.

Begin the Test By Surveying It

You will probably have a time limit on your test. Still, begin by reading the test instructions and listening to any instructions or corrections given in class. Knowing what you are doing will save time in the end. Get an idea of how long the test is. Make sure that you have all the pages by checking that the question numbers are sequential.

Ask Questions

If you really don't understand a question, either put up your hand or walk up and ask the instructor or teaching assistant. Don't just answer the question based on one interpretation when there is another reasonable interpretation. Ask for clarification. If you don't know a word in a question, ask for a definition. If it is a word that you should know, your instructor probably won't give you the definition, but it doesn't hurt to ask.

Pace Yourself

If the room does not have a clock, wear a watch. Allow yourself enough time to finish the test. For example, if you are supposed to answer 50 questions in 50 minutes, you should average no more than 1 minute per question. Periodically, check yourself to be sure that your pace is right.

Don't Cheat

Learning the material in your courses will have lifelong benefits to you. The knowledge that you gain from your college courses will allow you to better understand and solve a lifetime's worth of problems. Doing well on tests by looking at your "brilliant" friend's answers or by using cheat sheets will gyp you of useful knowledge. Cheating also degrades the value of an education for everyone. If college graduates have not learned the knowledge expected of them because they cheated, the value of a college education is lessened. Furthermore, most universities have severe penalties for cheating. You could fail the test, fail the course, or even be suspended from school. So, don't be tempted to cheat. Instead, learn the material, and there is no need to consider being dishonest.

Taking Multiple-Choice Tests

Watch the Wording of Questions

Words like always and never mean there are no exceptions. Something always occurs or it never occurs. Such alternatives are usually (although not always) wrong. Few facts in psychology are that absolute.

Pick the Best Answer

One answer may be correct under most circumstances and another answer may be correct under a more general set of circumstances. Select the answer that is most generally correct and that has the fewest exceptions. Don't immediately choose a, if a seems correct. Answer b may be correct also and perhaps even better. You are supposed to choose the best answer, not just one that is partly or possibly correct. Also, some instructors use double-answer questions. Both **a** and **b** may be correct and the correct answer is e, both a and b. Always read all of the alternatives before selecting the best one.

Watch for Negative Questions

Read the question carefully and note if it contains a negative, such as "not" or "isn't." Many students miss that little word and select an alternative that is true. What they don't notice is that the question asked the student to select the alternative that is <u>not</u> true. Allow yourself some extra time to answer "not" questions and be sure to double-check your answer carefully.

Mark out Incorrect Alternatives

Read each question and mark off the alternatives that you know are wrong. Don't be hasty about this. Read each alternative carefully, filling it in as the answer. If you're sure the answer is wrong, mark it out. Then, select the best choice among the items you did not eliminate.

Skip the Difficult Questions

If you are not certain about your answer, skip the question and go back to it later when you will know how much time you can afford to spend on it. (But don't forget to come back to the ones you omitted!)

Avoid Interference from Incorrect Alternatives

Research on memory has shown that it is sometimes harder to recognize (select) an answer that is embedded in other similar answers than to simply recall it from memory (Tulving & Thomson, 1973). Thus, for those difficult questions that you skipped, you might do better to turn the multiple-choice test into a short-answer test. When you go back to those questions, cover the alternatives and try to write what you think should be the correct answer. Then, look at the alternatives that you haven't eliminated as being wrong, and see which one best matches what you wrote. Choose that answer.

Make your Best Guess

After you have gone through the test twice and eliminated wrong alternatives, make your best guess among the remaining choices. Because you have already marked out alternatives that you know are wrong, your chance of getting the question correct has improved. It's 50% if there are only two remaining alternatives.

Don't Pay Attention to Patterns

Instructors usually don't look at the pattern of correct answers until after the test is printed. Some intentionally use a random-number sequence to determine the order of answers, so it's possible that the correct answer might be the same alternative on many consecutive questions, or that the correct answers might accidentally form some pattern. Select the best answer for each item and don't worry if there seems to be too many of one alternative or if the alternatives form a pattern.

Put your Answers on the Answer Sheet Carefully

If your answers need to go on a special answer sheet, it is probably a good idea to wait until you have circled the answers to all questions before transferring them to the answer sheet. Make sure that you are on the right question as you mark the answer sheet. After you have transferred your answers, take an extra minute to check to ensure that the circled answer for each question is what you placed on the answer sheet.

Check your Answers

When you finish, if you have time available, check your answers to each question. You may catch some mistakes.

Taking Essay Tests

Take a Few Minutes to Read all the Questions

This is particularly important if your instructor allows you to choose which of several questions you can answer. Look over all the questions and make a decision about which item you know the best. Start by answering your best questions. They will go quickly and allow you to build confidence.

Outline your Answers

Many essay questions have several parts. Jot down each part. Some instructors grade by assigning specific numbers of points to specific parts of the essay. Whether or not this is the case with your instructor, you will probably get more credit for your answer if you specifically address each point in your answer. It is probably a good idea to write a short heading and underline it for each part. This will force you to organize your answer in line with the question and it will also make grading easier for your instructor. He or she will see that you have answered all parts.

Don't Add Irrelevant Material

The point of essay answers is not to write everything you know that is tangentially related to a topic. The point is to write what you know that is directly related to the topic. Going off on tangents won't impress the graders with your knowledge. Such extraneous material is likely to annoy them because they have to search for the correct answer. Make it easy for graders by just giving relevant information in an organized form.

Don't Answer Questions that Weren't Asked

This is related to the irrelevant material discussed above. If you really know nothing about a topic, then you are in trouble and, chances are, you have not followed the guidelines listed above. Don't try to weasel out by answering some question other than what was asked. Write whatever you know about the topic and leave it at that. And study harder the next time!

Write Legibly

Some instructors (including this one) simply give up if they have difficulty reading an answer (and they are unlikely to assume that the correct answer is really there without reading it). Thus, try to write as legibly as possible. If you have poor handwriting, try printing your answers or try to write larger than usual. Whatever you can do to make your handwriting more legible will help you in the long run.

Taking Matching Tests

Understand the Rules

The most important point here is to understand the rules of the matching tests. If your instructor did not tell you, then ask. (You do have a right to know the constraints on the test.) Is each alternative used only once, or can some be used multiple times? Is there, in fact, a match for each item? Find out these things before you start.

Write in the Answers that You Know

The whole matching item might look overwhelming, but once you have written answers that you are sure of, you may do much better on the rest. This is much easier if each alternative is used only once. You can simply cross off those that you are sure of and you greatly reduce the number that you need to use for the remaining items. If alternatives can be used more than once, then you might look for items that are similar to those that you know and put in the same alternatives.

Work with one item at a time

Take a single item on the matching test and compare it with each alternative individually. You might even put the number of the item beside an alternative if you think it might match. Then go through those that you have put the item number beside and make it a multiple-choice test. Mark out the alternatives that seem less likely until you are left with only one in ideal circumstances, or more in less-than-ideal circumstances. If you cannot decide among several alternatives, simply guess. You have already improved your chances by eliminating many of the potential match items.

Learn from Your Errors

Understand Your Wrong Answers

Always look over your test when you get it back (or go and look at the key if your instructor posts one). Check your test and make yourself aware of which items you have gotten right and which are wrong. Don't be "sick of it" and not look at a test after it's over and graded. The test provides a great learning experience, particularly if your instructor gives a cumulative final. The material that you missed will probably be back on the final, so keep your tests to study for the final exam.

Use the Test Experience to Analyze Your Study Plan

If you met your goal on the test, then you know that you are studying appropriately. Keep doing what you have been doing; your study plan works! If you did worse than you realistically expected, then you either need to change your study plan, find more time for study, or change your goal. Changing your study plan should be the first step. Go back over your plan and see whether you could use some of your time more efficiently. Is your study group working or do they spend half the study time visiting? Are you really using those hours between classes? Are you following through on your study plan? For example, are you writing answers to questions or are you just looking at them and assuming that you know them? When you make an error on a question while studying, are you going back to really understand why you were wrong and why another answer is correct? If you really are giving the course all the time that you can and if you really have an efficient study plan that you are following, you may have to reset your goals. Perhaps, getting an A in the course is not realistic. Change your expectations to settle for a B (but don't settle for much less--there is always a way to improve your study plan).

IF YOU HAVE PROBLEMS

There are a number of things to do if you find you are not doing as well on your tests as you wish. Visit your instructor or your teaching assistant during office hours. They may have some specific ideas about how you can do better in the course you are taking. Don't be afraid to go to your instructor's office during office hours. Even when they are teaching large classes, most instructors are alone during office hours. Students rarely go to see them. Even if things aren't going badly, you should always feel free to visit your instructor and discuss either your progress in the course or an issue that is of interest to you. If you still have problems with a course, try your university's counseling center. They have a staff who is trained to help you. Use them, even if your problem is not severe. You probably have an advisor who can help you also. Go and talk with him or her when you begin to have difficulty. Find out about your school's drop policy. Can you still drop the course that is causing the problems without penalty? If you are overloaded (which you should know before classes start when you make up your schedule), drop the excess courses immediately. Don't think that you will start with more courses than you have time for and later drop the worst one. By that time, you have already spread yourself too thin and hurt your performance in all of your courses. Set up a reasonable load and then stick with it.

FINAL NOTE

It is true that all of this takes a long time. However, learning a great deal of new material, as is necessary in any college-level course, is not easy. The procedures suggested here will make you much more efficient than if you simply read and reread your text. These studying techniques will pay off, and as you get better at using them, they will become easier. The key point in all of this is to BE ACTIVE. The less time you spend passively reading and the more time you spend actively generating answers and testing yourself, the better you will do on tests in your course. And generating answers makes studying much more interesting than simply reading and reading and reading. The topics covered in this textbook are exciting and useful in everyday life. May you learn them well and use them for your entire lifetime!

REFERENCES

Bahrick, H. P., Bahrick, L. E., Bahrick, A. S., and Bahrick, P. E. (1993). Maintenance of foreign language vocabulary and the spacing effect. *Psychological Science, 4*, 316-322.

Balch, W. R., Bowman, K., and Mohler, L. A. (1992). Music-dependent memory in immediate and delayed word recall. *Memory and Cognition, 20*, 21-28.

Bransford, J. D., and Johnson, M. K. (1973). Consideration of some problems of comprehension. In William G. Chase (Ed.), *Visual information processing*. New York: Academic Press.

Craik, F. I. M., and Tulving, E. (1975). Depth of processing and the retention of words in episodic memory. *Journal of Experimental Psychology: General, 104*, 268-294.

Craik, F. I. M., and Watkins, M. J. (1973). The role of rehearsal in short-term memory. *Journal of Verbal Learning and Verbal Behavior, 12*, 599-607.

Cull, W. L., Shaughnessy, J. J., & Zechmeister, E. B. (1996). Expanding understanding of the expanding-pattern-of-retrieval mnemonic: Toward confidence in applicability. *Journal of Experimental Psychology: Applied, 2*, 365-378.

Druckman, D., and Bjork, R. A. (Eds.). (1994). *Learning, remembering, believing: Enhancing human performance.* Washington, D. C.: National Academy Press.

Fischhoff, B., Slovic, P., and Lichtenstein, S. (1977). Knowing with certainty: The appropriateness of extreme confidence. *Journal of Experimental Psychology: Human Perception and Performance, 3,* 552-564.

Foos, P. W., Mora, J. J., Tkacz, S. (1994). Student study techniques and the generation effect. *Journal of Educational Psychology, 86,* 567-576.

Furnham, A., & Bradley, A. (1997). Music while you work: The differential distraction of background music on the cognitive test performance of introverts and extraverts. *Applied Cognitive Psychology, 11,* 445-455.

Glover, J. A. (1989). Improving readers' estimates of learning from text: The role of inserted questions. *Reading Research Quarterly, 28,* 68-75.

Greenwald, A. G., Spangenberg, E. R., Pratkanis, A. R., and Eskenazi, J. (1991). Double-blind tests of subliminal self-help audiotapes. *Psychological Science, 2,* 119-122.

Haenggi, D., and Perfetti, C. A. (1992). Individual differences in reprocessing of text. *Journal of Educational Psychology, 84,* 182-192.

Jacoby, L. L. (1978). On interpreting the effects of repetition: Solving problems versus remembering solutions. *Journal of Verbal Learning and Verbal Behavior, 17,* 649-667.

Krueger, W. C. F. (1929). The effects of overlearning on retention. *Journal of Experimental Psychology, 12,* 71-78.

Krug, D., Davis, T. B., and Glover, J. A. (1990). Massed versus distributed repeated reading: A case of forgetting helping recall? *Journal of Educational Psychology, 82,* 366-371.

Linden, M., and Wittrock, M. C. (1981). The teaching of reading comprehension according to the model of generative learning. *Reading Research Quarterly, 17,* 45-57.

Locke, E. A., and Latham, G. P. (1990). *A theory of goal setting and task performance.* New York: Prentice-Hall.

McDaniel, M. A., Einstein, G. O., DeLosh, E. L., May, C. P., Brady, P. (1995). The bizarreness effect: It's not surprising, it's complex. *Journal of Experimental Psychology: Learning, Memory, and Cognition, 21,* 422-425.

Maki, R. H., and Serra, M. (1992). Role of practice tests in the prediction of test performance over text material. *Journal of Educational Psychology, 84,* 200-210.

Melton, A. W. (1970). The situation with respect to the spacing of repetitions and memory. *Journal of Verbal Learning and Verbal Behavior, 9,* 596-606.

Nitsch, K. E. (1977). Structuring de-contextualized forms of knowledge. (Doctoral dissertation, Vanderbilt University) as cited in J. D. Bransford. (1979). *Human cognition.* Belmont, Calif.: Wadsworth.

Paivio, A., Walsh, M., and Bons, T. (1994). Concreteness effects on memory: When and why? *Journal of Experimental Psychology: Learning, Memory, and Cognition, 20,* 1196-124.

Riefer, D. M.; & LaMay, M. L. (1998). Memory for common and bizarre stimuli: A storage-retrieval analysis. *Psychonomic Bulletin & Review, 5,* 312-317.

Runquist, W. (1983). Some effects of remembering on forgetting. *Memory and Cognition,, 11,* 641-650.

Rusche, K. M. (1984). The effectiveness of study skills training for students of different personality types and achievement levels. (Doctoral dissertation, Loyola University).

Saufley, W. H., Jr., Otaka, S. R., and Bavaresco, J. L. (1985). Context effects: Classroom tests and context independence. *Memory and Cognition, 13,* 522-528.

Schraw, G., and Roedel, T. D. (1994). Test difficulty and judgment bias. *Memory and Cognition, 22,* 63-69.

Smith, S. M., Glenberg, A., and Bjork, R. A. (1978). Environmental context and human memory. *Memory and Cognition, 6,* 342-353.

Tulving, E., and Thomson, D. M. (1973). Encoding specificity and retrieval processes in episodic memory. *Psychological Review, 80,* 352-373.

Van Meter, P., Yokoi, L., Pressley, M. (1994). College students' theory of note-taking derived from their perceptions of note-taking. *Journal of Educational Psychology, 86,* 323-338.

Introduction

CHAPTER 1 WHAT IS PSYCHOLOGY?

OBJECTIVES

Understand that:

I. Psychology is the systematic study of behavior and experience (p. 5)

Types of Psychologists

II. Psychology had its start in philosophy, and some philosophical issues are still important in psychology (p. 5)
    A. Free will vs. determinism (pp. 5-6)
        1. Does behavior have predictable natural causes or are some choices unpredictable? (p. 5-6)
    B. Mind-brain problem (p. 6-7)
        1. How does brain activity relate to behavior and experience? (p. 7)
    C. Nature-nurture issue (pp. 8)
        1. Are differences in behavior due to heredity or environment? (p. 8)
III. What psychologists do (pp. 8-10, Figure 1.4)
    A. Some psychologists teach and do research in universities (pp. 9-10)
        1. Biopsychologists are interested in the nervous system, effects of drugs and hormones, genetics, effects of brain damage, and drugs (p. 9)
        2. Psychologists interested in learning and motivation focus on how the outcomes of past behavior affects present behavior (p. 9)
        3. Cognitive psychologists study how people think and acquire knowledge (pp. 9-10)
        4. Developmental psychologists study behavioral capacities typical of different ages (p. 10)
        5. Social psychologists study how individuals influence each other (p. 10)
    B. Clinical psychologists and psychotherapists usually work in practice settings (p. 10)
        1. Clinical psychologists specialize in understanding and helping people with problems (p. 11)
        2. Psychiatrists are medical doctors who deal with emotional disturbance (p. 11)
        3. Psychoanalysts emphasize the methods of Freud (p. 11)
    C. There are other types of non-clinical applied psychologists (pp. 11-13, Table. 1.2)
        1. Industrial/organizational psychologists study people at work (pp. 11-12)
        2. Ergonomics (human factors) psychologists study people-machine interactions (pp. 12-13)
        3. School psychologists deal with the psychology of students (p. 13)
IV. Psychology is a good major to prepare for many careers (p. 13)
    A. Women receive over half of the doctorates in psychology (p. 14)
    B. Minority representation in psychology is growing, but the percentage is still small (p. 14)
The message: *Psychologists do very different things but they are dedicated to understanding psychological processes through research. (pp.14-15)*

Psychology Then and Now

V. The early era of psychology was 1879 to 1920 (p. 18)
    A. Wundt founded the first psychology laboratory in 1879 (p. 18)
        1. Psychological experience is composed of compounds (p. 18)
    B. Titchener tried to describe the structures of mind (p. 19)
    C. William James focused on how the mind produces useful behavior (p. 19-20)
    D. Early psychologists studied psychophysics, the relationship between perceived stimulus intensity and actual physical intensity (p. 20)
    E. Darwin's theory spurred the study of animal intelligence (pp. 20-21)
    F. Galton focused on human intelligence (pp. 21-22)

G. Mary Calkins and Margaret Washburn were early female psychologists (p. 22)
VI. Behaviorists dominated psychology from about 1920 to 1960 or 1970 (p. 22)
    A. John B. Watson argued that psychology should be totally objective (p. 23)
    B. Clark Hull tried to create an equation to account for maze learning (p. 23)
VII. Psychology today is very diverse (p. 23)
    A. There is increasing interest in differences among people (pp. 23-24)
    B. There has been increasing interest in understanding the brain (p. 24)

The message: *Psychologists don't have all the answers but they continue to search through research.* (p. 24)

COMPREHENSION CHECK

Answer these questions soon after reading the chapter. Circle the underlined best alternative. Check your answers on pp. 5-6 of the study guide. If you gave a wrong answer, try to write why it was wrong. Understanding your wrong answers can be a better learning experience than giving the right answer. Check your reasons on pp. 5-6 of the study guide.

Goals of Psychologists

1. Psychology is the systematic study of:
    a. conscious thought
    b. human behavior
    c. abnormal behavior
    d. behavior and experience
    e. techniques for manipulating and tricking people

Correct _____ If wrong, why? _____

2. According to determinism:
    a. choices cannot be predicted
    b. unpredictability implies a lack of causes
    c. everything people do has a physical cause
    d. much of human behavior is caused by random factors
    e. physical events have natural causes, but human decisions are guided by free will

Correct _____ If wrong, why? _____

3. Chaos theory proposes that:
    a. events aren't unpredictable; they could be predicted if we knew the many small causes
    b. unpredictability comes from a lack of causes
    c. human behavior results from indeterminism
    d. only large influences affect final outcomes
    e. human behavior is beyond the reach of the natural sciences

Correct _____ If wrong, why? _____

4. What do research studies, such as those measuring brain activity, say about the mind-brain problem?
   a. they show how mind controls the brain
   b. they constrain the answers that philosophers can give to this problem
   c. they show that mind and brain are two names for the same thing
   d. they indicate the independence of mind and brain
   e. they show that brain activity causes thoughts

Correct _____ If wrong, why? _____

5. A researcher attempts to determine whether a personality trait is inherited or learned. Which philosophical issue is she addressing?
   a. nature vs. nurture
   b. chaos theory versus indeterminism
   c. free will vs. determinism
   d. mind-brain problem

Correct _____ If wrong, why? _____

6. What does a biopsychologist study?
   a. the influence of the nervous system, drugs, genetics, and brain damage on behavior
   b. thinking and acquiring knowledge
   c. behavioral capabilities at different ages
   d. the influence of experience on behavior

Correct _____ If wrong, why? _____

7. A psychologist taking which approach would argue that "people differ from one another because some of them know more than others about a particular topic"?
   a. social
   b. clinical
   c. behavioral neuroscientist
   d. cognitive

Correct _____ If wrong, why? _____

8. A child's parents believe that boys are aggressive. Indeed, the son is aggressive. To what would a social psychologist attribute the child's aggressiveness?
   a. the child is living up to (or down to) the expectations of his parents
   b. the child's is part of his nature
   c. the child has been rewarded for past aggression
   d. the child has some subtle damage in a specific part of the brain

Correct _____ If wrong, why? _____

9. Which type of psychologist would try to help a person who has trouble making decisions?
    a. human factors psychologist
    b. developmental psychologist
    c. clinical psychologist
    d. school psychologist

Correct _____ If wrong, why? _____

10. Dr. Psyche has an M.D. degree and his specialty is helping people with emotional problems. He sometimes prescribes drugs for his patients. He is a:
    a. clinical psychologist
    b. psychiatrist
    c. psychoanalyst
    d. experimental psychologist

Correct _____ If wrong, why? _____

11. Women constitute:
    a. 11.4% of all psychologists
    b. just over 80% of all graduate students in psychology
    c. over 50% of all graduate students in psychology
    d. less than 30% of all psychologists, and the number is declining

Correct _____ If wrong, why? _____

Psychology Then and Now
12. Wundt's main question was:
    a. what are the components of experience?
    b. can questions about mind be answered philosophically?
    c. how does the mind produce useful behavior?
    d. how do the consequences of behavior strengthen behavior?
    e. why do some men become eminent?

Correct _____ If wrong, why? _____

13. How did Darwin's theory affect psychology?
    a. his work showed Hull that mathematical equations could be used to describe learning
    b. his finding that physical stimuli and perceived stimuli are not directly proportional began the study of psychophysics
    c. his work implied that animals have intelligence, and comparative psychologists began to study it
    d. his work showed that it was easy to measure animal intelligence
    e. women were finally allowed to earn Ph.D. degrees because of his theory

Correct _____ If wrong, why? _____

ANSWERS AND EXPLANATIONS FOR COMPREHENSION CHECK

First, cover the Other Alternatives section and write the correct answer beneath each question. If you are correct, great! If not, write why you think your answer is wrong in the blank below the question. The page where the topic is covered is given. Look at your book to see why you were wrong. Finally, look at the explanation given below and see how correct you were. You might also want to look at why the other answers are wrong to further your understanding. The Objective (pp. 1-2) related to each question is also given.

Correct Answer	Other Alternatives Are Wrong Because:
1. d (p. 5) Obj. I	a. unconscious thought is studied too, especially by psychoanalysts b. animals are studied, especially by biological psychologists c. normal behavior is studied too, e.g., do people have several kinds of memory e. psychologists try to understand why people act as they do, not to develop techniques for tricking them
2. c (pp. 5-6) Obj. II-A	a. if enough could be known, choices would be predictable b. many small causes may result in complex effects that seem unpredictable d. causes are not random; they are orderly and can be known e. determinism says that human behavior results from predictable causes
3. a (p. 6) Obj. II-A	b. events appear unpredictable because they result from many small causes c. all natural events result from many small causes d. many small influences affect outcomes e. this is the free-will position, not chaos theory
4. b (p. 7, Fig. 1.2) Obj. II-B	a,c,d,e. wrong because research cannot resolve the mind-brain problem
5. a (p. 8) Obj. II-C	b. asks whether apparently unpredictable events result from many small causes c. asks whether behavior has identifiable causes d. studies the relationship between mind and brain
6. a (p. 9, Table 1.2) Obj. III-A-1	b. cognitive psychologist c. developmental psychologist d. learning psychologist

7. d (pp. 9-10)
    Obj. III-A-3

    a. would emphasize influence of others, not knowledge
    b. emphasizes emotional influences, not knowledge
    c. would emphasize biological influences, not knowledge

8. a (p. 10)
    Obj. III-A-5

    b. it's not part of his inherited traits, he's probably learned
    c. a learning explanation in terms of consequences
    d. this is a biological explanation

9. c (p. 10, Table 1.1)
    Obj. III-B-1

    a. studies interactions between humans and machines
    b. studies changes with age
    d. works with children with academic difficulties

10. b (p. 11, Table 1.1)
    Obj. III-B-2

    a. an M.D. is needed to prescribe drugs; a clinical psychologist has a Ph.D
    c. no indication that he trained at a psychoanalytic institute
    d. experimental psychologists don't help people with emotional problems; they study perception, learning, memory, and thinking

11. c (p. 14)
    Obj. IV-A

    a. only 11.4% of the doctorates in clinical psychology are awarded to ethnic minorities
    b. just over 50% of graduate students are women
    d. over 50% with the percentage increasing

12. a (p. 18)
    Obj. V-A-1

    b. asked by philosophers prior to Wundt; Wundt tried to answer the questions experimentally
    c. asked by the functionalist, William James
    d. asked by the behaviorists
    e. asked by Francis Galton

13. c (p. 21)
    Obj. V-E

    a. Darwin influenced Hull's use of animals, but not Hull's use of mathematics
    b. Darwin didn't study sensations
    d. later psychologists tried to do this but not very successfully
    e. Darwin's theory did not help to improve the lot of women in psychology

LECTURE MATERIAL

Write a brief outline of the topics that your instructor covered in lecture. Be sure that you understand each topic; if not, ask your instructor or your teaching assistant to explain it to you. Be sure to process your lecture notes meaningfully. Write comments directly on your notes. Then write questions over the major concepts.

WAIT AT LEAST 24 HOURS BEFORE PROCEEDING.
LET FORGETTING OCCUR--IT WILL!!

SHORT-ANSWER ESSAY QUESTIONS

Write brief answers to each of the following. The answers are on pp. 8-9, but do try to write the answers yourself before looking at them.

Types of Psychologists

1. Explain how chaos theory can explain apparently unpredictable events.

2. Research studies cannot solve the mind-brain problem, but they can shed light on it. How?

3. Some psychological disorders are more common in large cities than in the country. Describe how the nature and the nurture viewpoints might explain this.

4. Your friend says that all psychologists are shrinks (which he explains means psychiatrists) and they all psychoanalyze you. Explain why he is wrong.

5. How do biopsychologists and cognitive psychologists differ?

6. How does the approach taken by learning psychologists differ from the approach taken by social psychologists?

7. Describe how the acceptance of women in psychology has changed from the 1890s to today.

8. Describe the types of settings in which psychologists work.

Psychology Then and Now

9. Describe the approach taken by most psychologists from about 1920 to 1970.

10. Why did early psychologists study sensation?

****
Find the questions that you wrote over lecture material and write answers to them.
****

ANSWERS TO SHORT-ANSWER ESSAY QUESTIONS

1. Many tiny influences can result in very different patterns of responses. Each small event has a cause and may such small events can add up to very different outcomes. So, as indicated in the text, each bounce of a golf ball is caused by physical principles but the final location of the ball appears unpredictable because we can't identify the small influences for each bounce. (p. 6)

2. Researchers can look for links between behavior and brain activity. For example, studies using PET scans show that different tasks result in different patterns of brain activity. This puts constraints on how philosophers should think about the mind-body problem. (p. 7)

3. *Nature:* People have a genetic predisposition to the psychological disorder. As the disorder worsens, they move to the big city to find a job and use the welfare services.
   Nurture: Life in crowded, impersonal cities causes the psychological disorder. (p. 8)

4. Psychologists with Ph.D. degrees may concentrate in many different areas. One type of psychologist, a clinical psychologist, usually works with people who have emotional problems. Psychiatrists have M.D. degrees, but they are only psychoanalysts if they complete specialized training at an institute of psychoanalysis. Relatively few clinical psychologists and psychiatrists are psychoanalysts. (pp. 8-9)

5. The biological psychologist looks for relationships between the nervous system and other biological systems and behavior. The cognitive psychologist studies the specific thought processes and knowledge necessary to perform various tasks. (pp. 9-10)

6. The learning psychologist is interested in studying observable behavior. Behavior occurs because of what consequences follow it in a given situation. The social psychologist stresses the role of others in influencing behavior. Social norms and expectations are important. (pp. 9-10)

7. In 1895, Mary Calkins completed her graduate work at Harvard University, but they would not grant a Ph.D. to a woman. Today, over 50% of the graduate students in psychology are women. (pp. 14, 22).

8. The largest percentage (about 40%) of psychologists work in settings that provide health care, such as hospitals, clinics, and independent private practices. A little over 33% work in academic institutions, including colleges, universities, and medical schools. Others work in a variety of settings: businesses, government, schools, and counseling centers. (p. 9, Fig. 1.4)

9 Behaviorism was the dominant school of psychology. The idea was that observable behavior, rather than elements of mind, should be studied. The main research question was: What do people and other animals do under various conditions. (pp. 22-23)

10. The philosophical reason was that they wanted to understand mental experience, and experience is primarily composed of sensations. The strategic reason was that they wanted to create a scientific psychology, and they began with questions that could be answered. (p. 20)

POSTTEST

Take this test with all of your books and notes out of sight. This should give you a good idea of how well you understand the material. The answers are on pp.12.

Matching

Put the letter of the type of psychologist on the right in the blank beside the description on the left.

1. _____ studies how people think and acquire knowledge

2. _____ studies man-machine interaction

3. _____ looks for relationships between factors that affect body functioning and behavior

4. _____ looks for emotional reasons for behavior

5. _____ emphasizes the effects that other people have on an individual's behavior

6. _____ stresses role of past experience on behavior

A. cognitive

B. biological

C. clinical

D. learning

E. human factors

F. social

Multiple-Choice

Circle the best alternative.

<u>Types of Psychologists</u>

1. Psychology is best defined as the study of:
   a. abnormality
   b. social influences
   c. consciousness
   d. human behavior
   e. behavior and experience

2. Prof. R is engaged in a debate with Prof. S. Prof. R argues that people are free to make choices and that their choices are unpredictable. Prof. S argues that choices are made because of past experience and that each choice could be predicted if we knew enough. Prof. R's arguments support _____ and Prof. S's arguments support _____.
   a. free will; determinism
   b. mind controls brain; brain controls mind
   c. determinism; free will
   d. brain controls mind; mind controls brain
   e. nurture; nature

3. Boys generally spend more time playing with toy guns and trucks than girls do. Which of the following reasons for this is consistent with the <u>nature</u> point of view?
   a. boys watch more violent television shows than girls do
   b. boys like to do what their fathers do and many fathers use guns and trucks
   c. boys have genes that make them prefer such toys
   d. society discourages girls from playing with such toys
   e. boys are given such toys so they have more opportunities to play with them

4. A clinical psychologist is:
   a. the same as a psychiatrist
   b. the same as a psychoanalyst
   c. any psychologist with a Ph.D.
   d. a psychologist who helps people with emotional problems
   e. any psychologist who administers and interprets tests

5. A psychoanalyst:
   a. is the same as a clinical psychologist
   b. is the same as a psychiatrist
   c. adheres to Freud's methods and theories
   d. has fewer years of formal training than a clinical psychologist
   e. always hold the Ph.D. degree

6. How is a psychologist different from a psychiatrist?
   a. there is no difference
   b. psychiatrists deal with helping people; psychologists do research in universities
   c. psychiatrists have M.D. degrees; psychologists have Ph.D. degrees
   d. psychologists use methods developed by Freud; psychiatrists do not
   e. psychologists can prescribe drugs; psychiatrists cannot

7. Which type of psychologist would be most interested in the genetic makeup of an individual?
   a. cognitive
   b. behaviorist
   c. biological
   d. psychoanalytic
   e. clinical

8. A child is constantly in trouble at school for disrupting the class. How would a learning psychologist view this situation?
   a. there is conflict in the child's home, and he unconsciously wants to hurt his parents
   b. the child may have damage to a specific part of his brain
   c. the child's diet is lacking in essential minerals and vitamins
   d. the child only receives attention (which is reinforcing) when he is disruptive
   e. other students expect the child to be disruptive, so he is

9. A psychologist believes that differences between males and females are due to society's expectations about how boys and girls behave. This psychologist takes which viewpoint?
   a. social
   b. cognitive
   c. physiological
   d. clinical
   e. behaviorist

10. African Americans, Hispanics, Asian Americans, and other minorities constitute about:
    a. about 11% of all doctorates in clinical psychology
    b. about 50% of all psychologists
    c. 25% of all clinical psychologists
    d. about 50% of all doctorates in clinical psychology
    e. 5% of all psychologists today, but the percentage is declining

Psychology Then and Now
11. What was Wundt's most lasting impact on psychology?
    a. his discovery that it takes time to shift attention
    b. he set the precedent for studying psychological questions with scientific data
    c. he correctly described the elements of mind
    d. he made self-observation into an exact science
    e. he mapped out the psychophysical functions relating psychology to physical stimuli

12. Mary Calkins, the first woman psychologist:
    a. received her Ph.D. degree from Harvard
    b. was never allowed to attend graduate classes
    c. performed poorly on her final examination for the Ph.D., so she never received her Ph.D.
    d. never received her Ph.D. because Harvard would not grant a Ph.D. to a woman
    e. completed a Ph.D. at Harvard, but was unable to find a job because she was a woman

13. How does the psychology advocated by the behaviorists differ from the psychology advocated by the structuralists?
    a. the behaviorists were more interested in sensation than the structuralists
    b. the behaviorists emphasized the study of animal intelligence, and the structuralists developed a psychology of human intelligence
    c. the behaviorists developed mathematical models of intelligence, and the structuralists developed nonmathematical models
    d. behaviorists emphasized learning, and the structuralists emphasized sensation

ANSWERS TO POSTTEST

Correct Answer	Questions Testing a Similar Concept	
	Comprehension Check	Short-Answer

Matching

(See Table 1.2, p. 9 for all)

	Comprehension Check	Short-Answer
1. A (pp. 9-10)	7	6
2. E (p. 13)	9a	--
3. B (p. 9)	6,8d	6
4. C (p. 11)	7b,9,10a	4
5. F (p. 10)	7a,8	8
6. D (p. 9)	6d, 8c	8

Multiple-Choice

	Comprehension Check	Short-Answer
1. e (p. 5)	1e	--
2. a (pp. 5-6)	2,3	1
3. c (p. 8)	5	3
4. d (p. 11, Table 1.1)	7b,9,10a	4
5. c (p. 11)	10c	4
6. c (pp. 10-11, Table 1.1)	10	4
7. c (p. 9, Table 1.2)	6,7c,8d	5
8. d (p. 9)	6d,8c	6
9. a (p. 10)	7,8	10
10 a (p. 14)	11a	--
11. b (p. 18)	12	10
12. d (p. 22)	--	7
13. d (pp. 19-20, 22-23)	12a,13b	9,10

CHAPTER 2 SCIENTIFIC METHODS IN PSYCHOLOGY

OBJECTIVES

Understand that:

Science and the Evaluation of Evidence

I. Scientists generally agree on how to evaluate competing theories (p. 29)
- A. There are ordered steps for gathering evidence (pp. 29-30, Fig. 2.1)
  - 1. Making a hypothesis (p. 29)
  - 2. Devising a method to test the hypothesis (pp. 29-30)
  - 3. Measuring the results (p. 30)
  - 4. Interpreting the results (p. 30)
- B. Experiments should be replicable (p. 30)
  - 1. A meta-analysis combines many studies and can show evidence for small effects (p. 30)
- C. The goal of research is to establish theories (p. 30)
  - 1. Theories should be comprehensive explanations of observable events, make new predictions, and be falsifiable (pp. 30-31)
- D. Theories should be parsimonious, that is, fit known facts with the simplest assumptions; (p. 31)
  - 1. A parsimonious explanation for Clever Hans' arithmetic skills that he watched his trainer and received cues (pp. 32-33)
  - 2. There is no scientific evidence for extrasensory perception (p. 33)
    - a. Evidence is often based on anecdotes (pp. 33-34)
    - b. Psychic stage performers use tricks and illusions (pp. 34-35)
    - c. Experiments have produced mixed results and positive results may not be replicable (p. 35)

The message: Scientific conclusions are tentative, subject to revision, and parsimonious (pp. 35-36)

Methods of Investigation in Psychology

II. Research follows some general principles (p. 37)
- A. Variables should be operationally defined (pp. 37-38)
- B. Samples should be representative and random (pp. 38-39)
  - 1. Cross-cultural studies pose special sampling problems (p. 39)
- C. Observers and subjects should be "blind" (pp. 39-40, Table 2.1)

III. Observational research designs don't show cause and effect relationships (p. 40, Table 2.2, p. 45)
- A. Naturalistic observation involves careful observation under natural conditions (p. 40)
- B. Case histories involve detailed studies of an individual (pp. 40-41)
- C. Surveys involve giving questionnaires to samples of individuals (p. 41)
  - 1. It is important to get a random and representative sample (p. 41)
  - 2. People may express opinions even if they know little about a topic (p. 41)
  - 3. Results depend upon how a question is asked (pp. 41-42)
  - 4. The surveyor may intentionally bias the questions to get a desired answer (pp. 42-43)
- D. A correlational study examines the relationship between two variables, without manipulating them (p. 43)
  - 1. Correlation coefficients are statistical measures of the relationship that range from -1 to +1 (pp. 43-44, Fig. 2.9)
  - 2. Correlations observed in everyday life may be illusory (p. 44)
  - 3. Correlation does not imply that one variable causes the other (pp. 44-45, Fig. 2.10)

IV. Experiments involve the manipulation of variables (p. 45)

A. Independent variables are manipulated and dependent variables are measures of behavior (pp. 45-46)
B. Experimental groups receive the treatment and control groups do not (pp. 46-47, Fig. 2.12)
  1. Subjects are randomly assigned to groups (pp. 46-47)
C. An example of an experiment is an investigation of the effects of televised violence on aggressive behavior (pp. 47-48)
  1. Adolescent boys were randomly assigned to watch violent films or not (p. 47)
  2. Boys who watched violent films were more aggressive than those who didn't (pp. 47-48)
V. Demand characteristics may produce self-fulfilling prophecies (pp. 48-49, Fig. 2.13)
A. Double-blind studies can reduce these (p. 49)
VI. Some experiments raise ethical issues (pp. 49-51)
A. Participants in research should give informed consent (p. 49)
B. Research with nonhuman animals raises special ethical issues (pp. 50-51)

The message: Our understanding of complex human behavior has been increased by sound research (p. 51)

Measuring and Reporting Results

VII. Descriptive statistics are mathematical summaries of results (pp. 53-54)
A. There are several measures of the central score (pp. 53-54)
  1. Mean is the arithmetic average (pp. 53-54)
  2. Median is the middle score in a set of ordered scores (p. 54)
  3. Mode is the most common score (p. 54)
B. Measures of variation refer to the spread of the scores (pp. 55-56)
  1. Range is the distance from the top to the bottom score (p. 55)
  2. Standard deviation measures the distance of scores from the mean (pp. 55-56, Fig. 2.20)
VIII. Inferential statistics allow inferences about larger groups from small samples (pp. 56-57, Fig. 2.22)
A. If a result is statistically significant, it probably did not occur by chance (p. 57)
  1. p values indicate how often results would occur by chance (p. 57)
  2. The lower the p value, the more convincing the results (p. 57)

The message: Psychologists need statistics because they often measure small, variable effects (p. 57)

COMPREHENSION CHECK

Answer these questions soon after reading the chapter. Circle the best alternative. Check your answers on pp.18-20. If you gave a wrong answer, try to write why it was wrong. Check your reasons on pp. 18-20.

Science and the Evaluation of Evidence

1. Which of the following is <u>not</u> an appropriate order for steps involved in gathering and evaluating evidence?
   a. gather the data, then make up a hypothesis
   b. make up a hypothesis, then devise an appropriate method
   c. interpret the results, then try to replicate them
   d. gather the data, then think of alternative explanations

Correct _____ If wrong, why? _____

2. If a result is replicable, it:
    a. may be found by a few investigators, but many investigators cannot get the same results
    b. is not falsifiable
    c. is interpreted so that everyone agrees with the interpretation
    d. can be found by anyone who repeats the same procedures
    e. is a small effect that can only be found in a meta-analysis

Correct _____ If wrong, why? _____

3. What are the criteria for good scientific theories?
    a. predict new discoveries and be vague
    b. not falsifiable, but parsimonious
    c. be stated so that all types of evidence would fit
    d. make accurate predictions and be parsimonious
    e. change a few simple facts into complex ones and fit known facts

Correct _____ If wrong, why? _____

4. Clever Hans was actually:
    a. able to add and subtract but not multiply or divide
    b. able to do simple arithmetic of all types and was also able to identify musical notes
    c. able to respond to subtle cues given by the examiner
    d. better at answering questions when the examiner was out of sight

Correct _____ If wrong, why? _____

5. Anecdotes are not good scientific evidence for ESP because they:
    a. usually involve prediction before the event
    b. show that accurate predictions could not be coincidental
    c. produce accurate predictions when the predictions were very specific and precise
    d. usually involve selective memory; people remember when predictions come true but not when they don't

Correct _____ If wrong, why? _____

Methods of Investigation in Psychology

6. Which of the following is the best operational definition of aggression?
    a. the number of times one person strikes another person during a 30-minute period
    b. how much physical force and verbal abuse is contained in a 30-minute period
    c. how much violence there is
    d. assaultive, offensive, and combative behavior

Correct _____ If wrong, why? _____

7. A researcher conducted a survey of all the customers at an expensive restaurant because she knows the owner and was able to get permission to do her survey there. She has
   a. selected a representative sample of the entire population
   b. used a random sample of the entire population
   c. conducted a cross-cultural study
   d. conducted single-blind study
   e. used a convenience sample

Correct _____ If wrong, why? _____

8. A news columnist asked readers to write in and indicate the importance of sex in their marriages. The responses were tallied and published. The columnist conducted:
   a. a correlational study
   b. an experiment
   c. a case history
   d. a survey

Correct _____ If wrong, why? _____

9. A researcher found that grade-point averages of college students are related to their family incomes. High GPAs generally go with higher incomes and low GPAs go with lower incomes. This study is:
   a. an example of an illusory correlation
   b. an experiment
   c. a correlational study
   d. a double-blind study

Correct _____ If wrong, why? _____

10. Generally the weight of clothing that people wear goes down as the outdoor temperature goes up. This relationship would produce a:
   a. negative correlation
   b. zero correlation
   c. very high positive correlation
   d. very low positive correlation

Correct _____ If wrong, why? _____

Questions 11 to 14 refer to the following:
An experiment was conducted to determine whether a new approach to psychotherapy (interactive scream therapy) is effective in helping couples with marital problems. Couples who came to a clinic were randomly assigned to two groups--one group was given the new interactive scream therapy for 6 months and he other was placed on a waiting list and given no treatment. After 6 months, couples in both groups rated their marital happiness and therapists rated the adjustment of each couple.

11. What is the dependent variable?
    a. the therapy program
    b. the couples
    c. the ratings
    d. the clinic

Correct _____ If wrong, why? _____

12. What is the term for the group who received the therapy program?
    a. the experimental group
    b. the dependent variable
    c. the independent variable
    d. the control group

Correct _____ If wrong, why? _____

13. Why did the experimenter use random assignment?
    a. to be sure that the subjects in the experiment were represented in the same proportions as subjects in the population
    b. to reduce the possibility that the two groups differed in the beginning
    c. to avoid demand characteristics
    d. to ensure informed consent

Correct _____ If wrong, why? _____

14. Instead of using random assignment, the researcher obtained ratings from couples who had signed up for and completed the new therapy and those who did not sign up. She found better adjustment in the therapy group. What type would the study be and what conclusion could be made?
    a. experiment; the improvement is caused by the therapy
    b. correlation; interactive scream therapy "cures" marital problems
    c. experiment; there is a relationship between signing up for this therapy and adjustment
    d. correlation; there is a relationship between signing up for this therapy and adjustment

Correct _____ If wrong, why? _____

15. Which of the following would be unethical in conducting research?
    a. an experiment uses mild shock; subjects were informed about the shock and agreed to participate
    b. an experiment involves eating disgusting things (such as cockroaches) but subjects are told they are eating shrimp
    c. an experiment uses small doses of marijuana that has been approved by the Human Subjects Committee
    d. an experiment in which behavior is manipulated

Correct _____ If wrong, why? _____

Measuring and Reporting Results

16. A group of scores is 5, 6, 4, 8, 1. What is the median?
    a. 4
    b. 4.8
    c. 8
    d. 5

Correct _____ If wrong, why? _____

17. The researcher finds a difference between a therapy group and a control group that is statistically significant at $p < .01$. This means:
    a. the difference would occur by chance more than 1% of the time
    b. the probability that the difference was due to therapy is 1/100
    c. the explanation that therapy helped is parsimonious
    d. the difference would occur by chance less than 1% of the time

Correct _____ If wrong, why? _____

ANSWERS AND EXPLANATIONS FOR COMPREHENSION CHECK

Correct Answer	Other Alternatives Are Wrong Because:
1. a (pp. 29-30, Fig. 2.1) Obj. I-A	b-d. the question asked for orders that are not appropriate; each of these is appropriate
2. d (p. 30) Obj. I-B	a. this would be considered replicated because a few investigators found it, but not replicable because most did not b. refers to theories, not results; theories are falsifiable if some set of observations would disconfirm them c. everyone may not agree with the interpretation, even though they can replicate the results e. a replicable result can be seen in other single experiments; meta-analysis combines many studies to look for small effects
3. d (pp. 30-32) Obj. I-C-1, I-D	a. theories should be precise, not vague b. they should be falsifiable c. should be able to imagine evidence that would falsify the theory e. parsimony suggests that simple is better; shouldn't make simple things complex
4. c (pp. 32-33) Obj. I-D-1	a. he probably wasn't doing any arithmetic; c is more parsimonious b. he probably couldn't do either; c is more parsimonious d. the examiner needed to be in the horse's sight
5. d (p. 33) Obj. I-D-2-a	a. specific predictions are not usually made b. coincidence can explain many apparently accurate predictions c. predictions are usually not specific or precise

6. a (pp. 37-38)
   Obj. II-A

b. how would physical force and verbal abuse be measured?
c. how is violence measured?
d. what is meant by assaultive, offensive, combative?

7. e (p. 38)
   Obj. II-B

a. it may be representative of people who eat in expensive
   restaurants, but not of the population
b. everyone in the population didn't have an equal chance of being
   selected, so it is not random
c. refers to comparing people from different societies
d. not used for surveys; refers to a situation in which either the subject
   or experimenter doesn't know the participant's group

8. d (p. 41)
   Obj. III-C

a. specific relationships were not studied
b. no independent variable was manipulated
c. not an in-depth study of an individual

9. c (p. 43)
   Obj. III-D

a. the correlation is not illusory; it has been objectively observed
b. a relationship was noted, but no variables were controlled or
   manipulated by the researcher
d. we don't know whether the experimenter knew which subjects were
   from high- and low-income families; the participants probably
   knew

10. a (pp. 43-44,
    Fig. 2.9
    Obj. III-D -1

b. the variables are related; correlation cannot be zero
c. the variables do not increase together; one goes up and the
   other goes down
d. the relationship is pretty strong so the correlation should be high;
   see c for why it is not positive

11. c (pp. 45-46)
    Obj. IV-A

a. the researcher controls the therapy program (gives it
   to some couples, not others), so it is the independent variable
b. the couples are the subjects or participants
d. the clinic is the site of the study, not a variable

12. a (p. 46)
    Obj. IV-B

b. dependent variable is the measure of behavior, not a group
c. the therapy group is one level of the independent variable, not the
   independent variable itself
d. control group is the one that is not treated, i.e., the no-therapy
   group

13. b (pp. 46-47)
    Obj. IV-B-1

a. this is a representative sample; random assignment refers to
   placing the sample into groups
c. demand characteristics could still be a problem if participants know
   they're supposed to improve
d. informed consent doesn't have to do with assignment to groups; it
   means that the participants knew what was required of them in the
   experiment and they agreed to do it

14. d (pp. 44-45)
   Obj. III-D, IV-C

    a. not an experiment because who got the therapy was not controlled by the experimenter; people who sign up for therapy may be different from people who don't

    b. correlational, but you cannot be sure that therapy is the only difference between the groups; the group who signed up may already be better adjusted or they may be more motivated

    c. not an experiment because the groups already existed; experimenter did not randomly assign couples to therapy

15. b (pp. 49-50)
   Obj. VI-A

    a. subjects knew they would be shocked and they agreed to participate; informed consent was obtained

    c. the Human Subjects Committee judged that the procedures were ethical

    d. by definition, experiments manipulate behavior, but such manipulation is usually short-lived

16. d (p. 54)
   Obj. VII-A-2

    a. scores must be rank ordered first, then the middle score is the median

    b. this is the average or mean

    c. highest score or top of the range

17. d (p. 57)
   Obj. VIII-A-1

    a. < means less than 1%--it's a rare event

    b. probability that difference is due to <u>chance</u> is less than 1/100

    c. statistical significance is unrelated to parsimony; a difference could be significant and the explanation still might not be the simplest

LECTURE MATERIAL

Don't forget to review your lecture material. Process each topic meaningfully. First, be sure that you understand the material in each lecture--if you don't, ask your instructor or teaching assistant. Associate the material with things that you already know and with your personal experiences. If you can make up mental images of any of the material, do so. Try to think of real-life applications of the concepts. Write comments on your notes. Then write questions to cover each concept.

WAIT AT LEAST 24 HOURS BEFORE PROCEEDING.
LET FORGETTING OCCUR--IT WILL!!

SHORT-ANSWER ESSAY QUESTIONS

Write brief answers to each of the following. The answers are on pp. 22-23, but do try to write the answers yourself before looking at them.

Science and the Evaluation of Evidence

1. Describe two factors that would help you decide whether a theory is a good one.

2. Explain why things like coincidence and subtle cues are more parsimonious explanations for incidents such as anticipating what your friend will say than is extrasensory perception.

3. Explain why anecdotes do not provide very strong scientific evidence.

Methods of Investigation in Psychology

4. Explain how a survey differs from a case history.

5. A researcher found that students who enrolled in a study skills class improved their GPAs more the next term than students who did not enroll. He concluded that GPAs increased because of the study skills class. What is wrong with this conclusion?

6. Describe how you would do a good experiment to see whether study skills classes help students. Indicate the independent and dependent variables.

7. Explain how a correlational study differs from an experiment both in terms of procedures and in terms of the types of conclusions that can be drawn.

8. For the study on televised violence and aggression in the "What's the Evidence?" section, explain why it is unlikely that the boys who watched the violent shows were more aggressive to begin with than the boys who watched the nonviolent shows.

9. Explain how demand characteristics might play a role in an experiment to test two types of therapy and how you might try to minimize them.

10. Explain what is meant by informed consent in experimental participation.

Measuring and Reporting Results

11. Describe how you would find the means in the study skills experiment you designed and explain what a statistically significant difference at $p < .05$ would mean.

****
Find the questions that you wrote over
lecture material and write answers to them.
****

ANSWERS TO SHORT-ANSWER ESSAY QUESTIONS

1. Theories should make specific predictions that can be tested in experiments that are replicable. In other words, a theory should be falsifiable. Theories should be parsimonious so that their explanations use generally accepted scientific principles. (pp. 30-32)

2. Scientists do not know how humans might receive "extrasensory" stimuli. Because there is no accepted explanation for this, it is not parsimonious. We do know that people in the same situation will have similar thoughts with some probability and that people and animals can read nonverbal cues in people. (p. 33)

3. Anecdotes rely on memory, which may not be accurate; the observer may exaggerate; coincidence may be the correct explanation; people generally remember when predictions came true and not when they didn't. (p. 33)

4. A survey involves asking questions of a lot of people; a case history involves a much more detailed study of one person. The survey should use a random sample, so that everyone in the population of interest has an equal chance of being selected. A case study selects a specific person because of some interesting characteristic. (pp. 40-41)

5. The researcher conducted a correlational study. Students who signed up for the study skills class may differ from those who didn't. The increase in GPA might have been due to something other than the class; perhaps those students were more motivated to improve and would have improved without the study skills class. (pp. 44-45)

6. Take a large group of students who are having difficulty in college. Randomly assign half of them to the study skills class. Look at the grades of both groups before the study skills class and look after the study skills class. The experimental group (who took the study skills class) should show a larger increase in grades than the control group (who did not take the class). The independent variable is whether the study skills class was taken or not; the dependent variable is the students' grades. (pp. 45-47, Fig. 2.12)

7. In an experiment, the researcher randomly assigns participants to specific groups. The groups should be equal in the beginning because of the random assignment. Any difference in the end should be due to the independent variable. The researcher has control over who gets which treatment. In a correlational study, the researcher compares existing groups, which may differ in more ways than the one the researcher is interested in. Differences might be due to any of these original differences. The researcher does not control who gets which treatment. (pp. 43-46)

8. The researcher used random assignment. That means that the boys were placed in the violent and non-violent groups just by chance. The degree of violence of the boys in the two groups should have been about equal at the start of the experiment. The violent group made more aggressive acts because they watched the violent film because otherwise they were equated in all respects to the non-violent group due to the random assignment to groups. (pp. 47-48)

9. People might improve simply because they expect the therapy to work and not because the therapy itself is effective. Some sort of "placebo" therapy could be used in a control group. Participants would be led to expect that it would help, but actually it would be ineffective. If the therapists rating improvement don't know who got which therapy, the experiment would be double blind. If the participants know whether they're getting therapy or not, but the raters don't, it's a single-blind experiment. (pp. 48-49, Table 2.1, p. 40)

10. Participants should know what will happen in the experiment before they participate. In addition, they must be given the right to withdraw if they do not wish to participate once they know what will happen. (p. 49)

11. Add all the grade point averages (GPAs) of the students in a group and then divide by the number of students in that group. Do this for junior-year grades of the group that had the study skills class and for the group that did not. A significant difference at the .05 level would mean that the observed difference in grades between the groups would occur by chance less than 5% of the time. (pp. 53-54)

POSTTEST
Take this test with all of your books and notes out of sight. This should give you a good idea of how well you understand the material. The answers are on p. 28.

Matching
Write the letter of the design on the right in the blank beside the description on the left.

Methods of Investigation in Psychology

1. _____ Ted has noticed that it seems to rain every time he has his car washed, but he hasn't collected precise data on this

2. _____ a psychologist studies all aspects of the memory of a person who has an exceptional memory

3. _____ the number of wrinkles was counted on people who smoke and people who don't smoke, and smokers were more wrinkled

4. _____ students were asked to answer questions about how much they use and plan to use microcomputers

5. _____ a random half of the participants in a weight-loss program were given exercise plans and half were not

6. _____ some students were given a marijuana brownie and others were given a placebo brownie; their social interactions were rated by observers who did not know who ate which

7. _____ one group of patients was given psychotherapy and the other was not; interviewers who did not know who received the therapy rated their adjustment

A. experimental study

B. correlational study

C. illusory correlation

D. double-blind study

E. survey

F. single-blind study

G. case history

Multiple-Choice

Circle the best alternative.

Science and the Evaluation of Evidence

1. Prof. R tried to repeat an experiment that he read about in a scientific journal using exactly the same procedures as the original experiment. His results were different. Therefore, the original experiment was not:
    a. double-blind
    b. parsimonious
    c. statistically significant
    d. replicable
    e. accurate in its predictions

2. You suggest a theory and your instructor says it is not parsimonious. She means that it:
   a. doesn't make sense
   b. would not lead to replicable experiments
   c. would not lead to statistically significant differences
   d. would lead to experiments with demand characteristics
   e. does not make simple scientific assumptions

3. How did Clever Hans solve arithmetic problems?
   a. with ESP
   b. by taking advantage of coincidence
   c. by watching the examiner for subtle cues
   d. by using his native abilities to do arithmetic
   e. by taking advantage of selective attrition

4. In one experiment, people who said they had ESP were tested over several days. Sometimes they performed above chance and sometimes below chance. The researcher concluded that ESP depends on mood--it can be either positive (above chance) or negative (below chance). What is wrong with the explanation?
   a. it is not parsimonious--performance will vary around chance
   b. it is too parsimonious--some factor other than ESP must be operating
   c. it is replicable--people should not vary around chance
   d. there are too many demand characteristics that force performance below chance
   e. differential attrition occurred, so chance performance dropped

5. Advertisers often use testimonials in which a single person tells how a product helped. Why are such reports not good evidence?
   a. they are replicable
   b. they involve objective observation
   c. they involve experimental-control group designs
   d. they ignore the cases where the product did not help
   e. improvement could not occur by coincidence

6. Experiments with ESP have:
   a. had a history of flawed procedures and nonreplicable results
   b. produced positive results that are easily replicated
   c. proved that ESP occurs for people who can read brain waves
   d. shown that most professional psychics have ESP

Methods of Investigation in Psychology

7. Sometimes an inert pill is given to experimental participants, but they are told that the pill is effective. This pill is called a:
   a. placebo
   b. dependent variable
   c. double blind
   d. mode

8. A random sample involves selecting:
   a. only those people who volunteer
   b. people so that the percentages in the sample match the percentages in the population
   c. people from one specific culture
   d. so that every individual has an equal chance of being chosen
   e. all the studies on a topic for a meta-analysis

9. It has been found that children who have encyclopedias in their homes get better grades in school than children without encyclopedias. Can you conclude that using an encyclopedia makes children do better in school?
   a. yes, this is an experimental study and encyclopedias are the independent variable
   b. yes, this is a correlational study and the correlation is a strong positive one
   c. no, this is a correlational study; something other than encyclopedias might help grades
   d. no, this is an experiment but there is no control group
   e. no, this is a survey and experimenter bias might affect the conclusion

10. If there is a high correlation between parents' use of physical punishment and children's aggressiveness, then we can conclude:
    a. physical punishment causes aggression
    b. aggressive children cause parents to use physical punishment
    c. a third factor in the family causes both
    d. both a and b must be true
    e. nothing can be said about causality

11. If a correlation between variables A and B is -1, then:
    a. there is no relationship
    b. A causes B
    c. increases in A are perfectly associated with decreases in B
    d. increases in A are perfectly associated with increases in B
    e. the mean of A is larger than the mean of B

12. A study was conducted to test a new hay fever drug. Patients were randomly assigned to experimental and control groups. For 6 weeks, experimental patients took the drug daily and control patients took nothing. Each patient recorded hay fever attacks. The drug users had fewer and less severe attacks. What is wrong with this study?
    a. the groups probably were not equal in the beginning
    b. demand characteristics may have caused the effect
    c. the experiment lacks a dependent variable
    d. random assignment wasn't used
    e. informed consent wasn't obtained

13. Which of the following would best improve the design in Question 12?
    a. use a placebo rather than a "nothing" group
    b. include an independent variable
    c. use more participants to increase selective attrition
    d. include a dependent variable
    e. avoid the use of random assignment

14. An experiment was conducted to test the effect of rewards on learning. One group of subjects was paid 10 cents for every word they memorized and the other group was not paid. Number of words memorized was measured. Which of the following is true?
    a. number of words memorized is the dependent variable
    b. payment or not is the dependent variable
    c. random assignment should ensure that the groups differ in the beginning
    d. number of words memorized is the independent variable
    e. the control group is the one that is paid

15. A good question for deciding whether an experiment is ethical or not is:
    a. would subjects have agreed to participate if they had known what was going to happen?
    b. will the subjects experience any discomfort?
    c. is there any manipulation of behavior involved?
    d. will any subjects agree to participate?
    e. would any subject withdraw from the experiment?

16. Participants in an experiment are often kept "blind" about the condition to which they've been assigned. This will help prevent:
    a. surveyor bias
    b. an illusory correlation
    c. random assignment
    d. demand characteristics
    e. informed consent

Measuring and Reporting Results

17. A researcher found that subjects who were paid for memorizing words remembered more than subjects who were not paid, $p < .01$. This means:
    a. the reward group recalled 1% more than the nonreward group
    b. the results were not statistically significant
    c. the results are not replicable
    d. the results may have occurred because of an illusory correlation
    e. a difference that large would occur less than 1% of the time by chance alone

18. A class of seven students received the following grades on a test: 65, 78, 90, 89, 64, 78, 60. Which is true?
    a. the mode is 90
    b. the mean is 63
    c. the median is 89
    d. the mode is 89
    e. the median is 78

ANSWERS TO POSTTEST

Correct Answer	Questions Testing a Similar Concept	
	Comprehension Check	Short-Answer

Matching

	Comprehension Check	Short-Answer
1. C (p. 44)	9a	--
2. G (pp. 40-41)	8c	4
3. B (p. 43)	8a,9c,14	5,7
4. E (p. 41)	8	4
5. A (pp. 46-47)	8b,9b,13,14a	6,7,8
6. D (p. 49)	9d	9
7. F (p. 49)	7d	9

Multiple-Choice

	Comprehension Check	Short-Answer
1. d (p. 30)	1c,2	--
2. e (pp. 31-32)	3	1,2
3. c (pp. 32-33)	4	2
4. a (p. 33)	3	2
5. d (p. 33)	5	3
6. a (p. 35)	5	2
7. a (p. 40)	--	9
8. d (p. 38)	7b,13a	4
9. c (pp. 44-45)	9,14	7
10. e (pp. 44-45)	9,14	7
11. c (pp. 43-44)	10	--
12. b (pp. 48-49)	7d,9d,13c	9
13. a (pp. 40, 49)	7d	9
14. a (pp. 45-46)	11	6
15. a (pp. 49-50)	15	10
16. d (pp. 48-49)	13c	9
17. e (p. 57)	16	11
18. e (pp. 53-54)	16	--

CHAPTER 3 THE BIOLOGICAL APPROACH TO BEHAVIOR

OBJECTIVES

Psychological Explanations at the Level of the Gene

I. Principles of Genetics (p. 63, Fig. 3.1-3.2, p. 63)
   A. Genes are transmitted from one generation to the next (pp. 63-64)
      1. People are either homozygous or heterozygous for genes (p. 64, Fig. 3.3, p. 64)
      2. Genes are dominant or recessive (p. 64, Fig. 3.4)
   B. Some genes are different from males and females (p. 65)
      1. Sex chromosomes determine sex (p. 65, Fig. 3.6)
      2. Sex-linked genes are found on the X chromosome (p. 65)
      3. Sex-limited genes affect one sex more than the other (p. 65)
   C. Specific genes can be identified and localized (p. 66)
      1. Huntington's and Alzheimer's diseases are caused by specific genes (p. 66)
II. Differences among individuals due to genetics are measured by heritability (p. 66)
   A. Monozygous and dizygous twins can be compared (pp. 66-67)
      1. Adopted children can be compared with their biological and adoptive parents (p. 67)
   B. Genetics can influence many types of behavior (p. 68)
   C. Heredity and the environment interact (p. 70)
      1. Just because something is under genetic control doesn't mean that the environment can't alter it (p. 70)
         a. PKU is a genetic disorder that can be altered by the environment (p. 70)
III. Genes are a product of evolution (p. 70)
   A. Reproductive advantage is the key to evolutionary success (p. 70, Fig. 3.12)
IV. The role of genetics can be studied by comparing animal species (p. 71)
V. Sociobiology is the study of social behaviors from a biological viewpoint (p. 72)
The message: *Most behaviors are influenced by an interaction of heredity and environment (p. 73)*

Explanations of Behavior at the Level of the Neuron

VI. The nervous system is composed of neurons and glia (p. 75)
   A. A neuron consists of a cell body, dendrites, and an axon (pp. 75-76, Figs. 3.15-3.16)
   B. Nerve impulses are called action potentials (p. 77)
      1. Inflow of sodium ions makes inside of axon positive (pp. 77-78, Figs. 3.17-3.19)
   C. Gaps between neurons are called synapses (p. 78, Fig. 3.20)
      1. Neurotransmitters are released from presynaptic endings (pp. 78-79, Fig. 3.21)
         a. Neurotransmitters from one animal can affect another animal (p. 81)
   D. Different neurotransmitters have different effects on behavior (pp. 81-82)
      1. Parkinson's disease occurs because neurons producing dopamine die (p. 81-82, Fig. 3.24)
The message: *Behavior is not determined by a single neuron but by patterns of activity shown by many nerve cells. (p. 82-83)*

Explanations of Behavior at the Level of the Nervous System

VII. Neurons are organized into the brain and nervous system (p. 85, Fig. 3.25)
   A. Spinal cord is connected to sensory and motor nerves (p. 86, Fig. 3.27)
   B. Autonomic nervous system consists of sympathetic and parasympathetic nervous systems (pp. 86-87)
   C. Endocrine system produces hormones that are similar to neurotransmitters (p. 87)
   D. Hindbrain consists of the medulla, pons, and cerebellum (p. 88, Fig. 3.30)

1. Medulla and pons receive sensory input and control life-preserving functions (p. 88)
   a. The reticular formation serves an arousal function (p. 88)
2. Cerebellum is important in movement and timing (p. 88)

VIII. Cerebral cortex is the "master area" of the brain (p. 90)
  A. Cortex consists of left and right hemisphere (p. 90)
    1. Cortical hemispheres are made of cell bodies, gray matter (p. 90)
    2. Axons covered with white insulation, called myelin, lie beneath the cortex (p. 90, Fig. 3.32)
  B. Brain is full of separate systems operating in parallel (p. 90)
    1. Damage to different areas of the visual cortex result in different deficits (p. 91, Fig. 3.33)
    2. Damage to the parietal lobe can lead to neglect or inattention (p. 91)
    3. A small amount of damage to the frontal lobe can results in loss of memory for a specific location (p. 92-93)
  C. Cerebral cortex consists of four lobes (pp. 93-94, Fig. 3.38)
    1. Occipital lobe is specialized for vision (p. 94)
    2. Parietal lobe is specialized for body senses (p. 94)
      a. Primary somatosensory cortex senses touch in different body areas (p. 94, Fig. 3.38)
    3. Temporal lobes are involved in hearing (p. 94)
    4. Frontal lobes have several different functions (p. 95)
      a. Primary motor cortex controls movement on opposite side of body (p. 95, Fig. 3.38, p. 94)
      b. Prefrontal cortex is critical for keeping track of memories and planning actions based on them (p. 95)
  D. Functional magnetic resonance imaging (fMRI) can be used to study brain activity (p. 95)

IX. Experience can modify brain anatomy (p. 96)
  A. Musical training begun at an early age modifies the cerebral cortex (p. 96)

X. Split-brain operations involve cutting the corpus callosum (p. 96)
  A. Helps epilepsy by stopping spread of seizures (p. 96)
  B. Fibers from each retina still go to each hemisphere (p. 97, Fig. 3.42, p. 98)
    1. Half of the optic nerves cross over to the other side of the brain (p. 97)
  C. Cutting the corpus callosum creates two separate hemispheres (pp. 97-98)
    1. Information presented to the right visual field (left hemisphere) can be named, but information presented to the left visual field cannot (p. 98, Fig. 3.42)

XI. There are many misconceptions about the brain (p. 99)
  A. Although the right and left hemispheres are specialized, all tasks rely on both hemispheres (p. 99)
  B. People use all of their brains; the idea that we only use 10% is a myth (p. 99)

The message: *Many specialized brain areas work together to produce conscious experience (p. 100)*

COMPREHENSION CHECK

Circle the best alternative. Check your answers on pp. 34-36. If you were wrong, look back at your text and write why you were wrong. Check your reasons and the reasons why other alternatives are wrong on pp. 34-36.

Psychological Explanations at the Level of the Gene

1. People who have the gene for Alzheimer's disease:
    a. will always develop the disease
    b. may develop the disease, depending upon the environment
    c. will develop the disease earlier than people who don't have the gene
    d. begin to develop the disease soon after birth

Correct _____ If wrong, why? _____

2. If neither F. Lat nor his wife can curl their tongue, which of the following would be evidence for high heritability of tongue-curling?
    a. none of their children will be able to curl their tongue
    b. half of their children will probably be able to curl their tongue
    c. all of their children should be able to curl their tongue
    d. either b or c, depending on whether F. Lat and his wife are heterozygous or homozygous

Correct _____ If wrong, why? _____

3. Men are much more likely to be color-blind than women because this is a sex-linked trait. This means that:
    a. the gene is sex limited; although both sexes carry it, it is more likely to show up in men
    b. it is not carried on a chromosome
    c. it is carried on the Y chromosome
    d. it is carried on the X chromosome

Correct _____ If wrong, why? _____

4. Huntington's disease:
    a. begins when individuals are teenagers
    b. can be prevented if the gene is found before the disease begins
    c. is caused by a single gene that can be identified
    d. results in progressive increases in memory loss

Correct _____ If wrong, why? _____

5. How could genetics affect people's preferences for dairy products?
    a. a single gene is directly responsible for the food preference
    b. genes control the ability to digest lactose
    c. genes produce differences in taste buds, which produce differences in food preferences
    d. genetics doesn't control this taste preference; it depends purely upon culture

Correct _____ If wrong, why? _____

6. Although people say evolution is the survival of the fittest, what really matters is not survival but:
    a. length of life
    b. environment
    c. health
    d. reproduction

Correct _____ If wrong, why? _____

7. According to sociobiology, why might women be less likely than men to have multiple sex partners?
    a. they have no need to pass their genes along
    b. by having multiple sex partners they are likely to have more trouble finding someone to help with rearing their children
    c. girls learn from an early age that they should take care of children
    d. it is part of a male plot to maintain their superiority

Correct _____ If wrong, why? _____

Explanations of Behavior at the Level of the Neuron

8. Which of the following is true?
    a. neurons are larger and more numerous than glia cells
    b. each neuron physically touches at least one other neuron
    c. neurons are all similar in shape and size
    d. neurons consist of a cell body, dendrites, and an axon
    e. neurons decrease dendritic branching with enriched experience

Correct _____ If wrong, why? _____

9. The action potential:
    a. occurs when positive sodium ions enter an axon
    b. becomes weaker as it travels down an axon
    c. can be speeded up by anesthetic drugs
    d. occurs when potassium enters the axon

Correct _____ If wrong, why? _____

10. What happens at the synapse between neurons?
    a. synaptic vesicles are released from postsynaptic endings
    b. presynaptic endings are destroyed by action potentials
    c. neurotransmitters are released from terminal buttons
    d. neurotransmitters excite the next neuron

Correct _____ If wrong, why? _____

11. Parkinson's disease:
    a. involves muscle twitches and hallucinations
    b. results from the death of axons that use dopamine
    c. can be helped by having the patient take dopamine
    d. results from a deficit in MPTP

Correct _____ If wrong, why? _____

Explanations of Behavior at the Level of the Nervous System

12. John is about to give a speech and his heart is racing, he is breathing rapidly, and he has "butterflies in his stomach." What part of his nervous system is controlling this reaction?
    a. parasympathetic nervous system
    b. spinal cord
    c. endocrine system
    d. sympathetic nervous system
    e. sensory nerves

Correct _____ If wrong, why? _____

13. A person has damage to the hindbrain. Which of the following would be least likely?
    a. the person may have difficulty with memory because of damage to the hippocampus
    b. the person may have difficulty walking a straight line because of cerebellum damage
    c. the person may not show much arousal because of damage to the reticular formation
    d. the person may die because of damage to the medulla and pons

Correct _____ If wrong, why? _____

14. Which is the best statement about how the brain works?
    a. it works as a whole with all brain areas contributing equally to functions
    b. various areas of the brain funnel their information into association areas where the senses are integrated
    c. although the entire brain doesn't work as a whole, all visual input is integrated into one area of the brain
    d. there are many separate modules that act in parallel with each other

Correct _____ If wrong, why? _____

15. The primary somatosensory cortex is:
    a. located in the frontal lobe
    b. the receiving area for touch from the same side of the body
    c. located in the parietal lobe
    d. located behind the cerebral cortex

Correct _____ If wrong, why? _____

16. How does cutting the corpus callosum control the seizures of epilepsy?
    a. it removes the part of the brain that is damaged
    b. it prevents seizures from spreading to the other hemisphere
    c. it prevents visual input from reaching the brain
    d. it prevents axons from the retina from crossing at the optic chiasm

Correct _____ If wrong, why? _____

17. If a person with a split-brain operation closes her right eye and looks at a picture as long as she wants with her left eye, where does the picture end up in her brain?
    a. in her right hemisphere because the axons from the retina cross at the optic chiasm
    b. in her left hemisphere because the axons from the retina go straight back at the optic chiasm
    c. both hemispheres-axons from the left side of the eye go to left hemisphere; axons from the right side of the eye go to right hemisphere
    d. both hemispheres-axons from the right side of the eye go to left hemisphere; axons from the left side of the eye go to right hemisphere

Correct _____ If wrong, why? _____

18. A right-handed, split-brain patient sees a pen very briefly in her left visual field. What will happen when she is asked to identify it?
    a. she will say it is a pen, and pick it out from among other objects with either hand
    b. she will not be able to say what it is, but she will pick it up with her right hand
    c. she will say it is a pen, and will be able to pick it up with her left hand
    d. she will not be able to say what it is, but she will pick it up with her left hand

Correct _____ If wrong, why? _____

ANSWERS AND EXPLANATIONS FOR COMPREHENSION CHECK

Correct Answer	Other Alternatives Are Wrong Because:
1. b (p. 63) Obj. I	a. some may not, depending upon the environment c. people who don't have the gene won't develop the disease d. it develops in old age, following a normal life
2. a (p. 64, Fig. 3.4, p. 64) Obj. I-A-1,2	b. would occur if one was heterozygous and the other homozygous for not curling; one can't be heterozygous because curling is dominant c. would occur if both carried two genes (homozygous) for tongue curling; can't be because neither can do it d. because tongue curling is dominant, it would show up with one gene; they must both have two recessive genes for an inability to curl
3. d (p. 65) Obj. I-B-2	a. located on the X chromosome; capable of altering either sex b. all genes are carried on chromosomes c. the Y chromosome is smaller and does not carry this gene at all; that is why a male is color-blind if he gets the gene from his mother

4. c (p. 66)
   Obj. I-C-1

a. begins in middle-aged people
b. as yet, it can't be prevented although research may someday lead to this possibility
d. results in loss of voluntary muscle control eventually leading to death; Alzheimer's disease shows progressive memory loss

5. b (p. 68)
   Obj. II-B

a. genes control the taste preference indirectly, not directly
c. differences in taste buds don't explain this
d. cultures do differ in their preference for milk products, but this is genetically controlled

6. d (p. 70)
   Obj. III-A

a. not how long one lives, but how many offspring one has
b. may determine reproductive success, but not evolution
c. health doesn't matter; it's number of offspring

7. b (p. 72)
   Obj. V

a. according to sociobiology, reproduction is the key to survival
c. probably true, but not the sociobiologists' explanation
d. unlikely; sociobiologists emphasize spreading of one's own genes

8. d (pp. 75-76, Figs. 3.15-3.16)
   Obj. VI-A

a. glia cells are more numerous

b. neurons do not actually touch each other
c. neurons differ in shape, depending on how many sources of information they have and where their impulses travel
e. studies with rats show that enriched environments result in an increase in dendritic branching

9. a (pp. 77-78)
   Obj. VI-B-1

b. the impulse remains at the same intensity
c. anesthetics prevent action potentials
d. potassium ions leave the axon as sodium enters

10. c (pp. 78-79, Fig. 3.21)
    Obj. VI-C-1

a. released from presynaptic endings
b. endings are part of structure; not destroyed
d. postsynaptic neurons may be either excited or inhibited

11. b. (p. 81, Fig. 3.24)
    Obj. VI-D-1

a. movement problems and depression, not hallucinations
c. dopamine does not cross blood-brain barrier, must use L-DOPA
d. a chemical that causes symptoms similar to Parkinson's

12. d (pp. 86-87)
    Obj. VII-B

a. has the opposite reactions; "calms" body down
b. part of nervous system that controls internal organs lies just outside of spinal cord
c. not part of nervous system; secretes hormones
e. carry sensory information to spinal cord

13. a (p. 88, Fig. 3.30)   b-d. each of these is a function of hindbrain, so they are likely
     Obj. VII-D

14. d (p. 90)   a. Lashley believed this but he worked with complex behavior
     Obj. VIII-B   b. this was believed in early 1900s, but modern research shows it isn't
                                   true
                               c. specific aspects of vision, e.g., shape, color, and motion, are
                                   processed in different areas of the brain

15. c (p. 94)   a. it is in parietal lobe
     Obj. VIII-C-2   b. from the opposite side of body
                               d. it is part of cerebral cortex

16. b (p. 96)   a. connection between hemispheres, not site of damage, is cut
     Obj. X-A   c. visual input still goes to one hemisphere, but not to both
                               d. optic chiasm is not interfered with in split brain

17. c (p. 97, Fig. 3.42, p. 98)   a. only axons from the right half of the left eye cross to the right
     Obj. X-B   hemisphere
                                    b. only axons from the left half of the left eye go straight back to the
                                        left hemisphere
                                    d. reversed-axons from the right side of an eye go to the right

18. d (p. 98)   a. only the right hemisphere "knows" the object; she needs to use her
     Obj. X-C-1   left hand
                               b. she'll pick it up with her <u>left</u> hand
                               c. she won't be able to say what it is; speech is in the left hemisphere
                                   and "pen" is in the right hemisphere

LECTURE MATERIAL

Don't forget to review your lecture material. Process each topic meaningfully. First, be sure that you understand the material in each lecture--if you don't, ASK your instructor or teaching assistant. Associate the material with things that you already know and with your personal experiences. If you can make up mental images of any of the material, do so. Try to think of real-life applications of the concepts. Put comments on your notes. Then <u>write</u> questions to cover each concept.

WAIT AT LEAST 24 HOURS BEFORE PROCEEDING.
LET FORGETTING OCCUR--IT WILL!!

SHORT-ANSWER ESSAY QUESTIONS

Write brief answers to each of the following. The answers are on pp. 38-40, but do try to write the answers yourself before looking at them.

Psychological Explanations at the Level of the Gene

1. What are the advantages of locating specific genes that are related to specific characteristics?

2. What have studies involving monozygous and dizygous twins shown about the role of genetics in behavior?

3. Genetics and environment interact. What is meant by this?

4. Give an example of an animal behavior that is controlled by genetics.

Explanations of Behavior at the Level of the Neuron

5. Describe how nerve impulses travel through neurons and describe what happens when an impulse reaches the end of a neuron.

Explanations of Behavior at the Level of the Nervous System

6. Describe the autonomic nervous system. How is it similar to the endocrine system?

7. How does the brain integrate information from all the different senses?

8. Name the four lobes of the cerebral cortex and describe the function of each.

9. Describe an example of how early experience changes brain structure.

10. How does a split-brain operation help epilepsy, and what are the major consequences of such an operation?

11. Describe the path of the nerve fibers from each eye to the two hemispheres of the brain.

12. "They say that we only use 10% of our brain." What does the textbook say about this?

****
Find the questions that you wrote over
lecture material and write answers to them.
****

ANSWERS TO SHORT-ANSWER ESSAY QUESTIONS

1. Finding a specific gene for a genetic disorder such as Huntington's disease would allow a person to know that they will develop the disease and to plan accordingly. The person may not want to have children. If genes can be identified, researchers may be able to develop a treatment to undo the damage. Problems may be preventable before they begin. (p. 66)

2. Monozygous twins, who share the same genetics, are more similar in characteristics such as having a predisposition toward schizophrenia, depression, and alcohol abuse than dizygous twins, who are less similar genetically. Even monozygous twins separated at birth and reared apart are very similar. They often share interests and hobbies. These similarities aren't conclusive evidence for genetics because the twins shared the prenatal environment. (pp. 66-67)

3. Although something is controlled by genetics, it doesn't mean that it can't be modified by the environment. Phenylketonuria (PKU) is a good example of a genetic disorder that is under environmental control. People who are homozygous for PKU are unable to break down a substance called phenylalanine. Phenylalanine accumulates in the brain and causes mental retardation. However, if the child stays on a diet that is low in phenylalanine, the child does not become mentally retarded. Thus, the environment (the diet) modifies the genetic condition. (p. 70)

4. The Kittiwake, a type of gull that lays its eggs on narrow ledges, shows many behaviors that must be genetic, including fighting over territory, using mud to form a barrier for its nest, and remaining motionless as a chick until it can fly. These behaviors are well adapted to life on narrow ledges and they occur even when nests are built on the ground, suggesting a genetic cause for the behaviors. (pp. 71)

5. Nerve impulses travel through the axons of neurons. The impulse is a positive charge inside an axon that occurs because sodium ions rush in. The impulse continues from the cell body end of the axon to the presynaptic ending, where the impulse causes neurotransmitters to be released into the synapse. (pp. 77-78, Figs. 3.17-3.21)

6. The autonomic nervous system lies just outside the spinal cord and it consists of two parts: sympathetic and parasympathetic. The sympathetic nervous system prepares the body to "fight or flee" by increasing heart and breathing rates and decreasing digestive processes. The parasympathetic nervous system does just the opposite; it decreases heart and breathing rates and increases digestion. The endocrine system consists of glands that secrete hormones that can function like neurotransmitters. Epinephrine is a hormone that does the same thing as the sympathetic nervous system. (pp. 86-87)

7. In the early part of the 20th Century, people believed that there were association areas that integrated information from the various senses. The parts of the brain were thought to funnel their specific information to association areas. But these areas were never found. Karl Lashley argued that the brain operates as a whole and that information did not need to be funneled to any one spot. However, he studied complex learning tasks. Today it is known that small areas of the brain specialize in different functions and each area works in parallel with other areas. Brain damage to specific areas produces different types of deficits that are as specialized as involving only shape, color, motion. attention, and very specialized memory loss. (p. 90)

8. Occipital: Vision, although specific areas contribute to different aspects of visual coding, including motion, shape, and color
   Parietal: Body senses, including touch, pain, temperature, and awareness of body part location. Primary somatosensory cortex is here
   Temporal: Hearing, emotional behavior, language comprehension.
   Frontal: Primary motor cortex controls fine movement; prefrontal area contributes to organization and planning of movements; left frontal lobe involved in language production. (pp. 93-95, Fig. 3.38, p. 95)

9. Any of these examples would work: (a) Violin players who start in childhood have a larger area of the somatosensory cortex devoted to the left hand. (b) The somatosensory cortex representing the finger used to read Braille is larger in blind people. (c) Children who maintain absolute pitch into adulthood have some areas of the temporal lobe enlarged. (p. 96)

10. The corpus callosum is cut so there are no connections between right and left cerebral hemispheres. This prevents seizures from spreading between the hemispheres. People generally behave normally, but if information is presented very briefly to one visual field, it gets into the opposite hemisphere. Right hemisphere cannot say what was seen but it can identify objects with the left hand. Left hemisphere can say what was seen but it is poor at spatial tasks. (pp. 96-98)

11. Information presented to each visual field gets into both eyes. For example, information in the left visual field goes onto the right side of each retina. The optic fibers on the nose side (right) of the left eye cross to the right hemisphere, and the fibers on the temple side (right) of the right eye go back to the right hemisphere. Hence, information from the left visual field goes to the right hemisphere and information from the right visual field goes to the left hemisphere. (If this is unclear, review p. 98 and Fig. 3.42)

12. First of all, no statement should be accepted without evidence. Who is "they"? We could not lose 90% of our brains and operate normally. More than 10% of the neurons in the brain are active at any given time. We use all of our brain, even if we don't seem to be thinking very well. In the 1920s, the function of the so-called "association areas" was not clear to researchers so they may have imagined those areas did nothing. The brain does include many small neurons. Early observers may have thought that those were immature and would develop later. There is no scientific evidence for the 10% claim. (p. 99)

POSTTEST

Take this test with all of your books and notes out of sight. This should give you a good idea of how well you understand the material. The answers are on p. 44.

Matching

Write the letter of the structure on the right in the blank beside the description on the left.

Explanations of Behavior at the Level of the Neuron

1. _____ tiny gap between one neuron and another
2. _____ widely branching structure of neuron that receives information
3. _____ contains nucleus of neuron
4. _____ spherical packets that contain neurotransmitters
5. _____ place where neurotransmitters are released from axon
6. _____ single, long, thin straight part of a neuron
7. _____ insulate neurons and remove waste products from brain

A. axon

B. glia

C. cell body

D. synaptic vesicles

E. synapse

F. terminal button

G. dendrite

Multiple-Choice: Circle the best alternative.

Psychological Explanations at the Level of the Gene

1. Neither Jane nor her husband Jim can taste PTC. Will their children be able to taste this bitter substance?
   a. about half will and half will not
   b. all should be able to taste PTC
   c. none of their children will be able to taste PTC
   d. either a or b, depending upon whether Jane and Jim are heterozygous or homozygous for the gene

2. If a gene shows its effects more in one sex than the other because certain hormones activate it, the gene is said to be:
   a. sex limited
   b. recessive
   c. dominant
   d. sex linked
   e. chromosomal

3. In order for a gene to be favored in evolution, it must affect the:
   a. health of the organism
   b. reproductive success of the organism
   c. appearance of the organism
   d. behavior of the organism

4. Which of the following statements would be most conclusive?
   a. similarities in monozygotic twins raised apart must be genetic
   b. lack of resemblance in some trait for monozygotic twins indicates a non-genetic influence
   c. similarities between adopted children and their adoptive parents indicates a genetic influence
   d. preferences and attitudes cannot be genetic because they are psychological
   e. if something is under genetic control, it cannot be modified by the environment

5. Which of the following fits with principles of sociobiology the least?
   a. sexual customs vary greatly from culture to culture
   b. reed bunting males help incubate the eggs more if the female hasn't mated with a neighboring male
   c. male lions kill young lions after driving off an old male
   d. women devote more effort to child care than men
   e. a goose that sees a hawk overhead utters an alarm call to warn other geese

Explanations of Behavior at the Level of the Neuron

6. Action potentials:
   a. occur when potassium ions enter the axon of a neuron
   b. make the inside of an axon negative relative to the outside
   c. become weaker as they travel down an axon
   d. generally travel away from the cell body
   e. can be increased in strength with anesthetic drugs

7. How does one neuron send its signal to another neuron?
   a. its terminal button touches the next neuron
   b. the two axons touch so that the action potential is passed from one to the next neuron
   c. the positively charged ions from one neuron stimulate the axon of the next
   d. the postsynaptic neuron receives stimulation directly from the dendrites of the presynaptic neuron

8. Loewi collected fluid around the heart after stimulating axons that slowed down the heart and then transferred the fluid to the heart of a second animal. What happened?
    a. nothing; fluid from one animal had no effect on another animal
    b. the second animal's heart sped up; that is, the fluid produced the opposite effect on the second animal
    c. neurotransmitters contained in the fluid stimulated the second animal's heart to slow
    d. myelin contained in the fluid stimulated the second animal's heart to slow
    e. axons contained in the fluid stimulated the second animal's heart to slow

9. Parkinson's disease can be helped by:
    a. taking pills that contain dopamine
    b. taking pills that contain MPTP
    c. injections of epinephrine
    d. injections of serotonin
    e. taking pills that contain L-DOPA

Explanations of Behavior at the Level of the Nervous System

10. The sympathetic nervous system:
    a. lies at the very top and very bottom of the spinal cord
    b. controls the peripheral nerves that communicate with the skin and muscles
    c. transmits impulses from the central nervous system to the muscles and glands
    d. increases heart rate and breathing rate
    e. increases digestive activities

11. Hormones differ from neurotransmitters in that hormones:
    a. affect the organs, neurotransmitters affect the nervous system
    b. affect only the cells close to where they are released; neurotransmitters are diffused throughout the body
    c. are released into the blood stream; neurotransmitters are released adjacent to the cell they are to excite or inhibit
    d. have only short-lived influence; neurotransmitters can have long-term influences
    e. have no effect on behavior; neurotransmitters can have large behavioral effects

12. Damage to which of the following is most likely to be fatal?
    a. cerebellum
    b. spinal cord
    c. medulla
    d. midbrain
    e. limbic system

13. The idea that all kinds of information is funneled to association areas of the cerebral cortex is:
    a. supported by recent research
    b. supported by the finding that faceblindness occurs with damage to specific parts of the inferior temporal cortex
    c. similar to Lashley's theory that behavioral function depends on all brain areas equally
    d. supported by the idea that the two hemispheres operate independently
    e. challenged by the finding that different sensory systems seem to operate independently and in parallel

14. A person who shows unilateral neglect:
    a. has a sensory deficit so that things in one visual field are not seen
    b. is unable to detect movement
    c. may lose spatial memory for just one specific location
    d. has a loss of attention rather than a loss of sensation
    e. is also unable to detect shape and color

15. What is concluded in your text about the relationship between brain and mind?
    a. they are inseparable; if a part of the brain is lost, that part of behavior and experience is lost
    b. "mind" is the central area where all sensations are funneled and organized
    c. the loss of any one specific part of brain will cause total disorganization of "mind"
    d. loss of large parts of the brain has little effect on "mind"; they seem to be separate
    e. both b and c are true

16. The primary somatosensory cortex is:
    a. in the temporal lobe
    b. the part of the brain that controls fine motor movement
    c. organized with a larger area devoted to more sensitive parts of the body
    d. in the occipital lobe
    e. contributes primarily to the organization and planning of movements

17. Based on evidence cited in the textbook, which of the following would you expect to be true of the brain of a famous violinist who began her career as a child?
    a. because of her increased occipital cortex she will be especially good at Braille
    b. the amount of somatosensory cortex devoted to her left hand is larger
    c. most areas of her brain will have become larger because of her extensive experience
    d. her brain is likely to be no different from anyone else's brain

18. A person who has epilepsy has a split-brain operation. Which of the following is true?
    a. the person's corpus callosum has been cut
    b. seizures will increase
    c. seizures will occur more often than before the operation, but they will be less severe
    d. the fibers from each retina will only go to one hemisphere
    e. the person's optic chiasm has been cut

19. A right-handed split-brain patient sees the word cupcake presented very briefly such that cup is in the left visual field and cake is in the right visual field. Which of the following will occur?
    a. she will say that she saw the word "cup"
    b. she will pick out a cup with her left hand
    c. she will say that she saw the word "cupcake"
    d. she will pick out a cake with her left hand
    e. both a and d

20. In Question 19, the word "cup" will fall on the:
    a. right side of both retinas and go to the left hemisphere
    b. left retina only and go to the right hemisphere
    c. left side of both retinas and go to the left hemisphere
    d. right side of both retinas and go to the right hemisphere
    e. right side of the left eye and left side of the right eye and go to both hemispheres

21. The idea that some people are right-brained and some people are left-brained:
    a. is correct; some people use their left hemisphere for all tasks and some use their right
    b. is wrong because most people only use 10% of their brains and that 10% is almost always in the left hemisphere
    c. is correct and based on the fact that small neurons are constantly maturing so that only 10% of the neurons in only one hemisphere are mature at any given time
    d. is wrong; all people are left-brained; the right hemisphere is virtually useless
    e. is wrong because all tasks involve both hemispheres to some extent

ANSWERS TO POSTTEST

Correct Answer	Questions Testing a Similar Concept	
	Comprehension Check	Short-Answer
Matching		
1. E (p. 78)	10	5
2. G (pp. 75-76)	8d,8e	--
3. C (pp. 75-76)	8	--
4. D (p. 78)	10a	5
5. F (p. 78)	10	5
6. A (p. 75-76)	8,9	5
7. B (p. 75)	8a	--
Multiple-Choice		
1. c (p. 64)	2	--
2. a (p. 65)	3a	--
3. b (p. 72)	6	--
4. b (p. 70)	--	2
5. a (p. 72)	7	--
6. d (pp. 77-78)	9	5
7. e (pp. 78-79)	10	5
8. c (p. 81)	--	--
9. e (p. 81)	11	--
10. d (p. 86)	12	7
11. c (pp. 86-87)	10	--
12. c (p. 88)	13d	--
13. e (p. 90)	14b	8
14. d (p. 91)	14a,c	8
15. a (pp. 92-93)	14	8
16. c (p. 94)	15	9
17. b (p. 94)	---	9
18. a (p. 96)	16	10
19. b (p. 97)	17,18	11
20. d (pp. 97-98)	17,18	11
21. e (p. 99)	--	12

CHAPTER 4 SENSATION AND PERCEPTION

OBJECTIVES

Understand that:

I. Sensation is the conversion of energy into nervous system responses (p. 104)

Vision

II. Vision involves reception of radiated energy (p. 105, Fig. 4.1)
   A. Receptors are specialized cells that convert energy (p. 105)
   B. Light passes through the cornea, pupil, and lens (pp. 105-106, Fig. 4.2)
      1. Elongated eyeballs cause nearsightedness; flattened eyeballs cause farsightedness (pp. 106-107, Fig. 4.4)
      2. Glaucoma is increased pressure in the eyeball which can damage the optic nerve (p. 106)
      3. The lens becomes cloudy with cataracts (p. 106)
   C. Receptors are located on the retina (p. 107)
      1. Rods are sensitive in dim light (p. 107, Table 4.1, p. 109)
      2. Cones are sensitive to color and give detailed vision (p. 107, Table 4.1, p. 109)
         a. Fovea consists of cones (p. 107)
   D. Dark adaptation occurs for both rods and cones (pp. 108-109, Fig. 4.8)
   E. Neural impulses travel through the bipolar cells, ganglion cells, and optic nerve to the brain (p. 110)
      1. The blind spot is where the optic nerve leaves the retina (pp. 110-111, Fig. 10)
      2. Binocular rivalry happens when left- and right-eye images conflict (p. 110)
III. Color vision depends on cones (p. 111)
   A. Young-Helmholtz theory or trichromatic theory -- three types of cones (pp. 111-112, Fig. 4.12)
   B. Opponent-process theory -- three two-color systems (pp. 112-113, Fig. 4.14)
      1. Can explain negative afterimages (p. 113, Fig. 4.15)
   C. Retinex theory -- retina and cortex interact to determine color vision (p. 114)
      1. Can explain color constancy (p. 114, Fig. 4.16)
   D. Color blindness occurs because of a deficiency in the cones (pp. 114-115)
The message: Vision is a construction, not a copy, of the outside world (pp. 115-116)

Nonvisual Senses

IV. In hearing, sound waves are translated into neural impulses (pp. 119-120)
   A. Path is eardrum, three tiny bones, cochlear fluid, basilar membrane, hair cells which are the receptors (pp. 119-120, Fig. 4.21)
      1. Conduction deafness occurs when sound waves aren't properly transmitted to the cochlea (p. 120)
      2. Nerve deafness occurs because of damage to the cochlea, hair cells, or auditory nerve (p. 120)
   B. Pitch perception depends on three mechanisms (p. 121, Fig. 4.22)
      1. Neurons fire in synchrony for low frequencies (frequency principle) (p. 121)
      2. Groups of neurons fire in synchrony for middle frequencies (volley principle) (p. 121)
      3. Different parts of basilar membrane vibrate for high frequencies (place principle) (p. 121)
   C. Sound is localized by differences in loudness and time of arrival at the two ears (p. 122, Fig. 4.23)
V. Receptors for vestibular senses are in inner ear (pp. 122-123, Fig. 4.24)
   A. Semicircular canals detect acceleration (p. 123)

B. Otolith organs detect tilt of the head (p. 123)

VI. The cutaneous senses depend upon receptors in the skin (pp. 123-124, Fig. 4.25)

    A. Receptors are dense on fingertips, lips, and other sensitive areas (p. 123)

    B. Pain receptors are bare nerve endings (p. 124)

        1. Intensity of pain depends on other sensory experiences (pp. 124-125)

            a. Gate theory of pain suggests that pain message pass through a gate which can be open or closed (pp. 124-125)

            b. Endorphins (endogenous morphine) decrease pain (pp. 125-126, Fig. 4.28)

            c. Capsaicin causes a burning sensation followed by a reduction in pain (p. 125)

VII. Chemical receptors are responsible for taste and smell (pp. 127-129)

    A. Taste receptors are taste buds on the tongue (p. 127, Fig. 4.29)

        1. Traditionally, the four primary tastes are sweet, sour, salty, and bitter (p. 127)

            a. There is evidence for distinct receptors (pp. 127-128)

    B. Olfactory (smell) receptors are on mucous membranes at rear of nose (p. 128, Fig. 4.30)

        1. The nose has at least 100 different receptors. (pp. 128-129, Fig. 4.30)

        2. Animals identify each other by pheromones (p. 129)

The message: *Senses are adapted to provide information about what is most important to a species (pp. 129-130)*

The Interpretation of Sensory Information

VIII. The perceived world is created from the real world (p. 132)

    A. A threshold is the minimum intensity that a person can detect half the time (pp. 132-133, Fig. 4.33)

        1. Sensory adaptation can change the threshold (p. 133)

            a. The absolute threshold is found when adaptation is maximal (p. 133)

        2. Observers' willingness to make false alarms can affect threshold (p. 133)

            a. This is studied in signal-detection theory (p. 133)

    B. Subliminal perception occurs below the conscious threshold (p. 134)

        1. Subliminal messages don't do many things they are claimed to do (pp. 134-135)

            a. They don't cause people to buy things (p. 134)

            b. Backward messages aren't understood (p. 134)

            c. Subliminal audiotapes don't cause behavioral changes (pp. 134-135)

        2. There is some evidence that stimuli that aren't conscious are processed (p. 135)

            a. Subliminal messages may cause weak behavioral changes that are short-lived (p. 135)

IX. People are very good at recognizing what things are (p. 135)

    A. Face recognition depends on both specific feature and how they fit together into an overall pattern (pp. 135-136)

    B. Feature detectors break patterns into simple components (p. 137)

        1. Cells that detect specific features have been found in animals (pp. 137-138, Fig. 4.39)

        2. Fatigued feature-detector cells produce illusions (pp. 137-138, Fig. 4.40)

    C. More complex identification depends on context (p. 139)

    D. Gestalt psychology suggested that we actively construct overall patterns (p. 139)

        1. Reversible figures are evidence for active organization (p. 140, Fig. 4.45)

        2. The Gestalt principles of proximity, similarity, continuation, closure, and good figure help to explain the organization of stimuli (pp. 140-141, Fig. 4.46)

    E. Gestalt principles also apply to hearing (p. 142)

    F. Feature detection and Gestalt principles are both important for perception (pp. 142-143)

X. Distance and movement are interpretations of changes on the retina (p. 143)
   A. Objects are perceived as constant in size and shape (p. 143, Fig. 4.50)
   B. Movement of an object doesn't occur when the eyes move (pp. 143)
      1. Induced movement occurs when the background moves and the object is stationary (p. 143)
      2. Stroboscopic movement occurs when stationary images are presented (p. 144)
   C. Several cues are used to perceive distance (p. 144)
      1. Retinal disparity occurs because the two retinas receive different images (p. 144)
      2. The eyes must converge more to focus on close objects (p. 144, Fig. 4.53)
      3. Other monocular cues involve only one eye (pp. 144-145)
         a. Object size, linear perspective, detail, interposition, texture gradients, and shadows can be used to judge distance in pictures (p. 145, Fig. 4.54)
         b. Motion parallax involves relative movement and requires real scenes (p. 146)
   D. Illusions occur because of misinterpretations (pp. 146-147, Fig. 4.56)
      1. Sometimes changes in distance are interpreted as size changes (p. 147, Fig. 4.58, 4.59)
      2. Interpreting two-dimensional drawings as three-dimensional can cause depth perception errors (pp. 147-148)
   E. People misjudge loudness when apparent distance changes also (p. 148)
   F. The strength of illusions may differ across cultures, depending on experience with objects (p. 149, Fig. 4.62)
   G. The moon looks much larger on the horizon than high in the sky (pp. 149-150)
      1. There are several theories of the moon illusion, but none explains completely (pp. 149-150)

The message: Perception depend on our experience and knowledge to build up an interpretation of sensory information (p. 150)

COMPREHENSION CHECK

Answer these questions soon after reading the chapter. Circle the best alternative. Check your answers on pp. 51-52. If you gave a wrong answer, try to write why it was wrong. Check your reasons on pp. 51-52.

Vision

1. The nervous system:
   a. builds a copy of the external stimulus in the brain
   b. registers the exact intensity and direction of every stimulus
   c. uses receptors to interpret information and to extract meaning
   d. translates external stimuli into internal representations

Correct _____ If wrong, why? _____

2. Prof. Quaalude is myopic. He:
   a. is farsighted
   b. has an eyeball that is flattened
   c. has a cornea that is too round
   d. has a faulty optic nerve
   e. has an eyeball that is elongated

Correct _____ If wrong, why? _____

3. John is a night watchman. He thinks he hears someone outside in the dim light. In order to see this as clearly as possible, he should:
   a. look slightly to the side of the fovea so rods will be stimulated
   b. look through his widened pupil so cones will be stimulated
   c. make the image fall on his fovea so cones will be stimulated
   d. be sure that the entire electromagnetic spectrum falls on his retina
   e. try to get the image into his blind spot so that his cornea will be clear

Correct _____ If wrong, why? _____

4. Dark adaptation takes much longer if you stare at a faint light while another light flashes in the periphery of your vision than if you just stare at the first light. Why?
   a. having the two lights stimulates more cones
   b. the second light stimulates cones, which take longer to adapt
   c. the second light stimulates rods, which take longer to adapt
   d. having two lights stimulates the ganglion cells as well as the bipolar cells
   e. the second light moves the stimulation from the first light from the blind spot

Correct _____ If wrong, why? _____

5. According to the opponent-process theory, we see green when:
   a. the medium wavelength cone is more active than the other two
   b. the cortex synthesizes a color from active areas of the retina
   c. particular ganglion cells are inhibited and others are excited
   d. we have a negative afterimage of a yellow light

Correct _____ If wrong, why? _____

Nonvisual Senses

6. Which of the following is the correct path of sound waves to the receptors for hearing?
   a. eardrum, cochlea, three tiny bones, hair cells, basilar membrane
   b. eardrum, three tiny bones, cochlear fluid, basilar membrane, hair cells
   c. three tiny bones, cochlear fluid, basilar membrane, eardrum, hair cells
   d. three tiny bones, basilar membrane, hair cells, eardrum, cochlear fluid

Correct _____ If wrong, why? _____

7. How does the human ear encode a tone of 10,000 hertz?
   a. the basilar membrane vibrates in synchrony; hair cells send impulses at that frequency
   b. the basilar membrane vibrates in synchrony with it, and groups of hair cells volley impulses in synchrony with the tone
   c. by the difference in time and loudness at the two ears
   d. the basilar membrane vibrates maximally at a specific location; those hair cells send impulses

Correct _____ If wrong, why? _____

8. If you have damage to your semicircular canals:
    a. you may have trouble with balance
    b. your vestibular sense would be poor
    c. your free nerve endings would not send impulses
    d. both b and c
    e. both a and b

Correct _____ If wrong, why? _____

9. Jalapeño peppers cause somewhat painful sensations because they result in the release of:
    a. endorphins
    b. capsaicin
    c. sodium lauryl sulfate
    d. substance P
    e. pheromones

Correct _____ If wrong, why? _____

10. The olfactory sense in humans:
    a. is very poor because the receptors are not sensitive
    b. is particularly important because of the role played by pheromones
    c. results from receptors that are called taste buds
    d. is limited to only four tastes: sweet, sour, bitter, and salty
    e. is stimulated by gaseous molecules that we inhale

Correct _____ If wrong, why? _____

The Interpretation of Sensory Information

11. An observer might often detect stimuli that are below the absolute threshold because:
    a. dark adaptation has occurred, lowering the threshold
    b. thresholds are defined as 50% detection, so observers will detect below-threshold stimuli half the time
    c. observers set a stringent criterion and make few false alarms
    d. evidence for subliminal perception can be found easily and such perception has been shown to have long-lasting influences on behavior

Correct _____ If wrong, why? _____

12. The feature-detector approach differs from the Gestalt approach because the feature-detector approach:
    a. suggests that we break stimuli down into components; the Gestalt approach argues that we perceive "wholes"
    b. relies on the measurement of thresholds; the Gestalt approach emphasizes optical illusions
    c. points out the importance of visual constancies; the Gestalt approach emphasizes reversible figures
    d. argues that aftereffects should not be found after fatiguing specific feature detectors; Gestalt approach argues that they should

Correct _____ If wrong, why? _____

13. Many computer printers produce letters that consist of unconnected small dots. Yet we see the patterns as complete letters. Which Gestalt principle is operating here?
    a. separation of figure and ground
    b. similarity
    c. closure
    d. reversible figure
    e. proximity

Correct _____ If wrong, why? _____

14. When a rectangular door is slightly open, it projects a trapezoidal image on the retina, yet you see it as rectangular. Why?
    a. size constancy makes it appear the same
    b. visual constancies cause you to interpret changes on the retina as actual changes in the size and shapes of objects
    c. shape constancy tells you that it has changed position, not shape
    d. convergence tells you that its shape has not changed
    e. because a door is a door even if it's ajar

Correct _____ If wrong, why? _____

15. Which depth cue could not be used by a person with one eye?
    a. size
    b. closer objects overlap farther objects
    c. amount of detail in objects
    d. convergence
    e. motion parallax

Correct _____ If wrong, why? _____

16. Jack, who is standing perfectly still, says that there is some wind because the leaves on the trees are moving; Jill, who is riding up the hill, says "No, the leaves aren't moving." How can this discrepancy be explained?
    a. Jill's vestibular system tells her that she is moving
    b. induced movement tells Jack that the leaves are moving
    c. Jack is having an illusion similar to the Mueller-Lyer illusion
    d. the background is stationary to Jill

Correct _____ If wrong, why? _____

17. The moon illusion:
    a. is not an illusion at all; the moon is larger when it is close to the horizon
    b. occurs because light rays bend differently near the horizon
    c. occurs because we interpret the horizon as being farther away than the overhead sky
    d. occurs because we are likely to compare the moon's size with objects at the horizon
    e. both c and d may be partly correct, but the moon illusion is difficult to explain

Correct _____ If wrong, why? _____

ANSWERS AND EXPLANATIONS FOR COMPREHENSION CHECK

Correct Answer   Other Alternatives Are Wrong Because:

1. d (p. 104)
   Obj. I

   a. the internal representation may not resemble the external stimulus in any way
   b. internal representations are related to external stimuli, but they aren't the same
   c. this is perception; receptors are responsible for sensation

2. e (pp. 106-107, Fig. 4.4)
   Obj. II-B-1

   a. myopic means nearsighted; presbyopia means farsighted
   b. this occurs in farsightedness
   c. cornea shape is unrelated to nearsightedness
   d. optic nerve goes from ganglion cells to brain

3. a (p. 107, Table 4.1, p. 109)
   Obj. II-C-2a

   b. cones cannot see well in dim light; a widened pupil makes it more likely that rods will be stimulated
   c. cones cannot respond in dim light
   d. the entire spectrum is not visible, only part of it
   e. blind spot is where axons leave retina; nothing can be seen there

4. c (pp. 108-109, Fig. 4.7)
   Obj. II-D

   a. second light would only stimulate rods
   b. rods take longer to adapt than cones
   d. both lights would stimulate both types of cells
   e. nothing can be seen in the blind spot; a second light wouldn't affect where the first one falls

5. c (pp. 112-113, Fig. 4.14)
   Obj. III-B

   a. Young-Helmholtz theory (emphasis on cones)
   b. retinex theory (emphasis on cortex)
   d. blue would produce a yellow afterimage

6. b (pp. 119-120, Fig. 4.21)
   Obj. IV-A

   a. three tiny bones are between eardrum and cochlea
   c. eardrum comes before three tiny bones
   d. eardrum comes first, cochlear fluid before basilar membrane

7. d (p. 121, Fig. 4.22)
   Obj. IV-B-3

   a. for low tones, below 100 hertz
   b. for medium tones, 100-5000 hertz
   c. this is how sound is localized

8. e (p. 123)
   Obj. V-A

   a. correct, but so is b
   b. correct, but so is a
   c. free nerve endings are receptors for pain and temperature, not vestibular sense
   d. b is correct, but c is incorrect

9. d (p. 125, Fig. 4.28)
   Obj. VI-B-1-c
   a. neurotransmitters that inhibit the release of substance P
   b. this is the chemical in the jalapeños that causes the release of substance P
   c. a chemical that weakens the response to sweet tastes
   e. odorous chemicals released by mammals

10. e (p. 128)
    Obj. VII-B
    a. each receptor is sensitive; we just don't have as many as other animals
    b. less important for humans than other animals
    c. taste buds are for taste, not smell
    d. olfactory means smell, not taste

11. b (p. 133, Fig. 4.34)
    Obj. VIII-A
    a. the absolute threshold is measured when dark adaptation is complete; it's the lowest measurable threshold
    c. a stringent criterion would result in more misses and fewer false alarms
    d. evidence for subliminal perception is not always found and, when it is, it is short-lived

12. a (pp. 137-142)
    Obj. IX-B
    b. feature detection emphasizes components, but not necessarily thresholds; Gestalt relies on more than illusions
    c. visual constancies not particularly relevant to features; reversible figures are one demonstration
    d. such fatigue is evidence <u>for</u> feature detectors

13. c (p. 141)
    Obj. IX-D-2
    a. involves picking out object from background
    b. tendency to see similar things as going together
    d. tendency to see parts as either figure or ground
    e. tendency to see things that are close as going together

14. c (p. 143, Fig. 4.50)
    Obj. X-A
    a. shape is emphasized here, not size
    b. we do not interpret changes as actual changes in objects
    d. convergence is a cue to distance
    e. a bad joke, but that's what shape constancy suggests

15. d (p. 144, Fig. 4.53)
    Obj. X-C-3
    a-c. all can be seen with one eye
    e. differential movement across retina can be seen with one eye, although not in a picture

16. a (p. 143)
    Obj. X-B
    b. occurs when background moves and object doesn't; object is moving here
    c. seeing lines with outward arrowheads as longer than lines with inward arrow heads; not relevant here
    d. background would be moving to Jill since she is moving

17. e (pp. 149-150)
    Obj. X-G
    a. moon is same size
    b. it is a psychological, not a physical effect
    c,d. both are possibly correct, but see e

LECTURE MATERIAL

Don't forget to review your lecture material. Process each topic meaningfully. First, be sure that you understand the material in each lecture--if you don't, ask your instructor or teaching assistant. Associate the material with things that you already know and with your personal experiences. If you can make up mental images of any of the material, do so. Try to think of real-life applications of the concepts. Put your own notes on your lecture notes. Then write questions to cover each concept.

WAIT AT LEAST 24 HOURS BEFORE PROCEEDING.
LET FORGETTING OCCUR--IT WILL!!

SHORT-ANSWER ESSAY QUESTIONS

Write brief answers to each of the following. The answers are on p. 55-56, but do try to write the answers yourself before looking at them.

Vision

1. What is the function of receptors? How are they involved in the relationship between the external and internal worlds?

2. Describe three differences between rods and cones other than their shapes.

3. Contrast the Young-Helmholtz, opponent-process, and retinex theories of color perception.

4. Explain what occurs in the cones when people are color-blind.

Nonvisual Senses

5. Explain how pitch is perceived for sounds of different frequencies.

6. According to the gate theory of pain, why do reports of pain differ so much, even when the physical damage is similar?

7. Describe evidence that suggests there are different receptors for different tastes.

The Interpretation of Sensory Information
8. How does the signal-detection approach to detection differ from the threshold approach?

9. What are the problems in studying subliminal perception? What does modern research suggest about the possibility of subliminal perception?

10. Contrast the Gestalt and the feature-detector approaches to perception.

11. Explain how Gestalt principles apply to hearing.

12. Assume that you have a negative afterimage of the U.S. flag. Describe what would happen if you looked at a white screen that is very close to you and then at one that is very far away. Use this example to explain how size and distance are related.

ANSWERS TO SHORT-ANSWER ESSAY QUESTIONS

1. Receptors convert physical energy into nerve impulses, or stimuli in the external world into internal stimuli. The internal experience is lawfully related to the external stimuli, but they are not perfectly related. (p. 105)

2. Rods are sensitive in dim light; cones are sensitive only in bright light. Rods are color-blind; cones respond to color. Cones are concentrated on the fovea at the center of the retina; rods are on the periphery. (pp. 107-108, Table 4.1, p. 109)

3. Young-Helmholtz theory holds that there are three types of cones that respond maximally to different colors. Opponent-process theory holds that higher-level cells are excited (speeded up) to one color and inhibited (slowed down) to another. Retinex theory stresses interpretation of color by the cortex. (pp. 111-114)

4. Usually, there is an abnormality in either the red or green cones (although other types of colorblindness also occur). If the problem is in the green cones (medium-wavelength), it is called deuteranopia; if it is in the red cones (long-wavelength), it is called protanopia. The abnormal cones don't respond properly to the red or green light, so the person has difficulty discriminating red from green. (pp. 114-115)

5. For low sounds (under 100 Hz), the basilar membrane vibrates in synchrony with the sound and nerve impulses are sent in synchrony. Middle sounds (100-5000 Hz) are coded in a similar manner, except that individual hair cells cannot send impulses that fast, so groups of cells volley and, as a group, send impulses that are in synchrony with the sound. High sounds (over 5000 Hz) cause maximum vibration at certain places on the basilar membrane, and only those hair cells send impulses to the brain. (p. 121, Fig. 4.22)

6. According to Melzack and Wall's gate theory, pain messages pass through a gate in the spinal cord. The brain can send messages to the spinal cord to open the gate and let the pain impulses through or to close the gate and block the pain. Although some of the details of this gate theory are wrong, the basic idea that the brain facilitates or inhibits the transmission of pain messages is correct. Distraction may help to close the gate, or distraction may cause the release of endorphins, which are natural painkillers that work in the brain. (pp. 124-125)

7. Cooling the tongue reduces sensitivity to sweet tastes, but not to other tastes. Chemicals such as sodium lauryl sulfate (an ingredient in toothpaste) weakens sensitivity to sweet and increases sensitivity to sour and bitter. (pp. 127-128)

8. Thresholds are found by determining the lowest-intensity stimulus that can be detected half of the time. Thresholds will vary depending upon other factors, such as degree of dark adaptation. Using signal-detection theory, both the ability to detect a stimulus and the observer's criterion are taken into account. An observer may detect more stimuli under some conditions, but if she also makes a lot of false alarms (detecting the stimulus when it isn't present), detection isn't any better; the criterion is simply less stringent (strict). (pp. 132-133)

9. One problem is identifying whether stimuli are really subliminal (below threshold) because subjects may or may not report seeing or hearing them, depending upon how cautious they are about their responses. There is evidence that the nervous system processes stimuli even though we are unaware of them, but these effects don't last very long. These can influence our perception of other stimuli, but there is no evidence that subliminal messages influence buying behavior or have any effect on breaking bad habits. (pp. 134-135)

10. The feature-detector approach argues that people break stimuli down into components, such as lines and angles. The brain then analyzes the components to decide what a stimulus is. The Gestalt approach argues that we take in whole stimuli rather than breaking them into components. (pp. 137-142)

11. There are reversible figures in sound as well as in vision. For example, a clock can sound like "tick, tock, tick, tock" or "tock, tick, tock, tick." People also lock onto one interpretation of a sound and cannot hear the other one. If they organize the words in a sentence in one way, they may organize the words in the next sentence in the same way until they discover that the organization doesn't make sense. (p. 142)

13. The negative afterimage has a certain size on your retina. If you look at a white piece of paper near your eyes, you will see a small image. If you look at a piece of paper far away, you will see a large image. In the far case, you assume that the actual size must be quite large for the afterimage to be that big on your retina and that far away. In the close case, you assume that the actual size is small because the distance is close. (pp. 113, 144-145)

POSTTEST

Take this test with all of your books and notes out of sight. This should give you a good idea of how well you understand the material. The answers are on p. 61.

Matching

Put the letter of the structure on the right in the blank beside the description on the left.

<u>The Eye and the Ear</u>

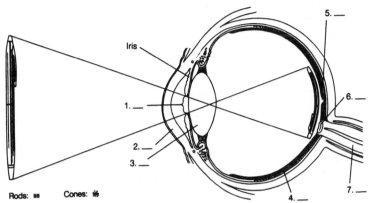

A. blind spot

B. fovea

C. semicircular canals

D. optic nerve

E. stirrup

F. eardrum

G. retina

H. cornea

I. hammer

J. anvil

K. pupil

L. lens

M. oval window

N. cochlea

O. round window

P. auditory nerve

Multiple -Choice

Circle the best alternative.

<u>Vision</u>

1. What is the relationship between what we sense and what is really there?
   a. there is a perfect relationship between external events and our internal representations
   b. models of external stimuli are created in the brain
   c. they are physically identical
   d. external stimuli are translated into a neural "language"
   e. for vision, internal copies are made but for other senses that are nonspatial, other types of representations are formed

2. When a person is farsighted:
   a. the lens does not become thin and flat as it should for distant objects
   b. he or she has myopia
   c. the eyeball is elongated
   d. the eyeball is flattened
   e. both b and c

3. Why can you see fine detail better if you look straight at an object than if you look out of the corner of your eye?
   a. the object falls on the fovea, where there are many rods
   b. the object falls on the periphery, where there are many cones
   c. the object falls on rods, many of which send impulses to the same ganglion cell
   d. the object falls in the blind spot, where detailed vision is good
   e. the object falls on the fovea, where there are many cones

4. Why does everyone have a blind spot in each eye?
   a. there are no rods or cones where the optic nerve leaves the retina
   b. there are no cones on the periphery of the retina
   c. the retina is organized with rods and cones at the front and ganglion cells at the rear
   d. the fovea contains no rods
   e. the rods on the far periphery contain no photopigments

5. Which of the following best supports retinex theory?
   a. negative afterimages occur in the opposite color
   b. people are usually red-green color-blind
   c. different cones show different levels of responding to different colors
   d. three different colors of light can be mixed to make all other colors
   e. the apparent color of an object depends upon the colors of the objects around it

6. Colorblind people:
   a. usually cannot distinguish any colors
   b. see green objects as red
   c. most often have trouble distinguishing yellow from blue
   d. most often have trouble distinguishing red from green
   e. do not have any photopigments in their cones

Nonvisual Senses

7. What happens to the basilar membrane when a low tone (below 100 Hz) is sensed?
    a. a very small area of it vibrates; the rest is relatively stationary
    b. it vibrates in synchrony with the sound waves
    c. it volleys in synchrony with the sound waves
    d. the left basilar membrane responds faster than the right one
    e. it will respond to more reflected sounds than with a higher tone

8. When a sound comes from directly overhead, it is difficult to localize because:
    a. it reaches one ear earlier than the other
    b. the basilar membrane is unable to respond to such a sound
    c. it sounds louder in one ear than the other
    d. it reflects off objects too much
    e. it reaches the two ears at the same time and with the same intensity

9. Why is it easier to read when your head is moving than when the page is moving?
    a. the vestibular system keeps your eyes focused when your head moves but not when the book moves
    b. the basilar membrane vibrates when your head moves, but not when the book moves
    c. the somatosensory system keeps your eyes focused when your head moves but not when the book moves
    d. the gate in the spinal cord prevents stimulation to the brain when your eyes move, but the signal gets through the gate when the book moves
    e. capsaicin is released when the head moves; this causes the release of substance P, which keeps the eyes focused when the head moves

10. Endorphins are:
    a. drugs made from the opium poppy that are similar to morphine
    b. neurotransmitters that cause the release of substance P and decrease pain
    c. used to decrease the sensitivity of the olfactory system
    d. neurotransmitters that occur naturally and are similar to morphine
    e. naturally occurring substances that cause the release of capsaicin in the body

11. The four types of taste buds are:
    a. scattered uniformly across the tongue
    b. are important for sensing the location of the substance on the tongue
    c. are interrelated, so that if one of them is affected by some chemical, all are affected
    d. are located almost exclusively along the sides of the tongue
    e. are unrelated to heat and cold so that changing the temperature does nothing to the taste

12. Pheromones:
    a. are used by animals to recognize one another
    b. are very important in human sexual behavior
    c. do not exist in humans
    d. are neurotransmitters that help to reduce pain
    e. cannot be detected by the human olfactory system

13. Which of the following claims about subliminal perception is true?
    a. people choose a picture that was presented subliminally more often than one that wasn't presented
    b. subliminal messages presented backward in songs can make people believe in the devil
    c. subliminal messages in movies influence people to buy snacks
    d. subliminal tapes can make people change their behavior; they are especially effective for increasing self-esteem

14. Which of the following supports the feature-detector model of pattern recognition?
    a. Hubel and Wiesel found that some brain cells responded only to angles
    b. some figures are reversible so that the background becomes the object
    c. things which are close together tend to be grouped into a unit
    d. we tend to "hear" missing syllables in speech
    e. stimuli are identified in context such that additional stimuli can either help or hurt identification

15. Gestalt psychologists:
    a. try to break stimuli into their basic components
    b. believe that perceptions depend on overall configurations
    c. argue that perception is simply the passive reception of energy
    d. emphasize the study of feature detectors
    e. believe in the theories of their founder, B. F. Gestalt

16.   K   K   K   K   K
       K   K   K   K   K
       K   K   K   K   K
       K   K   K   K   K

    Why are you more likely to see the above as columns of Ks rather than rows of Ks?
    a. figure-ground principle
    b. closure
    c. proximity
    d. continuity
    e. similarity

17. Which of the following is not a cue for distance?
    a. convergence of the two eyes
    b. different views seen by the two eyes
    c. haziness of objects
    d. curvature of the cornea when focusing
    e. size of objects

18. As the $100 bill that you just won blows away from you in the wind, you do not perceive it as becoming smaller. Why?
    a. you have size constancy
    b. you are not responding to visual constancies
    c. your eyes compensate by converging more and more to focus
    d. your lens is unable to change fast enough to notice the size change
    e. you assume that objects in the distance are moving closer

19. The Mueller-Lyer illusion is:
    a. seeing the moon as larger when it is closer to the horizon than when it is high in the sky
    b. seeing lines as longer when arrowheads point inward than when they point outward
    c. stronger for people who live in cities and more technological societies than for people from more rural cultures
    d. only experienced by people who have lots of experience with drawings of objects
    e. larger for adults than for children

ANSWERS TO POSTTEST

Correct Answer	Questions Testing a Similar Concept	
	Comprehension Check	Short-Answer

Matching

1. K (p. 106, Fig. 4.2)	3b	--
2. H (p. 106, Fig. 4.2)	2c, 3e	--
3. L (p. 106, Fig. 4.2)	--	--
4. G (p. 106, Fig. 4.2)	3d	--
5. B (p. 106, Fig. 4.2)	3a, 3c	--
6. A (p. 106, Fig. 4.2)	3e, 4e	--
7. D (p. 106, Fig. 4.2)	2d	--
8. I (p. 120, Fig. 4.21)	6	--
9. J (p. 120, Fig. 4.21	6	--
10. F (p. 120, Fig. 4.21	6	--
11. E (p. 120, Fig. 4.21	6	--
12. M (p. 120, Fig. 4.21	--	--
13. C (p. 120, Fig. 4.21	8	--
14. P (p. 120, Fig. 4.21	--	--
15. N (p. 120, Fig. 4.21	6	--
16. O (p. 120, Fig. 4.21	--	--

Multiple-Choice

1. d (pp. 104-105)	1	1
2. d (pp. 106-107, Fig. 4.4)	2a,b	--
3. e (pp. 107-108)	3c	2
4. a (pp. 110-111)	3e,4e	--
5. e (p. 114)	5b	3
6. d (pp. 114-115)	--	4
7. b (p. 121)	7a	5
8. e (p. 122)	7c	--
9. a (pp. 122-123)	8b	--
10. d (pp. 125-126, Fig. 4.28)	9a	6
11. d (p. 127, Fig. 4.29)	--	7
12. a (p. 129)	10b	--
13. a (pp. 134-135)	11d	9
14. a (pp. 137-139)	12,14	10
15. b (p. 139)	12	10
16. c (p. 141)	13e	10
17. d (pp. 144-145)	15	--
18. a (p. 143)	14a,b	12
19. c (pp. 148-149)	16c	--

CHAPTER 5 ALTERED STATES

OBJECTIVES
Understand that:

Sleep and Dreams

I. Rhythms of activity and inactivity are called circadian rhythms (p. 157)
  A. Some people are morning people and some are evening people (p. 158, Fig. 5.3)
  B. West-shift (going to bed later) is easier than east-shift (going to bed earlier) (p. 159, Fig. 5.5)
  C. The superchiasmic nucleus controls the circadian rhythms (p. 160, Fig. 5.6)
    1. It regulates the secretion of melatonin (p. 160)
II. Sleep must serve some function (p. 160)
  A. Repair and restoration might be one function (pp. 160-161)
    1. There are several weaknesses in this theory (p. 161)
      a. People don't need much more sleep after a day of extreme activity (p. 161)
      b. Some people get by with very little sleep (p. 161)
      c. People who go intentionally without sleep don't need much to be recovered (p. 161)
  B. Evolutionary or Energy Conservation theory suggests that sleep protects from danger (p. 161)
    1. Species vary in how much they sleep, but all sleep some (p. 161, Fig. 5.8)
III. Main stages of sleep are REM and non-REM (NREM) (pp. 162)
  A. Sleep cycles through four stages of (pp. 162-163, Fig. 5.10-5.11)
    1. Stages are 1-NREM, 2, 3, 4, 3, 2, 1-REM (pp. 162-163)
    2. A cycle through the stages takes 90-100 minutes (p. 163)
  B. Dreaming occurs during REM sleep (p. 163)
    1. Deprivation of REM sleep leads to anxiety, irritability, and impaired concentration (p. 164)
    2. REM sleep may improve memory storage and new learning may prompt extra REM sleep (p. 165)
IV. The content of dreams is usually related to recent thoughts and concerns (p. 166)
  A. The activation-synthesis theory suggests that the brain is active during sleep and that the brain tries to make sense of these sensations (p. 167)
    1. Blind people who could see at one time have visual dreams; those who have never seen or who have damage to the visual cortex don't have visual dreams (p. 167).
    2. Major postural muscles are paralyzed during REM sleep (p. 168)
V. Abnormalities of sleep (p. 168-170)
  A. Insomnia means lack of sleep (p. 168)
    1. A yoked control experiment showed that insomnia by itself doesn't cause tension, depression, and personal distress (pp. 168-169)
  B. People with sleep apnea awaken because they cannot breathe while asleep (p. 169)
  C. People with narcolepsy fall asleep during the day (p. 169)
  D. Sleep talking, sleepwalking, nightmares, and night terrors are fairly common (p. 170)
    1. Sleep talking is common and nothing to worry about (p. 170)
    2. Sleepwalking usually occurs in children (p. 170)
      a. Waking sleepwalkers poses no problems (p. 170)
    3. Night terrors are accompanied by extreme panic (p. 170)
      a. These are more common in children (p. 170)
  E. Periodic limb movement disorder or restless leg syndrome can cause poor sleep (p. 170)
  F. Hypersomnia is excessive but unrefreshing sleep (p. 170)
The message The brain is active even when sleeping (pp. 170-171)

Hypnosis

VI. Hypnosis is a state of increased suggestibility (p. 173)
   A. Mesmer founded hypnotism, calling it animal magnetism (p. 173)
   B. It can be induced in several different ways (p. 174)
      1. The first step is agreeing to try it (p. 174)

VII. Hypnosis can do a number of things (pp. 174-175)
   A. The distress of pain can be reduced (p. 174)
   B. Posthypnotic suggestions can help people to change their habits (p. 174-175)

VIII. Hypnosis cannot do other things that are claimed for it (pp. 175-176)
   A. Hypnotized people "remember" actual facts, but they mix in fantasies (p. 175)
   B. Hypnotized people don't relive childhood (p. 176)
   C. Hypnosis doesn't lead to recall from previous lives (p. 176)
   D. People under hypnosis may do strange (and dangerous) things, but so do people who are pretending to be hypnotized (p. 176)

IX. Hypnosis can result in distortions of perception (p. 177)
   A. People may claim that they don't hear or see stimuli, but those stimuli can still influence behavior (p. 177)

X. Hypnotized people and people pretending to be hypnotized show some different behavior (but there are lots of similarities too) (p. 178)
   A. Hypnotized people are puzzled by seeing double realities; pretenders don't report seeing double realities (p. 178)
   B. Criminal defendant Kenneth Bianchi was faking hypnosis, according to expert Martin Orne (p. 179)

XI. Meditation is another method of inducing a calm, relaxed state (p. 179)

The message: *Hypnosis enables people to relax and follow suggestions more than they usually do (p. 179-180)*

Drugs and Their Effects

XII. Most abused drugs increase activity at dopamine synapses (p. 182)
   A. Alcohol acts as a relaxant (p. 182)
      1. Excessive use damages the liver, aggravates medical conditions, and impairs memory and motor control (p. 182)
      2. Alcohol abuse is more common among Native Americans and African Americans than among people with European ancestry; people with Asian ancestry are lowest (p. 182)
   B. Tranquilizers help people to relax and fall asleep (p. 183)
      1. Benzodiazepines facilitate the neurotransmitter GABA (p. 183)
   C. Opiates bind to synapses that use endorphins which are naturally occurring brain chemicals (p. 183)
      1. Morphine is used as a pain killer in controlled doses (p. 183)
   D. Marijuana intensifies sensory experiences (pp. 183-184)
      1. THC, the active ingredient, attaches to receptors mostly in the hippocampus (p. 184)
   E. Stimulants heighten alertness and increase activity (p. 184)
      1. Caffeine can result in dependency (p. 184)
      2. Cocaine increases heart rate but it decreases brain activity (p. 184)
         a. Crack is cocaine that can be smoked (p. 185)
         b. Crack is very habit-forming because it enters the brain very rapidly (p. 185)
      3. Nicotine increases heart rate and blood pressure, but decreases breathing rate (p. 185)
   F. Hallucinogens induce sensory distortions (pp. 185-186)

XIII. Withdrawal effects and drug tolerance occur with extended use of drugs (p. 186)
   A. Withdrawal symptoms occur when habitual use ceases (p. 186)

1. Specific effects depend upon the drug (p. 186)
    a. Physical dependence occurs when people use the drug to reduce withdrawal effects (p. 186)
    b. Psychological dependence is a strong desire to use the drug but no physical withdrawal symptoms (p. 186)
  B. Drug tolerance means that more and more drug is required to get the same effects (p. 186)
    1. Tolerance may result from both automatic chemical changes and psychological effects (p. 186)

The message: Almost all drugs impair the brain's functioning in some way (p. 187).

COMPREHENSION CHECK

Answer these questions soon after reading the chapter. Circle the best alternative. Check your answers on pp. 67-69. If you gave a wrong answer, try to write why it was wrong. Check your reasons on pp. 67-69.

Sleep and Dreams

1. Which of the following provides evidence that our 24-hour sleep-waking cycle is the result of a built-in mechanism?
    a. some people sleep only 5-6 hours a night; others sleep 7-8 hours
    b. only a little more sleep is needed after a day of exertion than after a day of little activity
    c. people who live in an environment in which everything is constant still go to sleep and wake at about the same time each day
    d. prisoners who are forced to stay awake for long periods of time develop severe health problems

Correct _____ If wrong, why? _____

2. Jet lag occurs whenever you change time zones quickly. Which type of trip will result in the most difficult adjustment?
    a. Flying from Los Angeles to New York
    b. Flying for 1 1/2 hours but staying in the same time zone
    c. Flying from New York to Chicago
    d. Flying from New York to Los Angeles

Correct _____ If wrong, why? _____

3. Which of the following is evidence for the repair and restoration theory of sleep?
    a. the body increases its rate of cell division during sleep
    b. species that are less likely to be attacked sleep longer
    c. people can survive without sleep for 10 or 11 days
    d. people need only a little more sleep following a day of extreme activity than following a day of inactivity
    e. some people have hypersomnia

Correct _____ If wrong, why? _____

4. The evolutionary theory of sleep predicts which type of animal should sleep the least? One that is:
   a. unlikely to be attacked by other animals
   b. sleeping in a familiar environment
   c. able to complete its eating in a short time
   d. likely to be attacked by other animals

Correct _____ If wrong, why? _____

5. The high-school student who stayed awake for several days:
   a. was near death by the time he slept
   b. slept for many days when he finally went to sleep
   c. didn't fully recover until he had several nights of normal sleep
   d. slept longer than usual when he did go to sleep, but was fully refreshed upon awakening

Correct _____ If wrong, why? _____

6. REM sleep is also called paradoxical sleep because:
   a. the brain is very active, but heart rate, breathing rate, and temperature fluctuate greatly
   b. the brain is relatively inactive and the heart rate is very low
   c. the large muscles are very active but the temperature is very low
   d. the large muscles are relaxed and heart rate is low
   e. dreams occur here yet the times are much shorter than the perceived length of dreams

Correct _____ If wrong, why? _____

7. Electroencephalograph (EEG) waves:
   a. are similar when a person is in stage 4 sleep and awake
   b. become shorter and choppier as a person moves from stage 1 to stage 4 sleep
   c. become larger as a person goes into deeper sleep because a larger proportion of the active neurons are active at the same time
   d. are the largest when a person is very awake because the brain is most active

Correct _____ If wrong, why? _____

8. Which of the following is the proper order of sleep stages in a cycle?
   a. 1 (NREM), 2, 3, 4, 1 (REM), 2, 3, 4
   b. 1 (REM), 2, 3, 4, 1 (REM), 2, 3, 4
   c. 1 (REM), 2, 3, 4, 3, 2, 1 (REM)
   d. 1 (NREM), 2, 3, 4, 3, 2, 1 (REM)

Correct _____ If wrong, why? _____

9. Dreams:
   a. only occur in REM sleep
   b. may occur in NREM sleep but they are less vivid and visual than in REM sleep
   c. are almost always in color
   d. may occur in REM sleep but they are less vivid and visual than in NREM sleep
   e. never occur in blind people

Correct _____ If wrong, why? _____

10. People who have been selectively deprived of REM sleep:
    a. have difficulty waking up in the morning and falling asleep at night
    b. become very depressed
    c. often show REM rebound
    d. develop narcolepsy

Correct _____ If wrong, why? _____

11. Which of the following is not true?
    a. Dreams last about as long as REM sleep does
    b. Sleep talking occurs only during REM sleep
    c. People who have the same dream over and over report more anxiety, depression, and stress than do other people
    d. Night terrors are common among young children and usually occur during stages 3 and 4
    e. Restless leg syndrome is a common cause of poor sleep in people over 50

Correct _____ If wrong, why? _____

Hypnosis

12. The state of hypnosis is best described as a:
    a. condition of heightened suggestibility
    b. trance state that is similar to sleep
    c. power emanating from the hypnotist's body
    d. state in which the mind and body become separated

Correct _____ If wrong, why? _____

13. A well-established effect of hypnosis on perception is:
    a. the elimination of certain illusions as a result of suggestion
    b. the ability to become deaf
    c. a reduction in the distress of pain
    d. a large reduction in the intensity of pain

Correct _____ If wrong, why? _____

14. There are many myths about hypnosis. Which of the following is actually true?
    a. People can remember things very accurately that they cannot remember without hypnosis
    b. Hypnotized people can become stiff as a board
    c. People under hypnosis will do strange things that nonhypnotized people would never do
    d. Posthypnotic suggestions cause long-term behavior change
    e. Hypnotized people can remember most events from childhood

Correct _____ If wrong, why? _____

15. Orne detected that Kenneth Bianchi was faking because Bianchi:
    a. denied seeing a person that Orne suggested was sitting in the chair opposite him
    b. developed another personality after Orne told him that most multiple personalities have three, not two, personalities
    c. couldn't remember how the filter of his cigarette got torn off
    d. saw an imagined person and the whole chair in which the person was sitting at the same time

Correct _____ If wrong, why? _____

Drugs and Their Effects

16. Which drugs boost energy, heighten alertness, and increase activity?
    a. hallucinogens
    b. alcoholic beverages
    c. barbiturates
    d. stimulants
    e. opiates

Correct _____ If wrong, why? _____

17. Research has shown that the relationship between brain receptors and THC is that THC:
    a. attaches to specialized receptors, found mostly in the hippocampus
    b. doesn't attach to receptors but modifies neuronal membranes
    c. may attach to a few receptors but those are rare in the brain
    d. attaches to the same receptors as endorphins do

Correct _____ If wrong, why? _____

18. In rats, it has been shown that the coordination of rats after 24 injections of alcohol is better at the end if they have been tested after each injection. This shows that:
    a. alcohol is not addictive
    b. alcohol produces strong withdrawal symptoms
    c. tolerance results from more than simple repeated exposures to the drug
    d. drug tolerance depends on purely automatic chemical changes

Correct _____ If wrong, why? _____

ANSWERS AND EXPLANATIONS FOR COMPREHENSION CHECK

Correct Answer	Other Alternatives Are Wrong Because:
1. c (pp. 157-158) Obj. I	a. they still may have a 24-hour cycle b. problem for repair-restoration theory but not evidence for cycles d. but those who stay awake on their own usually don't; not evidence for 24-hour cycles
2. a (p. 159) Obj. I-B	b. this should not cause jet lag because time doesn't change c,d. going west is not as bad as going east; it's easier to go to bed later than earlier
3. a (pp. 160-161) Obj. II-A	b. evidence for evolutionary theory c, d, e. weakness of repair-restoration theory

4. d (p. 168, Fig. 5.8)
   Obj. II-B

   a. an animal that is a predator will sleep a lot
   b. should increase sleeping; no need to fear attack
   c. can sleep a lot because eating takes little time

5. d (p. 161)
   Obj. II-A-1-c

   a. consequences are not that serious
   b. sleep only a few more hours than normal
   c. usually recover after one night's sleep

6. a (pp. 162-163)
   Obj. III-A

   b. brain is active; heart rate fluctuates
   c,d. large muscles are very relaxed; temperature and heart rate
       fluctuate
   e. subjective time for dreams is about the same as REM periods

7. c (pp. 162-163)
   Obj. III-A

   a. stage 4 waves are much larger and slower Fig. 5.9, p. 190)
   b. they become longer and less choppy with sleep
   d. when the brain is active, neurons are out of synchrony and they
       cancel each other

8. d (p. 162-163)
   Obj. III-A-1

   a,b. goes from 4 to 3, not to 1
   c. the first stage is 1,NREM; REM later replaces Stage 1

9. b (p. 163)
   Obj. III-B

   a. some dreaming occurs in NREM sleep
   c. maybe, but people report color only about half the time
   d. NREM dreams are less vivid and visual
   e. visual dreams occur in people who had vision and lost it; people
       who never had vision dream about touch

10. c (p. 165)
    Obj. III-B-2

   a. characteristics of jet lag
   b. this can improve mood in depressed people
   d. . they show more REM the next night; they don't fall asleep
       suddenly during the day

11. b (p. 167-170)
    Obj. IV-A, V

   a,c,d,e are correct statements so they are not correct answers to the
       question which asked you to select the statement that was <u>not</u> true
   b. statement is wrong; occurs during non-REM also

12. a (p. 173)
    Obj. VI

   b. in terms of ability to move about and respond to stimuli, hypnosis
       is more like waking
   c. being a hypnotist requires no unusual personality traits
   d. people just become more suggestible under hypnosis

13. c (p. 174)
    Obj. VII-A

   a. illusions still occur, even when their cause is supposedly not
       perceived
   b. the behavior of hypnotized people suggests that they still hear, even
       when they say they don't
   d. the intensity of pain is changed only a little

14. b (p. 178)
    Obj. X
a. many memories that come out under hypnosis are wrong
c. nonhypnotized "pretenders" do strange things too
d. usually change is short-lived, but if there is long-term change, it's probably due to the person's resolve and not the hypnotic suggestion
e. many such "memories" are not accurate

15. b (p. 179)
    Obj. X-B
a. he didn't deny it; he actually shook hands with the person--a rare response for a hypnotized person
c. he said he couldn't remember which would be appropriate for a hypnotized person, but he repeated this three times for other hypnotists
d. actually hypnotized people do this; pretenders don't

16. d (p. 184)
    Obj. XII-E
a. causes hallucinations and sensory distortions actually a relaxant
b. may appear to stimulate because it inhibits some brain areas
c. results in sleep, a sedative
e. analgesics; these reduce pain

17. a (p. 184)
    Obj. XII-D-1)
b. scientists used to think this, but specific receptors have been found
c. THC receptors may be among the most numerous in the brain
d. opiates do this; anandamide is the neurotransmitter that binds to the same receptors as THC

18. c (p. 186)
    Obj. XIII-B-1
a. alcohol is an addictive drug
b. alcohol does produce withdrawal symptoms, but this drug tolerance example doesn't show this
d. if tolerance was purely automatic, then practice would have no effect

LECTURE MATERIAL

Don't forget to review your lecture material. Process each topic meaningfully. First, be sure that you understand the material in each lecture---if you don't, ask your instructor or teaching assistant. Associate the material with things that you already know and with your personal experiences. If you can make up mental images of any of the material, do so. Try to think of real-life applications of the concepts. Write your own notes on your lecture notes. Then write questions to cover each concept.

WAIT AT LEAST 24 HOURS BEFORE PROCEEDING.
LET FORGETTING OCCUR--IT WILL!!

SHORT-ANSWER ESSAY QUESTIONS

Write brief answers to each of the following. The answers are on pp. 71-72, but do try to write the answers yourself before looking at them.

Sleep and Dreams

1. Describe evidence that supports the idea that humans have built-in mechanisms that produce a 24-hour wake-sleep cycle.

2. Briefly describe the repair and restoration theory of sleep. Discuss two weaknesses of the theory.

3. Explain the evolutionary view of sleep.

4. Describe the stages of sleep including the EEG activity that accompanies them. Discuss two characteristics of REM sleep.

5. What are the effects of REM sleep deprivation?

6. What is narcolepsy? How does it differ from insomnia?

7. Discuss sleep talking, sleepwalking, and night terrors.

Hypnosis

8. Describe the modern view of hypnosis. How does it differ from Mesmer's view?

9. Describe how people imitating hypnosis are similar to and different from people who are actually hypnotized.

Drugs and Their Effects

10. Explain how crack differs from cocaine both in terms of the substance itself and in terms of its effects.

11. Explain how drug withdrawal symptoms might work to keep someone using the drug.

****
Find the questions that you wrote over lecture material and write answers to them.
****

ANSWERS TO SHORT-ANSWER ESSAY QUESTIONS

1. Two people spent several weeks in a cave in which the temperature was constant and they controlled their own lighting. They tended to go to sleep and awaken at their usual times even though there were no cues in the environment. (pp. 157-158)

2. The body needs sleep in order to repair and restore itself from the day's exertions. Cell division and the rate at which the body produces new proteins increase. One weakness is that we do not seem to need more sleep after a day of extreme activity than after a day of inactivity. Another weakness is that people vary greatly in the amount of sleep that they need. (Other weaknesses exist; see p. 161)

3. Sleep may have a restorative function, but it also occurs at a time when the animal is likely to be inefficient. How often and how long an animal sleeps depends upon whether it is a predator and can afford lots of sleep or a prey and can afford little sleep. It also depends upon whether meals are short or whether the animal must eat constantly. (p. 161)

4. Stage 1 (NREM) - stage 2 - stage 3 - stage 4 - stage 3 - stage 2 - stage 1 (REM). The cycle takes about 90 min. Brain waves go from short, choppy waves to long, slow waves at stage 4. During REM sleep, the person's EEG shows short, choppy waves; postural muscles are relaxed; and the person is hard to awaken. (pp. 162-163, Figs. 5.10-5.11)

5. People who are deprived of REM show anxiety, irritability, and difficulty in concentrating. When participants are allowed to sleep undisturbed, REM rebound occurs; they spend more time in REM than usual. Because REM sleep facilitates memory storage, deprivation of REM sleep may also slow down learning, at least in animal studies. (pp. 164-165)

6. Narcolepsy is a condition in which people fall asleep, often going into REM sleep, in the middle of the day. This is the opposite of insomnia. The person with insomnia cannot fall asleep at night; the person with narcolepsy falls asleep during the day. (p. 169)

7. Most people talk in their sleep sometimes. It occurs both during REM and NREM sleep and is not abnormal. Children are more likely to sleepwalk than adults. It occurs during stage 4 sleep because the muscles are too relaxed during REM sleep. Night terrors are fairly common in young children. The child usually awakens in an extreme state of panic and has a very high heart rate. These occur in sleep stages 3 and 4. (p. 169)

8. Hypnosis is considered to be a state of heightened suggestibility. People who are hypnotizable are likely to do what the hypnotist tells them without question. In terms of ability to move about and to respond to stimuli, it is more like waking than sleeping. Mesmer thought that the powers were within him, the hypnotist. In fact, hypnotizability seems to be due more to the subject's willingness to accept suggestions than to the hypnotist. (pp. 173-174)

9. People who are imitating hypnosis will tolerate pain without flinching, recall old memories, make their bodies stiff as a board and lie between two chairs, and show physiological changes when told to experience an emotion. However, they are not as inconsistent as actually hypnotized people who will report seeing a person sitting in a chair and also report seeing the entire chair. Real hypnotized people report seeing two images of the same person, but pretenders don't. (p. 178)

10. Cocaine can be sniffed or injected, but not smoked. In order to smoke it, the drug must have the hydrochloride removed, turning it into "freebase" cocaine, commonly called crack. Crack enters the brain more rapidly than cocaine, so it is more likely to be addictive. It is also more likely to   lead to mental confusion, heart attacks, lung disease, and neglect of daily activities. (p. 185)

11. Drugs usually provide the stimulus for pleasant emotional states. As drugs wear off, however, the user moves into the opposite state. Because drugs produce tolerance effects, initial highs grow weaker and weaker with use. Finally, users may need to take the drugs to avoid the negative, opposite states produced as the effects of drugs wear off. (p. 186)

POSTTEST

Take this test with all of your books and notes out of sight. This should give you a good idea of how well you understand the material. The answers are on p. 76.

Matching

Put the letter of the term in the blank beside the description.

Sleep and Dreams; Drugs and Their Effects

1. _____ medical condition in which people fall asleep in the middle of the day

2. _____ tranquilizers that facilitate neurotransmitter GABA

3. _____ bind to endorphin synapses in brain

4. _____ induce distortions of experience

5. _____ getting too much unrefreshing sleep

6. _____ trouble breathing while asleep

7. _____ difficulty in sleeping

A. sleep apnea

B. insomnia

C. narcolepsy

D. hallucinogens

E. benzodiazepines

F. opiates

G. hypersomnia

Multiple-Choice

Circle the best alternative.

<u>Sleep and Dreams</u>

1. What happened to the sleep cycles of the people who spent a few weeks in Mammoth Cave?
    a. they spontaneously adapted to a 28-hour day
    b. they slept for about 4 hours and stayed awake for about 4 hours
    c. they could not keep a set cycle; sleeping and waking times varied greatly from day to day
    d. they kept a 24-hour cycle, waking up and going to sleep at about the same time each day
    e. they were sleepy in the morning, but not at night

2. Sleep deprivation for a period of several days results in:
    a. dizziness, slurred speech, and hallucinations in everyone
    b. a loss of skill, such as that needed to play arcade games
    c. the need to sleep for 24 hours or more before recovery can occur
    d. minimal effects in some people who have control of the situation
    e. a total loss of ability to concentrate; even the simplest tasks cannot be completed

3. Which of the following is consistent with the repair and restoration theory of sleep?
    a. some people need much less sleep than other people
    b. only a little more sleep is needed after a day of exertion than after a day of inactivity
    c. people who stay awake are sleepier at night than in the morning
    d. people can go for 10 or more days without sleep
    e. the body increases the rate of cell division and new protein production during sleep

4. According to the evolutionary theory of sleep, some animals sleep more than others because they:
    a. are more active
    b. must expend more energy to kill their prey
    c. eat such low-calorie food that they must rest often
    d. are less vulnerable to attack
    e. have higher metabolic rates

5. Why is it better to shift work schedules from an eight-to-four shift to a four-to-midnight shift than the other way around?
    a. the body is better able to repair and restore when sleep occurs later than earlier
    b. it is like flying east--going toward the sunrise makes it easier to fall asleep than going away from it
    c. the direction of the shift is irrelevant as long as the lights are kept dim for the night shift
    d. it is like flying west--it is easier to go to bed later than usual
    e. this type of shift makes you feel safer in your bedroom, so you sleep better

6. Sam Snore volunteered for a psychology experiment in which he slept for two nights in the laboratory. On the first night, he was awakened every time he entered REM sleep. The result was that he had almost no REM sleep during that night. His EEG on the next night would show:
    a. more stage 4 sleep than usual
    b. more stage 2 sleep than usual
    c. less REM sleep than usual
    d. less stage 4 sleep than usual
    e. more REM sleep than usual

7. Bob seems to be deeply asleep, yet his brain waves resemble those of an alert, waking state. Bob is now in _____ sleep and just before this he was in _____.
    a. REM; a drowsy, awake state
    b. REM; stage 2 sleep
    c. Stage 4; stage 2 sleep
    d. Stage 2; stage 1 sleep
    e. paradoxical; stage 4 sleep

8. REM sleep:
    a. has been shown to help memory storage
    b. lasts longer during the first than during the second half of the night
    c. is the time when sleepwalking is most likely to occur
    d. is the only stage in which dreams occur at night
    e. is absolutely necessary; even a few nights of deprivation can cause death

9. The content of dreams is influenced by:
    a. experiences of the past day
    b. stimuli being experienced during sleep
    c. spontaneous brain activity
    d. all of the above

10. Why is it impossible for sleepwalking to occur during REM sleep?
    a. the postural muscles are so relaxed that they would not support a person
    b. the heart rate is so slow that there would not be enough blood flowing to the large muscles
    c. the part of the brain that is responsible for movement becomes inactive
    d. the EEG shows too much spontaneous activity for specific muscles to be stimulated
    e. the eye movements use so much energy that there is little left for coordinated movement

11. Which of the following is false?
    a. night terrors usually occur during Stage 3 or Stage 4 sleep
    b. most people talk in their sleep, at least some of the time
    c. the activation-synthesis theory of dreams suggests that the brain is actively organizing sensory information during dreams
    d. sleepwalking occurs in adults more often than in children
    e. dream content is often related to the day's activities

12. Narcolepsy involves:
    a. a failure to breathe while sleeping that may results in awakening many times each night
    b. very unpleasant dreams that keep children awake
    c. prolonged creepy-crawly sensations in the legs
    d. frequent awakenings during the night
    e. sudden attacks of extreme sleepiness during the day

Hypnosis
13. Mesmer's animal magnetism:
    a. worked because magnets redirected patients' flow of blood
    b. made physicians and scientists associate hypnosis with eccentrics
    c. was based on the idea that hypnosis is a state of enhanced suggestibility
    d. induced hypnotic trances, which redistributed brain activity
    e. worked with actual magnets, but not without them

14. Scientific studies have most strongly supported the contention that hypnosis can:
    a. reduce the distress of pain, although it reduces the intensity of pain only slightly
    b. make people totally deaf
    c. eliminate illusions if the hypnotist says to ignore the contextual stimuli
    d. give you physical strength that you would not have otherwise
    e. make you do things that you would never do otherwise

15. Hypnosis has been used to help people remember things. These memories:
    a. are extremely accurate
    b. often include things that the hypnotized person has made up
    c. are quite accurate under hypnosis, but become mixed with fantasy when the person comes out of hypnosis
    d. are very accurate if they involve the person's childhood; otherwise they are not accurate

16. Which of the following is true of people who are actually hypnotized as compared with people who are pretending?
    a. pretenders cannot tolerate pain without flinching
    b. when asked to sit down, pretenders look for a chair first; hypnotized people do not
    c. when told to experience anger, hypnotized people show physiological reactions, pretenders do not
    d. hypnotized people will imagine seeing someone sitting in a chair and also see the entire chair; pretenders do not report seeing the chair
    e. pretenders will report seeing a single individual in two places; hypnotized people will not report seeing the same person in two places

Drugs and Their Effects

17. Marijuana:
    a. is chemically similar to crack
    b. causes sexual debauchery
    c. facilitates transmission at synapses using GABA
    d. can help relieve glaucoma
    e. is gone from the body within 3 hours after use

18. Cocaine:
    a. increases heart rate, but decreases overall brain activity
    b. has no anesthetic properties
    c. has less of an effect after it is treated with ether
    d. is called a designer drug because people from high society use it
    e. is not addictive

19. Symptoms of withdrawal from opiate drugs include:
    a. sweating, sleeplessness, and possibly hallucinations and seizures
    b. nervousness and sleeplessness
    c. anxiety and heightened sensitivity to pain
    d. only mild withdrawal symptoms or no withdrawal symptoms occur

20. How are drug withdrawal and drug tolerance related?
    a. both are purely physiological effects
    b. both are purely psychological effects
    c. together they lead to decreased use of a drug
    d. increased tolerance makes a drug less effective so users may take more of the drug to fight withdrawal effects
    e. increased tolerance makes a drug more effective, so less of the drug is needed to eliminate withdrawal effects

ANSWERS TO POSTTEST

Matching

Correct Answer	Questions Testing a Similar Concept	
	Comprehension Check	Short-Answer
1. C (p. 169)	10e	6
2. E (p. 183)	--	--
3. F (p. 183	16e	--
4. D (pp. 185-186)	16a	--
5. G (p. 183)	3e	--
6. A (p. 169)	--	--
7. B (p. 168)	--	6

Multiple-Choice

1. d (pp. 157-158)	1	1
2. d (p. 161)	3d,5	2
3. e (pp. 160-161)	3	2
4. d (p. 161)	4	3
5. d (p. 159)	2	--
6. e (p. 164)	10	5
7. b (p. 162)	8	4
8. a (p. 165)	6	5
9. d (p. 166)	11c	--
10. a (p. 170)	6d	4,7
11. d (p. 170)	11	7
12. e (p. 169)	10e	6
13. b (p. 173)	12	8
14. a (p. 174)	13, 14	--
15. b (p. 175)	14a,e	9
16. d (p. 178)	14, 15	9
17. d (pp. 183-184)	17	--
18. a (p. 184)	16	10
19. c (p. 183)	16e,17d	11
20. d (p. 186)	18	11

CHAPTER 6 LEARNING

OBJECTIVES

Understand that:

Behaviorism

I. Behaviorists study measurable, observable behaviors (p. 191)
    A. Radical and methodological behaviorists differ in the degree to which they believe that mental processes exist and can be inferred (p. 191)
        1. Early behaviorists explained behavior in terms of stimulus-response connections (p. 192)
    B. Behaviorists made several assumptions (p. 193)
        1. All behavior is caused (determinism) (p. 193)
        2. Mental explanations do not explain causes of behavior (p. 193)
        3. Behavior is molded by the environment (p. 193)

The message: Behaviorists believe that your behaviors are caused by your present and past environments (p. 194)

Classical Conditioning

II. Pavlov first described classical conditioning (pp. 195-197)
    A. Unconditioned stimuli (UCS) produce unconditioned responses (UCR) (p. 196, Fig 6.3, p. 197)
        1. A neutral stimulus (CS) paired with the UCS causes a similar response (CR) (p. 196, Fig.6.3, p. 197)
    B. Many phenomena are associated with conditioning (p. 198, Fig. 6.4)
        1. Acquisition occurs when the CR is strengthened following UCS and CS pairings (p. 198)
        2. Extinction occurs if the CS is presented often without the UCS (p. 198)
        3. Spontaneous recovery occurs when extinguished responses return temporarily after a delay (p. 198)
        4. Stimulus generalization has occurred if CRs are made to stimuli that are similar to the CS (p. 199)
        5. Discrimination has occurred if the animal responds to some stimuli but not others (p. 199)

III. Drug tolerance can be explained by classical conditioning (pp. 199-200)
    A. Stimuli that precede the drug become CSs for a defense reaction by the body (p. 200)
    B. The drug has weaker effects because of this conditioned response (p. 200)

IV. There are differing explanations of classical conditioning (pp. 200-203)
    A. Pavlov thought that temporal contiguity caused conditioning (p. 201, Fig. 6.8)
    B. CSs are reacted to as signals, not as if they were UCSs (p. 201)
    C. Temporal contiguity is not the entire explanation (pp. 201-203)
        1. Animals don't respond much to a CS when other CSs predict the UCS (p. 202, Fig. 6.9)
        2. Animals don't learn about a CS if the UCS often occurs without it (p. 202)
    D. Both contingency and contiguity are important (p. 203)

The message: Classical conditioning creates signals that prepare us for what happens in our environment (p. 203)

Operant Conditioning

V. Thorndike first studied operant (instrumental) conditioning (pp. 205-206)
    A. Reinforcement increases the probability of a response (p. 206)

1. The law of effect states that a response that is followed by favorable consequences will be more likely in the future (p. 206)
2. Classical conditioning applies mostly to visceral responses; operant conditioning applies to skeletal responses, although the distinction sometimes breaks down (p. 206)
- B. Extinction, generalization, and discrimination occur in operant conditioning also (pp. 206-207)
- C. Some responses are more easily learned than others (p. 207)
  1. Some stimuli and responses show belongingness (p. 207)

VI. B. F. Skinner first demonstrated shaping (pp. 207-209)
- A. Shaping involves reinforcement of responses that become closer to the final response (pp. 208-209)
- B. In chaining, each response is reinforced by an opportunity to perform the next response (pp. 209-210)

VII. Response frequencies can be both increased and decreased (pp. 210-211, Table 6.2)
- A. Reinforcement increases response frequency (pp. 210-211, Table 6.2)
  1. Event that increases behavior is added in positive reinforcement (p. 210)
  2. Unpleasant event is removed in negative reinforcement (p. 211)
     a. Also called escape or avoidance learning (p. 211)
- B. Punishment decreases response frequency (pp. 210-211, Table 6.2)
  1. Event that decreases behavior is added for punishment (p. 210, Table 6.2)
     a. Also called passive avoidance learning (p. 210)
     b. Effective only if it is prompt and consistent, and if an alternative response is available (p. 211)
  2. Behavior removes that positive event is negative punishment (p. 210)
     a. Also called omission training (p. 210)
- C. A reinforcer is anything that increases responses (p. 212)
  1. Drive-reduction theory argues that reinforcers satisfy drives (p. 212)
  2. Premack principle states that more frequent responses can serve as reinforcers for less frequent responses (p. 212)
  3. Disequilibrium principle states that activities are reinforcing if we have spent less than our usual time on them (p. 212)
  4. Unconditioned reinforcers meet biological needs (p. 212)
  5. Conditioned reinforcers have been associated with unconditioned reinforcers (p. 212)
  6. Individuals learn what leads to what (p. 213)
- D. Reinforcement does not follow every response when a schedule is used (pp. 213-214, Table 6.3)
  1. Reinforcement is given after some set number of responses in fixed ratio (p. 213, Table 6.3, p. 214)
  2. Reinforcement is given on the average after some number of responses in variable ratio (pp. 213-214, Table 6.3)
  3. Reinforcement is given for the first response after some time period in fixed interval (p. 214, Table 6.3)
  4. Reinforcement is given on the average after some time period in variable interval (p. 214, Table 6.3)
  5. Extinction takes longer following intermittent reinforcement than following continuous reinforcement (p. 214)

VIII. Operant conditioning has practical applications (pp. 215-216)
- A. Animals are trained through shaping and reinforcement (p. 215)
- B. Reinforcements can be used to persuade people (p. 215-216)
- C. Applied Behavior Analysis can modify problem behaviors (p. 216)

D. Bad habits can be broken with operant conditioning (p. 216)

The message: Survival depends on the sensitivity of our behavior to its consequences (p. 217)

Other Kinds of Learning

IX. Taste-aversion learning can occur in a single trial and with long delays between UCS and CS (pp. 219-221, Fig. 6.18)

 A. Some CSs work better than others; e.g., tastes condition more to illness than lights and noises (pp. 219-221, Fig. 6.19)

X. Song learning in birds differs from classical and operant conditioning (p. 221)

 A. Birds learn to sing during an early sensitive period (p. 221)

 B. Birds learn to sing the songs of their own species (p. 221)

 C. Songs are learned by listening and perfected by practice (p. 221)

XI. Much learning occurs from observing others, according to social-learning theory (pp. 221-222)

 A. People model their behavior after others' behavior; they imitate (pp. 222)

 B. Some behaviors occur or do not occur because similar behaviors in other people have been reinforced (vicarious reinforcement) or punished (vicarious punishment) (pp. 222-223)

  1. Vicarious punishment doesn't work as well as vicarious reinforcement (p. 223)

 C. Self-efficacy may be necessary for imitation (p. 223)

  1. Much behavior is maintained through self-reinforcement (pp. 223-224)

The message: Many forms of learning influence your behavior (p. 224)

COMPREHENSION CHECK

Answer these questions soon after reading the chapter. Circle the best alternative. Check your answers on pp. 83-85. If you gave a wrong answer, try to write why it was wrong. Check your reasons on pp. 83-85.

Behaviorism

1. Which of the following is <u>not</u> a basic assumption of behaviorists?

 a. behavior should be explained by internal motivations

 b. behavior is molded by the environment

 c. explanations based on internal states are not useful

 d. determinism is the appropriate philosophy

Correct _____ If wrong, why? _____

Classical Conditioning

2. Every time the toilet in a neighboring apartment is flushed, your shower becomes very hot and you jump back. Soon you learn to jump back at the sound of the flushing even before the water gets hot. Which of the following is correct?

 a. pulling back from a painful stimulus is a conditioned reflex

 b. the flushing sound is the UCS

 c. jumping back at the sound is the UCR

 d. the flushing sound is the CS

 e. jumping back from the hot water is the CR

Correct _____ If wrong, why? _____

3. Which of the following would produce the best classical conditioning?
   a. an unfamiliar sound presented 1 sec. before the UCS
   b. a familiar sound presented 1 sec. before the UCS
   c. presentation of the CS many times without the UCS
   d. presentation of the CS immediately after the UCS

Correct _____ If wrong, why? _____

4. A child named Albert learned to fear a rat because the sight of it was paired with a loud, frightening sound. Later the child also showed fear of his mother's fur coat. Why?
   a. there was no contingency between the noise and the rat
   b. he formed a discrimination for the situations when the UCS would and would not occur
   c. stimulus generalization occurred from the furry rat to the similar coat
   d. extinction probably caused him to associate the coat with the noise
   e. spontaneous recovery occurred following extinction of the fear

Correct _____ If wrong, why? _____

5. An individual always takes a drug injection in his small, cramped room. One reaction of his body to the drug is an increase in heart rate. The conditioned response in this case is likely to be:
   a. a decrease in heart rate
   b. an increase in heart rate
   c. things in the small, cramped room
   d. the injection of the drug itself
   e. the injection procedure

Correct _____ If wrong, why? _____

Operant Conditioning

6. Thorndike's cats learned to escape the puzzle box because:
   a. positive reinforcement followed the correct response
   b. their learning curves showed a gradual increase
   c. visceral responses were changed by instrumental conditioning
   d. skeletal responses were changed by classical conditioning

Correct _____ If wrong, why? _____

7. How does extinction occur in <u>operant</u> conditioning?
   a. present the CS many times without the UCS
   b. present the CS many times without the UCS; then wait for a day and present the CS again
   c. withhold positive reinforcement following a correct response
   d. set up the situation so that the opportunity to make the next response is the reinforcement for each response

Correct _____ If wrong, why? _____

8. The lion in a circus stands up on a chair and from there jumps through a hoop that is on fire. No reinforcement is given until it goes to the center of the stage and stands on its hind legs. How was this animal trained?
   a. by shaping
   b. by reinforcing each successive approximation to the response
   c. by chaining the shaped responses
   d. by first giving positive reinforcement only when the entire sequence was correct
   e. a, b, and c

Correct _____ If wrong, why? _____

9. Many cars have loud, obnoxious buzzers that continue until the driver buckles the seat belt. Buckling the belt turns off the buzzer. This is an example of which type of operant conditioning?
   a. positive reinforcement
   b. negative punishment
   c. punishment
   d. negative reinforcement

Correct _____ If wrong, why? _____

10. What do psychologists currently believe about punishment?
    a. it is effective in the short run but not in the long run
    b. punishment can be effective if it is immediate and very severe
    c. punishment can be effective if it is immediate and there is an alternative response available
    d. punishment is never effective and should be avoided at all costs
    e. punishment sometimes reduces the behavior because attention is reinforcing

Correct _____ If wrong, why? _____

11. Your father promises you your own credit card if you do well in your first year at college. The credit card is:
    a. an unconditioned reinforcer
    b. valuable because you have been shaped to appreciate it
    c. a conditioned reinforcer
    d. an example of fixed-ratio reinforcement

Correct _____ If wrong, why? _____

12. Jake, a fly fisherman, finds that he gets an average of five bites per 50 casts. If getting bites is reinforcing, he is:
    a. on a fixed-ratio schedule of reinforcement
    b. on a fixed-interval schedule of reinforcement
    c. in a negative reinforcement situation
    d. on a variable-ratio schedule of reinforcement
    e. on a continuous reinforcement schedule

Correct _____ If wrong, why? _____

13. Jake, from question 13, goes fishing with Bud who, in the past, has gotten a bite with every cast. They go to a river where there are no fish and they get no bites. How long will each continue to cast?
   a. Jake will continue longer than Bud because he had been on intermittent reinforcement
   b. Bud will continue longer than Jake because he had been on intermittent reinforcement
   c. both will continue the same time because they are in a punishment situation
   d. Bud will continue longer because he was on a variable-interval schedule before and that prolongs extinction

Correct _____ If wrong, why? _____

14. A girl with a developmental disability is being taught to comb her hair, to brush her teeth, and to be generally neat and clean every day. She receives tokens that can be traded for goods and privileges. At first, almost any attempt at neatness earns a token, but later she must do more to earn a token. The girl is:
   a. being reinforced by the Premack principle
   b. receiving negative punishment
   c. receiving unconditioned reinforcers
   d. in an applied behavior analysis program
   e. being forced into disequilibrium by her behavior

Correct _____ If wrong, why? _____

15. If you eat a new food and then get sick because of the flu, you might dislike that food and avoid it in the future. Which of the following is true?
   a. you would also avoid the type of plate upon which the food was served
   b. classical conditioning could not have occurred because the delay between the taste and illness would be too long
   c. a conditioned taste aversion was acquired; the association between taste and illness is easily learned
   d. a conditioned taste aversion developed with taste as the UCS for illness

Correct _____ If wrong, why? _____

Social Learning

16. John was able to stop smoking after seeing that his racquetball partner was able to play better and not become short of breath after he stopped. John:
   a. was able to stop because of his poor self-efficacy
   b. changed his behavior because of vicarious reinforcement
   c. began to change his behavior because of positive reinforcement
   d. changed his behavior because of vicarious punishment

Correct _____ If wrong, why? _____

17. If you have received vicarious reinforcement for a behavior, you are likely to be successful at executing the behavior if you:
    a. have poor self-efficacy
    b. have doubts about your ability but are willing to try anyway
    c. use appropriate self-reinforcement
    d. have high self-efficacy
    e. both c and d

Correct _____ If wrong, why? _____

ANSWERS AND EXPLANATIONS FOR COMPREHENSION CHECK

Correct Answer	Other Alternatives Are Wrong Because:
1. a (p. 191) Obj. I	a. the emphasis was on observable behavior, not on unobservable internal states b-d. these are basic assumptions of behaviorists
2. d (p. 196) Obj. II-A-1	a. pulling back from a painful stimulus is an <u>un</u>conditioned reflex b. flushing sound is CS; response to it is learned (conditioned) c. jumping back from sound is CR; it is learned e. jumping back from hot water is UCS; it is not learned
3. a (p. 196) Obj. II-A-1	b. it is more difficult to learn CRs to familiar stimuli c. this will produce extinction if conditioning has already occurred; otherwise no learning will occur d. CS must precede the UCS for good conditioning
4. c (p. 199) Obj. II-B-4	a. there was a contingency; the appearance of the rat predicted the noise b. no; he responded in the new situation rather than discriminating it and not responding d. extinction refers to the reduction of CRs to a CS, not to responding to other stimuli e. the original fear was not extinguished; rat was not presented alone many times
5. a (p. 200) Obj. III-A	b. unconditioned response due to the drug itself; an opposite defense reaction is conditioned c. would be part of the conditioned <u>stimuli</u> d. this is the <u>unconditioned stimulus</u> e. part of the conditioned <u>stimuli</u>

6. a (pp. 205-206)
   Obj. V-A

b. curves plot the course of performance, they don't cause it; errors decreased
c. visceral responses are usually automatic and classically conditioned; not relevant to cats' behavior
d. skeletal responses are usually voluntary muscle movements and operantly conditioned

7. c (pp. 206-207)
   Obj. V-B

a. extinction in classical conditioning
b. would lead to spontaneous recovery in classical conditioning
d. chaining; can be done without extinction

8. e (pp. 207-211)
   Obj. VI-A,B; VIII-A

a,b. different terms for reinforcing small parts of the response
c. this is how the different responses would be linked
d. the whole sequence would never occur spontaneously, so reinforcement would never be given

9. d (p. 211, Table 6.2, p.210)
   Obj. VII-A-2

a. the buckling response removes an unfavorable consequence; it doesn't add a favorable one
b. the buckling response does not remove a favorable consequence
c. the buckling response does not add an unfavorable consequence

10. c (p. 211)
    Obj. VII-B-1-b V-A

a. this was Skinner's view; however, if an alternative response is available, punishment can work
b. very severe punishment is not necessary
d. it can be effective, and may be necessary to stop dangerous behavior
e. punishment is sometimes reinforcing because it is accompanied by attention; however, this increases the behavior, not decreases it

11. c (pp. 212-213)

    Obj. VII-C-5

a. doesn't satisfy a basic biological need, unless you eat and digest plastic
b. shaping refers to responses, not reinforcements
d. you aren't being reinforced for a set number of responses

12. d (pp. 213-214, Table 6.3)
    Obj. VII-D-2

a. he doesn't get a bite every 10th cast; it's on the average
b. number of casts, not time, is specified
c. refers to increasing a response because an unfavorable stimulus is removed; not relevant here
e. continuous means reinforcement for every response; not true here

13. a (pp. 213-214)
    Obj. VII-D-5

b. Bud has been on continuous reinforcement and that will produce faster extinction
c. refers to addition of an unfavorable stimulus; not relevant here
d. Bud has not been on any intermittent reinforcement schedule; he has been on continuous reinforcement

14. d (p. 216)
   Obj. VIII-C

   a. tokens are reinforcers; she isn't being allowed to do a preferred behavior
   b. no favorable stimuli are being removed if she is not neat
   c. tokens are conditioned, not unconditioned, reinforcers
   e. disequilibrium refers to the fact that any behavior that has been engaged in less often than usual can be reinforcing; getting her to increase hygiene isn't doing this

15. c (p. 219)
   Obj. IV-E-1

   a. visual stimuli are not easily associated with illness
   b. this type of long-delay learning does occur
   d. taste is the CS

16. b (pp. 222-223)
   Obj. XI-B

   a. he must have thought he was able to stop; he probably had high self-efficacy
   c. the positive benefits on his own health would be positive reinforcement, but at first he stopped because he saw his partner being reinforced
   d. the partner had a favorable, not an unfavorable, outcome

17. e (pp. 223-224)
   Obj. XI-C,1

   a. must have high self-efficacy; think you can do it
   b. this is low self-efficacy; not likely to succeed
   c. correct, but high self-efficacy is important too
   d. correct, but probably need self-reinforcement as well

LECTURE MATERIAL

Don't forget to review your lecture material. Process each topic meaningfully. First, be sure that you understand the material in each lecture--if you don't, ask your instructor or teaching assistant. Associate the material with things that you already know and with your personal experiences. If you can make up mental images of any of the material, do so. Try to think of real-life applications of the concepts. Write your own comments on your lecture notes. Then write questions to cover each concept.

WAIT AT LEAST 24 HOURS BEFORE PROCEEDING.
LET FORGETTING OCCUR--IT WILL!!

SHORT-ANSWER ESSAY QUESTIONS

Write brief answers to each of the following. The answers are on pp. 87-89, but do try to write the answers yourself before looking at them.

Behaviorism

1. Describe the three assumptions of behaviorism.

Classical Conditioning

2. Describe how a person might come to feel frightened at a corner after having had an auto accident at that corner.

3. John's girlfriend is trying to get him to wink on command. She blows a puff of air into his eye and then says "Hi ya." After doing this many times, John still doesn't blink to "Hi ya." Explain why not.

4. Describe one example of evidence that classical conditioning is not simply the result of temporal contiguity.

Operant Conditioning

5. Design an operant conditioning program to get a dog to press a lever to turn on a light.

6. Explain how negative and positive reinforcement differ.

7. Describe Skinner's view of punishment and also describe the more current view.

8. Describe the four schedules of reinforcement and describe the effect of intermittent versus continuous reinforcement on extinction.

9. Explain how shaping could be used to get prisoners to say things publicly that they don't believe.

Other Kinds of Learning

10. How does song learning in birds differ from classical and operant conditioning?

11. How would a social-learning theorist explain a child's learning to smoke cigarettes?

12. Describe the roles of self-efficacy and self-reinforcement in learning.

****
Find the questions that you wrote over lecture material and write answers to them.
****

ANSWERS TO SHORT-ANSWER ESSAY QUESTIONS

1. 1) All behavior has a cause that can be understood with scientific methods; 2) explanations based on internal causes and mental states are not useful; explanations should be based on external, observable events; 3) the environment molds behavior, and we are influenced by our surroundings (p. 193)

2. Classical conditioning could explain this. The fear at the sight of the corner is a conditioned response. Fear at the time of the accident is the unconditioned response to the unconditioned stimuli of loud noise and pain. The particular corner is the CS, but other corners may also produce fear through generalization. If only that corner produces fear, discrimination has occurred. (pp. 196-197)

3. For conditioning to occur, the CS ("Hi ya") needs to precede (predict) the UCS (puff of air). Simple contiguity is not enough; the UCS should be contingent upon the CS (the puff of air should only occur <u>following</u> the "Hi ya" stimulus). She should present the CS a second before the UCS and then John might wink on command. (p. 203)

4. If a CS has already been conditioned to a UCS, then a second, simultaneous, CS is not learned about because it is redundant and not informative. This is true even though it has temporal contiguity with the UCS. Another piece of evidence is that conditioning doesn't occur when the UCS occurs alone frequently without the CS, even though presentations of the CS are always followed by the UCS. (pp. 201, 203)

5. The dog would have to be shaped. First, a food reinforcement should be given whenever the dog looks toward the lever, then only when he moves toward it, and later when he touches it. Next, the dog would have to push the lever slightly to be rewarded. Finally, he would have to push it hard enough to turn on the light. (pp. 205-206, 207-209)

6. In positive reinforcement, the consequence of the behavior is that a favorable event occurs after the response. For example, money is given contingent upon some behavior. The goal is to increase the behavior that led to the positive event. In negative reinforcement, the behavior results in the removal of a negative event. For example, a shock is turned off as a result of a behavior. In negative reinforcement, the goal is to increase the likelihood of the behavior that led to the removal of the negative event. (pp. 210-211, Table 6.2)

7. Skinner argued that punishment may temporarily suppress a response, but that it is of no use in the long run. However, his animals were not given a response alternative. If an alternative response is available and if the punishment is immediate and consistent, punishment can be effective in the long run. (pp. 211-212)

8. <u>Fixed ratio</u>: Reinforcement is given after a set number of responses; e.g., FR 10 means reinforcement after every 10 responses.
   <u>Variable ratio</u>: Reinforcement after some number of responses, but the number is an average; e.g., VR 10 means reinforcement is given after an average of 10 responses, but not after the 10th, 20th, etc.
   <u>Fixed interval</u>: Reinforcement is given for the first response following some time interval; e.g., FI 5 sec. means that the first response after 5 sec. has passed would be reinforced.
   <u>Variable interval</u>: Reinforcement is given after a time interval, but it is an average interval; e.g., VI 5 sec. means that the intervals would average 5 sec., but would vary. Responding will continue longer without reinforcement after one of these schedules than after reinforcement following every response (continuous). (pp. 213-214)

9. This happened during the Korean War. The Chinese Communists ran essay contests, and soldiers who wrote the best essays won extra food or privileges. Soldiers who wrote negative comments about the United States were asked to elaborate on them. Many prisoners ended up denouncing the United States, making false confessions, and even revealing military secrets. Basically, a shaping process with positive reinforcements was used. (pp. 215-216)

10. Song learning is species specific, and occurs during an early sensitive period. Classical and operant conditioning use the same CSs for many animals and both forms of learning occur in adulthood as well as in childhood. Songs are learned just by listening, but there is some form of feedback in both classical (UCS) and operant (reinforcement) learning. (p. 221)

11. Much human learning occurs through imitation. The child sees his or her parents, other children, and TV personalities smoking, and they seem to be enjoying themselves. Thus, the child receives vicarious reinforcement, so he or she imitates these people and tries the behavior. (pp. 221-222)

12. Even if a person has received vicarious reinforcement for some behavior, the behavior may not be imitated unless self-efficacy is high. That is, a person must think that he or she can succeed at the behavior before trying it. When the behavior is attempted, some self-reinforcement (self-administered praise or reinforcers) will probably be necessary for the execution of the behavior to continue. (pp. 223-224)

POSTTEST

Take this test with all of your books and notes out of sight. This should give you a good idea of how well you understand the material. The answers are on p. 93.

Matching

Put the letter of the stimulus or response in the blank beside the description.

Classical Conditioning

1-4. Paul's Aunt Molly gave him a new sweater that makes him itch. Now just the sight of the sweater makes him itch.

1. _____ sweater on the skin
2. _____ itching at the sight
3. _____ sight of sweater
4. _____ itching with sweater on

A. conditioned response (CR)
B. conditioned stimulus (CS)
C. unconditioned response (UCR)
D. unconditioned stimulus (UCS)

5-8. Cryin' Bryan cringes when he sees lightning, although he has never been struck by lightning. The loud thunder that follows naturally makes him cringe.

5. _____ sound of the thunder
6. _____ cringing at thunder
7. _____ sight of lightning
8. _____ cringing at lightning

A. conditioned response (CR)
B. conditioned stimulus (CS)
C. unconditioned response (UCR)
D. unconditioned stimulus (UCS)

Multiple-Choice

Circle the best alternative.

Behaviorism

1. Which of the following would most likely be a statement made by a radical behaviorist?
    a. learning is a change in an individual's response to a stimulus
    b. we can tell what people have learned by asking how well they think they know material
    c. having people describe thoughts and ideas is the only real way to observe learning
    d. behavior is often unpredictable because of free will
    e. both b and c

Classical Conditioning

2. Our dog drools saliva whenever he hears the "doggy snacks" cupboard open. Which of the following is true?
    a. the sound of the cupboard is a UCS for salivating, which is the UCR
    b. the sound of the cupboard is the CS; the doggy snacks are the UCS
    c. salivating to the sound is the UCR; salivating to the snacks is the CR
    d. the snacks are the CS; salivating to the cupboard is the UCS
    e. the snacks are the UCS; salivating to the cupboard is the UCR

3. Which of the following is an example of spontaneous recovery?
    a. a dog hears a tone CS many times without the UCS
    b. a child who has learned to stop wetting the bed wakes up when he has stomach cramps as well as when he has a full bladder
    c. an alcoholic learns not to drink in the lab because he will become sick but learns that he can drink in the local bar
    d. a fear that was removed by presenting the object over and over without harm returns when the object hasn't been seen for weeks
    e. a dog salivates to the sound of any cupboard opening

4. Pavlov believed that the CS and UCS must be presented in temporal contiguity. What do psychologists believe today?
    a. temporal contiguity is even more important than Pavlov thought
    b. CS must predict the coming UCS
    c. long delays between CS and UCS make all learning impossible
    d. Presenting the UCS before the CS produces even stronger conditioning than presenting the CS first
    e. extinction will only occur if the UCS is presented without the CS

Operant Conditioning

5. Which of the following is an example of operant conditioning?
    a. a child fears the sight of dogs because she was once bitten by one
    b. a cancer patient feels sick when she sees the hospital where she receives a strong drug treatment
    c. a rabbit blinks its eyelid to a tone that has been paired with shock
    d. a chimpanzee pulls the lever on a slot machine to get banana chips
    e. a boy learns to wake up before wetting the bed, because a full bladder has been paired with a loud noise

6. What procedure would you use to train your dog to go to the bedroom, pick up your slippers, carry them to your favorite chair, go to the door, get the newspaper, and bring it to you?
    a. shaping
    b. classical conditioning
    c. chaining
    d. both b and c
    e. both a and c

7. I have learned to open my umbrella in order to stop the rain from soaking me. What type of contingency led to this learning?
   a. positive reinforcement
   b. negative punishment
   c. punishment
   d. negative reinforcement
   e. omission training

8. Which of the following would increase the likelihood that punishment would be effective?
   a. make sure that there are no alternative ways of getting reinforcement
   b. make a child's punishment intense and with no explanation
   c. make a child's punishment mild and accompany it with an explanation
   d. give a child as little attention as possible, except when punishing him
   e. Punish a behavior that is strongly motivated and give the animal no other way to satisfy the motivation

9. Dogs are frequently trained with verbal praise, such as "Good boy," as the reinforcer. What type is it?
   a. an unconditioned reinforcer
   b. a negative reinforcer
   c. a punisher
   d. an instrumental reinforcer
   e. a conditioned reinforcer

10. The disequilibrium principle states that:
   a. any high-frequency behavior can be used to reinforce a low-frequency behavior
   b. any behavior that has been performed less often than usual can reinforce behavior
   c. rare behaviors can never be used to reinforce more frequent behaviors
   d. conditioned reinforcers are more powerful than unconditioned reinforcers
   e. individuals learn what leads to what rather than automatically increasing reinforced behaviors

11. Which of the following is an example of a variable-interval schedule?
   a. Bertha gets one chocolate-chip cookie for every 10 sit-ups she does
   b. A pigeon gets food the first time it pecks a key after 10 sec. have passed
   c. Freddie gets a dime each morning that he makes his bed
   d. A gambler wins on 3 out of 10 poker hands on the average
   e. A fisherman gets a bite once every 15 minutes on the average

12. The drive reduction theory of reinforcement states that reinforcers:
   a. must satisfy some drive which may be biological or not
   b. must satisfy biological needs
   c. are discovered by trial and error; if they increase behavior, they're reinforcing
   d. work is only if a behavior has occurred less often than usual
   e. really work because they allow one to engage in a preferred behavior

13. Rats that have been shocked while drinking sweetened water from a tube that produces loud noises and bright lights will later:
    a. avoid tubes with noises and lights
    b. avoid sweet-tasting water
    c. avoid both sweet-tasting water and tubes with noises and lights
    d. avoid all sweet-tasting substances
    e. completely stop eating and drinking

14. Which of the following could be used to support the argument that bird song learning is different from operant conditioning?
    a. adult songs are UCSs not reinforcers
    b. songs are learned just by listening with no obvious reinforcer
    c. songs are learned by classical conditioning
    d. songs are not learned until adulthood, but operant conditioning occurs in childhood
    e. birds learn to sing whatever songs they hear

15. According to social-learning theory:
    a. we learn because of unconditioned reinforcement
    b. we usually learn because we are classically conditioned by society
    c. much human learning occurs because of imitation
    d. operant conditioning is irrelevant for human learning
    e. society could be improved through operant conditioning

16. Vicarious punishment:
    a. works better than vicarious reinforcement
    b. involves actual physical consequences to the learner
    c. affects behavior less than vicarious reinforcement
    d. does not involve a model
    e. is probably an important reason for engaging in "safe sex"

17. Although it is clear that the gymnast was reinforced for her excellent tumbling routine, most people would not imitate her. Why?
    a. vicarious reinforcement did not occur
    b. vicarious punishment occurred
    c. self-reinforcement doesn't work for gymnastics
    d. self-efficacy would be low for most people
    e. the gymnast would not be a good model

ANSWERS TO POSTTEST

Correct Answer	Questions Testing a Similar Concept	
	Comprehension Check	Short-Answer
Matching		
1. D (pp. 196-197)	2	2, 3
2. A (pp. 196-197)	2	2, 3
3. B (pp. 196-197)	2	2, 3
4. C (pp. 196-197)	2	2, 3
5. D (pp. 196-197)	2	2, 3
6. C (pp. 196-197)	2	2, 3
7. B (pp. 196-197)	2	2, 3
8. A (pp. 196-197)	2	2, 3
Multiple-Choice		
1. a (p. 191)	1	1
2. b (pp. 196-197)	2, 3	2, 3
3. d (p. 198)	4e	--
4. b (p. 201)	3	3, 5
5. d (pp. 205-206)	7	6
6. e (pp. 208-210)	9	6
7. d (p. 211)	10	7
8. c (pp. 211-212)	11	8
9. e (pp. 212-213)	12	--
10. b (p. 212)	15a,15e	--
11. e (p. 214, Table 6.3)	14d	9
12. a (p. 212)	12a, 12c	--
13. a (pp. 219-221)	15	--
14. b (p. 221)	--	10
15. c (pp. 221-222)	16	11
16. c (p. 223)	16d	11
17. d (p. 223)	17	12

CHAPTER 7 MEMORY

OBJECTIVES

Understand that:

Types of Memory

I. No one experiment characterizes all features of memory (p. 229)
   A. Ebbinghaus learned nonsense syllables and forgot quickly (pp. 229-230)
      1. Ebbinghaus forgot faster than college students today because he learned so many lists (p. 230)
   B. Interference from earlier (proactive) or later (retroactive) learning can cause forgetting (p. 231)
   C. Meaningful material is remembered better than nonsense material (p. 231)
   D. Distinctive material that stands out is remembered better than common material (pp. 231-232)
      1. This is called the von Restorff effect (p. 232)
   E. How much one remembers depends upon the type of test (pp. 232-233, Table 7.5, p. 253)
      1. In recall, material must be produced from memory (p. 232)
      2. In cued recall, hints are given to help remember (p. 232)
      3. In recognition, several items are given and the person picks the correct one (p. 232)
      4. In savings or relearning, the person relearns the material and the time is compared to the time to learn it originally (p. 233)
II. Information-processing model assumes that there are three basic types of memory (p. 233, Fig. 7.7.)
   A. Sensory store holds a very brief image of stimuli (p. 234)
   B. Short-term memory is available only a short time; long-term memory can be available at any time (p. 234, Fig. 7.9, p. 235)
      1. Retrieval cues help to bring out long-term memories (p. 234)
      2. Short-term memory capacity is limited but long-term memory is not (pp. 234-235)
         a. Chunking can increase the amount of information that can be held in STM (pp. 235-236, Fig. 7.11)
      3. Decay occurs in short-term memory if a person doesn't rehearse (pp. 236-237)
         a. Interference also causes forgetting from short-term memory (pp. 236-237)
   C. Information is transferred from short-term memory to long-term memory (pp. 237-238)
      1. This is called consolidation (p. 237)
      2. Simply holding information in short-term memory won't put it in long-term memory (pp. 237-238)
III. The information-processing model needs some modification (pp. 238-239)
   A. Working memory temporarily stores information, but it is also a system for working with information (p. 238)
      1. The central executive governs shifts of attention (p. 238)
      2. The phonological loop stores and rehearses speech (p. 238)
      3. The visuospatial sketchpad stores and manipulates visual and spatial information (p. 238)
IV. Psychologists make several other memory distinctions (p. 239)
   A. Semantic memory consists of factual information; episodic memory consists of specific events from a person's life (p. 239)
      1. Source amnesia occurs when a fact is remembered but the person doesn't know where or how it was learned (p. 239)
The message: Psychologists agree that memory consists of many processes (p. 239)

Memory Improvement

V. People remember events that were emotionally arousing, although such memories may not be accurate (p. 241)

VI. According to levels of processing, the number and type of associations formed is important for later memory (p. 242)

    A. Giving meaning to material results in a deep level of processing (pp. 242-243)

    B. Putting things into categories helps memory (p. 243)

VII. Learners must monitor whether they understand material (p. 243)

    A. People have some ability to predict future performance on text passages (p. 243)

VIII. The spacing of study of sets of material affects memory (pp. 244-245)

    A. The serial-order effect consists of a primacy effect and a recency effect (p. 244)

        1. The primacy effect is the tendency to remember things learned first (p. 244)

        2. The recency effect is the tendency to remember things learned last (p. 244)

    B. Studying with time between repetitions increases long-term retention (pp. 244-245)

        1. To remember for a longer time, study at various times and places with long intervals between studying (p. 245)

IX. Special coding strategies can help memory (pp. 245-247)

    A. The encoding specificity principle states that cues used during learning must be the same as the cues used for retrieval (pp. 245-246, Table 7.4)

    B. Mnemonic devices can help anyone to improve memory (pp. 246-247)

        1. Stories linking items can help (p. 246)

        2. Method of loci involves imagining things in known places (p. 246)

        3. With the peg method, you use rhymes of numbers instead of places (pp. 246-247)

The message: The more you know about a topic, the easiest it is to store and retrieve information related to it. (p. 247)

Memory Loss

X. Forgetting occurs normally for several reasons (p. 249)

    A. Forgetting occurs because of proactive and retroactive interference (p. 249)

    B. Memory traces may decay, although perhaps not from long-term memory (p. 249)

    C. Memories may be "forgotten" because the appropriate retrieval cues aren't used (p. 249)

XI. Amnesia is a severe loss of memory following brain damage (p. 250)

    A. Damage to the hippocampus can cause amnesia (pp. 250-251, Fig. 7.20)

        1. Anterograde amnesia is an inability to learn new things (p. 251, Fig. 7.21)

        2. Retrograde amnesia is the forgetting of events that occurred before the damage (p. 251, Fig. 7.21)

        3. Procedural memory may be spared in such amnesia (p. 251)

            a. The main problem is in memory for facts, declarative memory (p. 251)

    B. Damage to the frontal lobes produce a different type of amnesia (pp. 251-252)

        1. Korsakoff's syndrome occurs in chronic alcoholics who have a deficiency of vitamin B_1 (pp. 251-252)

        2. These patients have severe retrograde and anterograde amnesia (p. 252 , Fig. 7.21, p. 251)

        3. They tend to fill in gaps in memory with confabulations (p. 252)

            a. They have trouble working with memory, or reconstructing memory (p. 252)

    C. Amnesic patients perform normally on implicit memory tasks, but not explicit tasks (pp. 252-253)

        1. Implicit tasks don't require conscious recollection; explicit tasks do (p. 253, Table 7.5)

    D. Brain-damage amnesia shows that conscious awareness is not necessary for memory to influence behavior (p. 254)

XII. Infant amnesia refers to the fact that most adults can't remember anything from before age 3 1/2 (p. 254)
   A. Freud argued that infantile memories are repressed (p. 254)
   B. Early memories may be nonverbal and we later rely on language (p. 254)
   C. The hippocampus may not be mature enough to store factual memories (p. 254)
   D. A sense of self may be necessary before permanent memories can be formed (p. 254)
XIII. Elderly people experience some amnesia (p. 255)
   A. Older people show the largest deficits on complex tasks (p. 255)
The message: *There are many ways for memory to fail; it is impressive that memory is as accurate as it is. (p. 255)*

Reconstruction of Memory

XIV.   Memory is often reconstructed from bits of memory that remain (p. 258)
   A. Words not present on lists of related words are inferred and "remembered" (pp. 258-259)
   B. We use schemas to reconstruct stories (p. 259)
      1. Typical events are often reconstructed (p. 259)
      2. If material is highly schematic, unusual items may be better remembered, probably because they're distinctive (p. 259)
   C. Hindsight bias refers to remembering events as consistent with the outcome (pp. 259-260, Fig.7.25)
XV. Eyewitnesses often select the wrong person (p. 261)
   A. Lineups can be biased by the nature of the incorrect choices (foils) (p. 261)
XVI. Some psychologists warn that repressed memories for childhood sexual abuse may actually come from therapists' suggestions (pp. 261-262)
   A. Freud defined repression as moving a memory into the unconscious, but there is not good evidence that repression occurs (p. 262)
   B. Memory can be changed with suggestions (pp. 262-264)
      1. People report things that were suggested and not presented (pp. 262-263)
      2. People come to believe that events occurred when they are suggested by a relative (pp. 262-263)
      3. False evens that are more similar to actual experience are more likely to be implanted by suggestion (p. 263)
   C. Children are influenced more by suggestion than adults (p. 264)
The message: *Everyone reconstructs memory and misremembers some events. (p. 264)*

COMPREHENSION CHECK

Answer these questions soon after reading the chapter. Circle the best alternative. Check your answers on pp. 100-103. If you gave a wrong answer, try to write why it was wrong. Check your reasons on pp. 100-103.

Types of Memory

1. Oblivia Sue lost her bicycle lock and then bought a new one, which she used for several weeks. Finally, she found her old lock; but simply cannot remember its combination. What is the best explanation for her forgetting her old combination?
   a. the old combination is too distinctive
   b. proactive interference
   c. testing is by relearning rather than by recognition
   d. retroactive interference

Correct _____ If wrong, why? _____

2. After Ebbinghaus had been learning and recalling lists of nonsense syllables for months, he began to study forgetting. He learned a list and then tried to recall it after 24 hours. He forgot much more of the list than an average college student would. What is the best explanation for this?
   a. his declarative memory was fine, but his semantic memory was poor
   b. Ebbinghaus was probably less intelligent than the average student
   c. retroactive interference; the earlier lists caused rapid forgetting of the later lists
   d. proactive interference; the earlier lists caused rapid forgetting of the later lists
   e. Ebbinghaus had probably developed Alzheimer's disease

Correct _____ If wrong, why? _____

3. Which of the following is true about ease of memorizing?
   a. people who have more practice in memorizing similar things remember better
   b. distinctive events are easier to remember than less distinctive ones
   c. words that have little meaning are easier than words that are meaningful because there is less interference
   d. words that show the von Restorff effect are not well remembered

Correct _____ If wrong, why? _____

4. The questions in this exercise are using what method to measure your memory?
   a. recognition
   b. cued recall
   c. free recall
   d. savings
   e. relearning

Correct _____ If wrong, why? _____

5. Which memory store can only store images for less than a second?
   a. short-term memory
   b. long-term memory
   c. sensory store
   d. episodic memory store

Correct _____ If wrong, why? _____

6. You've just looked up a phone number and held it in memory while you dialed it. Now, the operator comes on and asks you what number you dialed and you are unable to tell her. What has happened?
   a. the number is still in your sensory store
   b. the number has faded from short-term memory
   c. the number is now in long-term memory
   d. the number was lost because you chunked it too much

Correct _____ If wrong, why? _____

7. Practice in short-term memory tasks can:
    a. expand short-term memory capacity
    b. actually hurt long-term memory
    c. help sensory memory as well as short-term memory
    d. improve the ability to chunk

Correct _____ If wrong, why? _____

8. Working memory:
    a. is broader than short-term memory involving a system of processing as well a storage
    b. occurs after a memory has been consolidated from short-term memory to long-term memory
    c. is the same thing as the phonological loop
    d. consists of memory for specific events in a person's life

Correct _____ If wrong, why? _____

9. Almost all memory researchers agree on which of the following?
    a. long-term memory should be divided into episodic and semantic
    b. source amnesia is the main cause of forgetting from long-term memory
    c. memory that stays in short-term store long enough is consolidated into long-term memory
    d. the visuospatial sketchpad is a separate system than the phonological loop
    e. memory is not a single store that we dump things into and later take them out

Correct _____ If wrong, why? _____

Memory Improvement

10. According to the levels-of-processing principle of memory, which of the following should be remembered best?
    a. a word that is repeated several times in short-term memory
    b. a word for which you produced a rhyme
    c. a word that you looked at to decide if it had an e in it
    d. a word that you related to yourself

Correct _____ If wrong, why? _____

11. If you want to remember something for a long time, what should you do?
    a. study it immediately before the test
    b. eat chocolates right before studying
    c. avoid self-monitoring of understanding
    d. study under condition that are as different as possible as the actual test conditions
    e. study several times with long intervals between studying

Correct _____ If wrong, why? _____

12. When you learned the word "spade," you thought of it as a type of card. Now you're trying to remember the word and you are given "shovel" as a cue, but it doesn't help you to remember. The best explanation is:
    a. encoding specificity principle
    b. working memory is different from reference memory
    c. depth-of-processing principle
    d. retroactive interference

Correct _____ If wrong, why? _____

13. The method of loci involves:
    a. avoiding mnemonic devices because they produce interference
    b. imagining what you want to remember in places that you already know
    c. use of the recency effect
    d. taking something that you know well, like the face of a coin, and using it to associate what you want to remember

Correct _____ If wrong, why? _____

Memory Loss

14. Damage to the hippocampus results in:
    a. in inability to learn new facts
    b. a loss of procedural memory
    c. anterograde, but no retrograde amnesia
    d. a total loss of all long-term memories developed before the damage
    e. total amnesia

Correct _____ If wrong, why? _____

15. A list of words is presented. Which would be an implicit test of the words?
    a. present a long list of words, half new and half old; ask subjects to say whether each word is old or new
    b. ask subjects to write down all the words they remember
    c. give the first three letters of the words and ask subjects to complete the stems with any word that comes to mind
    d. ask the subjects to relearn the words after some time period

Correct _____ If wrong, why? _____

16. Which of the following is characteristic of frontal lobe amnesia such as that associated with Korsakoff's syndrome?
    a. confabulation is common
    b. people remember when and where events occurred but they can't remember the details of the events
    c. people lose their sense of self and hence they can't remember
    d. procedural learning is the first to show the effects of amnesia
    e. it is particularly evident when the details from stories are tested

Correct _____ If wrong, why? _____

17. On which task would Korsakoff's patients do the best?
    a. describing their present life's situation, i.e., children's ages, length of marriage, location of present home
    b. describing what they had for dinner the night before
    c. remembering a list of words presented in the laboratory
    d. completing word stems with words that were previously presented
    e. describing what happened to them before age 3

Correct _____ If wrong, why? _____

The Reconstruction of Memory

18. After learning who was the murderer in a mystery novel, the reader thinks back and decides that she was pretty sure who actually did it after the very first chapter. This is an example of:
    a. savings
    b. retrograde amnesia
    c. von Restorff effect
    d. hindsight bias

Correct _____ If wrong, why? _____

19. Research has shown that incorrect suggestions given after a witnessed event:
    a. result of repression of the original event
    b. can lead to incorrect answers about the original event
    c. affect adults, but don't affect children
    d. after memory when it is measured by lineups, but suggestions don't affect verbal memory

Correct _____ If wrong, why? _____

20. False memories:
    a. are controversial when they are remembered in therapy after having been "repressed"
    b. can be implanted for emotional, real-life events, but not for simpler laboratory events
    c. are most controversial when the client has always known that she was abused
    d. are most easily implanted if the event is highly unusual for a person
    e. may develop because children have little memory for traumatic events

Correct _____ If wrong, why? _____

ANSWERS AND EXPLANATIONS FOR COMPREHENSION CHECK

Correct Answer	Other Alternatives Are Wrong Because:
1. d (p. 231) Obj. I-B	a. distinctiveness helps, not hurts, memory b. the old combination would cause forgetting of the new one if it was proactive c. method of testing not relevant
2. d (p. 231) Obj. I-A-1,B	a. Ebbinghaus measured declarative memory, and it was poor b. he was very creative for his times c. this is the reason, but it's proactive e. doubtful; his memory was generally good

3. b (pp. 231-232)
   Obj. I-D

   a. the earlier material would cause proactive interference
   c. meaningful words are more easily associated
   d. refers to distinctive events; these are easier

4. a (p. 232, Table7.5, p. 253)
   Obj. I-E-3

   b. would give you cues but have you produce response
   c. would have you produce answers in any order
   d. would have you relearn material and compare with time to learn originally
   e. same as d

5. c (p. 234, Fig. 7.9, p. 235)
   Obj. II-A

   a. lasts for 20-30 sec. without rehearsal
   b. lasts indefinitely
   d. type of long-term memory for personal events

6. b (p. 235, Figure 7.9)
   Obj. II-B-3

   a. moved out of sensory store before you could use it
   c. unlikely or you would remember it
   d. chunking allows you to remember more in short-term memory, not less

7. d (pp. 235-236)
   Obj. II-B-2-a

   a. more information can be learned, but capacity itself is not changed
   b. no evidence for this
   c. sensory memory is not affected by practice

8. a (p. 238)
   Obj. III-A

   b. is involved in consolidation; doesn't come after it
   c. the phonological loop is one part of working memory, not the whole concept
   d. this is episodic memory

9. e (p. 239)
   Obj. IV

   a-d. some theorists believe each of these statements, but there is wide agreement only on this statement e

10. d (pp. 242-243, Table 7. 3)
    Obj. VI

    a. rote repetition does little good
    b. fairly superficial level of processing
    c. very superficial level of processing

11. e (pp. 244-245)
    Obj. VIII-B-1

    a. this will produce good performance in the short run, but not for the long-term
    b. this may raise blood glucose briefly but not it won't help long-term memory into categories
    c. self-monitoring of understanding is necessary for good learning
    d. the encoding specificity principle states that the best memory will occur when the conditions of study and testing are as *similar* as possible

12. a (pp. 245-246, Table 7.4a)
   Obj. IX-A

   b. this is a problem with retrieval cues, not differences in memory store
   c. the word should have been processed semantically; you can't retrieve it now
   d. no new learning occurred during the interval; it's a retrieval problem

13. b (p. 246)
   Obj. IX-B-2

   a. method of loci is a mnemonic system
   c. very few people can remember detailed images; anyone can use method of loci
   d. people don't remember details on coins

14. a (pp. 250-251, Fig. 7.20)
   Obj. XI-A

   b. new skills can be learned
   c. some retrograde amnesia for memories occurring just before the brain damage
   d. some memories acquired long before the damage are normal
   e. no, because of b and d

15. c (pp. 252-253)
   Obj. XI-C

   a. recognition; an explicit test
   b. recall; an explicit test
   d. relearning; an explicit test

16. a (pp. 251-252)
   Obj. XIII

   b. they have trouble remembering when and where events occurred
   c. this is one explanation for childhood amnesia, not for frontal lobe amnesia
   d. procedural learning is rarely affected by amnesia
   e. true of the amnesia of old age; Korsakoff's have problems with important parts also

17. d (pp. 251-252)
   Obj. XI-C

   a. they confabulate, mixing old memories with guesses such episodic memory is very poor
   b-c. word lists containing more than about seven items cannot be remembered
   e. they would not be able to do this because of infantile amnesia

18. d (pp. 259-260)
   Obj. XIV-B

   a. refers to faster relearning the second time; no relearning here
   b. forgetting of earlier material; material here is reconstructed
   c. memory for distinctive things; reconstruction occurred here

19. b (p. 261)
   Obj. XVI-B-1

   a. although repression was important in Freud's theory, there is little evidence that it actually occurs
   c. children are affected by suggestions
   d. incorrect suggestions can influence all types of memory

20. a (pp. 261-262)
    Obj. XVI

b. when lists of related words are presented in the laboratory, people falsely "remember" non-presented words
c. these cases probably involve real, not false, memories
d. it's just the opposite; events that fit in with one's normal life are more easily implanted
e. children who have experienced traumatic events remember them fairly well

LECTURE MATERIAL

Don't forget to review your lecture material. Process each topic meaningfully. First, be sure that you understand the material in each lecture--if you don't, ask your instructor or teaching assistant. Associate the material with things that you already know and with your personal experiences. If you can make up mental images of any of the material, do so. Try to think of real-life applications of the concepts. Put notes in the left margin of your lecture notes. Then write questions to cover each concept.

WAIT AT LEAST 24 HOURS BEFORE PROCEEDING.
LET FORGETTING OCCUR--IT WILL!!

SHORT-ANSWER ESSAY QUESTIONS

Write brief answers to each of the following. The answers are on pp. 105-107, but do try to write the answers yourself before looking at them.

Types of Memory

1. Describe the research done by Ebbinghaus, including one of his findings.

2. Give one example of forgetting by retroactive interference and one example of forgetting by proactive interference.

3. Describe two characteristics of material that affect ease of memorizing, and give an example of each.

4. Describe two ways that short-term and long-term memory differ.

5. What are two problems with the traditional view that information moves from short-term memory to long-term memory following adequate time and rehearsal in short-term memory?

6. Describe working memory. How does it relate to reading comprehension?

Memory Improvement
7. Describe the effects of emotional arousal on memory.

8. According to the levels-of-processing principle, why is it useless to simply repeat a definition over and over?

9. Describe how the timing of study affects later memory.

10. Why does forgetting occur according to the encoding specificity principle?

11. Explain how you would use the method of loci to remember a grocery list.

Memory Loss
12. Discuss three reasons for normal forgetting.

13. What is the difference between retrograde and anterograde amnesia? From which type of amnesia did H. M. suffer?

14. Discuss the types of memory that are spared in most types of amnesia.

The Reconstruction of Memory

15. What is meant by reconstruction in memory? Give an example.

16. How is the suggestibility of memory related to the false memory controversy?

****
Find the questions that you wrote over lecture material and write answers to them.
****

ANSWERS TO SHORT-ANSWER ESSAY QUESTIONS

1. Ebbinghaus wanted to study how associations are formed in memory. He used nonsense syllables because they had no prior associations (as he thought; it turns out that they do). He would memorize a list and then test himself. He measured how quickly he forgot a list of syllables. He found that he forgot rapidly, forgetting about half of the syllables after an hour and still more after 24 hours. (pp. 229-230)

2. Retroactive interference: Last week you studied theories of learning and this week you are studying theories of interference. You forget the theories of learning because you learned about interference. Proactive interference: Last week you learned how to use the NIFTY-1 word processing program and this week you learned how to use the SUPER-W program. Your memory for the SUPER-W program will be impaired, because the NIFTY-1 will interfere. (p. 231)

3. Things that are meaningful and have lots of associates are remembered better than things that are not. For example, you can remember material presented in your own language better than material presented in a language that you don't understand. Material that is emotionally arousing is remembered better than material that is less arousing. However, information learned during emotional arousal is not always completely accurate. (pp. 231-232, 241)

4. <u>Capacity</u>: Only about seven chunks fit in short-term memory; long-term memory capacity is unlimited. (pp. 234-235)
   <u>Length of time that information is available</u>: Information is available for only a short time in short-term memory; it becomes less available after attention has shifted; information is potentially retrievable forever in long-term memory. (p. 236)

5. Rehearsing words in short-term memory for a shorter or a longer time has no effect on later memory for the words. Some brain damaged patients have very small short-term memory capabilities, yet they are able to form and retrieve long-term memories normally. (pp. 237-238)

6. Working memory both stores information and works with current information. It may be thought of as one's present region of attention. The central executive governs shifts of attention. The phonological loop stores and rehearses verbal information. The visuospatial sketchpad stores and manipulates visual and spatial information. People who can't hold as much in their phonological loops have more trouble understanding complex sentences than people who have larger phonological loops. (pp. 238-239)

7. People often remember many details about arousing events, such as news of an assassination or some major disaster. Although the memories may be vivid and intense, they are not necessarily accurate. Exciting events may be remembered because certain norepinephrine synapses are stimulated and because the sympathetic nervous system is aroused. (p. 241)

8. Rote repetition results in a very superficial level of learning. Studies have shown that simple repetition does not lead to an increase in later memory for the material. A deeper encoding in terms of meaning and understanding is necessary for later memory. Remember the SPAR system-- Process meaningfully. (pp. 242-244)

9. The serial order effect includes the primacy effect, which is the tendency to remember the first items of a list, and the recency effect, which is the tendency to remember the last items. Other timing effects have to do with spacing study over long periods of time, or learning right before a test. Spacing learning sessions over weeks results in slower learning than learning all in one session. However, the spaced learning will be remembered longer than the massed learning. Thus, to remember a long time, learning should be spaced over several sessions. (pp. 244-245)

10. The principle of encoding specificity argues that you must use retrieval cues that are similar to the way you originally thought about the material. If you place a word in memory in one way (e.g., thinking of ball as a dance) and try to pull it out in way (e.g., thinking of ball as a round, bouncy object), you won't retrieve it. (p. 245)

11. First, I would learn a list of 20 locations in order, buildings on a walk around campus, for example. Then I would imagine each item that I want to buy in one of those locations. For example, if the administration building comes first and I want to buy tomatoes, I would imagine tomatoes smeared all over the building. Then in the store, I would take an imaginary walk and "see" each thing that I want to buy. (p. 246)

12. Interference is one explanation for forgetting. People forget specific information because of other similar information that they learned before it (proactive interference) or because of other information learned after it (retroactive interference). A second explanation is decay, that is, the traces fade away. This may be a better explanation of forgetting from working memory than from long-term memory. A third possibility is that information is not forgotten but that the retrieval cues are not appropriate at a given time. The material is potentially retrievable with different cues at a later time. (pp. 249-250)

13. Retrograde amnesia means a loss of memory for events that occurred before the onset of the amnesia. Anterograde means an inability to learn new things, or to form new long-term memories. H. M.'s biggest problem was anterograde amnesia; he couldn't learn new facts. Although he had some trouble remembering events that happened a few years before his operation, H. M. could generally remember things that occurred before his amnesia. (p. 251, Fig. 7.21)

14. People with amnesia generally perform normally on tests that do not require explicit remembering. These implicit memory tests ask participants to simply respond to some stimuli that they have experienced before, like giving words for word fragments. Generally, the people with amnesia give as many previously seen words as normal participants do. People with amnesia are usually normal on procedural memory tasks. They remember how to do things even though they may not remember having learned to do them. (pp. 252-253)

15. We tend to fill in the gaps of memories by inserting things that should be true. We omit or distort other details to fit with our expectations. For example, students remember a Native American folk tale as more consistent with their expectations than it really was. People may omit unexpected events and include events that should have happened even though they didn't. (pp. 257-258)

16. Experiments show that people will incorporate false information from questions about events into their memory of the events themselves. Whether the memories actually change, or whether people have trouble identifying the source of the suggested information is not clear. The false memory controversy surrounds clients' remembering childhood sexual abuse during therapy. Some psychologists believe that certain therapeutic techniques suggest that abuse occurred when it did not and the client comes to believe this is an actual memory and not just a suggestion. (pp. 261-264)

POSTTEST

Take this test with all of your books and notes out of sight. This should give you a good idea of how well you understand the material. The answers are on p. 112.

Matching

Write the letter of the term on the right that best explains the forgetting in the description on the left.

1. _____ a person with Korsakoff's syndrome can't remember new things

2. _____ Mary remembers few facts about an important Civil War battle, so she just fills in the rest with what should have happened

3. _____ John forgot the Spanish that he learned in high school because he studied French in college

4. _____ When Amorfus learned the word *orange*, he thought of it as a color; now he can't remember it with *fruit* as a cue

5. _____ Perplexity tried to memorize a definition by repeating it over and over; now she can't remember it

6. _____ Equivocus forgot his new address because of his old, similar address

7. _____ H. M. has a poor memory for things that happened within the 3 years before his operation

A. retroactive interference

B. retrograde amnesia

C. anterograde amnesia

D. encoding specificity

E. proactive interference

F. reconstructive memory

G. levels-of-processing

Multiple-choice

Circle the best alternative.

Types of Memory

1. Susan learned German in college but she has not used it for two years. During this time, she has been studying French. Mary also learned German in college and she hasn't used it for two years either, but she has not learned any other languages in the two years. Who should remember German better and why?
   a. Mary; she will have less retroactive interference
   b. Susan; she will have less proactive interference
   c. Mary; she will have more retroactive interference
   d. Susan; she will have less retroactive interference
   e. Mary; she will have less proactive interference

2. Many students are dismayed because they feel that they have forgotten everything they learned in some courses. However, some weak memories are probably left. Which method would be most likely to show those weak memories?
    a. relearning
    b. cued recall
    c. recognition
    d. recall
    e. von Restorff effect

3. If you are given an English word and asked to give the French equivalent, your memory is being tested by:
    a. cued recall
    b. implicit test
    c. free recall
    d. recognition
    e. savings

4. If you meet someone and use her correct name immediately but cannot remember it a half-hour later, the name probably was in your:
    a. sensory store
    b. episodic memory
    c. short-term memory
    d. long-term memory
    e. semantic memory

5. If you glance at a bright scene on television and close your eyes and still see the exact image for less then a second, the image is in your:
    a. sensory store
    b. procedural memory
    c. long-term memory
    d. short-term memory
    e. episodic memory

6. Why can people hold about seven 5-letter words (35 letters) in short-term memory, but only seven unrelated letters?
    a. they use chunking so that each word is one unit
    b. words are tested by implicit memory; letters by explicit memory
    c. the seven letters are held in long-term memory, but the words are held in short-term memory
    d. the seven letters are held in short-term memory, but the words are held in long-term memory
    e. unrelated letters decay much faster than meaningful words

7. Why did Peterson and Peterson have subjects count backward during the delay interval in their experiment on short-term memory?
    a. to prevent passive decay
    b. to prevent rehearsal
    c. to prevent the use of visual imagery
    d. to interfere with the sensory store
    e. to increase the amount of proactive interference

8. The concept of working memory differs from the traditional concept of short-term memory in that working memory:
    a. does not store information, short-term memory is a storage system
    b. comes after the sensory store; short-term memory comes before it
    c. is forgotten because of interference; short-term memory forgotten because of decay
    d. has a limited capacity; short-term memory does not
    e. includes a processing system along with storage; short-term memory just stores information

Memory Improvement

9. According to levels-of-processing theory, which will lead to the best memory?
    a. repeating a word over and over for 5 sec.
    b. counting the number of vowels in a word
    c. looking to see whether a word contains an "e"
    d. producing a rhyme for a word
    e. producing a definition for a word

10. According to the encoding specificity principle, what type of cue will be best for the word *iron*, which you learned along with *sweep* and *wash*?
    a. metals
    b. i---
    c. had an "o"
    d. household chores
    e. rhymes with "my urn"

11. The Bahrick family studied foreign language vocabulary on a moderately frequent basis (every 2 weeks) or on an infrequent basis (every 8 weeks). The moderately frequent study led to:
    a. faster learning, but poorer retention
    b. slower learning, but better retention
    c. slower learning and poorer retention
    d. faster learning and better retention
    e. a total inability to learn

12. John needed to remember the last 10 presidents of the United States. He learned a rhyme beginning with "One is a bun" and then he changed the name of each president into something he could imagine. He imagined each modified name in the object paired with each number in his rhyme. John used:
    a. the method of loci
    b. the peg method
    c. a mnemonic device
    d. both a and c
    e. both b and c
    f.

Memory Loss

13. The patient H. M.:
    a. has damage to the cerebral cortex
    b. could not remember any information from before his operation
    c. has no short-term memory
    d. has great difficulty learning new facts
    e. cannot learn any new skills

14. Infant amnesia occurs because:
    a. childhood memories are repressed
    b. the hippocampus is immature so long-term memories aren't stored
    c. infants and young children don't have a sense of self yet
    d. early memories are nonverbal and later memories are verbal
    e. all of the above may be true, but there are problems with each explanation

Reconstruction of Memory
15. Which of the following is likely to occur in our recall of an event?
    a. incorrect suggestions given after the event will wipe out memory for the original event
    b. details that don't fit in with the rest of the story will be omitted or distorted
    c. it is either recalled word-for-word or not recalled at all
    d. we are very accurate at dating events based on their sharpness in memory
    e. the middle part is likely to be remembered better than the beginning and the end

16. A lineup measures memory in what way?
    a. recall
    b. cued recall
    c. savings
    d. relearning
    e. recognition

17. Which of the following is true about false memories?
    a. people distort things they've seen; they don't "add" things to memory because of suggestions
    b. more than half of the people tested in "lost in the mall study" believed that personal events occurred when they were only suggested
    c. memories are more likely to be implanted if they fit with one's personal experience than if they are not related
    d. children are less likely to have memories implanted than adults

ANSWERS TO POSTTEST

Correct Answer

Questions Testing a Similar Concept

Matching	Comprehension Check	Short-Answer
1. C (p. 251)	14c	13
2. F (p. 257)	--	15
3. A (pp. 231, 249)	1	2
4. D (p. 245)	12	10
5. G (p. 242)	10	8
6. E (pp. 231, 249)	1b, 2	2
7. B (p. 251)	14c	13

Multiple-Choice

	Comprehension Check	Short-Answer
1. a (pp. 230-231, 249)	1	12
2. a (p. 233)	4e	--
3. a (p. 234)	4b	--
4. c (pp. 236-237)	5a, 6	4
5. a (p. 236)	5	--
6. a (pp. 235-236)	6d, 7	4
7. b (pp. 236-237)	6	4
8. e (p. 238)	8	6
9. e (pp. 242-243)	10	8
10. d (p. 246)	12	10
11. a (pp. 244-245)	11	9
12. b (p. 246)	13d	--
13. d (pp. 250-251)	14	13
14. e (p. 254)	17e	--
15. b (pp. 258-259)	19	15
16. e (p. 261)	4	--
17. c (pp. 261-264)	20	16

CHAPTER 8 COGNITION AND LANGUAGE

OBJECTIVES

Understand that:

Thinking and Mental Processes

I. Cognitive psychologists study how people think and gain knowledge (p. 269)

    A. People are unaware of their thought processes (p. 269)

II. Categories are used to group similar things (p. 269)

    A. There are several different theories about the arrangement of categories (pp. 269-271)

        1. Categories are organized around prototypical members (pp. 269-270)

        2. Related concepts activate each other through a conceptual network in memory (pp. 270-271)

III. Mental images can be used to solve problems (pp. 272-273)

    A. Mental images are much like actual perceptions (pp. 272-273)

        1. The time it takes to rotate a mental image depends on how far it must be rotated (pp. 272-273)

    B. Cognitive maps are mental representations of spatial locations (p. 273)

        1. Cognitive maps are often distorted to be more regular than actual locations (p. 273)

IV. Attention limits people's abilities to perform everyday tasks (pp. 273-274)

    A. Different tasks have different attentional requirements (pp. 274-275)

        1. Visual search for familiar objects is done automatically and in parallel (p. 274)

        2. Visual search for unfamiliar objects is done slowly and serially (p. 274)

        3. The Stroop effect shows how preattentive processes in reading can interfere with performance (p. 275)

    B. Attention limits people's abilities to perform more than one task at once (p. 275)

        1. Attending to one stimulus temporarily prevents attention to another stimulus (the attentional blink) (p. 275)

The message: *Even though not directly observable, thought processes can be studied in the laboratory. (p. 277)*

Problem Solving, Expertise, and Error

V. Experts have a lot of practice in their fields (pp. 280-281)

    A. Experts recognize common patterns in their fields quickly (p. 281)

        1. They remember organized material from their areas easily (p. 281)

    B. Experts solve problems quickly by selecting relevant information (p. 281)

VI. Problem solving involves four phases (p. 281, Fig. 8.13)

    A. Problems need to be understood and simplified (pp. 281-282)

    B. Hypotheses should be generated (pp. 282-283)

        1. Algorithms can be used to generate all possibilities (p. 282)

        2. Heuristics generate likely possibilities (p. 282)

    C. Hypotheses should be tested and results checked (p. 283)

    D. Solutions should be generalized to similar problems (p. 283)

        1. People often fail to generalize to similar problems (p. 283)

VII. Some problems are solved insightfully (pp. 284-285)

    A. But people may still be making progress before a solution is found (p. 284)

    B. Insights in mathematics and science may come to anyone who has the data available (p. 285)

    C. Creative people are probably only creative in their own fields (pp. 285-286)

VIII. People often base decisions on illogical reasoning (p. 287)

    A. People are often overconfident about their answers (pp. 287-288)

B. They don't consider alternative hypotheses (pp. 288-289)

C. They often use representativeness and don't use the base rate (pp. 289-290, Table 8.1)

D. People overuse availability in memory to judge frequency (p. 290, Table 8.1)

  1. Illusory correlations can result from the availability heuristic (p. 290)

E. The way a question is worded affects its answer (pp. 290-291)

  1. People are more willing to take risks when dealing with a loss than with a gain (pp. 290-291)

IX. Gambling can be understood via knowledge about cognition and learning (pp. 292-294)

A. People overestimate the amount of control they have (p. 292)

B. People don't understand differences among long shot probabilities (pp. 292-293)

C. Gambling is reinforced on a variable-ratio schedule (p. 293)

D. Vicarious reinforcement is received by seeing others win (pp. 293-294)

  1. Seeing others lose doesn't do much because vicarious punishment isn't very effective (pp. 293-294)

E. Availability and representativeness heuristics play a role in gambling (p. 294)

  1. Gamblers' fallacy (the next one will be a winner) is an example of the representativeness heuristic (p. 294)

F. Self-esteem may be attached to proving oneself a winner (p. 294)

The message: Learning about common cognitive errors may help us make better decisions. (p. 295)

Language

X. Language makes humans unique (p. 297)

A. Some animals have learned rudimentary human language (pp. 298-299)

  1. Chimps use symbols but they don't show flexibility (pp. 298-299)

  2. Pygmy chimps show more flexible use of language (p. 299)

XI. Humans are specialized for learning language (pp. 299-300)

A. Some areas of the brain are critical for language comprehension and production (pp. 300-301)

B. Experience with language during child development is important (pp. 301-303)

  1. Children progress through different stages of language ability (pp. 301-302)

  2. Deaf and bilingual children show the importance of the language environment during development (pp. 302-303)

XII. Language comprehension is complicated, yet we do it easily (p. 304)

A. Missing sounds in words are filled in by the brain (p. 304)

B. People hear the same sounds differently, depending upon context (pp. 304-305)

C. Negatives are particularly difficult to understand (p. 305)

XIII. Reading is complicated too, but most of us read easily (p. 306)

A. Whole words are read faster than individual letters (p. 306)

B. The connectionist model involves interactive activation of higher-order and lower-order units (pp. 306-307, Fig. 8.35)

C. Eyes jump in saccades while reading (pp. 307-308)

  1. Nothing can be seen while the eye is moving (pp. 307-308)

  2. Readers take in about 11 letters per fixation (p. 308)

    a. Part of the next word is processed while each word is being read (pp. 308-309)

D. Good readers suppress irrelevant meanings faster than poor readers (pp. 309-310)

The message: Although nonhuman primates show some use of language, only humans are language "experts." (p. 310)

COMPREHENSION CHECK

Answer these questions soon after reading the chapter. Circle the best alternative. Check your answers on pp. 119-121. If you gave a wrong answer, try to write why it was wrong. Check your reasons on pp. 119-121.

Thinking and Mental Processes

1. The topic that would be least likely to be studied by a psychologist interested in cognition is how people:
   a. plan a vacation
   b. use their imagination to describe a scene
   c. change their behavior following reinforcement
   d. becomes experts on a new topic

Correct _____ If wrong, why? _____

2. Which of the following is an example of the use of conceptual networks in categorizing?
   a. a dog must have lungs because it is a mammal; mammals are animals; animals have lungs
   b. a dog is an animal because it has fur, a tail, and lungs
   c. a dog is an animal because it is similar to an average animal
   d. a dog is an animal because I memorized that fact in childhood

Correct _____ If wrong, why? _____

3. When people decide whether two objects that differ in orientation are the same or not:
   a. the difference in orientation has no effect
   b. they act as if they are watching a model rotate in their heads
   c. responses are faster if the two objects are in very different orientations than if they are in similar orientations
   d. people report that they do not use visual images

Correct _____ If wrong, why? _____

4. A common error in cognitive maps is:
   a. people align things along east-west and north-south axes more than they actually are
   b. people don't use higher-level categories in making location judgments
   c. street angles that are 90 degrees are distorted; people remember them as being more or less than 90 degrees
   d. they have many more details than actual maps

Correct _____ If wrong, why? _____

5. Finding the X in this display **OOOXOOOOO** is easier (and faster) than finding the X in this display **WHVXKYMZN**. The reason is
   a. processing circles is easier than processing angles
   b. preattentive processes (automatic and parallel search) can be used in the first display
   c. attentive processes (serial search) can be used in the first display
   d. interference from the Stroop effect

Correct _____ If wrong, why? _____

6. Doing two things at once is:
   a. not possible
   b. no problem; it's just as efficient as doing only one thing
   (c) no problem, if one thing is so routine that it requires no attention
   d. no problem, if you can delay the response to the second task by 200 milliseconds

Correct _____ If wrong, why? _____

Problem Solving, Expertise, and Error

7. Experts:
   (a.) attend to relevant features and ignore irrelevant ones
   b. are better at all types of memory tasks involving material from their area than novices
   c. are born with special talent
   (d.) solve problems better than novices almost entirely because they have more "tools" to use

Correct _____ If wrong, why? _____

8. Which of the following would be <u>least</u> useful in solving a problem that you can't answer quickly?
   a. try to answer a related question
   b. start to generate hypotheses
   c. try to solve a simpler version
   (d.) start with the assumption that the problem is not solvable

Correct _____ If wrong, why? _____

9. When people are asked to solve problems that are similar to just-solved ones, they:
   a. easily apply the same principles to the new problem
   b. apply the same principles if they've seen only one example, but don't if they've seen many examples
   c. sometimes use the prior experience if they had a variety of different examples
   d. can apply materials from a specific discipline, such as physics, to a more general discipline, such as math, but not vice versa

Correct _____ If wrong, why? _____

10. Creative problem solving is:
    a. a talent; either you have it or you don't
    b. unrelated to prior knowledge; discoveries are made without reliance on accumulated data
    c. similar to insight in that it is sudden and unrelated to a gradual move toward a solution or a discovery
    d. based, in part, on the availability of prior data
    e. both b and c

Correct _____ If wrong, why? _____

11. A patient shows most of the symptoms of a very rare disease and many of the symptoms of a common one. The doctor decides that it must be the very rare disease. In her decision, she has ignored:
    a. base-rate information
    b. the similarity of the symptoms to those in each category
    c. the fact that there may be an alternative hypothesis
    d. a heuristic that would be useful in solving the problem

Correct _____ If wrong, why? _____

12. The availability heuristic would lead to which error?
    a. thinking that a test for a rare disease that is 99% accurate would call only a few well people "sick"
    b. taking a risk when a question is phrased in terms of loss but not in terms of gain
    c. deciding that a student is a math major because he wears glasses, carries a calculator in his pocket, and is sort of a nerd even though only 1% of all students are math majors
    d. thinking that you are more likely to die in a plane than in a car crash because you have read about so many plane crashes lately
    e. saying you are 99% sure you're correct when the actual likelihood is 70%

Correct _____ If wrong, why? _____

13. People generally:
    a. avoid taking risks when considering a loss
    b. avoid taking risks when considering a gain
    c. take risks when considering a gain
    d. avoid risks in all cases if lives are involved, but take them if money is involved

Correct _____ If wrong, why? _____

14. A correct explanation for gambling is that people:
    a. don't pay attention to the representativeness heuristic
    b. are much more willing to accept a certain loss than they are to accept a slim chance of winning
    c. continue a behavior that has been reinforced on a fixed schedule longer than a behavior that has been reinforced on a variable schedule, even when reinforcement has ended
    d. overestimate the control that they have in chance events
    e. are more influenced by vicarious punishment (losing) than by vicarious reinforcement (winning)

Correct _____ If wrong, why? _____

Language

15. "Visiting relatives can be tiresome" can either mean that the relatives are visiting you or you are visiting the relatives. Thus, this sentence has:
    a. two deep structures and one surface structure
    b. two surface structures and one deep structure
    c. deep structures that are identical to surface structures
    d. deep structures that are unrelated to surface structures

Correct _____ If wrong, why? _____

16. The most recent attempts to teach language to animals have shown that:
    a. chimps can learn language and use it in the same way as children
    b. animals that supposedly understand and use language are really only using subtle cues
    c. young bonobos have shown evidence of actual language learning
    d. watching and imitating other animals who are being taught disrupts learning

Correct _____ If wrong, why? _____

17. Most psychologists believe that humans are specialized for language learning. Which of the following is support for that belief?
    a. the human brain contains areas specifically important for language comprehension
    b. children progress through stages of language learning
    c. deaf children deprived of language experience make up their own sign language
    d. all of the above provide support for human language specialization

Correct _____ If wrong, why? _____

18. Which of the following is an example of the Stroop effect?
    a. when asked to name the color of ink, students take a long time to say green when the word "red" is written in green ink
    b. seeing the letter 'O' in JOIN is faster than when students focus on the whole word than when they focus on the spot where the letter appears
    c. letters activate units in memory and the pattern of activation allows identification of the word
    d. poor readers keep several meanings of ambiguous words active for a longer time than good readers

Correct _____ If wrong, why? _____

19. Which of the following shows evidence that context affects our understanding of words?
    a. lecturers in scientific areas use fewer uhs and ers than lecturers in the humanities
    b. if there is a delay between a word with a missing first letter and the word that clarifies it (such as *ent and forest), people don't report the appropriate word (tent)
    c. adding a label such as "not cyanide" makes students less likely to select the container
    d. the word "rose" can refer to a flower or the past tense of rise depending on other words around it

Correct _____ If wrong, why? _____

20. During a fixation in reading, people:
    a. take in less than during a saccade
    b. can take in long sentences
    c. keep their eyes stationary for about seconds
    d. take in a window of about 11 characters

Correct _____ If wrong, why? _____

ANSWERS AND EXPLANATIONS FOR COMPREHENSION CHECK

Correct Answer	Other Alternatives Are Wrong Because:

1. c (p. 269)
   Obj. I

    a. planning is part of cognition
   b. imaging is part of cognition
   d. acquiring knowledge is part of cognition

2. a (pp. 270-271, Fig. 8.2)
   Obj. II-A-2

    b. using features to categorize
   c. prototype view of categorization
   d. true, but how is that fact represented in memory?

3. b (pp. 272-273, Fig. 8.3)
   Obj. III-A-1

    a. the larger the difference in orientation, the longer the time
   c. the closer together the orientations, the shorter the time
   d. people say that they do compare images in this task

4. a (p. 273)
   Obj. III-B-1

    b. use higher-level categories; for example, they say L.A. is west of Reno because California is west of Nevada
   c. angles that are not 90 degrees are remembered as being 90 degrees
   d. details are often omitted

5. b (pp. 274-275, Fig. 8.6)
   Obj. IV-A

    a. preattentive processes operate equally well on all kinds of features (find O in XXXOXXXX vs. QCPODBSG)
   c. attentive processes are used in the second display
   d. the response to the target stimulus X is the same in both displays

6. c (pp. 275-276)
   Obj. IV-B

    a. possible if one task requires no attention
   b. doing two things takes more attention unless one is very routine
   d. responding to a second stimulus 200 ms after a first one results in poor performance on the second stimulus

7. a (p. 281)
   Obj. V-A, B

    b. not all memory tasks; they don't remember random arrangements better, just organized ones
   c. experts need to put in about 10 years of practice
   d. also know which "tools" to use and when to use them

8. d (pp. 281-283)
   Obj. VI

    a-c. these should help problem solution
   d. not likely to help you see a solution, therefore, it is the least useful

9. c (p. 283)
   Obj. VI-D-1

    a. often the very same principles would work, but they are not used
   b. seeing several examples makes generalization more likely
   d. research shows just the opposite

10. d (p. 285)
Obj. VII

a. scientific discoveries may be based more on having available data than on talent
b. access to prior data is important
c. solutions to insight problems may first involve "getting warm"; creative discoveries may also be based on study of data and be gradual
e. both b and c are incorrect

11. a (p. 289)
Obj. VIII-C

b. the similarity of the symptoms and the diseases was considered
c. she did consider an alternative, the more common disease

d. she doesn't need to simplify; the number of hypotheses is small

12. d (p. 290)
Obj. VIII-D

a. base-rate fallacy; ignoring how many people 1% of a large number actually is
b. letting framing of questions affect decisions
c. use of representativeness; ignoring base rate
e. this is overconfidence

13. b (p. 291)
Obj. VIII-E-1

a. they are willing to take risks when a loss is involved
c. they tend to avoid risks if a gain is involved
d. situations involving lives and money show similar effects

14. d (p. 292)
Obj. IX-A

a. do pay attention; the gamblers' fallacy is an example of the representativeness heuristic
b. more willing to accept a slim chance of winning
c. variable schedules lead to more persistence during extinction
e. people are more influenced by vicarious reinforcement than vicarious punishment

15. a (pp. 304-305)
Obj. X

b. the sentence itself is the surface structure; there's only one
c. deep structure is the meaning; different from surface structure
d. they're not the same, but they're related

16. c (pp. 298-299)
Obj. X-A

a. chimps' language wasn't as flexible as human children's language
b. not true with the bonobos; they followed instructions given over headphones
d. it probably helped young bonobos to learn

17. d (pp. 299-301)
Obj. XI

a-c. each of these provides support for the idea that humans are specialized for language learning

18. a (pp. 275-276, Fig 8.8)
Obj. IV-A-3; XI-B

b. this is the word superiority effect
c. this is a simplified version of the connectionist model
d. this is a difference between good and poor readers, but it is not called the Stroop effect

19. d (pp. 304-305)
    Obj. XII-B

    a. not because of context but because there are fewer ways to say things in scientific areas than in the humanities
    b. this is an example where context <u>doesn't</u> affect understanding; context must come soon after an ambiguous word to clarify it
    c. evidence for the difficulty of understanding negatives; not necessarily evidence for context

20. d (pp. 307-308)
    Obj. XIII-C-2

    a. saccades are eye movements; nothing is taken in during them
    b. only about 11 characters
    c. fixations last from about 100 ms. to about 1 s

LECTURE MATERIAL

Don't forget to review your lecture material. Process each topic meaningfully. First, be sure that you understand the material in each lecture--if you don't, ask your instructor or teaching assistant. Associate the material with things that you already know and with your personal experiences. If you can make up mental images of any of the material, do so. Try to think of real-life applications of the concepts. Go through each day's lecture and add your own notes. Then write questions to cover each concept.

WAIT AT LEAST 24 HOURS BEFORE PROCEEDING.
LET FORGETTING OCCUR--IT WILL!!

SHORT-ANSWER ESSAY QUESTIONS

Write brief answers to each of the following. The answers are on pp. 124-126, but do try to write the answers yourself before looking at them.

Thinking and Mental Processes

1. Behaviorists argue that thinking cannot be studied because there is no way to measure it. Give an example of an experiment which could be used to argue against that view.

2. Explain how a person would know that a robin is a bird according to the prototype view and according to the conceptual network approach.

3. Describe an experiment that shows that mental images are similar to perceptions.

4. Cognitive maps are often distortions of actual spatial locations. Describe two ways in which they are distorted.

5. Discuss the conditions under which doing two things results in poorer performance than doing only one thing.

Problem Solving, Expertise, and Error

6. Describe two ways in which experts differ from novices.

7. Describe two things that a problem solver can do to understand a problem.

8. Explain the difference between an algorithm and a heuristic.

9. Discuss research on generalization of problem solution to other similar problems.

10. Discuss the characteristics of creative problem solving.

11. Under what conditions are people likely to be overconfident about their predictions?

12. Many people fail to consider alternative hypotheses when trying to solve a problem. Give one example of this.

13. Give an example of how rephrasing a situation involving risks would affect people's acceptance of risk.

14. Explain how gambling might be explained by understanding some principles of learning.

Language

15. Early attempts to teach language to non-human primates were not very successful, but later attempts have been more successful. Explain why.

16. The linguist Noam Chomsky and his followers have suggested that people are born with a built-in mechanism for learning language -- the language acquisition device. What was their argument in its favor? What additional evidence could you use to support their idea?

17. What is known about the role of context in the understanding of words with missing phonemes?

18. Describe the word-superiority effect and explain how the connectionist model can handle it.

****
Find the questions that you wrote over
lecture material and write answers to them.
****

ANSWERS TO SHORT-ANSWER ESSAY QUESTIONS

1. The time that thought processes take can be measured. More complex processes take longer than simple ones. For example, Sternberg did an experiment in which he presented one, two, or four numbers to be remembered. Then subjects decided whether a single number was in the memorized set. It took about 35 msec. to search each number in memory, suggesting that people compare the presented number against each one in memory. Sternberg concluded that the comparison processes was in series, not in parallel. (pp. 272-273)

2. The prototype view argues that people categorize by comparing objects with typical instances of categories. For bird, typical birds are robins and sparrows, so a person could quickly compare an actual robin with the prototypical bird, see the similarity, and call a robin a bird. The conceptual network approach would argue that we determine that a robin is a bird by noticing that robin is subordinate to (beneath) bird in the hierarchy in memory. (pp. 269-271)

3. People remember street angles as being 90 degrees (right and left turns), even when they are not 90-degree angles. They use higher-level categories to make judgments about lower-level locations, and sometimes these are incorrect. For example, Los Angeles is east of Reno even though California is generally west of Nevada. This type of error also results from people's tendencies to make locations fall more on north-south, east-west axes than they actually are. (p. 273)

4. If one of the tasks is demanding, then doing both tasks at once will result in poorer performance than doing one alone. If people must identify two patterns that are presented 100-200 ms apart, they identify the second pattern more poorly than the first pattern. Apparently, it takes about half a second to shift attention from one stimulus to another. (pp. 275-276)

5. Shepard and Metzler presented pictures of three-dimensional objects and asked subjects if they were the same or different. Each pair of objects was in the same orientation, or one was turned some amount relative to the other. The time to say "same" depended upon the difference in orientation. It appeared that subjects actually imagined one of the pictures turning in their head and then matched the image with the other picture. The farther they had to turn it, the longer it took, just as it would if they were actually moving an object. (pp. 272-273)

6. Experts recognize and remember organized patterns relevant to their expertise more quickly and accurately than novices. Experts know how to use their problem-solving tools appropriately, and immediately pick out relevant information and reject fruitless approaches. (pp. 279-281)

7. Try to solve a simpler version of the problem. If there are many objects involved, try to solve it with only one or two. Even if you can't come up with an exact answer, see if you can make a decent estimate. Use what you know to estimate about what the answer should be. (pp. 281-283)

8. An algorithm is a mechanical, repetitive procedure that will eventually lead to a correct answer. It tests all possible hypotheses. Heuristics are strategies for simplifying a problem. They are "rules of thumb" for solving various problems that often lead to correct answers. (p. 282)

9. People are often very poor at generalizing. They may be able to use probability to solve simple problems, such as those involving coin tosses, but they are poor at applying the same principles to real-world problems. People are better at generalizing if they have seen several different types of examples of problems than if they have only seen one type of example. Mathematics transfers to physics, but physics doesn't transfer to mathematics. We know that mathematics is applicable to many different areas, but we don't assume that this is true for physics. (p. 283)

10. Creative contributions involve both good solutions to problems and the selection of appropriate problems. Guessing that problems are important and solvable is part of creative problem solving. The formation of great theories may depend on having the appropriate data and persistence to keep trying to solve the problem, and not on some special talent. Creative individuals often sense that the old ways are not quite right, and they throw themselves into the work. (p. 285)

11. People tend to be overconfident when they predict events that are quite uncertain. This is particularly true about predictions of one's own performance. Students are overconfident about their performance in courses and athletes predict they'll have better seasons than they have. Government officials express great confidence in their predictions of future events, but they are actually no more accurate than people outside of the government. (pp. 287-288)

12. If subjects are told to find the rule for generating number sequences and are given 2,4,6 as an example, they immediately decide that the rule is "add 2" and ask if 6,8,10 or 190,192,194 fit the rule. They may not consider the alternative that any increasing sequence might be correct. (pp. 288-289)

13. People are more likely to accept a plan in which 200 out of 600 will live than a plan in which there is a one-third chance that all will live and a two-thirds chance you will save no one. However, if it is phrased as 400 out of 600 will die vs. a one-third chance that no one will die and a two-thirds chance that all will die, people prefer the second version. Phrasing in terms of gain (living) or loss (dying) changes people's willingness to accept risk. (pp. 290-291)

14. Gambling is reinforced on a variable-ratio schedule of reinforcement; occasionally a bet results in a win. Variable ratio schedules result in long persistence of responding in the absence of reinforcement. Gambling is also explained by social-learning theory. People tend to imitate behavior that they have seen reinforced in others, but they don't tend to stop behavior that was punished in others. Thus, hearing about someone winning the lottery will increase gambling. (pp. 292-294)

15. Very early attempts to teach spoken language to chimpanzees failed because chimpanzees do not have the appropriate vocal apparatus to speak. Later attempts to teach sign language or other symbols were more successful, although some scientists argued that the chimps simply imitated symbols used by their trainers. The chimps created nothing like a sentence. More recent attempts have used pygmy chimpanzees known as bonobos. These animals use symbols to describe objects and to relate past events. They make creative requests, but still they don't form full sentences. Bonobos may have greater language ability than other chimps, or learning by observation and imitation may be more effective than more formal training. (pp. 298-299)

16: The original observation was that the language that children hear does not provide enough information for them to learn the rules of grammar; therefore, children must be born with such rules. However, that argument does not explain how children learn different grammars associated with different languages in different cultures. Additional evidence for something like an innate language acquisition device could include the existence of specialized areas of the brain, developmental stages of language development, and effects of early experience (effects of deafness and bilingualism). (pp. 299-301)

17. Context can help to identify words with missing phonemes, but the appropriate context word must come soon after the word with missing sounds. Delayed context, however, can change your interpretation of a sentence, even if you have misinterpreted a word. (pp. 304-305)

18. Letters can be identified in words faster than alone. According to the connectionist model, incoming letters activate units corresponding to the letters, which in turn activate higher-level word units. Letter units aren't activated enough to identify the letters. However, the word units increase the activation of the lower-level letter units, allowing identification of the letters. (pp. 306-307)

POSTTEST

Take this test with all of your books and notes out of sight. This should give you a good idea of how well you understand the material. The answers are on p. 130.

Matching

Put the letter of the term in the blank beside the definition.

Problem Solving, Expertise, and Error

1. _____ strategy for simplifying a problem   A. gamblers' fallacy

2. _____ mechanical, repetitive procedure for   B. availability
   solving a problem
3 ._____ possibility that can be tested   C. heuristic

4. _____ how rare or common something is   D. representativeness

5. _____ assumption that events that haven't   E. base-rate information
   happened for a while are "due"
6. _____ item similar to category members   F. hypothesis
   belongs to it
7. _____ number of memories of an event   G. algorithm
   indicates how common the event is

Multiple-choice

Circle the best alternative.

Thinking and Mental Processes

1. Mental activity can best be measured by:
   a. asking subjects what they are thinking
   b. directly observing it
   c. having people judge how long it would take them to do a task
   d. measuring how long it takes to answer questions
   e. none of the above; it cannot be measured and cannot be studied scientifically

2. Categories are:
   a. very similar from culture to culture
   b. absolute so that an object either is or is not a clear member of a category
   c. completely organized by levels such that each feature is stored at the lowest possible level and not repeated at higher levels
   d. activated by related concepts
   e. clearly defined by critical features

3. According to the conceptual network view of categorization, which would take longer to respond "true" to: "A blackpoll warbler can fly" or "A bird can fly"?
   a. "A bird can fly," because it is more general
   b. "A blackpoll warbler can fly," because you need to infer that a blackpoll warbler is a bird
   c. "A bird can fly," because it is a more typical statement
   d. "A blackpoll warbler can fly," because it is lacking some of the features of a typical bird

4. In Shepard and Metzler's study in which students decided whether two drawings of blocks were the same or different, students:
   a. were more accurate in responding "same" than "different"
   b. took longer to say "same" when the two objects were many degrees different in orientation than when they were only a few degrees different
   c. took longer to say "same" when the two objects were only a few degrees different in orientation than when they were many degrees different
   d. made so many errors (over 97%) that reaction times were meaningless
   e. reacted as if they could not use mental images

5. Why do people respond incorrectly to the question "Is Rome north of Philadelphia"?
   a. people make geographical areas line up on north-south and east-west axes more than they actually do
   b. cognitive maps make angles closer to 90 degrees than they are
   c. central locations are more likely to be included in cognitive maps than less-central locations
   d. cognitive maps get more detailed with experience

6. People can do two things as fast as one thing if:
   a. they are able to perform tasks in series, rather than in parallel
   b. one task is so routine that is requires no attention
   c. the response to one task follows the other one by 200 ms
   d. one task is difficult but the other task is easy
   e. both tasks require cognitive effort

Problem Solving, Expertise, and Error

7. When chess experts were shown a chess board and asked to recall the pieces, they:
   a. recalled more poorly than novices; apparently their expertise got in the way
   b. remembered better than novices whether the pieces were arranged as in a game or randomly
   c. remembered more poorly than novices if the pieces were arranged as in a game, but better if they were arranged randomly
   d. remembered better than novices if the pieces were arranged as in a game, but about the same if they were arranged randomly

8. In which situation would a heuristic be most useful?
    a. you have no hypotheses about how to solve a problem
    b. you have committed yourself to one hypothesis
    c. you cannot think of a way to test a hypothesis
    d. you keep generating the same incorrect hypothesis
    e. you have too many hypotheses to test

9. Which of the following would be most useful in helping to understand a problem?
    a. try to answer a related question
    b. try to add complexity to the problem; think of many instances rather than just a few
    c. keep trying to retrieve the factual information; avoid making estimates of the answer
    d. sit back and try to use insight to solve the problem

10. Students who learned how to solve progression problems in physics were later asked to solve very similar math problems. They:
    a. solved them very quickly because they noted the similarity
    b. did not use their learning on the math problems; evidently they associated the solutions entirely with physics
    c. solved the math problems more quickly than students who learned math first and then were given physics problems
    d. gave correct solutions if the problems involved rigid things like guns and bullets, but not if water and hoses were used in the examples

11. Evidence that solutions to insight problems may involve a gradual progression toward the solution is shown by:
    a. people's inability to say whether or not they will be able to solve such problems
    b. people's ability to indicate whether or not problems have solutions, even without being able to solve them
    c. the fact that some people are never able to solve some insight problems
    d. the inability of students to calculate Kepler's results

12. Which of the following is an example of base-rate information?
    a. the population consists of 10,000 mosquitoes and 2 rare kwiny bugs
    b. the kwiny bug looks like a mosquito except it is a bit bigger
    c. the mosquito flies a bit faster than the kwiny bug
    d. a particular specimen looks exactly like a kwiny bug
    e. the bite of the kwiny bug soothes the skin rather than irritating it

13. You are quite sure that it rains every time you wash you car. In fact, this is probably not true, but it is most related to which heuristic?
    a. representativeness
    b. base-rate
    c. avoiding risk
    d. availability
    e. overconfidence

14. If you are like most people, which would you be more likely to select as your prize in a quiz show?
    a. win $5,000
    b. take a 25% chance of winning $20,000 with a 75% chance of winning nothing
    c. lose $2,000 that you've won
    d. take a 50% chance of winning $10,000 with a 50% chance of winning nothing
    e. all of the above are equally likely; people do not agree on their choices

Language

15. "Mary chased the man" and "The man was chased by Mary" have:
    a. a unique transformational grammar
    b. two deep structures but only one surface structure
    c. totally arbitrary speech sounds
    d. two surface structures but only one deep structure

16. Chimpanzees can:
    a. learn spoken language, but teaching them is very difficult
    b. learn to use many symbols in sign language
    c. not learn anything that resembles human language because they lack intelligence
    d. not learn sign language but they can learn spoken language
    e. learn and use language in the same way as children

17. The language acquisition device
    a. is a built-in mechanism for acquiring language in humans
    b. is a computer that generates sentences and answers questions
    c. is the typewriter used by bonobos when they learn to speak
    d. is the computer terminal used by the gorilla Koko when she "spoke" on the internet

18. The Stroop effect occurs because:
    a. it is very difficult to see the colors of ink
    b. people are so used to reading words that they cannot suppress the habit
    c. people do not take the frequency of things in the population into account
    d. people's thoughts are related to their categories

19. When students hear a sentence with part of a word missing, they report:
    a. exactly what was missing
    b. hearing a word that fits the sentence no matter when the relevant context word appears
    c. hearing the whole word, even the missing letter
    d. hearing the word with those sounds that occurs most frequently in the language, independently of context

20. Which of the following is consistent with the word-superiority effect?
    a. you can find letters faster by searching for letters rather than by reading words
    b. you can recognize the difference between C and J alone faster than in COIN and JOIN
    c. you can recognize the difference between C and J faster in XQCF and XQJF than in COIN and JOIN
    d. a single letter can be identified faster when people read the whole word than when they focus attention on the critical letter
    e. all of the above are consistent

ANSWERS TO POSTTEST

Correct Answer	Questions Testing a Similar Concept	
	Comprehension Check	Short-Answer

Matching

1. C (p. 282)	12	8
2. G (p. 282)	--	8
3. F (pp. 282-283)	8b	7
4. E (p. 289)	11a,12a,c	--
5. A (p. 294)	14a	--
6. D (p. 289)	12c,14a	--
7. B (p. 290)	12	--

Multiple-Choice

1. d (pp. 271-272)	--	1
2. d (pp. 269-270)	--	--
3. b (pp. 270-271, Fig. 8.2)	2	2
4. b (pp. 272-273, Fig. 8.3)	3	3
5. a (p. 273)	4	4
6. b (pp. 275-276)	6	5
7. d (p. 281, Fig. 8.12)	7b	6
8. e (p. 282)	--	8
9. a (p. 283)	8	7,9
10. b (pp. 283-284, Fig. 8.17)	9	9
11. b (pp. 284-285)	10c	--
12. a (p. 289)	11,12a,c	--
13. d (p. 290)	12	--
14. a (pp. 290-291)	13	13
15. d (p. 297)	15	--
16. b (pp. 298-299)	16	15
17. a (p. 300)	17	16
18. b (pp. 274-276, Fig. 8.8)	18	--
19. c (pp. 304-305)	--	17
20. d (p. 306)	--	18

CHAPTER 9 INTELLIGENCE AND ITS MEASUREMENT

OBJECTIVES
Understand that:

Intelligence and Intelligence Tests
I. Defining intelligence is difficult, so we can't tell if the tests measure it (p. 315)
    A. Original tests were developed to measure the ability to do well in school (p. 315)
        1. This definition is too narrow (p. 315)
    B. Spearman suggested that there is a general factor (*g*) in mental ability (pp. 315-316, Fig. 9.1, Table 9.1, p. 320)
        1. Spearman allowed that each task also requires specific (s) abilities (p. 316)
    C. Cattell distinguished between fluid and crystallized intelligence (p. 317, Table 9.1, p. 320)
    D. Gardner argued that people have multiple intelligences (p. 318, Table 9.1, p. 320)
    E. Sternberg's triarchic theory has three components of intelligence (pp. 318-319, Table 9.1, p. 320)
        1. Cognitive processes within an individual (p. 318)
        2. Identification of situations that require intelligence (p. 318)
        3. Relationship between intelligence and the outside world (p. 318)
    F. Intelligence tests have little relationship to theories of intelligence (pp. 319-320)
II. Intelligence tests attempt to measure probable performance in school (p. 320)
    A. The intelligence quotient (IQ) involves dividing mental age by chronological age (p. 320)
    B. Stanford-Binet asks questions that can be answered at different ages (p. 321)
    C. Wechsler tests give scores on verbal and performance (pp. 321-322)
    D. Raven's Progressive Matrices makes minimal use of language and facts (pp. 322-323)
    E. Scholastic Assessment Test predicts performance in college (pp. 323-325)
The message. *Test scores give overall summaries of abilities which can be useful but must be interpreted cautiously (p. 325)*

Evaluation of Intelligence Tests
III. Tests are standardized so that mean and standard deviation are set (pp. 327-328, Fig. 9.10)
    A. Norms are established so that scores corresponding to percentiles can be determined (p. 327)
    B. Tests are restandardized as society changes (p. 328)
        1. Tests are harder today than they used to be (p. 328)
IV. Tests must be reliable and valid (pp. 328-330)
    A. Reliability refers to the repeatability of the test (pp. 328-329, Figure 9.11; Table 9.4, p. 331)
        1. A correlation coefficient is used to measure reliability (pp. 328-329)
    B. Validity refers to whether a test measures what it claims to measure (p. 329, Table 9.4, p. 331)
        1. Content validity refers to whether questions accurately represent the information (p. 329)
        2. Construct validity refers to whether the test results correspond to theoretical expectations (p. 329)
        3. Predictive validity refers to whether test scores predict behavior (p. 329)
            a. Scores must vary over a substantial range for high predictive validity (p. 329)
    C. Utility refers the practical usefulness of a test (p. 330, Table 9.4, p. 331)
    D. Test scores can fluctuate, especially if reliability is low (pp. 330-331)
V. Groups differ in mean performance on IQ tests (pp. 331-332)
    A. Males and females have similar means, but males show more variability (p. 331)
    B. There are some differences among ethnic groups on tests (pp. 331-332)
        1. Differences among European Americans are due to genetics and environment (p. 332)

2. Differences among ethnic groups may not have a genetic basis (p. 332)
VI. Tests are biased against a group if they systematically underestimate abilities (pp. 332-333)
    A. Single items may be biased if they don't correlate with the whole test for a group of people (p. 333)
    B. Tests may be biased if they underestimate the performance of a group of people (p. 333)
    C. IQ tests predict performance in school equally well for minority groups and European Americans with the same test score (p. 334)
       1. This doesn't mean there are differences in innate ability (p. 334)
    D. Intelligence is influenced both by heredity and environment (pp. 334-335)
       1. People who are closely related have more similar IQ scores than more distant relatives (p. 335, Fig. 9.13)
          a. IQs of identical twins are more similar than fraternal twins (p. 335)
       2. Identical twins adopted into different families have similar IQs, but the environments are usually similar also (pp. 335-336)
       3. Adopted children's IQs correlate with their biological parents' IQs (p. 336, Fig. 9.14)
    E. It is not clear whether ethnic differences in IQ are influenced by genetics (p. 337)
       1. African-American children raised in European-American homes score only slightly higher than the average for African-American children (p. 338)
       2. The degree of European ancestry in African Americans does not predict IQ scores (p. 339)

The message: *The present research doesn't support either a genetic or an environmental reason for ethnic group differences (pp. 339-340)*

COMPREHENSION CHECK

Answer these questions soon after reading the chapter. Circle the best alternative. Check your answers on pp. 135-137. If you gave a wrong answer, try to write why it was wrong. Check your reasons on pp. 135-137.

Intelligence and Intelligence Tests

1. The *g* factor identified by Spearman:
   a. consists of tasks that girls excel in
   b. involves crystallized intelligence
   c. involves dealing with abstract concepts and perceiving relationships
   d. is all the knowledge that a person has acquired
   e. is evidence for defining intelligence as independent abilities

Correct _____ If wrong, why? _____

2. Which of the following is <u>not</u> part of Sternberg's triarchic theory?
   a. crystallized and fluid intelligence must be distinguished
   b. identification of situations that require intelligence
   c. relationship between intelligence and the outside world
   d. cognitive processes within an individual

Correct _____ If wrong, why? _____

3. A person who remembers all of the batting averages for major league baseball players over the last 5 years, but who can't remember a short grocery list, can best be explained by which theory of intelligence?
   a. Spearman's *g*
   b. Cattell's crystallized vs. fluid intelligence
   c. Gardner's theory of multiple intelligences
   d. Stanford-Binet's IQ theory

Correct _____ If wrong, why? _____

4. IQ tests are:
   a. measures of innate potential
   b. explanations for why people do well or poorly in school
   c. useless for predicting school success
   d. not very reliable
   e. measurements of current performance

Correct _____ If wrong, why? _____

5. How do the Wechsler tests differ from the Stanford-Binet?
   a. the WISC-R has an average of 200; Stanford-Binet is 100
   b. WISC-R can be used with adults; Stanford-Binet cannot
   c. Wechsler tests give scores on more component abilities than the Stanford-Binet
   d. Wechsler tests don't involve factual information; Stanford-Binet test does
   e. Wechsler tests give only a single score; Stanford-Binet gives multiple scores

Correct _____ If wrong, why? _____

6. Scores on the Scholastic Assessment Test have just increased in 1995. Why?
   a. a smaller more select group of students took it than in previous years
   b. students can now take the test on the computer
   c. many students attend coaching classes which raise scores by 100 points or more
   d. the scores have been readjusted to bring the average back to 500

Correct _____ If wrong, why? _____

7. How are the Progressive Matrices different from the Wechsler tests?
   a. they require knowledge of more specific facts
   b. they can be used with blind people
   c. they make minimal use of language
   d. they provide scores on several distinct abilities
   e. they are not as "culture-fair"

Correct _____ If wrong, why? _____

8. Standard IQ and related tests:
   a. correlate positively with crude biological variables
   b. are inaccurate because they are not based on research
   c. focus on the ability to learn rather than on knowledge
   d. are useless because they don't correlate with how fast people process information

Correct _____ If wrong, why? _____

Evaluation of Intelligence Tests

9. Susan, who is 10, performs better than 84% of the other 10-year-olds who took the Stanford-Binet. Her IQ would be:
   a. 84
   b. 16
   c. 100
   d. 116

Correct _____ If wrong, why? _____

10. To standardize a test means to:
    a. check to see if people get the same score twice
    b. establish the rules for administering the test and for interpreting its scores
    c. see if the test predicts what it is supposed to predict
    d. make sure that all items are very similar, so that if people get one correct, they will get all correct

Correct _____ If wrong, why? _____

11. I have designed a new test for admission to law school. I measure the size of a person's wrist, and if it is larger than 85% of the people's, the student is admitted. My test has:
    a. reliability but not validity
    b. validity but not reliability
    c. content validity but not reliability
    d. neither reliability nor validity
    e. both reliability and validity

Correct _____ If wrong, why? _____

12. If a test has construct validity, it means that the test:
    a. predicts a certain behavior in a setting outside of the test
    b. has utility
    c. contains questions that accurately represent the information that the test is supposed to measure
    d. measures a concept that corresponds to a theoretical expectation

Correct _____ If wrong, why? _____

13. Research has shown that IQ tests are biased against:
   a. females as compared to males
   b. twins who were reared apart and unrelated people
   c. African Americans and East Asians
   d. non-English-speaking immigrants to the U.S.

Correct _____ If wrong, why? _____

14. Identical twins are more similar in IQ scores than fraternal twins whether they were raised together or apart. Which of the following is consistent with the conclusion that IQ is determined by heredity?
   a. twins whose parents thought they were identical but who really are fraternal are only as similar as other fraternal twins
   b. parents treat identical twins more similarly than they treat fraternal twins
   c. environments of twins reared apart are actually very similar
   d. twins are exactly the same age; random pairs of children are not

Correct _____ If wrong, why? _____

15. Which of the following provides evidence against genetics in the IQ difference between European and African Americans?
   a. there is no correlation between IQ scores and amount of European ancestry in African Americans
   b. African Americans consistently score lower than whites
   c. African-American children adopted into upper-middle class homes score only slightly higher on IQ tests than other African-American children
   d. African-American children's test scores do not improve when they are tested by an African-American tester using appropriate dialect

Correct _____ If wrong, why? _____

ANSWERS AND EXPLANATIONS FOR COMPREHENSION CHECK

Correct Answer	Other Alternatives Are Wrong Because:
1. c (pp. 315-316) Obj. I-B	a. general intelligence, not gender-specific b. part of intelligence--skills and knowledge one a already has; *g* argues for general factor d. includes ability to acquire new knowledge also e. Spearman argued that there is a general factor
2. a (pp. 318-319) Obj. I-E	a. Cattell's theory; not part of Sternberg's triarchic theory b-d. general abilities included in triarchic theory
3. c (p. 318) Obj. I-D	a. general ability; should be good at memory in general b. memory ability should be more general; good at memorizing all types of things d. the IQ is a measure of intelligence; not a theory

4. e (p. 320)
Obj. II-A

   a. no reason to assume this
   b. they don't explain performance, although they are reasonable predictors
   c. predict school success fairly well
   d. have high reliability

5. c (pp. 321-322)
Obj. II-B, C

   a. both have means of 100
   b. WISC-R is the children's test
   d. both test some factual knowledge
   e. Wechsler tests give scores on several component abilities

6. d (p. 324)
Obj. II-E

   a. a wider range of students have been taking the test in recent years
   b. true, but this doesn't explain the change in scores
   c. many students are coached but this only increases scores by 20-30 points

7. c (pp. 321-323)
Obj. II-C, D

   a. no specific facts are tested
   b. neither test can be used with blind individuals
   d. Matrices provide only one score
   e. presumably they are more fair because they do not require many language skills and they do not test facts

8. a (p. 325)
Obj. II-message

   b. they are the product of decades of research
   c. a criticism is that they focus too much on knowledge
   d. they do show a positive correlation with information processing speed

9. d (p. 327, Fig. 9.10)
Obj. III-A

   a. performs better than 84%; this is not her score
   b. performed worse than 16%, this is not her score
   c. this is average; she performed better than 50%

10. b (p. 327)
Obj. III

   a. test-retest reliability; not part of standardization
   c. validity; not part of standardization
   d. tests need a variety of items; items should be correlated with each other, but not all the same

11. a (pp. 328-329)
Obj. IV

   b. won't predict performance, but is reliable because I'd get about the same value every time
   c. questions don't represent information a law student knows; is reliable, see b
   d. it is reliable; see b
   e. not valid-see b and c above

12. d (p. 329)
Obj. IV-B-2

   a. this is predictive validity
   b. means that test is useful for practical purposes
   c. this is content validity

13. d (pp. 332-333)
   Obj. VI-B

a. females score about the same as males on IQ tests although males scores are more variable
b. genetics is irrelevant in bias
c. East Asians have higher than average scores and African Americans have lower than average scores but an intelligence test is only biased if it under predicts school performance

14. a (pp. 335-336)
   Obj. VI-D-1-a

b,c. environmental explanations for identical-twin similarities
d. explains why twins' IQs are more similar than random pairs, but not why identical twins are more similar than fraternal twins

15. a (p. 339)
   Obj. VI-E-2

b. doesn't say anything about genetics or environment because both differ
c. these results show a disappointingly small environmental influence; they don't argue against genetics they environment
d. doesn't argue against genetics

LECTURE MATERIAL

Don't forget to review your lecture material. Process each topic meaningfully. First, be sure that you understand the material in each lecture--if you don't, ask your instructor or teaching assistant. Associate the material with things that you already know and with your personal experiences. If you can make up mental images of any of the material, do so. Try to think of real-life applications of the concepts. Write your own comments on your lecture notes. Then write questions to cover each concept.

WAIT AT LEAST 24 HOURS BEFORE PROCEEDING.
LET FORGETTING OCCUR--IT WILL!!

SHORT-ANSWER ESSAY QUESTIONS

Write brief answers to each of the following. The answers are on pp. 139-140, but do try to write the answers yourself before looking at them.

Intelligence and Intelligence Tests

1. Explain how the theories of intelligence of Spearman and Cattell are similar and how these two theories differ from Gardner's theory.

2. How does Sternberg's theory differ from those of Cattell and Spearman?

3. Describe the WISC-R and the WAIS-R and explain how they differ from the Stanford-Binet.

4. Explain why Raven's Progressive Matrices should be more "culture-fair" than the Stanford-Binet and the Wechsler tests.

Evaluation of Intelligence Tests

5. What does it mean to standardize a test? Why must tests be restandardized periodically?

6. Discuss the relationship between reliability and validity.

7. Discuss the differences between content, construct, and predictive validity. How do these concepts differ from utility?

8. What type of evidence would be necessary to decide that a specific test item is biased against a group of individuals?

9. Discuss whether IQ and other aptitude tests are biased against groups of people.

10. Describe how the role of genetics in a characteristic, such as IQ, can be studied.

11. Discuss evidence related to the role of environment in the differences in IQ between African Americans and European Americans.

```
****************************************************************
```
Find the questions that you wrote over lecture material and write answers to them.
```
****************************************************************
```

ANSWERS TO SHORT-ANSWER ESSAY QUESTIONS

1. Spearman's and Cattell's theories assume that people use the same components of intelligence in tasks in different areas. Although they disagree on what or how many components of intelligence there are, they assume that the same components are used in different tasks. Gardner, on the other hand, assumes that there are different types of intelligence that are used for different tasks. (pp. 315-318, Table 9.1, p. 320)

2. Sternberg focuses less on the structure of intelligence and more on its function. He asks how people process information and engage in intelligent behavior. Sternberg's theory has three components: the cognitive processes that occur within an individual, the ability to identify repeated and novel situations and to make correct responses to them, and the ability to adapt to or change the environment. (pp. 315-319, Table 9.1, p. 320)

3. The WISC-R is the children's version and the WAIS-R is the adult's version. They include a number of different parts to assess different types of knowledge and abilities. A score is given for each of the 12 sections and also for Verbal, Performance, and Total IQ. The Stanford-Binet yields an overall IQ score, along with three subscores. However, it doesn't report as many subcomponents as the Wechsler tests. (pp. 321-322)

4. The matrices involve very little language, so a person who does not understand English or who has poor verbal skills can still complete the tests (assuming they can understand the instructions). They also do not test specific knowledge, but rather ask people to look for relationships among nonverbal items, so they should be less dependent upon what a person has been taught than the other tests. (pp. 320-323)

5. Standardization sets norms, or determines the mean performance and sets up the standard deviation. It also involves the selection of test items that test a variety of information but that all correlate to the total score. Over the years, some items become too easy, so they must be changed so that not everyone gets them correct. (pp. 327-328)

6. Reliability refers to the consistency of a test or how likely it is that a person will get the same score twice. A test can be very reliable (showing high consistency) but still not be useful or valid. A test that is not reliable, however, cannot be valid, because if the scores vary too much, they cannot predict performance. (pp. 328-329)

7. Generally, validity refers to whether a test measures what it is supposed to measure. A test has content validity if its questions represent the information that the test is supposed to measure. Construct validity refers to whether the test results are consistent with what would be expected from a theoretical construct. Predictive validity indicates that the test predicts behavior in a setting outside of the test. Utility refers to whether a test is useful, that is, whether its results can aid in improving selection or education. (p. 329)

8. An item is biased if it systematically underestimates the abilities of one group relative to another, that is, if it is easy for individuals from one group but difficult for another group. An item may also be biased if it correlates with the whole test score better for one group than for another. For example, if an item using a football field is answered correctly more often by men than by women and if the item correlates with the entire test better for men than for women, then the item is probably biased against women and it should be replaced by another item. (pp. 332-334)

9. A biased test systematically underestimates the performance of a group, so a person should perform better than the test score would predict. This is true for immigrants who do not speak English as their first language. It is also true of older women who take college entrance tests. They do better in college than the tests predict. Some ethnic groups score higher on standardized tests than other ethnic groups. This does not necessarily mean the tests are biased, however, because they do tend to predict school performance for the ethnic groups. School grades, however, may be biased and unfair for someone from a culture other than the majority culture. (pp. 332-334)

10. The role of genetics can be estimated by comparing differences in IQ for people who are either very similar or different in genetics and environment. If the role of genetics is high, people who are very similar genetically (such as identical twins) should be very similar in IQ no matter how different their environments are. If the role of genetics is low, similarity in environment should predict similarity in IQ. (pp. 334-337)

11. African-American children adopted into upper middle-class European-American families have IQs that are slightly above the averages for non-adopted African-American children. However, the size of the environmental effect here is disappointing. The amount of European ancestry in African-American children does not predict their IQs; it should if genes associated with European Americans produce higher IQs. (pp. 337-339)

POSTTEST

Take this test with all of your books and notes out of sight. This should give you a good idea of how well you understand the material. The answers are on p. 144.

Matching

Put the letter of the test in the blank beside the description.

1. _E_ general term for measure of person's probable performance in school

    A. WAIS-R

2. _C_ nonverbal test in which patterns are completed

    B. SAT

3. _G_ another college entrance test, not discussed in chapter

    C. Progressive Matrices

4. _M_ _D_ first practical intelligence test for English-speaking children

    D. Stanford-Binet

5. _A_ _D_ intelligence test for adults that contains verbal and performance items

    E. IQ

6. _B_ college entrance test that has a theoretical mean of 500

    F. WISC-R

7. _A_ intelligence test for children that gives scores on subabilities

    G. ACT

Multiple-choice

Circle the best alternative.

Intelligence and Intelligence Tests

1. Which of the following is most consistent with Spearman's theory of intelligence?
    a. intelligence consists of a general ability to perceive and manipulate relationships, plus some specific abilities
    b. intelligence consists entirely of factual information
    c. intelligence consists of cognitive processes, identification of situations requiring intelligence, appropriate use of intelligence in the world
    d. intelligence consists of unrelated specific abilities
    e. intelligence consists of the ability to plan approaches to problems

2. Jimmy remembers things well and has learned skills taught in the first grade. However, he doesn't have much potential to go far beyond these very basic skills. Jimmy has:
    a. high fluid intelligence but low crystallized intelligence
    b. a high *g* factor but low crystallized intelligence
    c. a low *g* factor and high fluid intelligence
    d. high fluid intelligence and high crystallized intelligence
    e. high crystallized intelligence but low fluid intelligence

3. A 30-year-old adult who has an IQ of 130 did what on the Stanford-Binet?
    a. performed as well as the average 39-year-old
    b. performed better than half of the other adults
    c. performed toward the left end of the normal distribution
    d. performed better than most other adults
    e. performed as well as the average 23-year-old

4. If an adult tells you that her Verbal IQ is 110 and her Performance IQ is 120, she must have taken which test?
    a. WISC-R
    b. WAIS-R
    c. Raven's Progressive Matrices
    d. Stanford-Binet
    e. TAT

5. Theoretically, why should the Progressive Matrices test be more culture-fair than the Wechsler tests?
    a. the matrices have more subtests
    b. the matrices are balanced so that males and females score about the same
    c. the matrices call for no verbal responses and no specific information
    d. the matrices are more interesting than the Wechsler tests
    e. the matrices have much higher reliability than the Wechsler tests

6. SAT scores:
    a. can be improved by 100 points or more through coaching
    b. predict college performance much better than high school grades
    c. have increased recently because the students taking the test are much smarter than those who took earlier tests
    d. significantly improve the prediction of college success when combined with high-school grades
    e. cannot be changed through coaching

7. IQ tests:
    a. measure differences among people; they don't explain them
    b. probably measure a single quantity
    c. measure inborn limits and capacities
    d. are based on precise meanings of "intelligence"
    e. explain why some people do better in school than others

Evaluation of Intelligence Tests

8. To say that someone is in the 70th percentile on a test means that she:
    a. scored higher than 70% of the norm group
    b. is 2 standard deviations above the mean
    c. got 70% of the questions correct on the test
    d. falls within the "gifted" range of intelligence
    e. falls within the "retarded" range of intelligence

9. I have a test that accurately predicts who will learn statistics quickly. My test has:
    a. predictive validity but not reliability
    b. content validity but not predictive validity
    c. predictive validity and reliability
    d. neither validity nor reliability
    e. reliability but not predictive validity

10. Which of the following is evidence for a biased test item?
    a. a judge suggests that African-American children may respond differently than European-American children because of differences in their cultures
    b. the item is missed by most test-takers
    c. the item correlates well with the entire test
    d. the item correlates with the entire test better for one group than for another group

11. The Stanford-Binet and the Wechsler tests are biased against people who do not speak English well because:
    a. such people do better in school and on the job than their scores predict
    b. such people score lower than the average population
    c. such people do about the same in school as other people with the same score
    d. the tests do not have high content validity for them
    e. the tests are too reliable for them

12. The difference between the IQs of African- and European Americans:
    a. has been increasing in the last few years
    b. is about 25 points on the Wechsler tests
    c. predicts differences in their school grades
    d. is not caused by environmental differences
    e. is greater when African Americans who have more European ancestry are compared European Americans

13. If genetics plays no role in a trait, then:
    a. identical twins reared in very different environments should be more similar than unrelated people
    b. fraternal twins reared together should be much more similar than identical twins reared together
    c. adopted children should look more like their biological parents than their adoptive parents
    d. identical twins reared apart should be less similar than fraternal twins reared together
    e. disadvantaged children adopted in higher-income homes should perform the same as other disadvantaged children

14. Identical twins reared apart are more similar in IQ than fraternal twins reared apart. A researcher who believes in the influence of environment more than heredity might explain this in what way?
    a. identical twins are more similar genetically
    b. the environments of the identical twin pairs were more similar
    c. the identical twins were raised in genuinely different environments
    d. the adoptive parents of the fraternal twin pairs were more similar than the adoptive parents of the identical twin pairs
    e. both c and d

15. African-American children reared in upper middle-class European-American homes scored:
    a. higher than the average of European-American children on IQ tests
    b. about 15 points lower on IQ tests than the average of African-American children
    c. about the same as other African-American children in Minnesota
    d. much higher than the average African-American child in the United States
    e. much higher than European-American children adopted into the same homes

16. Performance on Raven's Progressive Matrices and amount of European ancestry in African-American children are:
    a. highly correlated, giving good evidence for the importance of environment in race differences in IQ
    b. highly correlated, giving good evidence for the importance of genetics in race differences in IQ
    c. uncorrelated, giving evidence that genetics may not be important in ethnic differences in IQ
    d. negatively correlated, giving good evidence for the importance of genetics in ethnic differences in IQ
    e. uncorrelated, giving good evidence for the importance genetics in ethnic differences in IQ

ANSWERS TO POSTTEST

Correct Answer	Questions Testing a Similar Concept	
	Comprehension Check	Short-Answer

Matching

Correct Answer	Comprehension Check	Short-Answer
1. E (p. 315)	4	--
2. C (pp. 322-323)	7	4
3. G (p. 324)	--	--
4. D (p. 321)	5	3, 4
5. A (pp. 321-322)	5	3
6. B (pp. 323-324)	6	5
7. F (pp. 321-322)	5	3

Multiple-Choice

Correct Answer	Comprehension Check	Short-Answer
1. a (pp. 315-317)	1	1, 2
2. e (p. 317)	1a, 2	1, 2
3. d (p. 321)	5a, 9c	3
4. b (pp. 321-322)	5	3
5. c (pp. 322-323)	7	4
6. d (pp. 323-324)	6	--
7. a (p. 315)	4	--
8. a (pp. 327-328)	9	--
9. c (pp. 328-329)	11, 12	6, 7
10. d (pp. 332-334)	--	8
11. a (p. 333)	13	8, 9
12. c (p. 334)	15	11
13. d (pp. 335-336)	14	10
14. b (pp. 334-336)	14	10
15. c (pp. 337-339)	15	11
16. c (p. 339)	15	11

CHAPTER 10 DEVELOPMENT

OBJECTIVES

Understand that:

The Fetus and the Newborn

I. Prenatal development depends upon the health of the mother (p. 346)

    A. Low birth weight babies may do poorly because they have other disadvantages (p. 346)

    B. Fetal alcohol syndrome is marked by stunted growth and other abnormalities (pp. 346-347; Fig. 10.4)

II. Newborn's capacities are limited, but they do have some sensory and learning abilities (p. 347)

    A. They spend more time looking human faces than at other objects (p. 348, Fig. 10.5)

        1. Very young infants keep looking at the same object (p. 348)

        2. Older infants shift their eyes but they keep looking back at the same object (p. 348)

    B. Infants show a fear of heights soon after they begin to crawl (p. 348)

    C. Young infants can discriminate one sound from another (pp. 348-349)

    D. Very young infants show learning and memory (p. 349)

        1. They respond more to their mother's than to an unfamiliar voice (p. 349)

        2. They can learn a response and remember it for days (p. 349)

    E. Piaget argued that infants don't understand object permanence, but more recent researchers have found evidence that they know objects still exist if tested differently (p. 350, Fig. 10.10)

        1. Infants as young as 6 months look longer at impossible events involving disappearing objects (p. 351, Fig. 10.11)

    F. Measurement of staring time has shown other capacities in infants (p. 352)

        1. Infants stared longer at displays that had an impossible number of objects (p. 352, fig. 10.12)

        2. Infants turn to recordings of their own name more than other names (p. 352)

        3. Older infants are surprised when two halves of an object don't move together (p. 352)

The message*: Researchers have discovered that infants have many capacities even though their motor control is poor (p. 352).*

Development of Thinking and Reasoning.

III. Piaget studied how children's thought processes differ from those of adults (pp. 354-355)

    A. Piaget uses some special terminology (pp. 354-355)

        1. Behavior is based on schemata that change with development (pp. 354-355)

        2. Development occurs through assimilation and accommodation (p. 355, Fig. 10.14)

    B. Piaget proposed four stages of development (pp. 355-356, Table 10.2, p. 361)

        1. Sensorimotor stage lasts from birth to 1 1/2 years (p. 355, Table 10.2, p. 361)

            a. Children begin to develop a concept of self (p. 355)

        2. Preoperational stage lasts from 1 1/2 to 7 years (pp. 355-356,Table 10.2, p. 361)

            a. Early preoperational stage children accept that appearances are reality (p. 356, Fig. 10.15)

            b. Preoperational children tend to have egocentric thought (pp. 356-357)

            c. Preoperational children develop an understanding of other people's knowledge (pp. 357-358)

            d. Concept of conservation is not understood (p. 358, Figs. 10.17, 10.18, 10.19, p. 361, Table 10.1, p. 359)

        3. Concrete operations stage lasts from 7 to 11 years (p. 360, Table 10.2, p. 361)

a. Children can perform mental operations on concrete objects (p. 360)
    4. Formal operations stage begins at age 11 (p. 360, Table 10.2)
        a. Now children use logical and systematic planning for abstract problems (p. 360)
  C. Children may have abilities related to later stages, but they may only be able to use them on simpler tasks (p. 362)
  D. Vygotsky argued the children have a zone of proximal development that is important in education (p. 362)
IV. Children's level of moral reasoning depends upon reasoning ability (p. 362)
  A. Kohlberg suggested that moral reasoning develops in stages (pp. 362-363, Table 10.3, p. 364)
  B. Kohlberg has been criticized (p. 365)
    1. Reasoning is just the beginning; does it lead to moral behavior? (p. 365)
    2. Moral obligation may be a primitive, natural concept and not one that occurs after other stages (p. 365)
    3. Kohlberg's studies looked at moral reasoning from a "justice" orientation, not a "caring" orientation (pp. 365-366)

The message: *The universe is complicated and children construct hypotheses to understand it (p. 366).*

Social and Emotional Development

V. There are two main types of research designs for studying development (p. 368)
  A. Cross-sectional designs compare groups of different ages at one time (p. 368, Table 10.5, p. 369)
    1. Cohort effects refer to differences due to the time of growing up rather than age (p. 369)
  B. Longitudinal designs compare the same individuals when they are at different ages (p. 368, Table 10.5, p. 369)
    1. This allows the researcher to know who has left the study (p. 369)
VI. Erikson proposed eight stages of social and personality development (pp. 370-371; see Table 10.6 for stages)
  A. Basic trust vs. mistrust occurs first (p. 370)
  B. Autonomy vs. shame and doubt occurs from about ages 1 to 3 (p. 370)
  C. Initiative vs. guilt occurs from about ages 3 to 6 (p. 370)
  D. Industry vs. inferiority is the conflict from ages 6 to 12 (pp. 370-371)
  E. Adolescents fact a conflict between identity vs. role confusion (p. 371)
  F. Intimacy vs. isolation is the conflict of young adults (p. 371)
  G. Generativity vs. stagnation occurs in middle adulthood (p. 371)
  H. The conflict in old age is between ego integrity vs. despair (p. 371)
VII. Infants develop attachments to their mothers (pp. 371-373)
  A. Harlow's studies with monkeys suggest that this is due to contact comfort (pp. 371-372)
  B. Infants differ in their styles of attachments to parents and care-givers (pp. 372-373)
VIII. Parents may be authoritative, authoritarian, permissive, or uninvolved (p. 374)
  A. The effects on children may differ in different ethnic groups (p. 374)
IX. Forming friendships is important for social and emotional development (pp. 374-375)
  A. Children tend to be popular, rejected, or controversial (pp. 374-375)
  B. Birth order may have some small effects on development (p. 375)
X. Adolescence begins when the body shows signs of sexual maturation (p. 375)
  A. An identity crisis occurs as adolescents decide what kind of lives they will lead (pp. 375-376)
  B. Adolescents believe they are "special"; bad things won't happen to them (p. 376)
    1. Teens often do not use contraceptives, thinking the won't become pregnant (p. 376)
XI. Adults wonder what they will achieve and contribute to society and their families (p. 377)
  A. Most adults are satisfied with their jobs, but they could be more satisfied (p. 377)

B. People become aware that they won't accomplish their goals and have a midlife transition (pp. 377-378)

XII. A problem in old age is maintaining dignity and self esteem (pp. 378-379)

    A. Adjustment to retirement can be a problem (p. 379)

    B. Older people desire to maintain control over their lives (p. 379)

XIII. Death is a principal source of anxiety (p. 379)

    A. Dying people may go through stages of adjustment (p. 379)

The message: People confront different crises at different ages, but decisions made at one age affect later life (p. 380).

Growing Up the Same and Different

XIV. Temperaments differ at birth and remain fairly consistent (p. 382-383)

    A. Genetics plays a role because monozygotic twins are more similar in temperament than dizygotic twins (p. 383)

    B. Environment also plays a role (p. 383)

        1. Temperament may alter the environment, which affects temperament (p. 383)

XV. The family plays a large role in children's social and emotional development (p. 383)

    A. The quality of daycare and quality of home life affect development (p. 383-384)

        1. One of these must be of high quality for satisfactory development (p. 383-384)

    B. Nontraditional families don't produce children different from traditional families (p. 384)

    C. Children have difficulty following divorce, especially in the beginning (p. 384)

        1. Children who were well adjusted before the divorce and whose parents displayed minimal conflict did better (p. 385)

XVI. There are relatively few consistent sex differences (pp. 385-386)

    A. Most sex differences emerge in social situations (pp. 386)

        1. Boys' play is more competitive than girls' (p. 387)

        2. Males and females have different styles and different needs (p. 387)

            a. Men are more demanding; women are more cooperative (p. 387)

            b. Men are concerned about status with other men (p. 387)

            c. Women expect listeners to express sympathy about problems (p. 387)

    B. Society teaches gender roles (pp. 386-387)

        1. Children pass along gender roles to each other (p. 386-387)

XVII. Minority children face different pressures than others (p. 387-388)

    A. Immigrants undergo acculturation (p. 387-388)

    B. Minority groups may show full assimilation to American culture or they may develop biculturalism (p. 388)

The message: Temperament, family influences, gender, and ethnic and cultural diversity lead to a diversity of behavior (p. 388).

COMPREHENSION CHECK

Answer these questions soon after reading the chapter. Circle the best alternative Check your answers on pp. 152-154. If you gave a wrong answer, try to write why it was wrong. Check your reasons on pp. 152-154.

The Fetus and the Newborn

1. Low-birth-weight babies typically show low achievement and often have behavior problems. The best reason for this is:
   a. impaired brain development
   b. that the mother is usually malnourished during pregnancy
   c. that the mother is usually unmarried
   d. that they have a number of disadvantages

Correct _____ If wrong, why? _____

2. Which of the following is a difference between infants and adults in terms of vision?
   a. adults look at human faces more than at other patterns but infants do not
   b. infants look at very different types of objects than adults
   c. infants shift their attention to new stimuli less than adults
   d. infants shift their attention from one stimulus to another much more than adults

Correct _____ If wrong, why? _____

3. When an infant sucks, the sound "ba" is produced. He increases his sucking rate and then decreases it as the sound is repeated. The experimenter then changes the sound to "pa." What is the infant likely to do?
   a. continue sucking at the same rate because he can't discriminate any speech sounds
   b. decrease his sucking rate because the new sound catches his attention
   c. continue sucking at the same rate because he can't discriminate "pa" and "ba"
   d. increase his sucking rate because he hears a new sound

Correct _____ If wrong, why? _____

4. Piaget interpreted infants' not reaching for a hidden object as a failure in object permanence. The correct explanation for this is that infants:
   a. don't know that objects continue to exist even when we can't see them
   b. may concentrate so much on seen objects than they ignore unseen ones
   c. quickly forget where things are hidden
   d. may show object permanence under some test conditions but not others

Correct _____ If wrong, why? _____

Development of Thinking and Reasoning

5. An infant takes a new rubber ducky and immediately puts it in her mouth in exactly the same way as she sucks her rattle. Piaget would say that:
   a. accommodation of the ducky to the sucking schema has occurred
   b. assimilation of the ducky to the sucking schema has occurred
   c. the infant is in the preoperational stage
   d. the infant has added a new schema to handle the ducky
   e. the infant is in the zone of proximal development

Correct _____ If wrong, why? _____

6. Children gain some concept of self during the first stage of development. What is the evidence for this?
   a. infants over 1 1/2 years touch a spot of rouge on their face when they see themselves in the mirror
   b. infants over 1 1/2 years touch the red spot on the mirror when they see themselves with rouge on their face
   c. 4-year-olds select the same cup as an informed adult rather than an uninformed adult
   d. children tend to draw a pile of blocks as they see them even when you ask them to draw the blocks as you see them from the other side

Correct _____ If wrong, why? _____

7. I take two equal-sized cans of Coke and pour one into a tall, thin glass and another into a shorter, fatter glass. Janie then tells me that there is more coke in the tall, thin glass. Janie is:
   a. in the concrete operations stage
   b. in the sensorimotor stage
   c. in the formal operations stage
   d. in the preoperational stage
   e. showing conservation

Correct _____ If wrong, why? _____

8. Several studies have been done to determine whether children who fail Piaget's tasks can pass the same tasks when they are set up more simply. After such practice, children can often pass the more difficult versions of the tasks. This shows that:
   a. the stages are distinct; children are either in one or the other
   b. the shift between the stages is sudden
   c. transitions from one stage to the next require a major reorganization of the child's way of thinking
   d. each stage seems to merge gradually into the next stage
   e. both a and b

Correct _____ If wrong, why? _____

9. John feels that he should be helpful to a new employee because one day that employee may become his boss and he would want his boss to owe him. John's moral reasoning is in which of Kohlberg's stages?
   a. social-contract legalistic
   b. universal ethical principle
   c. law and order
   d. instrumental relativist
   e. punishment and obedience

Correct _____ If wrong, why? _____

10. A weakness of Kohlberg's theory is:
    a. people often go back to earlier stages
    b. high-level moral reasoning does not necessarily go with moral behavior
    c. people progress through the stages in very different orders
    d. the differences between men's and women's moral reasoning are very great
    e. it emphasizes a "caring" approach to moral reasoning too heavily

Correct _____ If wrong, why? _____

Social and Emotional Development

11. An investigator wished to study the relationship between intelligence and age in adults. She started
    with a group of 40 20-year-olds and tested their intelligence. She (and later her students)
    continued to test this group every 5 years for the next 60 years. What type of study is this?
    a. longitudinal
    b. cohort
    c. cross-sectional
    d. a combination of longitudinal and cross-sectional

Correct _____ If wrong, why? _____

12. Perplexity is 16 years old. She is trying to decide whether she wishes to apply herself in school so
    that she can enter medical school or whether she wants to have fun in school and not bother about a
    career. Perplexity is in which of Erikson's stages?
    a. ego integrity vs. despair
    b. generativity vs. stagnation
    c. intimacy vs. isolation
    d. industry vs. inferiority
    e. identity vs. role confusion

Correct _____ If wrong, why? _____

13. Harlow reared infant monkeys with various types of artificial mothers. Which of the following is
    true?
    a. as long as the mother provided contact comfort, the infants developed normal sexual and social
       behavior
    b. infants spent more time clinging to a cloth mother, whether or not it provided nourishment
    c. infants developed a strong attachment to whichever mother provided nourishment
    d. infants who did not have a real mother were irreversibly harmed socially and sexually

Correct _____ If wrong, why? _____

14. An authoritarian parenting style is associated with:
    a. withdrawn children
    b. children who have a lack of self-control
    c. children who are socially cooperative
    d. withdrawn or assertive children depending upon the ethnic group
    e. African-American children doing well in school; European-American children doing poorly

Correct _____ If wrong, why? _____

15. Controversial children are those who are:
    a. popular with other children, but not with parents
    b. avoided by other children
    c. popular when young, but become rejected when they get older
    d. liked by some children, but rejected by others

Correct _____ If wrong, why? _____

16. Job satisfaction:
    a. generally decreases the longer one has worked at a job
    b. is high if people are asked if they are satisfied with their job, but lower if they are asked if they would seek the same job again
    c. is high if people are asked if they would seek the same job again, but lower if people are asked if they are satisfied with their job
    d. is unrelated to how satisfied people are with their life
    e. increases during the midlife transition

Correct _____ If wrong, why? _____

17. A dying person promises to leave all of his money to a worthwhile charity if God will save him. According to Kubler-Ross, he is in what stage?
    a. depression
    b. acceptance
    c. denial
    d. bargaining
    e. anger

Correct _____ If wrong, why? _____

Growing Up the Same and Different

18. Differences in temperament that exist in infancy are:
    a. largely gone by the time a child is 7
    b. due to the environment; genetics plays no role
    c. unrelated to measures of fear tested a few months later
    d. fairly consistent through childhood

Correct _____ If wrong, why? _____

19. Following divorce:
    a. almost all children act depressed for more than 5 years
    b. girls have more adjustment problems than boys, particularly if they live with their mother
    c. adjustment is best if children live with the opposite-sex parent
    d. African-American children have more adjustment problems than European-American children
    e. boys become aggressive toward other children

Correct _____ If wrong, why? _____

20. Gender roles are:
    a. gradually disappearing in today's society
    b. mostly defined by biology
    c. often learned from other children
    d. almost entirely learned from parents

Correct _____ If wrong, why? _____

ANSWERS AND EXPLANATIONS FOR COMPREHENSION CHECK

Correct Answer	Other Alternatives Are Wrong Because:
1. d (p. 346) Obj. I-A	a. probably not, because when twins are compared in the same environment the low-birth-weight twin usually catches up to the higher-birth-weight one b. true, but this isn't necessarily the cause of the poor development later c. true, but mother's marital status per se doesn't cause the later problems
2. c (p. 348, Fig. 10.5) Obj. II-A	a. very young infants also look at human faces b. both spend more time looking at more complex forms d. they shift attention less; even later, infants may shift attention, but they move back to the original stimulus
3. d (p. 348-349) Obj. II-C	a. infants can discriminate speech sounds b. new sounds are novel and infants increase their sucking rate c. infants do discriminate between "pa" and "ba"
4. d (p. 351; Fig. 10.11) Obj. II-E-1	a. Piaget's explanation; could be correct, but so could b or c b. possibly correct, but so are a and c c. possibly correct, but so are a and b
5. b (p. 354-355) Obj. III-A	a. an old schema was applied here because she sucked in exactly the same way; accommodation involves modifying an old schema c. an infant is in the sensorimotor stage d. an old schema, sucking, was used e. this is Vygotsky's term for the distance between what children can do themselves and what they can do with help
6. a (p. 355) Obj. III-B-1-a	b. this shows that they don't understand that it is themselves in the mirror; no concept of self c. shows they understand other people's knowledge; not evidence for concept of self; 4-year old not in first stage of development d. an example of egocentric thought
7. d (p. 358, Table 10.1, p. 361) Obj. III-B-2-d	a. if so, she should know they are the same b. if so, she shouldn't be able to talk c. she would show conservation at this age e. she is not showing conservation (notice the term is not conversation)

8. d (p. 361)
   Obj. III-C

   a. shows that the distinction is less certain; children appear to be in one stage on one task, but in the next stage on another task
   b. the shift appears to be more gradual
   c. Piaget's belief; this contradicts it; child shows thought patterns from both stages at same time
   e. both a and b are wrong; they are Piaget's beliefs, which these results contradict

9. d (p. 362-363, Table 10.3, p. 364)
   Obj. IV-A

   a. he's not arguing that it's best for society
   b. b. he's not thinking about highest ethical principles
   c. he's not doing it because it is the law
   e. there are no immediate consequences

10. b (p. 365)
    Obj. IV-B-1

    a. people usually do not go back
    c. people progress in the same order
    d. there are some sex differences, but they are not great
    e. Kohlberg's levels are based on a "justice" orientation

11. a (p. 368, Table 10.5, p. 369)
    Obj. V-B

    b. cohort effects refer to similarities in environment while growing up; occur with cross-sectional studies
    c. would have tested different-age people all at once
    d. purely longitudinal; same people tested many times

12. e (p. 371)
    Obj. VI-E

    a. during old age
    b. during middle age
    c. during young adulthood; she's only 14
    d. during preadolescent years

13. b (pp. 371-372)
    Obj. VII-A

    a. neither male nor female isolates showed appropriate sexual behavior; females became poor mothers
    c. nourishment was much less important than the contact comfort provided by the cloth mothers
    d. infants raised with artificial mothers were fairly normal if they played with other infants

14. d (p. 374)
    Obj. VIII-A

    a. related to authoritarian European-American parents, but not African-American parents; d is a better answer
    b. related to a permissive parenting style
    c. related to an authoritative parenting style
    e. related to an authoritative parenting style; it's European-American children who are likely to do well in school

15. d (p. 374-375)
    Obj. IX-A

    a. definitions refer to children's liking, not parents'
    b. these are called "rejected" children
    c. status tends to be fairly consistent from year to year

16. b (p. 377)
   Obj. XI-A

   a. new employees are less satisfied than older ones
   c. is high if asked about satisfaction, lower if asked about taking the same job again
   d. people who are satisfied with their life are usually satisfied with their job and vice versa
   e. tie when person learns that goals won't be met; not likely to increase job satisfaction

17. d (p. 379, Table 10.11)
   Obj. XII-A

   a. people lose hope in this phase
   b. psychologically ready to die
   c. people deny that death will occur
   e. people grow abusive and ask "Why me?"

18. d (pp. 382-383)
   Obj. XIV

   a. differences are still there at 7 1/2
   b. monozygotic twins are more similar than dizygotic, so genetics plays a role
   c. more difficult infants were more afraid later

19. e (p. 384)
   Obj. XV-C

   a. some did, but many felt better after a year or two
   b. boys had more problems
   c. generally better with same-sex parent
   d. it's the opposite; European-American children seem to have more problems

20. c (p. 383)
   Obj. XVI-B-1

   a. may be changing, but differences are still there
   b. a few aspects are, but most aren't biological
   d. also role models, television, other children

LECTURE MATERIAL

Don't forget to review your lecture material. Process each topic meaningfully. First, be sure that you understand the material in each lecture--if you don't, ask your instructor or teaching assistant. Associate the material with things that you already know and with your personal experiences. If you can make up mental images of any of the material, do so. Try to think of real-life applications of the concepts. Write your own notes on your lecture notes. Then write questions to cover each concept.

WAIT AT LEAST 24 HOURS BEFORE PROCEEDING.
LET FORGETTING OCCUR--IT WILL!!

SHORT-ANSWER ESSAY QUESTIONS

Write brief answers to each of the following. The answers are on pp. 156-158, but do try to write the answers yourself before looking at them.

The Fetus and the Newborn

1. Describe the relationship between low birth weight and later development.

2. For many years, it was thought that newborn infants could not learn. Describe some evidence that shows that infants can learn.

Development of Thinking and Reasoning

3. Explain what Piaget meant by the terms "assimilation" and "accommodation."

4. Describe how a child in the concrete operations and a child in the formal operations stage would decide which two colors of paint would make a certain shade of brown.

5. Briefly describe Kohlberg's theory of moral development.

Social and Emotional Development

6. Describe what Harlow found out about early attachment in monkeys.

7. Describe how a securely attached infant reacts in the Strange Situation test and also in other real-world situations.

8. Discuss the "personal fable" of teenagers.

9. Describe the midlife transition.

10. Discuss how people adjust to retirement.

Growing Up the Same and Different

11. Briefly, describe the effects of day care on the development of children.

12. Describe the situations in which sex differences are most likely to occur.

****

Find the questions that you wrote over lecture material and write answers to them.

****

ANSWERS TO SHORT-ANSWER ESSAY QUESTIONS

1. Children who are born with low birth weight tend to have lower academic achievement and behavior problems later in life. This does not mean the low birth weight causes these problems, however. The postnatal environments of low birth weight children are often not very good. When twins who vary in birth weight are compared, the twin with low birth weight tends to catch up to the heavier twin, suggesting that low birth weight per se may not be the cause of later problems. (p. 346)

2. Infants less than 3 days old could turn on a tape recording of their mother's voice by sucking on a nipple at certain times and certain rates. By sucking at different times and rates, they could turn on a recording of another woman's voice. The infants increased their sucking in order to turn on their mother's voice, but they decreased it when it resulted in turning on the other woman's voice. This shows that the infants recognized their mother's voice and they learned what to do to turn it on. The fact that the recognized their mother's voice so early suggests that the infants had learned their mother's voice even before birth. (p. 349)

3. Children try to use old ways of behaving in new situations. In Piaget's terms, they assimilate objects to a specific schema (an organized way of interacting with the world). Sometimes these old ways don't quite work, so they need to modify their behavior in order to interact with a new object. This modification of a schema is called accommodation. (p. 354-355)

4. The concrete operations child would haphazardly select two colors and mix them. This child might try some combinations twice and never try other combinations. The formal operations child would test pairs of colors systematically--mix #1 with #2, #3, #4, #5, #6, #7, and #8.Then she would mix #2 with #3, #4, #5, #6, #7, and #8. This systematic process would be continued until the correct combination was found. (p. 360)

5. As children grow older, their moral reasoning becomes less related to immediate rewards and punishments and more related to abstract principles. There are six stages, with the highest level of morality based on ethical principles such as a respect for human life and justice. Kohlberg argues that these changes occur because the child becomes more and more able to reason abstractly. (p. 360)

6. Before Harlow's experiments it was thought that attachment to the mother occurred because she was the source of nourishment. However, his studies showed that it was contact comfort that was important. Young monkeys send more tie on a terry cloth covered artificial mother than on a wire mother whether the terry cloth mother provided milk or not. These infants with artificial mothers, however, didn't grow up normally. They were inadequate mothers and they didn't know how to interact properly with other monkeys. (pp. 362-363, Table 10.3, p. 364)

7. In the Strange Situation, a mother and an infant come into a room with many toys. Then a stranger enters and the mother leaves the room. Later the mother returns. A securely attached infant uses the mother as a base for exploration, showing her toys and making eye contact with her. When the mother leaves, the infant may cry, but only a little. When the mother returns, the infant goes to her with apparent delight, cuddles with her, and then returns to the toys. Such infants also show secure attachment patterns to fathers, grandparents, and other care-givers. They relate well to playmates.

8. Teenagers are likely to believe that they are special and that bad things only happen to other people, not to them. This has been called the "personal fable"; it may lead to risky behaviors such as having sex without contraceptives. (p. 376)

9. People realize that they may never be able to meet some of the goals that they have not yet met. Illusions are discarded and people may become discontented. They may accept this and channel their energies into things they can accomplish or they may change their routine and modify their lives. Others may become depressed and turn to alcohol as a means of escape. (pp. 377-378)

10. People who had activities and interests outside of work adjust better than people without such outside interests. There is often a period immediately after retirement when people enjoy doing things they never had time for before. They may soon realize that they can't achieve all of their goals, and may set more realistic goals. Older people need to feel that they have control of their lives, even if their health begins to deteriorate. (pp. 378-379)

11. In many cultures, it is not expected that mothers will stay home with their young infants; however, in North America and Europe, this was the prevalent custom. Children who come from good homes develop adequately either at home or in a good day care center. Children from disadvantaged homes who have good day care actually develop better than the same children who stay at home with their mothers. Very early day care is not harmful if it is of good quality. (p. 383-384)

12. Important differences between males and females emerge in social situations. Boys compete with each other, whereas girls tend to cooperate. Boys exchange insults and make threats and boasts. Girls exchange compliments and make suggestions rather than demands. (pp. 386-387)

POSTTEST

Take this test with all of your books and notes out of sight. This should give you a good idea of how well you understand the material. The answers are on p. 162.

Matching

Write the letter of the term on the right in the blank beside the description on the left.

1. _C_ distance between what children can do for themselves and what they can do with help

2. _B_ awareness that many goals will never be reached

3. _F_ alternation between membership in one culture and in another

4. _A_ transition to feeling a part of the culture of one's new country

5. _E_ people's tendency to be active or inactive, outgoing or reserved

6. _D_ belief that one is special; bad things only happen to other people

A. acculturation

B. midlife transition

C. zone of proximal development

D. personal fable

E. temperament

F. biculturalism

Multiple-choice

Circle the best alternative.

The Fetus and the Newborn

1. Infants with low birth weight:
    a. may catch up in development to infants with higher birth weights if they experience similar environments
    b. have irreversible brain damage
    c. tend to be overachievers; have higher academic achievement than higher-birth-weight counterparts
    d. usually have environments that are similar to infants with higher birth weights
    e. have a lower risk of dying that heavier infants

2. Infants tend to shift their attention:
    a. much more often than adults; they have very low attention spans
    b. away from faces and other complex objects
    c. away from familiar things like their mother's voice
    d. toward objects that were previously seen and are now covered
    f. back toward objects they saw before

3. An infant sees a toy car go down a slope and emerge from behind a screen in either a possible (a hidden box is above the slope) or impossible (a hidden box blocks the slope) situation. What happened?
    a. infants stared longer at the possible than at the impossible event
    b. infants stated equally long at both events
    c. infants over 6 months stated longer at the impossible event; infants under 6 months stared longer at the possible event
    d. because infants don't have object permanence, they didn't stare at either event; they assumed that the car was gone when it went behind the screen
    e. infants stared longer at the impossible than at the possible event

Thinking and Reasoning

4. Which of the following is an example of egocentric thought, as Piaget described it?
    a. Johnny argues that his sister should not touch his toys
    b. Michael draws a pile of blocks as he sees them, even when ask to draw how they would look from your side
    c. Diane looks for the candy under the cup indicated by an "informed" adult
    d. Susie grasps at the new puppy and tries to shake him like a rattle
    e. Jamie doesn't hunt for Easter eggs because he assumes that hidden objects are gone

5. Susie in 4d above is showing:
    a. a lack of conservation
    b. assimilation
    c. concrete operational thought
    d. object permanence
    e. an inability to accommodate

6. A child in the formal operations stage can do which of the following that cannot be done by a child in the concrete operations stage?
    a. show conservation
    b. have the concept of object permanence
    c. be able to assimilate
    d. solve problems systematically
    e. distinguish between "pa" and "ba"

7. Piaget argued that children in the preoperational stage fail conservation tasks because they lack the necessary mental processes. More recent research has shown that:
    a. children understand relevant concepts; they just can't apply them to more complex tasks
    b. children who can show conservation of number with a few items fail when the number is increased
    c. giving children water to pour and balls of clay to squash speeds up their understanding of conservation
    d. Piaget overestimated the abilities of young children
    e. young children can easily deal with abstract conservation concepts, if they are presented properly

8. The military overthrows a dictator because he gives rights to a minority and the law states that they have no rights. The military's moral reasoning is probably at what level?
    a. law and order
    b. punishment and obedience
    c. social contract
    d. interpersonal concordance
    e. universal principles

9. A weakness of Kohlberg's theory is that:
    a. people seem to progress through the stages in the same order
    b. people usually don't go back to earlier stages
    c. in societies throughout the world, people begin at Kohlberg's first stage
    d. differences between males and females are not great
    e. criminals often show high-level moral reasoning, but their behavior is not moral

Social and Emotional Development

10. Today's 20-year olds score higher on an IQ test than today's 60-year olds. To say that this is due to a cohort effect means that:
    a. IQ declines with age
    b. the groups of 60-year olds is a dull group and the 20-year olds are a bright group
    c. the effects are due to the longitudinal design
    d. there is a correlation, but cause cannot be determined
    e. the effects may be due to health and education differences while the groups were growing up

11. Michael is 21 and he is trying to decide whether to marry now or wait until he has finished graduate school. He is in which of Erikson's stages?
    a. intimacy vs. isolation
    b. identity vs. role diffusion
    c. ego integrity vs. despair
    d. generativity vs. stagnation
    e. identity foreclosure vs. identity achievement

12. When monkeys who had been reared with artificial mothers became mothers, they:
    a. were normal
    b. were overly attached to their infants and did not let them develop much independence
    c. were "super-moms," even better than normally reared mothers
    d. constantly clung to their infants, apparently trying to make up for the lack of contact in their own infancy
    e. they rejected their infants

13. Authoritative parents tend to have children who:
    a. lack a sense of social responsibility
    b. get mixed reactions from their peers, liked by some but rejected by others
    c. show self-reliance and self-control
    d. are withdrawn
    e. have serious identity crises

14. Adolescent outbursts of vandalism and delinquency:
    a. occur in all cultures
    b. are most common in teens who are particularly obedient to their parents
    c. occur during the midlife transition
    d. occur only for teenagers who believe strongly in the personal fable
    e. are most common at age 16

15. J. Q. Med has just turned 40. He decides that his life isn't going anywhere. He has always wanted to sail around the world so he quits his job, buys a boat and takes off. J. Q. has experienced:
    a. a "honeymoon period"
    b. a failure in gender role identity
    c. an autonomy vs. shame and doubt crisis
    d. midlife transition
    e. an ego integrity vs. despair crisis

16. The "honeymoon period" of retirement refers to:
    a. the last few years before death, when marriage becomes more meaningful
    b. the desire of retirees to have close family ties
    c. the period following the loss of a spouse
    d. the period immediately following retirement in which the retiree tries to do all the things that he or she hasn't had time for
    e. the period early in retirement when both spouses are still living

17. M. N. has been told that he is dying of cancer. He becomes very abusive toward the doctor and the nurses. He is in which of Kubler-Ross's stages of death?
    a. bargaining
    b. acceptance
    c. depression
    d. denial
    e. anger

Growing Up the Same and Different

18. In which situation will a child probably develop most normally?
    a. the child comes from a disadvantaged home and day care is poor
    b. the child comes from a disadvantaged home and stays at home with mother
    c. the parents have just been divorced and the mother goes to work for the first time
    d. the child comes from a disadvantaged home and goes to a good day care
    f. the mother is unmarried and poor

19. Gender roles:
    a. are entirely biologically based
    b. are learned, although some aspects have biological bases
    c. are learned entirely from parents and other adults who visit the home
    d. do not exist in most societies

20. If an immigrant to the United States is able to alternate between his native culture and that of the United States, he is showing:
   a. biculturalism
   b. total assimilation
   c. bilingualism
   d. difficulty with acculturation
   e. gender role identity

ANSWERS TO POSTTEST

Correct Answer	Questions Testing a Similar Concept	
	Comprehension Check	Short-Answer

Matching

1. C (pp. 375-376)	5e	--
2. B (pp. 377-378)	16e	9
3. F (p. 376)	--	--
4. A (p. 376)	--	--
5. E (pp. 375-376)	18	--
6. D (p. 376)	--	--

Multiple-choice

1. a (p. 376)	1	1
2. e (p. 348)	2	--
3. e (p. 356)	4	--
4. b (p. 355)	--	--
5. b (p. 360)	5b	3
6. d (p. 360)	7a, 7c	4
7. a (p. 358)	8	--
8. a (p. 362-363, Table 10.3)	9	5
9. e (p. 369)	10	6
10. e (p. 369)	11b	--
11. a (pp. 370-371, Table 10.6)	12c	--
12. e (p. 374)	13	6
13. c (p. 374)	14	--
14. e (p. 375)	--	--
15. d (pp. 377-378)	16e	9
16. d (pp. 377-378)	--	--
17. e (p. 379, Table 10.11)	17	--
18. d (p. 384)	--	11
19. b (pp. 386-387)	20	12
20. a (p. 388)	--	--

CHAPTER 11 MOTIVATION

OBJECTIVES

Understand that:

General Properties of Motivated Behavior

I. Motivated behaviors are goal-directed (p. 393)
II. There are many different types of definitions of motivation (pp. 394-396, Table 11.1)
  A. Lorenz believed that instinctive energy compels behavior (p. 394)
  B. Drive-reduction theories propose that motivation is an internal state or irritation that energizes behavior (p. 394)
    1. Homeostasis is the maintenance of biological conditions at an optimum level (p. 395)
  C. Incentive theories propose that incentives "pull" organisms (p. 395)
    1. Intrinsic motivation involves engaging in a behavior for its own sake; extrinsic motivation includes rewards and punishments (pp. 395-396)
III. People have many different types of motives (p. 397)
  A. Primary motivations result from biological needs; secondary motivations result from learning (p. 397)
  B. Maslow proposed that motivations are arranged in a hierarchy of needs (pp. 397-398, Fig. 11.3)

The message: There are many types of motivation (p. 398)

Motivation and Biological States: The Case of Hunger

IV. Food selection depends upon physiological, social, and cognitive factors (pp. 400-402)
  A. Some taste preferences are biologically based (pp. 400-401)
  B. People prefer familiar tastes (p. 401)
  C. Taste aversions develop to foods that preceded illness and to foods that evoke repulsive associations (pp. 401-402)
V. Hunger is partly controlled by physiological mechanisms (p. 402)
  A. Satiety (a full feeling) is controlled by stomach distention (pp. 402-403)
  B. Hunger is controlled by glucose in blood stream (p. 403, Fig. 11.9)
    1. Insulin promotes movement of nutrients out of the bloodstream into cells (pp. 4403-404)
      a. If insulin is low, as in diabetes, nutrients enter cells very slowly (pp. 403-404)
    2. Glucagon converts stored energy back into blood glucose (p. 404)
      a. If insulin is consistently high, glucagon can't move glucose back into the bloodstream (p. 404)
  C. In the long run, the brain controls weight at a given set point (p. 405, Fig. 11.12)
VI. Hypothalamus is important in regulating weight (pp. 405-406, Fig. 11.13)
  A. Lateral hypothalamus is critical for starting meals (p. 405)
    1. Damage results in difficulty in digestion (p. 405)
  B. Ventromedial hypothalamus controls the speed of digestion and insulin secretion (p. 405)
    1. Damage results in rapid digestion and weight gain (p. 405)
  C. Paraventricular hypothalamus is important for sensing stomach distention (pp. 405-406)
VII. Eating disorders occur when motivational mechanisms go awry (p. 406)
  A. Obesity is an excessive accumulation of body fat (p. 406)
  B. People sometimes overeat in response to emotional problems (pp. 406-407)
    a. This probably isn't a cause of obesity (pp. 406-407)
  C. Genetics are involved in obesity (p. 407)
  D. Overweight people may expend less energy (pp. 407-408)
  E. The best way to lose weight is to eat less (p. 408)

1. Increasing energy expenditure helps too (p. 408)
    F. Normal weight people (especially women) often diet to become thinner (pp. 408-410)
       1. People who are dieting may eat more after breaking their diets (pp. 409-410, Fig. 11.17)
    G. Anorexia nervosa involves steady weight loss (pp. 410-411)
       1. Social pressure to be thin contributes to anorexia (pp. 410-411)
    H. Bulimia involves eating binges (p. 411)
The message: Motivations are controlled by a complex mixture of physiological, social, and cognitive forces (p. 412)

Sexual Motivation

VIII. Sexual motivation depends upon physiological drive and incentives (p. 413)
    A. Human sexual behavior shows great variability (p. 413)
       1. People think that excessive means "more than they do" (p. 414)
    B. Human sexual behavior varies across cultures (pp. 416-417)
    C. Sexual customs have changed over the years (pp. 415-416)
    D. AIDS has made people more cautious in their sexual behavior (pp. 417-418)
IX. Sexual arousal involves four physiological stages (pp. 418-419, Fig. 11.27)
X. Sexual orientation is a preference for male or female partners (p. 419)
    A. Sexual anatomy is determined by testosterone (male hormone) during early development (p. 419)
    B. The number of homosexuals is difficult to determine (p. 421)
    C. Many homosexuals are well adjusted and content (p. 421)
    D. A section of the anterior hypothalamus is smaller in homosexual men (pp. 422-423)
The message: Sexual motivation results from a combination of biological factors and experiences (p. 423)

Achievement Motivation

XI. Need for achievement is striving for competitive success and excellence (p. 425)
    A. The Thematic Apperception Test (TAT) has been used to measure this need (p. 426)
    B. People with a high need for achievement set moderately difficult goals (p. 426)
       1. People dominated by fear of failure prefer very easy and very difficult tasks (p. 426)
    C. High, realistic goals are the best motivators (p. 427)
XII. Need for achievement varies with age and sex (pp. 428-429)
    A. Preschool children don't show distress at failure (p. 428)
    B. Women sometimes score lower on need for achievement than men (pp. 428-429)
XIV. The structure of a job can encourage or discourage achievement motivation (pp. 429-430)
The message. Need for achievement is different from other motives in that it is never satiated (p. 430)

COMPREHENSION CHECK

Answer these questions soon after reading the chapter. Circle the best alternative. Check your answers on pp. 168-170. If you gave a wrong answer, try to write why it was wrong. Check your reasons on pp.168-170.

General Properties of Motivated Behavior

1. Which of the following is <u>not</u> consistent with a drive theory of motivation?
    a. a very hungry animal will work harder than a less hungry animal
    b. a hungry animal will seek food to achieve need reduction
    c. a rat will run faster to get tasty food than to get less-tasty food
    d. a thirsty child will produce many behaviors

Correct _____ If wrong, why? _____

2. Which of the following is an example of an extrinsically motivated behavior?
    a. you eat something quickly because it tastes so good
    b. a college student spends hours on a paper because the topic is so interesting
    c. a worker works extra hard because a bonus is expected soon
    d. a monkey figures out how to open a device "just for the fun of it"

Correct _____ If wrong, why? _____

3. According to Maslow's hierarchy of needs, a person who is desperately thirsty will try to satisfy:
    a. the need for self-actualization
    b. social needs
    c. needs at all levels
    d. physiological needs only _physical_
    e. secondary needs

Correct _____ If wrong, why? _____

Motivation and Biological States: The Case of Hunger

4. Taste preferences in humans:
    a. develop during the 2nd year of life
    b. can be related to abnormal biological functioning
    c. are purely psychological; they aren't related to biology
    d. are almost always related to the amount of nutrition in food
    e. are very similar across ethnic groups

Correct _____ If wrong, why? _____

5. A person with uncontrolled diabetes has low insulin levels. Which is most likely?
    a. a high percentage of what the person eats will be stored as fats
    b. the person probably has low glucagon levels
    c. the person has damage to the ventromedial hypothalamus
    d. a low percentage of each meal is converted to fats

Correct _____ If wrong, why? _____

6. A physician argues that overweight people have high set points and, therefore, cannot lose weight. By this he means that:
    a. their brain mechanisms are maintaining a constant, high weight
    b. they are set in their ways and unlikely to change through diets
    c. they have damage to the lateral hypothalamus
    d. satiety occurs too quickly in overweight people

Correct _____ If wrong, why? _____

7. Damage to which structure will result in a rat that loses a lot of weight and then maintains a very low body weight?
    a. ventromedial hypothalamus
    b. lateral hippocampus
    c. lateral hypothalamus
    d. ventromedial hippocampus

Correct _____ If wrong, why? _____

8. It has been argued that people become overweight because they eat to overcome emotional problems. Which of the following is true about this argument?
    a. it is true, because people "binge" when they are anxious
    b. it is probably not the reason for their being overweight, because overweight people do not have more emotional problems than normal-weight people
    c. it is probably true, because most overweight people have low self-esteem
    d. it is true, genetics has been linked to the increased anxiety and consequently to obesity

Correct _____ If wrong, why? _____

9. In the study in which subjects were either given a milkshake or not and then offered ice cream, the dieters:
    a. ate much less ice cream if they had a milkshake first, because they were not as hungry
    b. ate much less ice cream if they had a milkshake first, because of the "what-the-heck" effect
    c. ate the same amount or even more ice cream when they had a milkshake first, because of the "what-the-heck" effect
    d. didn't eat any ice cream if they had a milkshake first, because they had already exceeded the limits of their diets

Correct _____ If wrong, why? _____

10. Anorexia nervosa:
    a. results in very low energy levels
    b. is most common in women over 25
    c. is usually accompanied by a pathological fear of fatness
    d. occurs in women with poor self-control
    e. involves frequent episodes of binge eating

Correct _____ If wrong, why? _____

Sexual Motivation
11. How is the sex drive similar to hunger?
    a. both depend on physiological drives and incentives
    b. both drives are easily aroused in the absence of incentives
    c. incentives for both vary greatly, and people understand other people's preferences
    d. Masters and Johnson described four similar stages of arousal for both drives

Correct _____ If wrong, why? _____

12. In his pioneering research on sexuality, Kinsey found that:
    a. people agreed pretty much on what was excessive masturbation
    b. number of orgasms for an individual person declines with age
    c. the range of variation in male sexual activity was great; the range of variation in female sexual activity was very limited
    d. most people consider their behavior normal and anything above that to be excessive
    e. about 2.8% of the men reported themselves as being homosexual

Correct _____ If wrong, why? _____

13. Vaginal intercourse:
    a. is less likely to result in the transmission of the AIDS virus than anal intercourse
    b. will not lead to transmission of the AIDS virus, even if one partner is infected, so heterosexuals have nothing to fear
    c. has been less affected by the threat of AIDS than by the threat of other venereal diseases
    d. is safe between homosexual males if a condom is worn

Correct _____ If wrong, why? _____

14. Homosexuality in men:
    a. may occur because the mother secretes estrogen during pregnancy
    b. means that a man would prefer to be a woman
    c. was taboo in ancient Greek and Roman society
    d. appears to be related to genetics
    e. is caused by a part of the anterior hypothalamus being small

Correct _____ If wrong, why? _____

Achievement Motivation

15. How can the need for achievement be measured?
    a. have people tell stories about pictures in the Thematic Apperception Test
    b. ask people whether they are strongly motivated for success
    c. measure how much people achieve
    d. have people play a video game of a set difficulty

Correct _____ If wrong, why? _____

16. People with a strong fear of failure:
    a. put little effort into easy tasks
    b. put extraordinary effort into tasks if the goal is to "do your best"
    c. increase their efforts following feedback, no matter how they did
    d. react to feedback by reducing their efforts
    e. try harder when they're told they'll be evaluated

Correct _____ If wrong, why? _____

17. What has been found about young children's reactions to failure?
    a. they don't become discouraged; they assume they'll succeed next time
    b. they become discouraged very quickly, much quicker than adults
    c. they fear failure more than they seek success, even when they first enter school
    d. girls are encouraged to set higher personal goals than boys, so they fail more often and have more fear of failing

Correct _____ If wrong, why? _____

ANSWERS AND EXPLANATIONS FOR COMPREHENSION CHECK

Correct Answer	Other Alternatives Are Wrong Because:

1. c (pp. 394-395)
   Obj. II-B

a,b,d. all consistent with drive theory
c. tasty food should not reduce drive more than less tasty food; this is consistent with incentive theory

2. c (pp. 395-396)
   Obj. II-C-1

a,b,d. all intrinsically motivated; there is no external reward

3. d (pp. 397-398)
   Obj. III-B

a. lower-level needs must be satisfied before the desire to fulfill one's potential motivates
b. social needs are higher than physiological; they can't motivate until physiological are fulfilled
c. lower-level needs must be met before higher-level needs can motivate
e. won't satisfy secondary until primary are met

4. b (pp. 400-402)
   Obj. IV

a. some preferences are present at birth
c. abnormal biological conditions can influence preferences, such as a need for salt if the boy excretes salt too quickly
d. we often reject unfamiliar, nutritious foods
e. ethnic groups may differ in their food preferences

5. d (pp. 403-404)
   Obj. V-B-1

a. fats are stored when insulin is high
b. has the opposite effect as insulin; not low in both
c. this would produce high insulin levels

6. a (p. 405)
   Obj. V-C

b. may be true, but it isn't what is meant by "set point"
c. this would result in low body weight, not high
d. satiety means feeling full, so this would result in low weight

7. c (p. 405)
   Obj. VI-A

a. damage to this structure increases insulin, which converts glucose to fat and makes an animal hungry; causes weight gain
b,d. hippocampus is involved in memory

8. b (pp. 406-407)
   Obj. VII-B

a. people do binge, but this is not the cause of obesity; it usually happens in people who are dieting

c. this is true for a minority of overweight people, but not the majority

d. genetics plays a factor in obesity but it results in increased secretion of a protein and not in anxiety

9. c (pp. 409-410, Fig. 11.17)
   Obj. VII-F-1

a. this was true for nondieting people; dieters ate more

b. the "what-the-heck" effect led them to eat more; they had already gone off their diets

d. they ate ice cream following the milkshake, either as much as without the milkshake or more

10. c (pp. 410-411)
    Obj. VII-G

a. energy levels tend to be very high

b. most common in teenage years and early 20s

d. anorexic women usually have high self-control

e. bulimia; anorexics usually eat little food

11. a (p. 413)
    Obj. VIII

b. for many people, the sex drive is only aroused in the presence of incentives; people get hungry whether or not they see food

c. incentives probably vary more for the sex drive; people don't understand others' preferences

d. they described the stages of sexual arousal

12. d (p. 414)
    Obj. VIII-A

a. people varied greatly in what they thought was excessive

b. can't tell; Kinsey's sample was cross-sectional so he interviewed different people at different ages

c. females also showed a great deal of variability

e. Kinsey actually reported that 13% were homosexual; a more recent survey found 2.8%

13. a (pp. 417-418)
    Obj. VIII-D

b. transmission can occur, although it is less likely than with anal intercourse

c. AIDS has had more affect on sexual practices because it is life threatening

d. only women have vaginas; two males cannot have vaginal intercourse

14. d (pp. 421-422, Fig. 11.30)
    Obj. X-D

a. estrogen is secreted, but testosterone is important for male development

b. this is sexual identity; usually not related to sexual orientation

c. they considered it typical for men to engage in occasional sexual activities with other men

e. this was smaller in homosexual men, but it may not be the cause; homosexual life-style may cause brain difference

15. a (pp. 425-426) b. people may say yes because it is socially desirable to say yes
    Obj. XI-A c. this would mix up ability and the desire to achieve
                d. the difficulty should be chosen by the person to see if easy, unrealistic, or realistic high goals are set

16. d (p. 426) a. they put normal or extraordinary effort into easy tasks
    Obj. XI-B-1 b. "do your best" is not an effective goal for anyone
                c. they decrease their effort
                e. true of people high in need for achievement

17. a (p. 428) b,c. they don't become discouraged if they don't succeed
    Obj. XII-A d. boys are generally encouraged to set higher personal goals

LECTURE MATERIAL

Don't forget to review your lecture material. Process each topic meaningfully. First, be sure that you understand the material in each lecture--if you don't, ask your instructor or teaching assistant. Associate the material with things that you already know and with your personal experiences. If you can make up mental images of any of the material, do so. Try to think of real-life applications of the concepts. Write notes in the left column on your lecture notes. Then write questions to cover each concept.

WAIT AT LEAST 24 HOURS BEFORE PROCEEDING.
LET FORGETTING OCCUR--IT WILL!!

SHORT-ANSWER ESSAY QUESTIONS

Write brief answers to each of the following. The answers are on pp. 172-173, but do try to write the answers yourself before looking at them.

General Properties of Motivated Behavior

1. What do motivated behaviors have in common?

2. Explain how motivation involves both physiological drives and incentives.

3. Discuss why Maslow's hierarchy of needs theory cannot explain why a starving person would give food to a needy child.

Motivation and Biological States: The Case of Hunger

4. Discuss factors involved in people's food preferences.

5. Explain how insulin levels are related to hunger.

6. Discuss two reasons for obesity.

7. Explain how anorexia nervosa and bulimia are similar and how they differ.

Sexual Motivation

8. Name and describe Masters and Johnson's four stages of sexual arousal.

9. Discuss evidence that suggests a role for genetics in homosexuality.

Achievement Motivation

10. Explain how goal setting is related to the need for achievement.

11. Discuss sex differences and the need for achievement.

Find the questions that you wrote over lecture material and write answers to them.

ANSWERS TO SHORT-ANSWER ESSAY QUESTIONS

1. Motivated behaviors are directed at reaching a goal. However, they vary from time to time, from situation, and from person to person. Most behavior is motivated by more than one thing. (p. 393)

2. Motivation depends upon a drive to reduce needs; e.g., when a person is hungry she seeks food. Homeostasis is the idea that we are motivated to maintain a state of equilibrium, keeping states fairly constant. But motivation also depends on incentives, or external stimuli; e.g., a person may eat snacks because they are there and look good, not because she is hungry. The overjustification effect occurs because people do some things because of intrinsic motivation and adding an external incentive might actually reduce their tendency to do them. (pp. 394-395)

3. Maslow's theory holds that lower-level needs must be satisfied before higher-level needs can motivate behavior. A starving person has not fulfilled basic physiological needs, so social needs to help others should not be motivating him. (pp. 397-398, Fig. 11.3)

4. Bodily needs can affect taste preferences; e.g., if a person has a salt deficiency, salty foods may be preferred. People generally prefer familiar tastes; they tend to like foods that are flavored in ways that they are used to. Associations can affect food preferences; people will avoid foods that are associated with repulsive things, even though the foods are perfectly nutritious. (pp. 400-402)

5. When insulin levels in the bloodstream are low, glucose does not enter the body's cells and people feel hungry. When insulin levels are moderate, glucose enters the body's cells and people are not very hungry. When insulin levels are high, glucose enters the body's cells but a high percentage of it is converted into fat; people feel hungry. This is what occurs when the ventromedial hypothalamus is damaged. (pp. 403-404, Fig. 11.10)

6. First, there is some evidence for a genetic component to obesity. In mice, there is a specific gene that causes the secretion of excessive amounts of a protein. This protein may alter the activities of the digestive system or it may affect the brain. A similar thing may happen in people, although research hasn't confirmed this yet. Second, overweight people may expend less energy than normal-weight people. People with the lowest energy expenditure were the most likely to gain weight during the next 2 to 4 years. (pp. 406-408)

7. Anorexics and bulimics both starve themselves, but bulimics also have periods of eating binges after which they may force themselves to vomit. Thus, bulimics alternate between starving and eating binges, but anorexics just starve themselves. Both groups have an exaggerated fear of becoming fat, and both are preoccupied with food. Both disorders are more common in women than in men. (pp. 410-411)

8. Excitement: Penis becomes erect, vagina is lubricated, breathing becomes rapid and deep, heart rate, blood pressure increase.
   Plateau: Excitement remains fairly constant.
   Climax or orgasm: Excitement becomes intense followed by relief in the form of orgasm.
   Resolution: Body returns to unaroused state. (pp. 418-419, Fig. 11.27)

9. If one twin is homosexual, then the other twin is more likely to be homosexual if the pair is monozygotic than if the pair is dizygotic. Homosexuality is more common among dizygotic twins than among adopted brothers. However, gay men do not have a higher percentage of lesbian relatives than men who are not gay, and gay women do not have a higher percentage of gay relatives than women who are not lesbians. Thus, if there is a genetic component to homosexuality, it must be different for men and women. (pp. 421-422, Fig. 11.30)

10. People who are high in need for achievement tend to set moderately difficult goals that they have some probability of achieving and that they will feel proud to have achieved. They tend to make little effort on easy tasks, and they put forth extra effort when they are being evaluated. When they receive feedback, they tend to increase their effort, no matter what the results were. People who prefer very easy or very difficult tasks may have a high fear of failure. (p. 426)

11. According to some studies, men generally score higher on need for achievement than women. This may be due to social influences later in life. Goals set by high school girls are about as high as those set by boys. Within several years after high-school, girls lower their goals perhaps because they come to believe that men resent and dislike successful women. In 1972, Horner argued that women show a fear of success, but more recent studies have not shown this. (pp. 428-429)

POSTTEST

Take this test with all of your books and notes out of sight. This should give you a good idea of how well you understand the material. The answers are on p. 177.

Matching

Put the letter of the term on the right in the blank beside the description on the left.

General Properties of Motivated Behavior

1. __E__ an external stimulus that "pulls" an animal   A. extrinsic motivation

2. __A__ based on rewards and punishments separate from the act itself   B. self-actualization

3. __B__ need to achieve one's full potential as a human being   C. overjustification effect

4. __D__ maintenance of equilibrium   D. homeostasis

5. __F__ engaging in an act for its own sake   E. incentive

6. __C__ decline in inherent interest in doing an act after rewards are withdrawn   F. intrinsic motivation

Multiple-choice

Circle the best alternative.

General Principles of Motivation

1. Drive reduction theory argues that people and animals act:
    a. in order to find an outlet for excessive libido
    b. because they are pulled by incentives
    c. because they develop specific hungers for particular behaviors
    d. because they have a kind of irritation that energizes behaviors
    e. differently depending upon their level in the hierarchy of needs

2. Ravin is having stomach contractions, there is little food in his intestines, and the amount of glucose and fats in his bloodstream is low. He immediately takes off for the nearest fast-food restaurant and orders two jumbo cheese-bacon burgers. He eats until he can eat no more. At this point, his stomach feels full and some food has reached his intestines. This process of bringing the body into equilibrium is:
   a. an overjustification effect
   b. homeostasis
   c. an incentive system
   d. a breakdown in libido
   e. instinctive energy

3. Which of the following best supports an incentive view of motivation?
   a. a hungry rat runs to the end of a maze to get food
   b. a thirsty child turns on the garden hose to get water
   c. a woman eats a piece of birthday cake although she is not hungry
   d. a bear licks its paw to remove a thorn
   e. a diver surfaces as quickly as is safe when he runs out of air

4. A fifth-grader has just learned how to do some simple programming on his dad's computer. Now, his class at school is learning programming and he gets gold stars for doing well. If the overjustification effect occurs, what is likely to happen this summer when he no longer gets stars for programming?
   a. he will work less hard than before the reward
   b. secondary motivation will make him work harder at programming than before his class began programming
   c. he will continue at about the same rate as before he was rewarded
   d. he will work harder than before the reward
   e. both b and d

5. According to Maslow's theory, a person who has fulfilled all basic, social, and esteem needs is motivated by the need for:
   a. libido
   b. sensation seeking
   c. drive reduction
   d. self-actualization
   e. homeostasis

Motivation and Biological States: The Case of Hunger

6. A rat has a much higher than average weight, it seems to be hungry all the time, and most of what it eats is stored as fat. This rat probably has damage to the:
   a. set point
   b. lateral hypothalamus
   c. libido
   d. ventromedial hypothalamus
   e. insulin-producing center

7. Which of the following is <u>least</u> likely to cause a person to be overweight?
    a. high levels of insulin
    b. a particular gene that results in excessive secretion of a specific protein
    c. damage to the ventromedial hypothalamus
    d. depression
    e. expending less energy than normal-weight people

8. Injecting insulin in a person whose levels are normal will result in:
    a. a decrease in appetite
    b. a high percentage of each meal being stored as fat
    c. the body's fat supplies being converted to glucose
    d. a low percentage of each meal being stored as fat
    e. both c and d

9. When people are dieting, what happens to their appetite?
    a. it often increases after they have eaten some rich food
    b. it is increased by exercise, showing that dieters should conserve energy and exercise less
    c. it gradually decreases until the drive to eat is gone
    d. it is not influenced by emotional distress
    e. their blood glucose levels are increased which increases appetite

10. Which of the following is true of anorexia nervosa?
    a. it is more common among Asian cultures than among Western cultures
    b. it is related to sexuality in women, but not in men
    c. there is almost always damage to the lateral hypothalamus
    d. it reflects a pathological fear of fatness
    e. it involves frequent binge eating

Sexual Motivation

11. Which of the following is true about sexual behavior?
    a. Kinsey found that most people had similar sexual behaviors
    b. Kinsey found that homosexual experiences were very rare, particularly in men
    c. a higher percentage of women than men report an interest in various sexual activities
    d. the percentage of people having multiple sex partners increases with age
    e. most people think their sexual behavior is normal; anything in excess of it is excessive

12. In today's society in the United States:
    a. about 10% of the people report a predominantly homosexual orientation
    b. about 80% of the heterosexuals having multiple sexual partners use condoms consistently
    c. people in their 50s and 60s report having sex less often than younger people
    d. the threat of AIDS has not really changed sexual behavior
    e. there are more homosexual women than men

13. What is the order of Masters and Johnson's four stages of sexual arousal?
    a. plateau, excitement, climax, resolution
    b. excitement, plateau, orgasm, resolution
    c. plateau, climax, resolution, excitement
    d. resolution, excitement, orgasm, plateau
    e. excitement, orgasm, plateau, resolution

14. Homosexual men:
    a. developed their homosexuality because they were exposed to estrogen as fetuses
    b. have larger clusters of neurons in the anterior hypothalamus than heterosexual men
    c. are less common than homosexual women
    d. are more likely to have male relatives who are gay than heterosexual men
    e. have a mistaken sexual identity

Achievement Motivation

15. How does the Thematic Apperception Test measure the need for achievement?
    a. people look at pictures and tell a story about them; the number of times that a striving for goals is mentioned is counted
    b. people read a story and are asked to complete it; the number of times that people mention quitting or failure is counted
    c. people are asked to toss rings over a peg from different distances; the number of successes is counted
    d. people are asked to toss rings over a peg from different distances; the distance is measured
    e. people are asked whether they are strongly motivated to succeed

16. People who are high in need for achievement:
    a. choose easy tasks to avoid failure
    b. decrease their efforts following positive feedback, but increase them following negative feedback
    c. prefer difficult but not impossible tasks
    d. put forth less effort when they are being evaluated than when they are not
    e. are most highly motivated by "do your best" goals

17. People who have a strong fear of failure are likely to choose which of the following tasks?
    a. an intermediately difficult task that they'll win at half the time
    b. a very difficult task that they'll never accomplish
    c. a difficult task that they have a realistic chance of accomplishing
    d. either a or c
    e. either b or c

18. Which person will probably be most successful in meeting her goal?
    a. Jane, who has an IQ of 90, but who says she will get all A's
    b. Greta, who will do her best
    c. Maria, who says she will try to pass all her courses
    d. Helen, who has an above average IQ and who publicly says she will get all A's
    e. Sally, who says she will get all A's, but who never is in class to find out how she is doing

19. Which of the following is true about women and the need for achievement?
    a. high-school women set much lower goals than high-school men
    b. women today show more fear of success than women in the 1960s
    c. women tend to have a stronger need for achievement than men
    d. women's fear of success probably differs from one historical era and one culture to another
    e. sex differences in need for achievement are clearly biological

ANSWERS TO POSTTEST

Correct Answer	Questions Testing a Similar Concept	
	Comprehension Check	Short-Answer
Matching		
1. E (p. 395)	-	2
2. A (p. 395)	2	--
3. B (p. 397)	3a	3
4. D (p. 395)	--	--
5. F (p. 395)	2b,d	--
6. C (p. 396)	2	--
Multiple-Choice		
1. d (p. 394)	1	2
2. b (p. 395)	--	--
3. c (p. 395)	2	2
4. a (p. 396)	2	--
5. d (pp. 397-398, Fig. 11.3)	3	3
6. d (p. 405)	7d	--
7. d (pp. 406-407)	8	6
8. b (pp. 403-404)	--	5
9. a (pp. 408-410)	9	6
10. d (p. 410)	10	7
11. e (p. 414)	12	--
12. c (p. 415)	13	--
13. b (pp. 418-419)	--	8
14. d (p. 421)	14	9
15. a (pp. 425-426)	--	--
16. c (pp. 426-427)	16	10
17. b (pp. 426-427)	16	10
18. d (p. 427)	--	10
19. d (pp. 428-429)	17d	11

CHAPTER 12 EMOTIONS, HEALTH PSYCHOLOGY, AND COPING WITH STRESS

OBJECTIVES

Understand that:

Emotional Behaviors

I. Emotions are difficult to define (p. 435)
   - A. But emotions play an important role in decision making (p. 435)
     - 1. Patients with prefrontal cortical damage show less emotion and have trouble making decisions (p. 435)

II. Emotion is related to physiological arousal. (p. 436)
   - A. Autonomic nervous system is involved in emotion. (p. 437, Fig. 12.2)
     - 1. Sympathetic nervous system increases arousal. (p. 437, Figs. 12.2, 12.4)
     - 2. Parasympathetic nervous system decreases arousal. (p. 437-438, Figs. 12.2, 12.4)
   - B. Opponent-process principle proposes that emotions swing from one state to the opposite as the original stimulus is removed. (p. 438, Fig. 12.5)
   - C. Polygraph measures sympathetic arousal. (p. 439)
     - 1. Polygraph administrators can identify lying more accurately than most people, but they also identify innocent people as lying. (pp. 440-441, Fig. 12.8)
     - 2. Guilty-knowledge test reduces number of innocent people identified as lying. (p. 441)
       - a. Paper and pencil integrity tests can identify dishonest people, but they also misidentify highly honest people. (pp. 441-442)

III. The postulated relationship between physiological arousal and experiencing the emotion differs for different theories. (p. 442, Figure 12.9, Table 12.1, p. 446)
   - A. James-Lange theory proposes that sympathetic arousal is necessary for emotion. (pp. 442-443)
     - 1. We probably don't determine our emotional state by differences in physiological states. (p. 442)
       - a. We may judge our own facial expressions. (p. 443, Fig. 12.10)
   - B. Cannon-Bard theory argues that emotion results from sensory information; autonomic arousal is independent. (p. 443)
   - C. Schachter and Singer proposed that emotion is the label given to arousal. (p. 444)
     - 1. A problem with this experiment is that people given placebo injections also felt emotion (p. 444, Fig. 12.11, p. 445)

IV. There may be a limited set of basic emotions. (p. 445)
   - A. Basic emotions should emerge early in life, have biological bases, and be the same for people of different cultures. (pp. 445-446)
   - B. Facial expressions can communicate emotional states. (pp. 446-447)
   - C. People from many cultures show similar expressions. (pp. 447-448, Fig. 12.16)
   - D. If basic emotions exist, then different emotions should be affected by different types of brain damage. (p. 449, Fig. 12.18)

V. Self-reported happiness may be related to personality and genetics (p. 450)

The message: Defining basic emotions is scientifically important but continues as a challenging problem for psychologists (p. 451)

Anger and Violent Behaviors

VI. Understanding anger and violence is important for humanity (p. 453)
   - A. Anger usually doesn't lead to physical aggression. (p. 453)
   - B. Anger occurs when one feels mistreated. (p. 453)
     - 1. The frustration-aggression hypothesis proposes that anger is displayed when an individual is frustrated. (p. 453)

2. All unpleasant events may lead to the impulse to fight or flee. (p. 453)
VII. Violent people are characterized by biographical and biological characteristics (pp. 453-454)
    A. Biographical information can predict the likelihood of violent behavior (p. 454)
        1. Several factors are correlated with violent behaviors (p. 454)
            a. Experience with physical abuse as a child, neighborhood violence, and television violence all are correlated with the tendency toward violence (pp. 454-455)
    B. Biological factors such as gender, age, and hormones are also important (p. 455)
VIII. Rape is sexual contact obtained through violence, threat, or intimidation (p. 457)
    A. In college, many rapes are date rapes (p. 457)
    B. Convicted rapists have a history of hostility and violence against both men and women (p. 457)

The message: *Controlling violence will require both improving socioeconomic conditions and applying psychological principles (pp. 457-458)*

Health Psychology

IX. Health psychology is concerned with how behaviors influence health and wellness (p. 459)
X. Stress results from emotional responses. (p. 459)
    A. Selye's concept of stress is that it is the response of the body to demands. (pp. 459-460)
        1. Responses to stress are alarm, resistance, and exhaustion. (pp. 459-460)
            a. Persistent stress can lead to the general adaptation syndrome. (p. 460)
    B. Posttraumatic stress disorder results from extreme stress. (p. 460)
    C. We must be able to measure stress to look at its effects on health. (p. 461)
        1. Social Readjustment Rating Scale is one measure of stressful events. (p. 461, Table 12.2)
            a. This scale is subject to many criticisms. (pp. 461-462)
    D. Stress depends upon how events are interpreted. (p. 462, Fig. 12.25)
XI. Psychosomatic illnesses are related to stress. (p. 463)
    A. Heart disease may be linked to personality type. (p. 463)
    B. Stress may influence the immune system and be related to cancer. (p. 464)

The message: *Behavior and biology act together to determine health and illness (p. 465)*

Coping with Stress

XII. Monitoring strategies involve attending to a stressful event and trying to take effective action (p. 468)
    A. Predictability and control reduce stress (p. 468)
        1. We assume that things won't get worse (p. 468)
        2. We can prepare for predictable events (p. 469)
    B. Inoculation involves practice coping with a small-scale or simulated stressful experience (p. 469)
    C. Social support can be helpful in dealing with stress (pp. 469-470)
        1. Talking about an experience may to reduce stress (p. 470)
    D. People often cope by creating false beliefs (p. 470)
        1. Slightly unrealistic optimism may be the best attitude (pp. 470-471)
XIII. Blunting strategies help manage our reaction to stress (p. 471)
    A. Relaxation can reduce stress (p. 471)
    B. Exercise can reduce stress (p. 472)
    C. Distraction can help to reduce pain (p. 472)

The message: *Emotions are linked with biological, motivational, and cognitive functioning; changes in these functions will affect emotion and vice versa (p. 472)*

COMPREHENSION CHECK

Answer these questions soon after reading the chapter. Circle the best alternative. Check your answers on pp. 183-185. If you gave a wrong answer, try to write why it was wrong. Check your reasons on pp. 183-185.

Emotional Behaviors

1. The pilot of your airplane just announced that the plane would have to land suddenly and you should tighten your seat belt and put your head between your knees. What will happen to your autonomic nervous system?
   a. the parasympathetic nervous system will become more activated
   b. some parts of the sympathetic nervous system will be activated
   c. some parts of the parasympathetic nervous system will be activated
   d. the sympathetic nervous system will become more activated

Correct _____ If wrong, why? _____

2. The opponent-process principle could best explain which of the following?
   a. one person reacts to a stimulus with anger; another responds with fear
   b. a person who is depressed often feels angry
   c. a person feels very relieved after a terrible event is over
   d. the physiological response to fear is different from the physiological response to anger

Correct _____ If wrong, why? _____

3. The polygraph test:
   a. measures only the electrical conduction of the skin
   b. is close to 90% accurate in detecting lies
   c. is most accurate when the guilty-knowledge test is used
   d. is no more accurate than a person trying to detect lying
   e. is a measure of parasympathetic nervous system activity

Correct _____ If wrong, why? _____

4. When hiking, you suddenly notice a rattlesnake preparing to embed his fangs into you. You promptly beat all known records for the 40-yard dash to get away. According to the James-Lange theory, you:
   a. are afraid because you perceive your heart pounding and you are running away
   b. run away because you are afraid
   c. decide that you are afraid at the same time as your body reacts to the fear
   d. have probably been classically conditioned to fear rattlesnakes

Correct _____ If wrong, why? _____

5. How would the Cannon-Bard theory explain the above situation?
   a. you interpret the sympathetic nervous system arousal as fear because of the situation
   b. you are afraid because you run away
   c. your forebrain triggered the body reaction, which you then interpreted as fear
   d. your fear and the sympathetic arousal happened simultaneously but independently

Correct _____ If wrong, why? _____

6. How does Schachter and Singer's theory of emotions differ from the James-Lange view?
    a. body states are not relevant in the Schachter-Singer theory
    b. body states and the perception of emotion are independent in the Schachter-Singer view
    c. a given body state always leads to the same emotion in the Schachter Singer theory
    d. a given body state may lead to different emotions depending upon interpretation in the Schachter-Singer theory
    e. Schachter and Singer argue that facial expressions can induce emotions; James-Lange theory says they cannot

Correct _____ If wrong, why? _____

7. In different cultures, gestures and facial expressions:
    a. are similar enough that many can be identified cross-culturally
    b. are used in exactly the same situations
    c. are very different; most of the expressions in some cultures are unknown in other cultures
    d. are the same but their interpretation is very different

Correct _____ If wrong, why? _____

Anger and Violent Behaviors

8. Which of the following is most consistent with the frustration-aggression hypothesis?
    a. a person who is insulted sometimes attacks the person who insulted him; but at other times, he leaves the room
    b. a foul odor makes someone run from a room
    c. a man who is locked out of his house kicks a passing dog
    d. a rat that can avoid shocks does not attack another rat even though it is frequently shocked
    e. a husband gives his wife the "silent treatment" after she says she doesn't want him to go to the poker party with his friends

Correct _____ If wrong, why? _____

9. Violent behavior:
    a. can be accurately predicted with interviews
    b. can be prevented by severe punishment during childhood
    c. is likely to occur in people who have stronger than normal physiological responses to arousal
    d. is unrelated to the amount of violence watched on television
    e. is associated with not feeling guilty after hurting someone

Correct _____ If wrong, why? _____

Health Psychology

10. According to Selye, what are the stages that the body goes through in response to stress?
    a. resistance, alarm, general adaptation syndrome
    b. exhaustion, alarm, resistance
    c. general adaptation syndrome, resistance, alarm
    d. alarm, resistance, exhaustion

Correct _____ If wrong, why? _____

11. PTSD:
    a. is a fairly new disorder seen only since the Vietnam War
    b. occurs only in cases involving tough combat
    c. develops anytime someone experiences severe stress
    d. may involve nightmares, constant unhappiness, anger, and guilt
    e. is purely psychological; there are no physiological effects associated with the disorder

Correct _____ If wrong, why? _____

12. The Social Readjustment Rating Scale:
    a. measures the number of unpleasant events in a person's life
    b. measures the stressful events that cause illness
    c. is related to the likelihood of illness
    d. is a very accurate way to measure stress

Correct _____ If wrong, why? _____

13. Psychosomatic illnesses: ~ related to stress
    a. are imagined illnesses
    b. are illnesses such as heart disease that are related to stress
    c. occur because emotions lead directly to illness
    d. are not caused by genes and toxic substances

Correct _____ If wrong, why? _____

14. What does the most recent evidence say about people with Type A personalities?
    a. they are more likely to get cancer than Type B people
    b. their impatience and competitiveness leads to heart disease
    c. they usually live in cultures where time isn't very important
    d. they may be more susceptible to heart disease because they show more depression and anger

Correct _____ If wrong, why? _____

Coping with Stress

15. Which of the following would be effective in dealing with a stressful situation, such as a loss of a job?
    a. keep the person distracted by constantly thinking about working
    b. convince the person that others were really at fault
    c. have the person join a support group whose members have all lost jobs
    d. make the person understand that he really had no control over the situation
    e. have the person think about other people who are better off

Correct _____ If wrong, why? _____

16. Which of the following is <u>not</u> true about predictability? It:
   a. can make it easier to cope because we can prepare for it at the right time
   b. may not be helpful if you can't do anything about the event
   c. may make an event less stressful if we also perceive that we have control
   d. helps coping only if people actually exert control over the event

Correct _____ If wrong, why? _____

17. Coping by having false beliefs:
   a. only works for minor stresses, and not in life-death situations
   b. only works if people compare themselves with someone else
   c. is basically unhealthy; such beliefs interfere with mental health
   d. can help people to gain a feeling of mastery over their lives

Correct _____ If wrong, why? _____

ANSWERS AND EXPLANATIONS FOR COMPREHENSION CHECK

<u>Correct Answer</u>   <u>Other Alternatives Are Wrong Because:</u>

1. d (p. 437; Fig. 12.2)   a. relaxing situations increase parasympathetic
   Obj. II-A   b. sympathetic responds as a unit
                                  c. parasympathetic would become less active

2. c (p. 438, Fig. 12.5)   a. better explained by Schachter-Singer theory
   Obj. II-B   b. probably true, but irrelevant to opponent-processes
                                  d. necessary for James-Lange theory to be correct

3. c (p. 439)   a. measures heart rate and breathing rate also
   Obj. II-C   b. will accurately detect lying about 75% of the time, but will also
                                     "detect" innocent people
                                  d. it is more accurate then people
                                  e. it measures sympathetic activity

4. a (pp. 442-443, Table   b. commonsense view; James-Lange is opposite
   12.1, p. 446)
   Obj. III-A   c. Cannon-Bard view
                                  d. may be true, but irrelevant to James-Lange

5. d (p. 443, Fig. 12.10,   a. this is the Schachter-Singer view
   Table 12.1, p. 446)   b. this is the James-Lange view
   Obj. III-B   c. brain sends message to autonomic nervous system and forebrain at
                                     same time

6. d (pp. 442-445, Table   a. body states are necessary for an emotion
   12.1, p. 446)
     Obj. III-A, C   b. perception does depend upon body state
                              c. different emotions can come from same body state, depending upon
                                 interpretation
                              e. both theories would agree that expressions might be related to body
                                 states, but these theories are aimed at physiological arousal

7. a (pp. 447-448)   b. similar expressions are used, but they may be used in somewhat
     Obj. IV-C   different circumstances
                              c. many of the expressions are very similar
                              d. people of different cultures can interpret each other's expressions
                                 fairly accurately

8. c (p. 453)   a. consistent with Berkowitz' theory that unpleasant events lead to
     Obj. VI-B-1   either fighting or fleeing
                              b. an unpleasant event but no evidence of frustration
                              d. even unpleasant stimuli don't always lead to aggression
                              e. frustration doesn't lead to calm aggressive behaviors

9. e (p. 454)   a. interviews are only a little better than chance
     Obj. VII-A-1   b. severe punishment may increase future violent behavior
                              c. likely to occur in people with <u>weaker</u> than normal responses
                              d. watching violence is associated with violent behavior

10. d (pp. 459-460)   a, c. alarm is first; general adaptation syndrome is the result of last
     Obj. X-A-1   phase
                              b. alarm is first; exhaustion is last

11. d (p. 460)   a. it has been recognized following wars throughout history
     Obj. X-B   b. can occur following extreme stress due to any cause
                              c. doesn't develop in everyone having the same stressful experience
                              e. Vietnam veterans with PTSD did show elevated endorphin levels
                                 after watching dramatized combat

12. c (p. 461)   a. pleasant events can be stressful, too
     Obj. X-C-1   b. events may not cause illness; this is a correlation
                              d. it is probably not very accurate

13. b (p. 463)   a. not imagined; they are physiologically very real
     Obj. XI   c. emotions don't lead directly to illness; they lead to other behaviors
                                 that may increase illness
                              d. cancer can be considered a psychosomatic illness, but its primary
                                 causes are genetic and toxic substances

14. d (p. 463)
   Obj. XI-A
   - a. more likely to get heart disease than Type B
   - b. later research has not shown this
   - c. probably more likely in cultures where time is important because they are always in a hurry

15. c (pp. 469-470)
   Obj. XII-C
   - a. distraction is usually used for pain; the person should think about something other than the problem
   - b. this would make it worse; it would increase perceived loss of control
   - d. lack of control usually increases, not decreases,. stress
   - e. needs to think of people who are worse off

16. d (p. 468)
   Obj. XII-A
   - a-c. are true
   - d. they don't actually have to exert control; they just need to perceive that they can exert control

17. d (pp. 470-471)
   Obj. XII-D
   - a. medics in Vietnam used it while risking their lives
   - b. this was one strategy used by women with breast cancer; they also searched for meaning in the experience, and tried to regain a feeling of mastery
   - c. such illusions can improve a person's self-image and contribute to mental health

LECTURE MATERIAL

Don't forget to review your lecture material. Process each topic meaningfully. First, be sure that you understand the material in each lecture--if you don't, ask your instructor or teaching assistant. Associate the material with things that you already know and with your personal experiences. If you can make up mental images of any of the material, do so. Try to think of real-life applications of the concepts. Put your own comments in the left column of your lecture notes. Then write questions to cover each concept.

WAIT AT LEAST 24 HOURS BEFORE PROCEEDING.
LET FORGETTING OCCUR--IT WILL!!

SHORT-ANSWER ESSAY QUESTIONS

Write brief answers to each of the following. The answers are on p. 187-189, but do try to write the answers yourself before looking at them.

Emotional Behaviors

1. Describe recent research that suggests how emotions might be related to decision making.

2. Explain how a lie-detector test is supposed to work and describe a better way to arrange the test.

3. Schachter and Singer's experiment on cognitive factors in emotion is frequently cited, but what problem is there in the interpretation of that experiment?

4. Describe what happened in the study in which subjects were made to frown smile by holding pens in their lips.

5. What has been found when gestures and facial expressions are studied in different cultures?

Anger and Violent Behaviors

6. Why is happiness difficult to measure in a behavioral way? What problems does this cause for the study of happiness?

7. Describe the original frustration-aggression hypothesis and Berkowitz's modification of it.

8. Describe factors that are related to the accuracy of prediction of violent behavior.

Health Psychology

9. Describe the effects of prolonged stress on the body.

10. Explain some of the problems that are associated with the conclusion that the Social Readjustment Rating Scale predicts illness.

11. Explain how cancer might be considered a psychosomatic illness.

Coping with Stress

12. Describe how predictability and control can help in coping with stress.

13. How can exercise help to reduce stress?

14. Describe how beliefs can serve as coping strategies.

****

Find the questions that you wrote over lecture material and write answers to them.

****

ANSWERS TO SHORT-ANSWER ESSAY QUESTIONS

1. Damage to the prefrontal cortex seems to result in a loss of emotion. In addition, people who have such damage have trouble making decisions and following plans. One hypothesis is that problems with decision-making occur because of the inability to experience emotions. The patients can't follow through and imagine how they would feel if they made one decision or another, or how they would feel after carrying out a plan. (p. 437)

2. When a person is nervous, the sympathetic nervous system increases breathing rate, heart rate, and sweating. The polygraph measures these variables, which should be higher when a person is lying than when telling the truth. However, polygraph tests result in a number of errors in which innocent people are called guilty. (37% in one study). The "guilty-knowledge" test helps to eliminate these. It asks about specific facts that only the guilty party would know, so an innocent person would not be judged guilty. (pp. 438-439)

3. Participants who were given placebo injections showed about as much emotion as subjects who were given epinephrine. Therefore, an appropriate conclusion may be that people in a euphoria situation act happy and people in an anger situation act angry. (pp. 443-444)

4. Subjects who were made to smile by holding a pen between their teeth rated cartoons as funnier than subjects who were make to frown by holding a pencil in their lips. (p. 443)

5. Facial expressions are pretty much the same, although their frequency and the situations in which they are used differ somewhat. People from one culture are fairly accurate in their interpretations of other cultures' expressions. (pp. 447-448)

6. Although anger is often linked to specific behaviors, happiness is not linked to specific behaviors. This means that the only way to measure happiness is to ask people if they are happy. People have different criteria for happiness, and so one person's low rating may actually mean the same level of happiness as another person's higher rating. (pp. 459-460)

7. Whenever individuals experience frustration. (because something prevents them from reaching some goal), they respond with aggression. Berkowitz modified this by saying that all unpleasant events lead to the impulse to fight or flee. Whether one fights or flees depends upon the circumstances. (p. 453)

8. Predictions of the behavior of people in long-term institutions that are based on interviews are not much more accurate than chance. However, predictions based on specific biographical information, such as physical abuse during childhood, history of committing violent acts, having a relative who has been committed to a psychiatric hospital, and watching violence on television, can be more accurate. (pp. 453-456)

9. According to Selye, reactions to stress go through an alarm, a resistance, and an exhaustion phase. This final phase leads to general adaptation syndrome, which results in weakness, fatigue, loss of appetite, and loss of interest. Continuing stress results in an increase in epinephrine in the body. Posttraumatic stress disorder may result from prolonged exposure to traumatic experiences. (pp. 459-460)

10. People who score higher on this scale are more likely to become ill; but the scale asks about symptoms of illness, so, of course, people with higher scores are more likely to be ill. The scale does not ask about stress from unchanging problems, such as poverty. It also ignores stress from things you worry about, but that do not happen. It may be inappropriate to add together the scores from various events. Having three mildly stressful events is probably not the same as having one very stressful event. In addition, the same event may be stressful for some people but not for others. (pp. 461-462)

11. People's behavior influences the onset and spread of cancer. Lung cancer is related to smoking. Women who examine their breasts can detect breast cancer early to prevent spreading. Severe depression affects the immune system, making depressed people more vulnerable to the spread of tumors. After the onset of cancer, stress weakens the ability of the immune system to attack cancer cells. (p. 464)

12. We assume that a predictable event won't get any worse or, if we have control, that we can control it if it does. We are able to prepare ourselves for predictable events. We need not be constantly aroused if an event is predictable; we can relax during "safe" periods. However, if we can't do anything about a predictable negative event. (such as developing Huntington's disease), we may prefer not to know about it. (p. 469)

13. Exercise can help relaxation. It is particularly helpful to deal with nervousness about an upcoming stressful event. Exercise also helps because people who are in good physical condition react less strongly to stressful events than people who are not in such good condition. (p. 472)

14. Most normal, happy people have a sort of personal fable throughout their lives. They distort bad news to make it seem good, they downplay their weaknesses, and they deny the seriousness of situations. For example, medics in the Vietnam war thought of themselves as invulnerable. Women who had a breast removed looked for meaning in the experience, believed that they knew why they had developed cancer and how they could avoid a recurrence, and compared themselves with others who are worse off. Having slightly unrealistic optimism might be the best attitude for coping with stress. (p. 472)

POSTTEST

Take this test with all of your books and notes out of sight. This should give you a good idea of how well you understand the material. The answers are on p. 193.

Matching

Put the letter of the method of coping with stress beside the description.

Coping With Stress

1. __C__ you know a tornado is coming, you can prepare for it

2. __E__ being in a quiet place with all sources of stimulation removed

3. __F__ a man's wife provides care and concern in a stressful situation

4. __B__ a person recovering from a heart attack thinks that his recovery is much faster than average

5. __A__ a person who will have surgery sees a film of the surgery and imagines what it will be like

6. __D__ a patient in a hospital feels little pain because he has an interesting view outside the window

A. inoculation

B. distorted beliefs

C. predictability

D. distraction

E. relaxation

F. social support

Multiple-choice

Circle the best alternative.

Emotional Behaviors

1. Your sympathetic nervous system has just been activated. What are you most likely to do?
    a. fall asleep
    b. breath harder and perspire
    c. slow your breathing and heart rate
    d. increase your salivation and digestion rate
    e. feel sorry for something in your environment

2. Why would a scuba diver's first encounter with sharks be more frightening than later encounters, according to the opponent-process theory?
    a. the fear state (A) is stronger initially than the rebound state
    b. the fear state (A) increases with more exposures, but the rebound state gets weaker
    c. there is no rebound state as the person repeats an experience
    d. the rebound state occurs later and later with repeated exposures

3. Which question is a polygraph examiner likely to ask in a guilty-knowledge test?
    a. Have you ever stolen anything?
    b. Did you steal the money from the grocery store on March 21?
    c. Did you rob the gas station as well as the grocery store?
    d. How much money was taken from the store? $50? $100? $200? $1,000?
    e. Are you lying?

4. Godzilla, Frankenstein, a werewolf, King Kong, the creature from the black lagoon, and Dracula all enter your room. How does the James-Lange theory relate your emotions to your behavior?
    a. you perceive the stimuli, are afraid, run away, and then respond physiologically
    b. you feel afraid, and this causes increased sympathetic arousal, which will produce a running response
    c. the stimuli provoke a specific sympathetic nervous system response that you label as "fear"
    d. you aren't really afraid, because epinephrine would be secreted and it produces "cold" emotions
    e. your thalamus simultaneously activates your sympathetic nervous system and sends a message to your cortex that indicates fear

5. Which of the following results from Schachter and Singer's experiment are inconsistent with their theory about cognitive interpretation of emotion?
    a. the groups that were informed about the drug's effects showed little emotion
    b. subjects who were not informed about the drug's effects showed euphoria in that condition and anger in the "angry" condition
    c. the same physiological state was interpreted differently by different subjects
    d. subjects who got a placebo showed almost as much emotion as subjects who got epinephrine

6. Forcing people to make facial expressions by having them move specific facial muscles or holding pencils in their mouths:
    a. does not result in any change in emotions, because there is no sympathetic nervous system arousal
    b. tends to make people feel happier or sadder
    c. makes people sadder, but has no effect on behavior, such as the ratings of cartoons
    d. has some behavioral results, but they are almost entirely due to demand characteristics

7. Across cultures, facial expressions and gestures:
    a. are similar, but people from one culture cannot interpret expressions from another culture
    b. are the same, because they are entirely controlled by genetics
    c. are similar in westernized cultures, but totally different in non-Western cultures, such as Japan
    d. can be identified with perfect accuracy
    e. are similar, but the frequencies with which they are used differ

8. Happiness differs from anger in that:
    a. people who say they are happy all mean about the same thing; people who say they are angry may mean different things
    b. happiness involves sympathetic nervous system arousal; anger does not
    c. anger has more observable behaviors associated with it than happiness
    d. when people become happy, it doesn't always lead to observable behavior; when people become angry it usually leads to observable physical attacks

Anger and Violent Behaviors

9. How are anger and aggression related?
    a. people become aggressive far more often than they become angry
    b. when people became angry at family and friends, they usually also display aggression toward them
    c. aggression is more context specific, in that the same level of anger won't always trigger aggression
    d. anger is related to how much violence one watches on television, but actual aggression is not

10. Berkowitz proposed a theory of aggression that is more comprehensive than frustration-aggression theory. Which of the following best describes his theory?
    a. all aggression is caused by frustration, which occurs when a motivated behavior is disrupted
    b. unpleasant stimuli that lead to aggression do so automatically
    c. both frustration and biological factors are important in aggression
    d. all unpleasant events give rise to the impulse to fight or flee; circumstances determine which will happen
    e. aggression will only occur when something goes wrong and there is no one to blame

Health Psychology

11. According to Selye's theory of stress, a person who has had many long-lasting stressful events during the past few months is likely to:
    a. be in the resistance stage
    b. develop the general adaptation syndrome
    c. be in the alarm stage
    d. have reduced epinephrine levels
    e. be less susceptible to disease than someone not so stressed

12. Who is likely to have the highest score on the Social Readjustment Rating Scale?
    a. Oblivia, who just took out a mortgage of $50,000
    b. Dr. Quaalude, who just got married
    c. Erasmus, who just got married and who changed his job
    d. Perplexity, who just graduated from college
    e. Ed Just, who got a speeding ticket and is having trouble with his boss

13. Which of the following conclusions from the Social Readjustment Rating Scale is most appropriate?
    a. high stress scores cause illness
    b. day-to-day problems are more related to illness than major crises
    c. there is a relationship between high stress scores and illness
    d. people of different ages and circumstances respond in a similar manner to the stressful events on the scale
    e. events that people worry about but that don't happen produce the highest scores on the scale

14. People with Type A personality:
    a. are more likely to live in countries in which time is not important and the pace is relaxed than in more time-conscious countries such as the United States
    b. show less increase in heart rate and blood pressure in competitive situations than people with Type B personality
    c. vary in how they handle work assignments, but not in how they behave in leisure activities, such as fishing
    d. develop heart disease because they avoid competitive tasks
    e. often have low scores on the Social Readjustment Rating Scale

15. Which is true about the relationship between emotional states and cancer?
    a. emotional factors are more important in cancer than genes and exposure to toxic substances
    b. severe depression may play a role in cancer by suppressing the immune system
    c. studies consistently show that stress in humans increases the spread of cancer
    d. cancer is most related to anger, rather than to impatience and competitiveness as originally thought
    e. stress influences the onset of cancer more than the course of the cancer following the onset

Coping with Stress

16. Which is the least likely explanation for why prediction and control can help in coping with stress?
    a. prediction allows an animal or human to prepare for the event
    b. control helps people, but only if they actually exert control, such as turning off an annoying noise
    c. a predictable and controllable event probably will not get any worse; an unpredictable event might
    d. if an event is predictable or controllable, a human or animal does not need to be in a constant state of preparation
    e. if an event is controllable, a human or animal can work harder to control it if it does get worse

17. A person who fears dental work is given a series of mild shocks to the teeth before going to the dentist to help her in coping with the stress associated with dental work. The technique being used here is:
    a. social support
    b. distraction
    c. inoculation
    d. control
    e. exercise

18. A man who has a stroke "knows" that it happened because he had not been exercising enough. He begins exercising to avoid a recurrence. He is coping by:
    a. unrealistic optimism
    b. distraction
    c. inoculation
    d. relaxation
    e. social support

Answers to Posttest

Correct Answer	Questions Testing a Similar Concept	
	Comprehension Check	Short-Answer

Matching

1. C. (p. 469)	16	12
2. E. (p. 469)	--	13
3. F. (pp. 469-470)	15	--
4. B. (p. 470)	17	14
5. A. (p. 472)	--	--
6. D. (p. 472)	15a	--

Multiple-Choice

1. b. (pp. 437-438, Fig. 12.2)	1	--
2. a. (p. 438, Fig. 12.5)	2	--
3. d. (p. 441)	3	2
4. c. (pp. 442-443, Fig. 12.9)	4,5b,6	--
5. d. (p. 444, Fig. 12.11, p. 445)	6	3
6. b. (p. 443)	--	4
7. e. (pp. 447-448)	7	5
8. c. (pp. 453-455)	--	6
9. c. (p. 453)	8	7
10. d. (p. 453)	8	7
11. b. (p. 459)	10	9
12. c. (pp. 461-462, Table 12.2)	12	10
13. c. (pp. 460-462)	12	10
14. e. (p. 463)	14	--
15. b. (p. 464)	13d	11
16. b. (p. 469)	16	12
17. c. (p. 472)	--	--
18. a. (p. 472)	17	14

CHAPTER 13 PERSONALITY

OBJECTIVES

Understand that:

Conceptions of Personality

I. Personality consists of consistent ways in which people's social behaviors differ (p. 477)

II. Psychodynamic theories propose that motivations are important and these often are unconscious (p. 478)

    A. Freud proposed the first psychodynamic theory (p. 478)

        1. Personality is the interplay of conflicting forces, some of which are unconscious (p. 478)

    B. Jung's psychodynamic theory argues for an unconscious that reflects the experiences of human ancestors (p. 478)

    C. Adler suggested that people are guided by a natural striving for superiority (p. 478)

III. The trait approach proposes that people have consistent personality characteristics that can be measured and studied (p. 479)

    A. Masculinity, femininity, and adrogyny can be called personality traits (pp. 479-480)

    B. External versus internal locus of control is a personality trait (p. 479)

IV. Most of personality is learned in a situation-by-situation basis (pp. 480-481)

    A. For example, gender roles are learned because of society's expectations (pp. 480-481)

    B. This approach relates specific behaviors to specific experiences (p. 481)

V. Humanistic psychology emphasizes consciousness, values and abstract beliefs (p. 481)

    A. Humanists do not use determinism and reductionism to explain behavior (p. 481)

    B. Growth experiences, the moments when people identify transition points, are important (p. 481)

    C. Rogers believed that people naturally try to achieve self-actualization, the achievement of full potential (p. 482)

        1. Children develop a self concept (actual self), but they also have an ideal self (p. 482)

        2. People should relate to others with unconditional positive regard (p. 482)

    D. Maslow described the self-actualized personality (pp. 482-483)

The message: *Approaches to personality are global views that must be converted into scientifically testable hypotheses (p. 483)*

Grand Theories of Personality

VI. Freud developed psychoanalysis which explains and deals with the interplay of conscious and unconscious forces (pp. 485-486)

    A. Freud's evidence was based on his inferences (p. 486)

        1. His interpretation with respect to sexual fantasies changed (p. 486)

        2. Freud did not seek parsimonious explanations (pp. 486-487)

    B. Freud proposed five stages of psychosexual development (pp. 487-488)

        1. Oral stage-- libido (psychosexual energy) focused on stimulation of mouth (p. 487)

        2. Anal stage-- libido focused on bowel movements (p. 487)

        3. Phallic stage-- libido focused on genitals (p. 487)

        4. Latent period-- libido is suppressed (p. 488)

        5. Genital stage-- libido focused on sexual intercourse (pp. 488)

    C. Personality consists of conflicting parts-- id, ego, superego (p. 488, Fig. 13.11)

        1. Defense mechanisms keep some thoughts from consciousness (pp. 489-490, Fig. 13.12)

            a. Repression-- motivated forgetting (p. 489)

            b. Denial-- refusal to believe facts (p. 489)

c. Rationalization-- try to prove that actions are rational (pp. 489-490)

d. Displacement-- diverting behavior to less threatening target (p. 490)

e. Regression-- a return to more juvenile means of escaping (p. 490)

f. Projection-- attributing one's own undesirable characteristics to others (p. 490)

g. Reaction formation-- presenting the self as opposite (p. 490)

h. Sublimation-- transformation of unacceptable urges into acceptable, even admirable, ones (p. 490)

D. The unconscious makes itself felt in everyday life (pp. 490-491)

   1. Slips of the tongue are related to present motivations (pp. 491-492)

E. Freud popularized psychotherapy and paved the way for other approaches (p. 492)

F. Neo-Freudians have remained faithful to some aspect of Freud's theory and changed others (p. 492)

VII. Carl Jung put more emphasis on people's search for meaning in life (pp. 492-493)

A. He added the concept of the collective unconscious (p. 493)

VIII. Alfred Adler's individual psychology proposed that people try to overcome weaknesses (p. 493)

A. Striving for superiority is a main motivation in life (p. 493)

B. Mental illnesses come from faulty life styles (pp. 494-495)

   1. People need to develop a social interest (p. 494)

C. The idea of inferiority complex has become part of the common culture (p. 495)

The message: The psychodynamic theorists were interested in building major theories of how personality fits together (p. 495)

Personality Traits

IX. Psychologists investigate how people differ (p. 497)

A. Nomothetic approach seeks general laws about behavior (p. 497)

B. Idiographic approach concentrates on intensive studies of individuals (p. 497)

X. Psychologists distinguish between traits and states (p. 497)

A. A trait is a consistent, long-lasting tendency in behavior (p. 497)

B. A state is a temporary activation of behavior (p. 497)

XI. Psychologists try to identify broad personality traits (pp. 498)

A. Many researchers agree on the "big five" personality traits (pp. 498-499)

   1. Neuroticism is the tendency to experience unpleasant emotions easily (p. 498)

   2. Extraversion is the tendency to seek new experiences and enjoy company (p. 498)

   3. Agreeableness is a tendency to be compassionate (p. 499)

   4. Conscientiousness is a tendency to show self-discipline (p. 499)

   5. Openness is the tendency to enjoy being exposed to new ideas (p. 499)

B. There is both support for and evidence against the "big five" (pp. 499-500)

   1. The five traits are satisfactory in describing men's and women's personalities (p. 499)

      a. Some traits, such as openness, don't vary much in some cultures (p. 499)

      b. People are fairly stable across adulthood (p. 499)

   2. There are also problems with the concept of "big five" (pp. 499-500)

      a. Most data depend on written responses to questionnaires (p. 499)

      b. The five-factor structure is not theoretically satisfying (p. 499)

      c. The selection of five, rather than 7 or 8, traits is arbitrary (p. 499)

XII. Heredity has a moderate influence on personality (pp. 500-501)

A. Monozygotic twins are more similar than dizygotic twins on some traits (p. 500, Fig. 13.18, p. 500)

B. Biological parents are more similar to their children than adoptive parents (p. 501, Fig. 13.19, p. 501)

C. Personality variation may come from the unshared environment, the part the differs among family members (p. 501)

The message: Individual personalities are all different and individuals may show different personalities in different situations (p. 501)

Personality Assessment

XIII. People accept general and vague personality descriptions of themselves (pp. 503-504)

XIV. Standardized personality tests are administered according to specified rules and they are scored in prescribed ways (p. 504)

XV. Objective personality tests are based on simple pencil and paper responses (p. 504)

    A. The MMPI measures tendencies toward psychological disorders (p. 504)

        1. It was constructed by comparing people with mental illness and people who didn't have mental illnesses (p. 504)

        2. The MMPI-2 is a recent revision of the MMPI (pp. 504-505)

        3. The same norms are used for different ethnic groups, although this may not be appropriate (pp. 505)

        4. MMPI includes a lie scale and measures other types of deception (pp. 505-506)

        5. Test results classify people, but don't tell anything about degree of disorder (p. 506)

    B. 16-PF test results in a personality profile (pp. 506-507, Fig. 13.22, p. 508)

XVI. Projective tests ask people to respond to ambiguous stimuli (pp. 507-508)

    A. Rorschach invented the inkblot test (pp. 508-510, Fig. 13.23)

        1. Its interpretation may depend on the psychologist's expectations (pp. 509)

        2. An objective scoring method has improved reliability (pp. 509-510)

    B. Thematic Apperception Test (TAT) involves telling stories about pictures (p. 510)

        1. It has low reliability perhaps because it measures present concerns (p. 510)

XVII. Handwriting analysis and doll play may tell us little about personality (pp. 510-511)

XVIII. The emotional Stroop test may allow objective measurement of anxieties (p. 511)

XIX. Personality tests should only be used for purposes for which they have been shown to be useful (pp. 511-512)

    A. Low baserates of some disorders will result in many people being diagnosed as mentally ill when they are not (pp. 511)

    B. Employers should only use personality tests if they clearly allow better selection than of employees than without the tests (p. 512)

The message: Personality tests can only measure a few aspects of personality (p. 512)

COMPREHENSION CHECK

Answer these questions soon after reading the chapter. Circle the best alternative. Check your answers on pp. 200-202. If you gave a wrong answer, try to write why it was wrong. Check your reasons on pp. 200-202.

Conceptions of Personality

1. Which personality theorist has a view most similar to that of Hobbes, who argued that humans are selfish and must be restrained by government?

    a. Maslow

    b. Rogers

    c. Adler

    d. Freud

Correct _____ If wrong, why? _____

2. A person who is androgynous:
    a. has many masculine and many feminine traits
    b. has more masculine than feminine traits
    c. believes that he or she has control over the outcomes of behavior
    d. learned a gender role early in life as part of the playground culture

Correct _____ If wrong, why? _____

3. Which of the following is <u>not</u> characteristic of the self-actualized personality?
    a. treat people with unconditional positive regard
    b. a good sense of humor
    c. a self-centered outlook
    d. an accurate perception of reality
    e. follow own impulses

Correct _____ If wrong, why? _____

Grand Theories of Personality

4. According to Freud's psychodynamic theory:
    a. all neurotic behavior can be traced to sexual abuse
    b. libido focuses on different parts of the body
    c. catharsis is what happens if the libido becomes fixated
    d. the unconscious has no thoughts, memories or emotions
    e. the unconscious never manifests itself in everyday life

Correct _____ If wrong, why? _____

5. According to Freud, the Oedipus complex occurs during which stage?
    a. phallic stage
    b. oral stage
    c. anal stage
    d. genital stage
    e. latent stage

Correct _____ If wrong, why? _____

6. Dan is angry with his boss, but he goes home and yells at his wife, who becomes crabby with her daughter, who starts tormenting the dog. What defense mechanism is being used?
    a. repression
    b. regression
    c. reaction formation
    d. projection
    e. displacement

Correct _____ If wrong, why? _____

7. John sees an attractive young woman. His _____ wants to have sex with her immediately; his _____ says absolutely not, he shouldn't even think such thoughts; his _____ tries to mediate between the other two.
   a. id, superego, ego
   b. superego, ego, id
   c. id, libido, superego
   d. id, ego, superego
   e. ego, id, libido

Correct _____ If wrong, why? _____

8. Karen Horney, an influential neo-Freudian, differed with Freud's views on:
   a. the existence of an ego
   b. the importance of peak experiences
   c. the importance of unconditional positive regard
   d. the importance of sexual motivation
   e. the role of self-actualization

Correct _____ If wrong, why? _____

9. Which of the following is not a correct pairing?
   a. Adler--collective unconscious
   b. Jung--universal symbols in art, religions, and dreams
   c. Adler--individual psychology
   d. Adler--inferiority complex
   e. Horney--importance of cultural influences

Correct _____ If wrong, why? _____

10. Adler believed that:
    a. we inherit archetypes as part of our collective unconscious
    b. each person is aware of his or her own style of life
    c. people with a strong social interest are very outgoing and friendly
    d. everyone has a natural striving for superiority
    e. personality theorists should study the parts of personality

Correct _____ If wrong, why? _____

Personality Traits
11. John always seems to be fidgety and anxious. John's anxiety is probably:
    a. state anxiety
    b. trait anxiety
    c. the result of extraversion
    d. the result of too much openness to experience

Correct _____ If wrong, why? _____

12. Which of the following is <u>not</u> one of the "big five" personality dimensions?
    a. androgyny
    b. extraversion
    c. agreeableness
    d. openness to experience
    e. neuroticism

Correct _____ If wrong, why? _____

13. A valid criticism of the "big five" personality traits is that:
    a. the traits change a great deal with age
    b. the traits do not correlate with each other very well
    c. the trait structure works well for women but not for men
    d. choosing only 5 traits is arbitrary

Correct _____ If wrong, why? _____

14. What is the role of imitating parents in personality development?
    a. it is strong because adopted children's personalities are much like their adopted parents'
    b. it is strong because adopted children's personalities correlate with their biological parents more than with their adoptive parents
    c. it is strong because unrelated children growing up in the same family are very similar
    d. it is weak because dizygotic twin pairs are more similar than monozygotic pairs
    e. it is weak because parents and their adopted children's personalities don't correlate

Correct _____ If wrong, why? _____

Personality Assessment

15. Experiments have been done in which students took tests and were given personality feedback. Generally, what was their opinion of the feedback?
    a. they believed it only if it had direct relevance to their answers on the test
    b. they rarely believed the feedback from so-called experts
    c. less than 20% rated a vague and general description as "good to excellent"
    d. about 90% rated a vague and general description as "good to excellent"
    e. about 90% rated a strange, unflattering description as "good to excellent"

Correct _____ If wrong, why? _____

16. The original MMPI:
    a. was developed by asking questions that fitted with the developers' theory of personality
    b. has high validity, so that a clinician can use it alone to evaluate psychological problems
    c. asks questions that are answered differently by people with various psychological disorders and other people
    d. asks a series of open-ended questions
    e. is not valid because most people lie

Correct _____ If wrong, why? _____

17. In the Thematic Apperception Test, you would be asked to:
    a. describe what you see in inkblots
    b. tell stories about people in pictures
    c. free-associate in Freud's sense
    d. answer questions that can be used to make a personality profile
    e. describe what people of the opposite sex are doing in pictures

Correct _____ If wrong, why? _____

18. A psychologist administering a Rorschach will:
    a. begin with very clear instructions about what the client should say
    b. only record what you say and not things you do with the cards
    c. almost always administer it using double-blind methodology
    d. show more reliability using objective scoring than using subjective interpretations
    e. be able to identify your specific disorder with about 95% accuracy

Correct _____ If wrong, why? _____

ANSWERS AND EXPLANATIONS FOR COMPREHENSION CHECK

Correct Answer	Other Alternatives Are Wrong Because:
1. d (p. 477, Fig. 13.1) Obj. I, II	a. believed in self-actualization, an innate goodness b. argues that people have good, noble goals c. many people have strong social interest
2. a (p. 479) Obj. III-A	b. this would be a masculine person c. external locus of control, unrelated to androgyny d. gender roles may be learned from other children, but an androgynous person shows both male and female trait
3. c (p. 483) Obj. V-D	a,b,d,e. all are characteristics c. they are problem centered
4. b (p. 486, 487) Obj. VI-B	a. Freud once thought this, but decided it was sexual fantasies, not actual abuse c. catharsis is release of tension related to unpleasant experiences; fixation means that people continue to be preoccupied with pleasure related to the stage d. unconscious does have these, but it's less logical e. it does in slips of the tongue; unconscious motivations can influence such errors
5. a (p. 486) Obj. VI-B-3	b. sensual pleasure from mouth area c. pleasure from bowel movements d. interest in others' and own genitals e. sexual interest is suppressed

6. e (p. 490)
   Obj. VI-C-1-d

a. Dan would place anger with boss into unconscious
b. Dan would behave in a more juvenile way
c. Dan would be very friendly toward his boss to hide the anger
d. Dan would argue that everyone hates his or her boss

7. a (p. 488, Fig. 13.11)
   Obj. VI-C

b. id contains sexual urge; superego is like a conscience; ego deals with reality
c. libido is general sexual energy; superego doesn't mediate, it is restrictive
d. ego is the mediator; superego is the restrictive part
e. id contains sexual urges; ego mediates and deals with reality; libido is sexual energy

8. d (p. 492)
   Obj. VI-F

a. she agreed that ego existed
b. in humanistic psychology--moments when people feel truly fulfilled
c. in humanistic psychology--unqualified acceptance of others
e. fulfillment of potential in humanistic theories

9. a (pp. 492-493)
   Obj. VII, VIII

a. this was Jung's term for the cumulative experience of previous generations
b-e. are correct

10. d (p. 493)
    Obj. VIII-A

a. this is Jung's idea
b. people may not be aware of their style of life
c. refers to striving to benefit the human race
e. people should be viewed as wholes

11. b (p. 497)
    Obj. VII-A

a. seems to be more temporary; a transient condition
c. directing interest in others; unrelated to anxiety
d. enjoyment of new experiences; wouldn't cause anxiety

12. a (pp. 498-499)
    Obj. X-A

a. relates to personality differences between men and women, important but not one of the big five; conscientiousness is missing here
b-e. all are "big five" personality dimensions

13. d (p. 499)
    Obj. XI-B-2

a. they change very little with age
b. they aren't supposed to correlate with each other; they should be nearly independent
c. the traits work well for both men and women

14. e (p. 501, Fig. 13.19)
    Obj. XII

a. adopted children and their adoptive parents are not similar
b. this is evidence for no family environment effect
c. they are not very similar, arguing against family environment as an important influence
d. monozygotic twins are more similar, showing a genetic influence

15. d (p. 503)
    Obj. XIII
    a. test questions don't have to be related to feedback
    b,c. 90% rated it "good to excellent"
    e. only about 20% rated this description "good to excellent"

16. c (p. 504)
    Obj. XV-A-1
    a. questions were chosen by trial and error; they just found questions that were answered differently by different groups
    b. validity not that high; should be used with other measures
    d. projective tests do this; MMPI is objective
    e. a lie scale is included, and if the score is too high, test results will not be used

17. b (p. 510)
    Obj. XVI-B
    a. Rorschach
    c. people are given pictures because they often don't talk spontaneously
    d. 16-PF test results in such a profile
    e. people in pictures are mostly of one's own sex

18. d (p. 509)
    Obj. XVI-A
    a. the instructions are intentionally vague
    b. some psychologists will record all behaviors
    c. they should, but most psychologists already know what disorder the person shows
    e. can tell whether people have some sort of problem but not specifically which one

LECTURE MATERIAL

Don't forget to review your lecture material. Process each topic meaningfully. First, be sure that you understand the material in each lecture--if you don't, ask your instructor or teaching assistant. Associate the material with things that you already know and with your personal experiences. If you can make up mental images of any of the material, do so. Try to think of real-life applications of the concepts. Don't forget to put your own notes on each day's lecture notes. Then write questions to cover each concept.

WAIT AT LEAST 24 HOURS BEFORE PROCEEDING.
LET FORGETTING OCCUR--IT WILL!!

SHORT-ANSWER ESSAY QUESTIONS

Write brief answers to each of the following. The answers are on pp. 204-206, but do try to write the answers yourself before looking at them.

Conceptions of Personality

1. Discuss the basic difference between the psychodynamic and humanistic approaches to personality.

2. Describe the two ways in which a person could be androgynous with Bem's original scoring method. How has this been changed?

Grand Theories of Personality

3. Describe Freud's five stages of sexual development.

4. Explain why people use defense mechanisms.

5. Describe how slips of the tongue have been increased so that they could be studied under different motivating conditions.

6. How did Jung and Freud disagree?

7. Describe Adler's individual psychology.

Personality Traits

8. Discuss the difference between the nomothetic and idiographic approaches to personality.

9. What type of support has been obtained for the "big five" personality traits?

10. Discuss the role of family environment in personality.

Personality Assessment

11. Describe how the developers of the MMPI guarded against lying. How do employers do a similar thing on job applications?

12. What is the problem with using tests, such as the MMPI-2, that have fairly good reliability and validity as the only means of diagnosing individuals?

****
Find the questions that you wrote over lecture material and write answers to them.
****

ANSWERS TO SHORT-ANSWER ESSAY QUESTIONS

1. Psychodynamic theorists agree with Hobbes that basic human instincts are selfish; these instincts are part of the id. Other parts of personality are necessary to keep these instincts from showing up fully. Humanist theorists side with Rousseau and argue that humans are good by nature; a person's full potential emerges in self-actualization. People strive for perfection, and when their true selves emerge, they are basically good, caring people. (pp. 477-478)

2. A person could be androgynous either because he or she checked many feminine traits and many masculine traits or because he or she checked few of either. Today, androgyny is usually defined as being high in both masculine and feminine traits. (p. 479, Table 13.1)

3. Oral stage: Libido attaches itself to mouth area and infant derives pleasure from sucking.
   Anal stage: Libido attaches itself to anal area and infant derives pleasure from bowel movements.
   Phallic stage: Libido is in genital area and child shows interest in genitals. Oedipus complex occurs because male child wishes to have mother's affection and get rid of father.
   Latent stage: Child is so traumatized by Oedipus complex that libido becomes latent or hidden. Child suppresses sexual interest.
   Genital stage: Libido is in genital area and child takes interest in own and others' genitals. (pp. 487-488, Table 13.3)

4. Personality is made up of the id, which is motivated by biological instincts; the superego, which is highly moral and punishing; and the ego, which mediates between id, superego, and reality. Ego can exclude some of id's impulses from consciousness, and thus avoid some of the guilt caused by superego. Defense mechanisms reduce anxiety by dealing with the conflict between id and superego. (p. 488-489)

5. Motley and Baars manipulated motivation either by having a sexy female experimenter or by having male subjects hooked up to a shock apparatus. They were asked to read and remember pairs of syllables, some of which would be related to shock or sex if the first letters were interchanged. "Shock" subjects make shock-related errors and "sex" subjects made sex-related errors. (p. 491, Fig. 13.13)

6. Jung put greater emphasis on people's search for meaning in life than Freud did. Jung argued that there was a deeper level of unconscious called the collective unconscious; Freud disagreed. (p. 493)

7. It is the psychology of a person as a whole. Adler argued that people strive for superiority, and if they don't succeed in overcoming helplessness in childhood they may develop an inferiority complex. The plan for achieving superiority determines a person's style of life. If a person contributes to the welfare of the human race, he or she has developed social interest. (pp. 493)

8. The nomothetic approach seeks general laws about how personality influences behavior. Groups of people are compared and statistical analysis is used. The results are meant to be generalized to the population. The idiographic approach focuses on intensive studies of individuals. The results are not meant to be generalized to the population. (p. 497)

9. The five-factor description characterizes personality in both men and women. It works in many languages and cultures, although some cultures may not show enough variation in some of the traits for the description to be meaningful. The "big five" traits seem to be fairly stable across age. (pp. 498-499)

10. Adopted children's personalities generally do not correlate with the personalities of their adoptive parents. Unrelated children growing up in the same home do not develop similar personalities. These findings suggest that personality development is not dependent upon family environment. However, many researchers believe that much of the variation in personality may be due to unshared environment which is the environment that differs from family member to family member. This is difficult to test. Overall, the research suggests a limited role for family environment in personality development. (p. 500-501, Figs. 13.18, 13.19)

11. Some questions should be answered the same by everyone; if you answer differently, you must be lying. The number of such answers are added up to give a score on the lie scale. Employers sometimes do a similar thing on job applications by asking applicants about experience in doing nonexistent tasks. (pp. 505-506, Table 13.5)

12. Tests should be used as aids and not the sole method of diagnosis. Even if a test correctly identifies 95% of the people with a disorder and incorrectly diagnoses 5% of the normal population, it is misdiagnosing more people than it is correctly diagnosing. This is because the total population of normal people is much greater than the population of people with fairly rare disorders. (pp. 511-512)

POSTTEST

Take this test with all of your books and notes out of sight. This should give you a good idea of how well you understand the material. The answers are on p. 210.

Matching

Put the letter of the approach in the blank beside the description.

Conceptions of Personality, Grand Theories of Personality

1. _____ "indivisible" psychology or psychology of person as a whole

2. _____ psychodynamic psychology with decreased role for sex; increased role for culture

3. _____ people are basically good and are motivated toward self-actualization

4. _____ approach that includes collective unconscious

5. _____ personality is interplay among forces, many of which are not consciously recognized

6. _____ consistent ways in which people's social behavior differ

A. humanistic

B. psychodynamic

C. Jung's theory

D. personality

E. neo-Freudian approach

F. individual psychology

Conceptions of Personality

1. Which approach to personality would agree with Rousseau that humans are good by nature?
   a. Freud's approach
   b. psychodynamic
   c. the ancient Greeks' approach
   d. humanistic
   e. neo-Freudian

2. Behaviorism and psychoanalysis share which assumptions that differ from humanistic psychology?
    a. parsimony and reductionism
    b. determinism and parsimony
    c. "all behavior is learned" and parsimony
    d. determinism and "all behavior is learned"
    e. reductionism and determinism

3. In humanistic psychology, the moment an adolescent clearly decides about a profession is called:
    a. peak experience
    b. self-actualization
    c. growth experience
    d. reaction formation
    e. resolution of the Oedipus complex

4. Unconditional positive regard means:
    a. encouraging a person to act on every impulse
    b. leading a person toward self-actualization
    c. trying to change behavior rather than thoughts
    d. complete, unqualified acceptance of a person
    e. a natural drive to achieve one's own potential

5. Maslow thought that people with self-actualized personalities showed all except:
    a. openness to all kinds of experiences
    b. avoidance of ambiguous perceptions
    c. independence and creativity
    d. good sense of humor
    e. treating people with unconditional positive regard

6. Recent conceptualizations of androgyny:
    a. define it as being equal in male and female traits
    b. define it in terms of biological maleness and femaleness
    c. suggest that one can be high in maleness or femaleness, but not both
    d. put masculine and feminine at opposite poles of a single dimension
    e. define it as being high in both male and female traits

Grand Theories of Personality
7. Johnny, who is 8, has absolutely no interest in girls or anything related to sex. According to Freud, Johnny would be in what stage?
    a. latent
    b. anal
    c. oral
    d. genital
    e. phallic

8. Mr. Ku absolutely hates people of other races, yet he sets up free food programs and medical clinics in areas where they live. Which defense mechanism is he using?
   a. denial
   b. reaction formation
   c. displacement
   d. projection
   e. repression

9. If a person has just been sexually aroused, what type of slip of the tongue is most likely?
   a. breast in bed for best in bread
   b. hot shock for shad bock
   c. big pit for pig bit
   d. square meal for mare squeal
   e. all of the above are equally likely

10. In the revision of his theory, what did Freud believe about sexual abuse?
    a. it was responsible for all neurotic behavior
    b. sexual abuse rarely occurs, because patients almost never report it
    c. sexual abuse is the cause of sublimation
    d. sexual abuse is part of the collective unconscious
    e. his patients misled him into believing they had been sexually abused

11. Adler argued that:
    a. people create a master plan for reaching peak experiences
    b. universal symbols occur in art, dreams, and hallucinations
    c. penis envy occurs because of the collective unconscious
    d. everyone has a natural striving for superiority
    e. people become maladjusted if they don't have a peak experience

12. Which of the following is mispaired?
    a. style of life-Adler
    b. inferiority complex-Jung
    c. collective unconscious-Jung
    d. Oedipus complex-Freud
    e. social interest-Adler

Personality Traits

13. Which two traits do most personality theorists agree are the most powerful?
    a. assertiveness and self-discipline
    b. neuroticism and extraversion
    c. conscientiousness and agreeableness
    d. openness to experience and extraversion
    e. conscientiousness and warmth

14. Evidence for a role of genetics in personality includes the finding that:
   a. dizygotic twins are more similar than monozygotic twins
   b. parents' level of extraversion is more similar to their biological children than to their adopted children
   c. unrelated children adopted into the same families don't develop similar personalities
   d. there is little relationship between arousal levels and personality
   e. unshared environments differ from one sibling to another

Personality Assessment

15. Which of the following is <u>not</u> necessary for a standardized test?
   a. it was developed from a specific theoretical viewpoint
   b. items are clear and unambiguous
   c. the mean and range of scores is determined for a large number of people
   d. it is administered according to specific rules
   e. the normal range of scores can be determined

16. The MMPI was devised empirically, which means that:
   a. it was based on a theory about personality disorders
   b. it was revised recently to improve its validity today
   c. items were simply given to groups having different disorders and similar answers given by similar groups were identified
   d. it was normed on many different ethnic groups
   e. it was designed to detect deception

17. Why would a psychologist use a projective test rather than just asking a person to talk about himself or herself?
   a. the projective test will be much higher in validity
   b. the projective test will make it much easier to decide if a person has a severe mental disorder
   c. the projective test should be more effective in getting a person to start talking
   d. different psychologists will come to different conclusions from an interview but not from a projective test

18. Which of the following is the psychologist least likely to do when giving a Rorschach?
   a. notice whether you rotate each card
   b. record how long you study each card
   c. suggest that you should try to see the inkblot as one object
   d. notice whether you say anything about color or movement
   e. count how many responses you give

ANSWERS TO POSTTEST

Correct Answer	Questions Testing a Similar Concept	
	Comprehension Check	Short-Answer

Matching

Correct Answer	Comprehension Check	Short-Answer
1. F (p. 493)	9,10	7
2. E (p. 492)	8,9e	--
3. A (p. 482)	3	1
4. C (pp. 492-493)	9b,10a	6
5. B (p. 478)	4	1,3
6. D (p. 477)	--	8

Multiple-Choice

Correct Answer	Comprehension Check	Short-Answer
1. d (pp. 477-478, Fig. 13.1)	1	1
2. e (p. 481)	--	1
3. c (p. 481)	8b	1
4. d (p. 482)	3a	1
5. b (p. 483)	3	--
6. e (p. 479)	2	10
7. a (p. 488)	5e	3
8. b (p. 490)	6c	4
9. a (p. 491)	4e	5
10. e (p. 486)	4a	--
11. d (p. 493)	9,10	7
12. b (p. 493)	9,10	6,7
13. b (p. 498)	12	9
14. b (pp. 500-501)	14	10
15. a (p. 504)	--	--
16. c (p. 504)	16	--
17. c (p. 508)	17,18	--
18. c (p. 509)	18	--

CHAPTER 14 SOCIAL PSYCHOLOGY

OBJECTIVES
Understand that:

Social psychologists study how people influence each other. (p. 516)

Social Perception and Cognition
I. First impressions influence perceptions of individuals (p. 517)

II. Stereotypes are generalizations about groups of people (pp. 517-518)

    A. People's judgments of others are often unreliable and inaccurate (p. 517)

    B. Prejudice is a negative attitude about a group (pp. 518-519)

        1. Prejudice may be overcome by having people work toward common goals (pp. 519-520)

III. Attribution is the process of assigning causes to behavior (p. 520)

    A. Behavior is attributed to internal or external causes (p. 520)

        1. Consensus information involves comparing behavior to that of others (pp. 520-521)

        2. Consistency information involves comparing behavior across time (p. 521)

        3. Distinctiveness involves comparing behavior toward different objects or people (p. 521)

    B. We often assume that behavior results from internal causes (pp. 521-522)

        1. The fundamental attribution error is an overemphasis on internal causes for other people (p. 521)

        2. The actor-observer effect makes people more likely to attribute internal causes to other's behavior than to their own (p. 521)

    C. Attributions for our own behavior may produce a self-serving bias (p. 522)

        1. We may adopt self-handicapping strategies as excuses for failures (p. 522)

The message: *We make guesses about reasons for people's behaviors and those (sometimes wrong) guesses influence how we interact with others (pp. 522-523).*

Attitudes and Persuasion
IV. An attitude is a learned like or dislike of something or somebody (p. 524)

    A. Attitudes are usually measured with rating scales (p. 524)

        1. These are imperfect because people use the scale differently (p. 524)

    B. Often attitudes are only weakly related to behavior (pp. 524-525)

        1. High self-monitors change their behavior to make the right impression (p. 525)

V. Attitudes can be changed by central and peripheral routes (p. 525)

    A. Attitudes are often difficult to change (pp. 525-527)

    B. Messages sometimes have a delayed effect on attitudes (p. 527)

        1. The sleeper effect is a delayed attitude change after an initial rejection (p. 527)

        2. Minorities can change attitudes in the long run if they are outvoted at first (p. 527)

    C. The way a message is presented can affect its effectiveness (pp. 527-528)

    D. Some people are more easily persuaded than others (pp. 528-529)

        1. Intelligent people are persuaded by complex messages, but less intelligent people are more easily persuaded by poorly supported ideas (p. 529)

        2. The forewarning and inoculation effects reduce persuasion (p. 529)

VI. Several techniques are used to persuade us to do what other people would like us to do (pp. 529-530)

    A. The foot-in-the-door technique involves increasing a modest request to a large one (p. 530)

    B. The door-in-the-face technique begins with a large request and then scales it down to a smaller, more reasonable one (p. 530)

C. The low-ball technique begins by making a favorable deal and then making more demands (p. 530)
D. The that's-not-all technique begins with an offer that is quickly improved (p. 530)
VII. Cognitive dissonance theory says that changes in behavior precede changes in attitude (pp. 530-531)
    A. People who lie for little money are more likely to change their attitudes than people who lie for more money (pp. 531-532)

The message: Our attitude about something is based on its importance and the type of information we have; our behavior can be affected by persuasion strategies used by other people (p. 532)

Interpersonal Attraction

VIII. People have a need to have relationships with other people (p. 535)
    A. People crave long-term relationships (p. 535)
    B. Temporary relationships are cultivated for limited purposes (p. 535)
        1. People who face a future difficulty like to be with others facing the same difficulty (pp. 535-536)
IX. Long-lasting relationships are developed with relatively few others (p. 536)
    A. People choose friends who live close to them; this is called proximity (p. 536)
    B. The more exposure to something, the more it is liked; this is familiarity (p. 536)
    C. People choose friends who are similar to themselves; this is similarity (pp. 536-537)
    D. We tend to be attracted to people who confirm our self-evaluation (p. 537)
    E. Exchange or equity theory says that each party should get the best deal possible in the relationship (p. 537)
X. Selection of a marriage partner is different because it may include raising children (p. 538)
    A. Physical attractiveness is important in dating, especially at first (pp. 538-539)
        1. Physical attractiveness may be important because of its relation to good health (p. 538)
    B. The sociobiological approach can explain different preferences of men and women (pp. 540-541)
        1. Men prefer younger, fertile mates (p. 540)
        2. Women need mates who are fertile, healthy, and who have substantial resources (pp. 540-541)
XI. Despite romance and passion, many relationships end (p. 541)
    A. Dating couples tend to become more confident of each other's experiences and preferences (but not more accurate) (p. 541)
    B. Similarity of attitudes and personalities, together with other factors, contribute to long-lasting romantic relationships (pp. 541-542)

The message: Learning about what influences interpersonal attraction may help us make better choices of friends and spouses (p. 542)

Interpersonal Influence

XII. Conformity is the tendency to do what others are doing (p. 544)
    A. People will conform to a group of 3-4 as much as to a group of more (p. 544-545)
    B. Having an ally reduces conformity (p. 545)
XIII. People sometimes accept responsibility toward others and sometimes not (p. 546)
    A. Bystanders often will not help if others are present because of diffusion of responsibility (pp. 546-547)
    B. Social loafing means working less hard when sharing work with others (p. 547)
XIV. Decisions of groups may differ from decisions of individuals (pp. 548-549)
    A. Groups usually come to more extreme decisions than individuals; this is called the group polarization effect (p. 548)

B. Groupthink occurs when group members do not question others' ideas and don't ask probing questions (pp. 548-549)

The message: Conformity can be helpful to society, but we need to be alert to situations when conformity can be harmful to ourselves or others (p. 549)

The Power of the Social Situation

XV. Much behavior is controlled by social situations (p. 551)
    A. Behavior traps force people into self-defeating behaviors (p. 551)
        1. Escalation of conflict occurs when people continue a behavior to avoid defeat (pp. 551-552)
        2. Situations like the prisoner's dilemma result in uncooperative behavior (pp. 552-553, Fig. 14.17)
        3. The commons dilemma involves overuse of limited resources (pp. 553-554, Fig. 14.19)
    B. Milgram found that many people showed obedience to authority and would "punish" another person (pp. 555-557)
        1. The ethical issues raised by his study resulted in clearer rules for treating research subjects (p. 556)

The message: Knowing about behavior traps can help us make better choices about social situations and environments (p. 557)

COMPREHENSION CHECK

Answer these questions soon after reading the chapter. Circle the best alternative. Check your answers on pp. 217-219. If you gave a wrong answer, try to write why it was wrong. Check your reasons.

Social Perception and Cognition

1. Which of the following is <u>not</u> true about forming impressions of new acquaintances?
    a. physically attractive people are likely to be judged more favorably
    b. facial expressions and body movements are more likely to be used than conflicting verbal information
    c. information that is learned first is more influential than information that is learned later
    d. information that is learned last is more influential than information that is learned earlier

Correct _____   If wrong, why? _____

2. Stereotypes probably get started because people:
    a. discount internal causes if there is an external cause as stated in the discounting principle
    b. do not remember the behavior of minority groups
    c. rely on consistency information more than distinctiveness information
    d. remember unusual behaviors of minority groups

Correct _____   If wrong, why? _____

3. The fundamental attribution error involves overemphasizing:
    a. external as opposed to internal causes of behavior
    b. distinctiveness rather than consensus information
    c. internal as opposed to external causes of behavior
    d. consensus rather than distinctiveness information

Correct _____   If wrong, why? _____

4. Self-handicapping refers to:
   a. creating external causes for our failures
   b. a tendency to attribute internal causes to others people's behavior but external causes to one's own behavior
   c. attributing emotional arousal to external stimuli
   d. creating internal causes for our successes

Correct _____ If wrong, why? _____

Attitudes and Persuasion

5. Measurement of attitudes is:
   a. often done on a Likert scale
   b. very accurate because people are aware of their attitudes
   c. similar across cultures in that people tend to use rating scales in the same way
   d. more accurate for implicit attitudes than for explicit ones
   e. useful because they accurately predict behavior

Correct _____ If wrong, why? _____

6. The central route to persuasion:
   a. is more likely to be followed for decisions that are unimportant
   b. involves paying attention to a speaker's appearance and reputation
   c. involves paying attention to the evidence and logic behind a message
   d. involves paying attention to the sheer number of arguments and not to their quality

Correct _____ If wrong, why? _____

7. How can a minority group best influence public opinion?
   a. by making themselves seem as different as possible from the public
   b. by presenting very frightening messages telling people that disaster is imminent and there is nothing they can do about it
   c. by forewarning people that they will hear a persuasive message
   d. by beginning with a weak message and then strengthening it
   e. by repeating a single, simple message over and over

Correct _____ If wrong, why? _____

8. An example of the foot-in-the-door technique is:
   a. a volunteer worker first asked me to give $100, and when I said no, she asked for $10
   b. a salesman places his briefcase in the door so that I can't close it until I have heard his spiel
   c. a beggar follows a pedestrian up the street constantly asking him for money
   d. a survey worker asks if I will answer a simple question, and after I do that, she asks if I will fill out a long questionnaire
   e. a salesman tells me the price of an item, and then immediately adds that another item will also be included in the price

Correct _____ If wrong, why? _____

9. According to cognitive dissonance theory, what is the relationship between attitude change and behavior change?
   a. attitudes must be changed before behavior can be
   b. attitude change and behavior change are unrelated
   c. behavior only changes if people are forewarned about attempts to change attitudes
   d. if behavior is changed, then attitude change will follow

Correct _____ If wrong, why? _____

Interpersonal Attraction

10. If people are led to expect severe shocks, with whom would they prefer to wait?
    a. other people, whether or not those people expect shock
    b. alone; people know that misery increases misery
    c. other people who are also expecting shock
    d. most people say they don't care

Correct ___C___ If wrong, why? _____

11. The likelihood of developing a friendship is increased by:
    a. proximity; people who live close together are more likely to become friends
    b. familiarity; people who are very familiar as children are likely to develop romantic relationships
    c. dissimilarity because opposites attract
    d. having a dominant person who gets a better deal from the relationship than the other person

Correct _____ If wrong, why? _____

12. What is the relationship between physical attractiveness and attraction?
    a. opposites attract; generally people who are very different in attractiveness have the strongest relationships
    b. attitudes and personality are much more important than attractiveness in determining how much people like dating partners
    c. while personality and attitudes may draw two people together initially, physical attractiveness is what determines whether they stay together
    d. people like physically attractive dating partners better than unattractive ones

Correct ___d___ If wrong, why? _____

13. With respect to romantic partners, women are more likely than men to prefer:
    a. someone younger than themselves
    b. casual sex partners
    c. multiple partners
    d. partners who have wealth

Correct _____ If wrong, why? _____

Interpersonal Influence

14. In which situation would you expect a true subject to conform the most?
    a. two people give a wrong answer
    b. seven people give a wrong answer
    c. five people give a wrong answer, and one person gives the correct one
    d. four people give a wrong answer
    e. b and d would be about equal

Correct _____ If wrong, why? _____

15. Would you expect to get help faster if your car broke down on a highway that has relatively few travelers or on a busy highway?
    a. on the busy one, because of bystander intervention
    b. on the lightly traveled highway, because of the ambiguity on the busy one
    c. on the busy one, because of diffusion of responsibility
    d. on the busy one, because of social loafing
    e. on the lightly traveled one, because of diffusion of responsibility

Correct _____ If wrong, why? _____

16. A group of professors is trying to decide what to do about academically deficient students. Each writes down what he or she thinks is appropriate, but in the end the group decides on more severe action than the average recommendation of the individuals. What has happened?
    a. the group polarization effect
    b. social loafing
    c. bystander intervention
    d. a peremptory challenge
    e. volunteerism

Correct _____ If wrong, why? _____

17. Which of the following is an example of groupthink?
    a. cooperating with a group to help in a major disaster
    b. competing with a group that has different goals from yours
    c. failing to challenge the assumptions of group members
    d. gathering information before making a group decision

Correct _____ If wrong, why? _____

The Power of the Social Situation

18. If nations act as people do in the prisoner's dilemma, what will happen in a nuclear arms race?
    a. each nation will build more weapons, because that is the best for the individual nation
    b. all nations will stop building such weapons, because this is best for each individual nation
    c. all nations will continue to build weapons, because that is best for the nations as a group
    d. communication among nations will probably increase the nuclear buildup

Correct _____ If wrong, why? _____

19. What happened in the experiment in which students could take nuts out of a bowl in which the nuts would double every 10 sec.?
    a. they competed and grabbed nuts for themselves immediately
    b. they cooperated and waited until there were many nuts and then divided them
    c. they took more nuts sooner when working as individuals than when working in a group
    d. they cooperated, just as they do in the prisoner's dilemma
    e. both b and d

Correct _____ If wrong, why? _____

20. In Milgram's experiment in which "teachers" shocked "learners":
    a. subjects did not obey unless they were sadists
    b. many normal people continued to give shocks, although they had misgivings about it
    c. whether or not the experimenter was in the room was irrelevant for obedience
    d. more people quit the experiment when a confederate followed orders than when they worked alone

Correct _____ If wrong, why? _____

ANSWERS AND EXPLANATIONS FOR COMPREHENSION CHECK

Correct Answer	Other Alternatives Are Wrong Because:
1. d (p. 517) Obj. I	a-c. these are true d. information learned first is more influential
2. d (p. 518) Obj. II	a. true, but such external attributions should not lead to stereotypes b. they remember unusual behaviors c. information used to decide about internal and external attributions; not necessarily relevant to stereotypes
3. c (p. 521) Obj. III-B-1	a. overemphasis of internal causes b,d. information used in making attributions; neither distinctiveness nor consensus necessarily overemphasized
4. a (p. 522) Obj. III-C-1	b. this is the actor-observer effect c. may be an example of misattribution if cause is wrong d. refers to explanations for failure, not success
5. a (p. 524) Obj. IV-A	b. people are often unaware of attitudes c. cultures differ in how they use rating scales d. people are unaware of implicit attitudes, so they are difficult to measure e. attitudes often do not predict behavior
6. c (p. 525) Obj. V	a. peripheral is followed for unimportant decisions b. this is the peripheral route d. this is the peripheral route

7. e (p. 527)
   Obj. V-B-2

  a. attitudes are changed more by people who are similar
  b. frightening messages are usually effective only if people can do something about the disaster
  c. forewarning effect reduces persuasion
  d. inoculation effect reduces persuasion

8. d (p. 530)
   Obj. VI-A-1

  a. this also works, but is opposite of foot-in-door
  b. foot-in-door doesn't refer to forceful entry
  c. foot-in-door doesn't refer to persistent asking
  e. this is the that's-not-all technique

9. d (p. 530)
   Obj. VII

  a. theory says the opposite
  b. attitudes do change if behavior does
  c. forewarning effect; decreases attitude change

10. c (p. 536)
   Obj. VIII-B-1

  a. they want to be with others undergoing same experience
  b,d. prefer to wait together

11. a (p. 536)
   Obj. IX-A

  b. this is an exception to the familiarity rule; people are very familiar as children don't develop romantic relationships
  c. similar people are usually attracted to each other
  d. equity theory argues that both people should get a fair deal

12. d (pp. 538)
   Obj. X-A

  a. similarity is the rule; according to the equity principle, both parties should be about equally attractive
  b. physical attractiveness is most important
  c. it's just the opposite; attractiveness is more important initially

13. d (p. 540)
   Obj. X-B-2

  a. men prefer younger partners who will be fertile for more years
  b. men are more likely to have casual sex partners
  c. men spread their genes more with multiple partners

14. e (pp. 545)
   Obj. XII-A

  a. at least three are needed for maximum conformity effect
  b. conformity will occur but no more than with four people
  c. having an "ally" reduces conformity
  d. about the same amount of conformity occurs with four and seven people

15. e (p. 546)
   Obj. XIII-A

  a. refers to whether people will help; not an explanation of why they help
  b. a car breakdown should be equally ambiguous on both types of highway
  c. diffusion should lead to less help; people assume others will help
  d. refers to tendency to work less hard in a group, not to whether bystanders will help

16. a (p. 548)
    Obj. XIV-A

b. not a matter of how much effort an individual puts forth, but of a group's influence on decisions
c. refers to whether people will help; both may be due to diffusion of responsibility
d. refers to lawyers' rights to reject potential jurors; not relevant to group decision making
e. people's tendency to help others; not relevant to group decision making

17. c (pp. 548-549)
    Obj. XIV-B

a,b. groupthink involves decision making
d. information, especially dissenting opinions, is not gathered when groupthink occurs

18. a (pp. 532-533, Fig. 14.17)
    Obj. XV-A-2

b. best for group, not individuals; if one country has weapons and others don't, that country can dominate
c. not best for group; possibility of nuclear war
d. communication should foster cooperation

19. a (p. 554)
    Obj. XV-A-3

b. cooperative response, but not what people do
c. groups are usually more greedy than individuals
d. in this commons dilemma and the prisoners dilemma, people behave competitively
e. b and d are wrong

20. b (pp. 555-556, Fig. 14.23)
    Obj. XV-B

a. over half obeyed; they were "normal"
c. obedience increased when the experimenter was in the room
d. obedience increased when a confederate obeyed

LECTURE MATERIAL

Don't forget to review your lecture material. Process each topic meaningfully. First, be sure that you understand the material in each lecture--if you don't, ask your instructor or teaching assistant. Associate the material with things that you already know and with your personal experiences. If you can make up mental images of any of the material, do so. Try to think of real-life applications of the concepts. Write your own notes on each day's lecture notes. Then write questions to cover each concept.

WAIT AT LEAST 24 HOURS BEFORE PROCEEDING.
LET FORGETTING OCCUR--IT WILL!!

SHORT-ANSWER ESSAY QUESTIONS

Write brief answers to each of the following. The answers are on pp. 221-222, but do try to write the answers yourself before looking at them.

Social Perception and Cognition

1. Discuss the factors that are important in first impressions.

2. What is an attribution, and what types of information are important in making internal and external attributions?

3. Give some reasons for why people tend to make external attributions for their own behavior and internal attributions for the behavior of others.

Attitudes and Persuasion

4. Describe the two routes to persuasion and discuss the conditions under which each might be used.

5. Contrast the foot-in-the-door, door-in-the-face, and that's-not-all techniques for persuasion.

6. Describe cognitive dissonance theory.

Interpersonal Attraction

7. Describe three things that are important in who dates whom.

8. Describe how equity theory applies to romantic relationships and friendships.

Interpersonal Influence

9. How is social loafing related to bystander apathy?

10. Explain why the group polarization effect occurs.

The Power of the Social Situation

11. What's a real-life example of the "commons dilemma?" Why is it a "behavior trap?"

12. Describe Milgram's experiment on obedience and discuss what we can learn from such an experiment.

****

Find the questions that you wrote over lecture material and write answers to them.

****

ANSWERS TO SHORT-ANSWER ESSAY QUESTIONS

1. First impressions are based on physical attractiveness, people's nonverbal behaviors, and information that is learned first. In addition, expectations that are derived from stereotypes about groups of people influence first impressions. (p. 517)

2. Attribution is the process of assigning causes to someone's behavior. *Consistency information* (how much a person's behavior varies), *consensus information* (how similar a person's behavior is to that of other people), and *distinctiveness information* (how much a person's behavior depends upon the situation) are important. Behaviors that are high in consistency, dissimilar to those of other people, and not distinctive to a situation are attributed to internal causes. (pp. 520-521)

3. This actor-observer effect may occur because people who are watching someone assume that behavior results from characteristics within that person. It might occur because we know that our own behavior is not consistent across situations, but we know less about others' behavior. Another possibility is that we attribute unexpected behaviors to external events and our own behavior is not unexpected. A third explanation is that we do not see ourselves as objects, so we tend to focus on the environment, or external stimuli. (p. 521)

4. When people hear persuasive arguments, they sometimes evaluate the evidence and logic behind the message. This is called the central route to persuasion, and it occurs for serious decisions. An alternative route that is used for less serious decisions is the peripheral route to persuasion. People pay more attention to the speaker's appearance and reputation, and to the sheer number of arguments regardless of their quality. (p. 525)

5. The foot-in-the-door technique involves getting agreement for a small request first and then making a much larger request. The door-in-the- face technique is the opposite; begin with the large request and then scale down to the smaller one. The that's-not-all technique makes a better offer before the person has responded to the first one. With each technique, the second request is more likely to be agreed to than if the first was not made. (p. 530)

6. The idea is that if people behave in ways that are inconsistent with their beliefs, they will change their beliefs. The original theory argued that tension builds up if people's behavior and attitudes do not match. They reduce this tension by adopting a new attitude that justifies their behavior. (p. 531)

7. Similarity is important. Couples tend to resemble each other in age, social class, religion, intelligence, etc. Proximity is important. People tend to date people who live close to them. For first dates, physical attractiveness is important; people like physically attractive dates better than less attractive dates. (pp. 536-537)

8. Equity theory assumes that social relationships are transactions in which partners exchange "goods." Each partner wants to get the best deal possible. Partners look at the pluses and minuses of relationships and decide whether the exchange seems fair. (p. 537)

9. Both may occur because of diffusion of responsibility because people in groups do less than individuals. Bystanders are less likely to help strangers in trouble when there are more, rather than fewer, people around. They assume either that others will help or that it may not really be an emergency situation. In social loafing, people do less work in a group than alone, perhaps because their own efforts won't be evaluated. (pp. 546-547)

10. If the members of a group generally agree on a position at the beginning, they often move toward the extreme because of diffusion of responsibility (the group is responsible, not me), because individuals hear many reasons for their position, and because they receive reinforcement from the group for agreeing. (p. 548)

11. The commercial fishing industry is an example of the "commons dilemma." Limiting catches is necessary to prevent declines in oceanic populations due to overfishing. It's a "trap" because of an individual fisherman's temptation to increase his catch without risk of penalty; if all fishermen behave the same way, the resource will be depleted and then no-one will have fish. (pp. 553-554)

12. Students served as teachers in what they thought was an experiment on obedience. They presented word pairs to a "learner" who made many mistakes in his recall of the pairs. Students were to administer a higher shock level following each mistake. Over half of the students continued and administered the highest shock level. This shows that people have such great respect for authority that they may carry out unreasonable and dangerous instructions. (pp. 555-556)

POSTTEST

Take this test with all of your books and notes out of sight. This should give you a good idea of how well you understand the material. The answers are on p. 227.

Matching

Put the letter of the term in the blank beside the description.

Persuasion; Interpersonal Influence; The Power of the Social Situation

1. __E__ results in decisions that are more extreme than the average of the individuals' decisions
       A. prisoner's dilemma

2. __F__ overuse of resources that have a fixed rate of replacement
       B. foot-in-the-door

3. __B__ beginning with a small request and escalating to a much larger one
       C. groupthink

4. __C__ failure to challenge assumptions and ask probing questions
       D. door-in-the-face

5. __D__ beginning with a large request and scaling it down
       E. group polarization effect

6. __A__ situation in which competition is pitted against cooperation
       F. commons dilemma

7. __H__ assuming that someone else will do what's needed
       G. conformity

8. __G__ changing behavior to be consistent with a group's standards
       H. diffusion of responsibility

Multiple-choice

Circle the *best* alternative.

Social Perception and Cognition

1. According to the primacy effect in impression formation, you will be more influenced by:
   a. physical characteristics than by nonverbal behaviors
   b. ordinary information than by unusual information
   c. information received first, rather than that received later
   d. peripheral rather than central traits
   e. nonverbal behaviors than by physical characteristics

2. 75% of the people you meet belong to group X and 25% belong to group Y. Members of both groups perform an equal number of unusual acts. When asked to decide which group does more unusual things, you will say:
   a. Group Y, because unusual acts committed by a minority group stand out
   b. Group X, because unusual acts committed by a majority group stand out
   c. Group Y, because unusual acts committed by a majority group stand out
   d. they are equivalent, because they actually are
   e. Group X, because unusual acts committed by a minority group stand out

3. Which of the following is an internal attribution?
   a. John failed the test because he had to work last night
   b. Mary forgot the party because she was so busy at work
   c. Sally invited me over for dinner because she owed me a favor
   d. Fred hung up on me because he has a short temper
   e. both a and b

4. The actor-observer effect is shown in which of the following?
   a. Jane left the party because she is not very friendly; I left it because people were using drugs
   b. Mike failed the test because it was too difficult; I failed it because I am basically stupid
   c. John dropped the tray because he is a klutz; I dropped the tray because I am clumsy
   d. Sally fell because it was slippery; I fell because my boots don't have good tread
   e. all of the above

5. People sometimes intentionally put themselves at a disadvantage on tasks so they can attribute their:
   a. successes to external factors
   b. failures to internal factors
   c. failures to external factors
   d. successes to internal factors
   e. outcomes to the fundamental attribution error

Attitudes and Persuasion

6. The measurement of attitudes:
   a. is very accurate and reliable
   b. is rarely done with subjective rating scales
   c. results in good prediction of behavior for high self-monitors
   d. may be inaccurate because people may not be aware of their attitudes
   e. is fairly constant across cultures so that a rating scale in one culture is interpreted similarly in other cultures

7. The sleeper effect refers to:
   a. persuasion via a superficial approach
   b. persuasion via careful evaluation of evidence
   c. a change in attitude by a high self-monitor
   d. changing attitudes after noticing that behaviors and attitudes don't match
   e. changing attitudes after initial rejection of a message

8. The foot-in-the-door technique is one trick to facilitate persuasion. What is another way that involves doing just the opposite?
   a. have an expert give the message
   b. start with a small request and then make a large one
   c. begin by arguing the opposite and gradually make arguments that support the desired view
   d. begin with a very large request and then scale it back
   e. make the arguments in a way that people don't know that they are being persuaded

9. According to the cognitive dissonance theory, people:
   a. will change their behavior only after their attitudes have changed
   b. try to understand and explain their behavior
   c. change their attitudes to reduce the tension that results from inconsistent attitudes and behaviors
   d. will like an activity if they receive a large payoff for doing it
   e. will dislike an activity if they avoid it because of a severe threat

Interpersonal Attraction

10. In the experiment in which subjects were either made afraid of the upcoming shock or not made afraid:
    a. the subjects chose to wait alone in both conditions
    b. the subjects chose to wait together in both conditions
    c. the highly anxious subjects were more likely to choose together, but only with other anxious subjects
    d. the highly anxious subjects wanted to wait with other people whether or not the other people were in the same experiment
    e. both b and d

11. People's friends in a graduate housing project were mostly people:
    a. who lived near them
    b. who looked like them
    c. who lived in other buildings
    d. of the same sex
    e. who had the same occupational goals

Interpersonal Influence

12. In Asch's experiment, subjects were to judge the length of bars after hearing other people give a wrong answer. What happened?
    a. people rarely conformed, because the situation was not ambiguous
    b. people conformed much more if there were seven other people than if there were only three
    c. people conformed even if there was only one other person
    d. everyone conformed if there were seven other people
    e. most people did not conform if they had an "ally" who gave the correct answer

13. Under which situation would you most expect social loafing to occur?
    a. an individual shooting while playing on a basketball team
    b. a person who has a unique specialty doing something in a group
    c. people thinking up unusual uses for a brick when they know that others will know how many uses they gave
    d. people clapping as part of a group

14. The city council is discussing whether a license to operate a new bar should be approved. Each member is slightly against approval. What is the group decision likely to be and why?
    a. in favor of the license because of groupthink
    b. a split vote because of social loafing
    c. against the license because of the group polarization effect
    d. a split vote because of the group polarization effect
    e. in favor of the license because of social loafing

15. Military strategists all agreed on a plan to attack an island. No one questioned whether it was reasonable and whether they would succeed. What happened during that meeting?
    a. peremptory challenges
    b. diffusion of responsibility
    c. social loafing
    d. groupthink
    e. fundamental attribution error

The Power of the Social Situation

16. Situations like gas wars in which one gas station lowers prices and then other nearby stations must do the same or lose customers are similar to the:
    a. dollar auction
    b. prisoner's dilemma
    c. commons dilemma
    d. door-in-the-face technique
    e. that's-not-all technique

17. Today, a Human Subjects Committee may still approve Milgram's procedures. Why?
    a. few psychologists and psychiatrists predicted that subjects would actually "shock" others
    b. there was no possibility of physical harm to any participants, and that is all that concerns Human Subjects Committees
    c. researchers abide by less-strict human subjects regulations than when Milgram did his study
    d. none of Milgram's subjects were upset by the procedures, so there is no reason for concern

ANSWERS TO POSTTEST

	Questions Testing a Similar Concept	
	Comprehension Check	Short-Answer

Matching

	Comprehension Check	Short-Answer
1. E (p. 548)	16	10
2. F (p. 553)	19	--
3. B (p. 530)	8	5
4. C (pp. 548-549)	17	--
5. D (p. 530)	8a	5
6. A (pp. 552)	18	--
7. H (pp. 546-547)	15	9
8. G (p. 544)	14	--

Multiple-Choice

	Comprehension Check	Short-Answer
1. c (p. 517)	1c	1
2. a (p. 518)	2	--
3. d (p. 520)	3	2,3
4. a (p. 521)	4d	3
5. c (p. 522)	4	--
6. d (pp. 524-525)	5	--
7. e (p. 527)	--	--
8. d (p. 530)	8	8
9. c (p. 531)	9	6
10. c (p. 536)	10	7
11. a (p. 536)	11a	7
12. e (pp. 544-545)	14	--
13. d (p. 547)	16b	9
14. c (pp. 548-549)	16	10
15. d (pp. 548-549)	17	--
16. a (p. 552)	--	--
17. a (p. 556)	20	12

CHAPTER 15 ABNORMALITIES AND THERAPIES I: GENERAL PRINCIPLES

OBJECTIVES

Understand that:

Overview of Abnormal Behavior

I. Defining abnormal behavior can be difficult (pp. 561-562)
    A. Different disorders occur in different cultures (pp. 562-563)
    B. Different views can be used to explain abnormal behavior (p. 563)
        1. Psychological disorders may result from biological disorders (p. 563)
        2. Psychological disorders may be due to early experiences (p. 563)
        3. Psychological disorders may result from stressful environments (p. 564)
II. DSM-IV classifies disorders (pp. 564-565)
    A. People often have symptoms that don't fit in a disorder classification (pp. 564-565)
        1. One-third to one-half of all people endure some diagnosable disorder at some point in their lives (p. 564, Fig. 154.4)
            a. Percent of people who "have a problem" depends upon classification of borderline cases (p. 565)
    B. DSM-IV has axes of classification (p. 565)
        1. Axis I lists disorders that have an onset after infancy and have some likelihood of recovery (p. 565, Table 15.1)
        2. Axis II lists disorders that persist throughout life (p. 565, Table 15.2)
        3. Axis III lists physical disorders (p. 565)
        4. Axis IV indicates how much stress the person has had to endure (p. 565)
        5. Axis V evaluates level of functioning (p. 565)
    C. DSM-IV allows clinicians to make differential diagnoses (pp. 565-566)
The message*: People who qualify for psychological diagnoses are not very different from normal (p. 568)*

Psychotherapy

III. Freud founded psychoanalysis to bring out unconscious material (p. 569, Table 15.3)
    A. Free association--patient says whatever comes to mind (p. 569-570)
    B. Dreams represent wish fulfillment (p. 570)
        1. Manifest content of dreams is the surface content (p. 570)
        2. Latent content of dreams is the hidden, symbolic content (p. 570)
    C. Transference--patient reacts to therapist as someone else (p. 571)
IV. Behavior therapists assume that behavior is learned and can be unlearned (p. 571, Table 15.3)
    A. Behavior modification is an effective way to treat anorexia nervosa (p. 652)
    B. Bed-wetting can be helped through classical conditioning (pp. 569-570)
    C. Aversion therapy involves punishment for inappropriate behavior (p. 572)
V. Some therapies focus on thoughts and beliefs (p. 572)
    A. Rational-emotive therapy assumes that abnormal behavior is due to irrational thoughts (p. 573)
    B. Cognitive therapy strives to have people discover their inappropriate beliefs and change them (p. 573, Table 15.3)
    C. Cognitive-behavior therapy attempts to change behavior but puts emphasis on people's interpretations of situations (pp. 573-574)
VI. Person-centered therapy is the best-known humanistic therapy (p. 574, Table 15.3)
    A. The therapist provides an atmosphere in which the client can freely explore feelings (p. 574)
VII. Family systems therapy involves working with the entire family (p. 575, Table 15.3)

VIII. New methods make therapy less costly and less time-consuming (pp. 575-577)
   A. Many therapists combine approaches and use eclectic therapy (p. 575)
   B. Brief therapies usually have time limits (pp. 575-576)
      1. HMOs sometimes force therapy to be too brief (p. 576)
   C. Group therapy sessions are less expensive and they allow individuals to relate to others with similar problems (p. 576)
   D. Self-help groups do not include a therapist (p. 577)
IX. The effectiveness of therapy can be determined by comparing treated and non-treated people (pp. 577-578)
   A. Psychotherapy patients do show more improvement than nontreated people (p. 578, Fig. 15.7)
   B. All kinds of therapies are helpful (p. 579)
      1. The type of therapist is not critical (p. 579, Fig. 15.8)
      2. Experienced therapists are not necessarily better than non-professionals (p. 579)
         a. However, professional therapists are always willing to listen and they keep conversations confidential (p. 580)
         b. Trained therapists can diagnose biological problems (p. 580)
   C. More therapy sessions do not necessarily mean more improvement (pp. 580-581)
   D. Therapies help because they rely on a therapeutic alliance between therapist and client (p. 581)
      1. Commitment to change by the client is necessary (p. 581)
X. Guidelines for choosing a psychotherapist (p. 581)
The message: Various types of therapy are about equally effective but some therapists differ in effectiveness and some therapists match some clients better than others (p. 581)

Social and Legal Issues in the Treatment of Troubled People

XI. Older mental hospitals were much like prisons (p. 584)
   A. Drugs and advances in psychotherapy allow hospitals to offer short-term care (p. 584)
   B. Deinstitutionalization refers to moving people from hospitals to community-based treatment centers (p. 584)
XII. There are a number of legal issues related to treatment (p. 585)
   A. Psychologically disturbed people can refuse treatment (p. 585. Fig. 15.10)
      1. A person who is dangerous to society can be involuntarily committed to a mental institution (pp. 585-586)
         a. Deciding who is dangerous is difficult (p. 586)
XIII. People are not responsible for their behavior if they are "insane" (pp. 586-588)
   A. Under the M'Naghten rule, people must not realize that they are committing a crime (p. 587)
   B. Under the Durham rule, a defendant is not responsible if suffering from a mental disease or defect (p. 587)
   C. The Model Penal Code says that the person must suffer from a mental disease and not realize that he or she has committed a crime (pp. 587-588)
XIV. Community psychologists attempt to prevent disorders from occurring or from becoming worse (p. 588)
   A. Society can take some actions to prevent disorders (p. 588)
The message: The insanity defense and other legal issues are complicated, difficult topics that require political decisions by society as a whole (p. 588)

COMPREHENSION CHECK

Answer these questions soon after reading the chapter. Circle the *best* alternative. Check your answers, pp. 233-235. If you gave a wrong answer, try to write why it was wrong. Check your reasons, pp. 233-235.

Overview of Abnormal Behavior

1. The American Psychiatric Association's definition of psychological disorder is:
    a. anything that is different from average
    b. behavior associated with distress, disability, or with increased risk of death, pain, or loss of freedom
    c. patterns of behavior that a particular culture regards as troublesome or unacceptable
    d. any unusual behavior that is caused by a biological disorder

Correct _____ If wrong, why? _risk of death_

2. According to DSM-IV, if someone has an Axis I disorder:
    a. the disorder is a part of the person himself or herself and therapy is unlikely to help
    b. the person is doing worse now than at some point in the past
    c. there is a physical problem, such as diabetes
    d. he or she would also score high on the Axis V scale of level of functioning

Correct _____ If wrong, why? _time →_

Psychotherapy

3. In psychoanalysis:
    a. the therapist uses hypnosis to gain access to the patient's unconscious
    b. the therapist explains the universal meaning of symbols in a dream
    c. the therapist uses free association to censor embarrassing thoughts
    d. the patient may begin to treat the therapist as someone else when transference occurs

Correct _____ If wrong, why? _____

4. How do behavior therapies differ from psychoanalysis and humanistic therapies?
    a. behavior therapists attack the behavior, not the thoughts
    b. behavior therapies dwell more on the discovering hidden meanings than the other two
    c. behavior therapists tend to stick with the same procedure longer (even its not working) than the other two
    d. the goals of behavior therapy are broader and more vague than the goals of the other two

Correct _____ If wrong, why? _____

5. Bed-wetting has been treated most effectively with:
    a. classical conditioning
    b. behavior modification
    c. aversion therapy
    d. rationale-emotive therapy

Correct _____ If wrong, why? _____

6. How does rational-emotive therapy differ from cognitive therapy?
   a. cognitive therapy deals with changing cognitions; rational-emotive therapy deals mainly with changing emotions, with the idea that changes in thoughts will follow
   b. cognitive therapists usually use Freud's methods; rational-emotive therapies don't
   c. rational-emotive believes emotions lead to thoughts; cognitive believes thoughts lead to emotions
   d. rational-emotive therapists often contradict their patients' irrational beliefs; cognitive therapists have patients explore evidence behind their thoughts

Correct _____ If wrong, why? _____

7. Person-centered therapy:
   a. tries to increase the incongruence between a person's self-concept and his or her ideal self
   b. tries to direct a person toward worthy goals
   c. directs the client away from inappropriate thoughts toward more appropriate ones
   d. includes unconditional positive regard
   e. was pioneered by Ellis

Correct _____ If wrong, why? _____

8. A therapist helps his clients to set specific goals for changing behavior, and then he works with them to change their interpretation of problems. What type of therapy is this?
   a. rational-emotive therapy
   b. family systems therapy
   c. cognitive-behavior therapy
   d. person-centered therapy
   e. aversion therapy

Correct _____ If wrong, why? _helps change their thoughts_____

9. Dr. Therup often interprets his clients' dreams; sometimes tries to get them to understand whether they are playing the role of child, adult, or parent; uses reinforcement for appropriate behavior; and tries to get them to change their irrational thoughts. Dr. Therup is a(n):
   a. psychoanalyst
   b. eclectic therapist _- role therapy_
   c. multiple personality
   d. family therapist
   e. brief therapist
   more than just a psycho analyst

Correct _____ If wrong, why? _more than just_____

10. What is the advantage of family systems therapy?
    a. it is cheaper because the whole family shares the expense
    b. a deadline is used so both therapist and the family are motivated to bring therapy to a successful conclusion
    c. communication and unreasonable demands within a family can be dealt with
    d. a therapist is not needed; people "treat" each other

Correct _____ If wrong, why? _____

11. Which of the following is true about the effectiveness of psychotherapy?
    a. people who receive no therapy improve at about the same rate as people who are treated
    b. people who receive psychotherapy show greater improvement than about 80% of untreated people
    c. therapy works best with patients who have vague, general complaints
    d. success depends a lot on the therapy; some are much better than others
    e. trained therapists produce much more improvement than "caring" individuals

Correct _____ If wrong, why? ___go for the facts — too vague___

12. In all psychotherapies:
    a. the therapist does most of the talking
    b. clients must make some commitment to change
    c. the more coordinated the treatment, the more improvement
    d. the therapist and client concentrate on the reasons behind behaviors

Correct _____ If wrong, why? _____

Social and Legal Issues in the Treatment of Troubled People

13. State mental hospitals:
    a. have changed today so that they can provide quality short-term care
    b. have had a steady increase in patients since 1950
    c. are more costly than alternative care
    d. promote psychological adjustment better than alternative care

Correct _____ If wrong, why? __—this promoting alternative care / adjustment__

14. Patients with mental disorders:
    a. must be confined to mental institutions if they are seriously disordered
    b. can be institutionalized against their will using preventive detention laws if they lack capacity to make informed decisions concerning treatment
    c. can refuse the right to treatment even if they have been involuntarily committed to a hospital
    d. were not discharged from hospitals during deinstitutionalization

Correct _____ If wrong, why? _____

15. In which case should a person be called insane according to the original M'Naghten rule?
    a. Fred understood that he was committing a crime, but he couldn't stop himself
    b. John, who has brain damage, did not know that what he was doing was wrong
    c. Michael, who is schizophrenic, says that he knew what he was doing was wrong, but he could not control his impulses
    d. Brian committed a bizarre crime that he agreed was wrong, but that is the only evidence for insanity

Correct _____ If wrong, why? _____

16. Which of the following is not a primary prevention strategy?

    a. a program is set up in a popular bar and people who drink nightly are identified; these people are then treated for early signs of alcoholism

    b. funding of child-care programs is instituted

    c. people who lose their jobs are given counseling and education to help them get back into the work force

    d. classes for disadvantaged pregnant women are begun; those programs teach about the dangers of using drugs while pregnant and also about how certain viruses and infections can affect fetuses

Correct _____ If wrong, why? _____ *others are educating/stopping* *a is only identifying one problem.*

Answers and Explanations for Comprehension Check

Correct Answer	Other Alternatives Are Wrong Because:
1. b (p. 562) Obj. I	a. this would include unusually happy or successful people too c. some societies may be intolerant of behaviors that are quite normal in other societies d. biological causes are only one point of view
2. b (p. 565) Obj. II-B-1	a. this describes Axis II, things like mental retardation and personality disorders c. physical problems are on Axis III d. a person with an Axis I disorder would be unlikely to score highly on the level of functioning scale
3. d (p. 569) Obj. III-C	a. Freud used hypnosis at first, but then he decided it didn't work b. what each symbol means to the individual is important c. thoughts are totally uncensored; person says whatever comes to mind
4. a (p. 571, Table 15.3) Obj. III, IV, VI	b. psychoanalysis searches for hidden meanings, and behavior therapy doesn't at all c. behavior therapists often change after a few sessions if something isn't working; psychoanalysts and humanists change much less d. goals are more specific
5. a (pp. 571-572) Obj. IV-B	b. uses reinforcements; although some reinforcement occurs here, therapy is mainly based on classical conditioning c. punishments for bedwetting aren't very effective d. a "talk" therapy; usually used with adults
6. d (p. 573) Obj. V-A,B	a. both deal with changing thoughts or beliefs b. neither use Freud's methods c. both believe that cognitions must be changed

7. d (p. 574)
    Obj. VI
    a. tries to increase <u>congruence</u>--a match between
        self-concept and ideal self
    b. it is nondirective--therapist encourages client to seek own goals
    c. nondirective; all the person's thoughts are appropriate in the therapy
        setting
    e. Carl Rogers; Ellis pioneered rational-emotive therapy

8. c (p. 573)
    Obj. V-C
    a. would try to change irrational beliefs, but not necessarily set goals
        for changing behavior
    b. would work with several family members
    d. wouldn't set behavioral goals; wouldn't try to change
        interpretations
    e. emphasis here is on changing interpretations, not punishing
        inappropriate behavior

9. b (p. 575)
    Obj. VII-A
    a. he may be, but he uses more types of therapy
    c. unlikely, unless a distinct personality goes with each of his
        therapies
    d. not necessarily; unless he treats families rather than individuals
    e. not necessarily; his therapy may go on for a long period with no
        deadline

10. c (p. 575)
    Obj. VII
    a. reason why group therapy developed; family would probably pay
        costs for individual therapy anyway
    b. maybe, but only if brief therapy is used
    d. true with a self-help group; therapist involved in family therapy

11. b (pp. 577-578,
    Fig. 15.7)
    Obj. IX
    a. recent studies show that treated people do better
    c. works best with specific, clear-cut problems
    d. studies show that various forms of therapy produce similar results
    e. they produced about equal benefits

12. b (p.581)
    Obj. IX-D-1
    a. true for some therapies, not for others
    c. this wasn't true in the Fort Bragg study; the well-coordinated
        program was just more expensive
    d. not true for all therapies, especially not behavior therapy

13. c (p. 584)
    Obj. XI
    a. although this is their goal today, few have changed so they can
        accomplish this
    b. the number has dropped because of drugs
    d. other forms of care are often more effective

14. c (p. 585)
    Obj. XI, XII
    a. not true in many states; in some states they must be dangerous to
        themselves or others
    b. preventive detention can only be used when a person is dangerous
        to society
    d. many mentally ill people were discharged and they now live in
        nursing homes, prisons, are homeless, or are struggling

15. b (p. 587)
    Obj. XIII-A

    a. not according to original rule; he had to be unaware that what he had done was wrong

    c. insane according to Durham rule, but knew he had done wrong

    d. knew he was wrong; not insane according to Model Penal Code—need more than bizarre crime

16. a (p. 588)
    Obj. XIV

    a. a secondary prevention program because alcoholism caught in early stages

    b-d. all primary prevention programs; changing the environment before the mental disorders occur

LECTURE MATERIAL

Don't forget to review your lecture material. Process each topic meaningfully. First, be sure that you understand the material in each lecture--if you don't, ask your instructor or teaching assistant. Associate the material with things that you already know and with your personal experiences. If you can make up mental images of any of the material, do so. Try to think of real-life applications of the concepts. Write comments on each day's lecture notes. Then write questions to cover each concept.

WAIT AT LEAST 24 HOURS BEFORE PROCEEDING.
LET FORGETTING OCCUR--IT WILL!!

SHORT-ANSWER ESSAY QUESTIONS

Write brief answers to each of the following. The answers are on pp. 236-238, but do try to write the answers yourself before looking at them.

Overview of Abnormal Behavior

1. Discuss the three components of the biopsychosocial model of abnormal behavior.

2. Describe how DSM IV categorizes psychological disorders.

Psychotherapy

3. If you go to a therapist who uses psychoanalysis, what would you expect?

4. How does person-centered therapy differ from the psychoanalytic therapy that you described above?

5. Describe a behavioral therapy for anorexia nervosa.

6. Treating people in groups has become increasingly common. Describe three types of such treatment.

7. Evaluate the effectiveness of psychotherapy.

8. Discuss the things that all forms of psychotherapy have in common.

Social and Legal Issues in the Treatment of Troubled People
9. How have mental hospitals changed since the 1950s?

10. Discuss the issues related to whether a psychologically disturbed person can refuse treatment.

****
Find the questions that you wrote over lecture material and write answers to them.
****

ANSWERS TO SHORT-ANSWER ESSAY QUESTIONS
1. One component is that psychological disorders result from biological disorders, including things like genetics, brain damage, hormonal abnormalities, disease, and the effects of drugs. The psychological component is that people react unfavorably to events. The disorder then is in the way they act or feel. The third component involves how other people act toward or expect of a mentally ill person. (p. 563)

2. Clients are classified along five axes. Axis 1 lists disorders that have a particular time of onset and a realistic probability of recovery. Axis 2 lists disorders that persist throughout life, such as personality disorders and mental retardation. Axis 3 lists physical disorders, such as diabetes or cirrhosis of the liver. Axis 4 involves an evaluation of stress. Axis 5 is an overall evaluation of the person's level of functioning. (p. 565)

3. The therapist would ask me to lie down on a couch and say anything that comes to mind. I would be asked to free associate and not censor or omit anything. The therapist would interpret what I say. I might also be asked to describe my dreams, and the therapist would find meaning in them. He would try to look beyond the manifest content and find the latent content of my dreams. He would also expect me to show transference. (p. 569)

4. The humanistic therapist would not try to interpret or direct the therapy as the psychoanalytic therapist would. The humanistic therapist would not look for unconscious motives, but rather she would allow the client to explore his own feelings. The humanistic therapist would show unconditional positive regard and be totally accepting of everything the client says. In person-centered therapy, the "cure" comes from the client himself; in psychoanalytic therapy, the "cure" comes from the interpretation and direction of the therapist. (pp. 569, 574, Table 15.3)

5. Reinforcement is given whenever the client exhibits a target behavior, in this case whenever weight is gained. In one successful case, a woman was confined to a hospital room and was not allowed to leave. She was reinforced for weight gain with radio or television, reading material, the opportunity to leave the room, or the right to have visitors. (p. 571)

6. In group therapy, a group of 7-8 people with similar problems are treated at once. They can spread the cost of the therapy among group members and they also can work on interpersonal relationships. Self-help groups are similar to group therapy, except there is no therapist. People talk with each other and try to help each other. Family systems therapy is a special type of group therapy in which entire families are treated to improve communication and interaction among family members. Each family member often has problems, and all must be resolved for an individual to be helped. (pp. 575, 577)

7. An early assessment of therapy suggested that treated people were no better off than people who were not treated. However, more recent studies have shown that the average psychotherapy patient improves more than 80% of all untreated people. All the common, mainstream therapies are about equal in effectiveness. There is some evidence that an inexperienced lay person can be as helpful as a licensed therapist. (pp. 578-579)

8. Psychotherapy requires a commitment to change one's life. A therapeutic alliance is formed between the therapist and the client that is characterized by acceptance, caring, respect, and attention. Clients talk about beliefs, emotions, and actions and gain self-understanding. The therapist conveys an expectation that the client will improve. Actual improvement, however, may depend largely on the client's commitment to work on problems outside the therapy sessions. (p. 581)

9. Older mental hospitals were large hospitals built by states to house severely disturbed people who would probably never return to society. These hospitals often resembled prisons. The advent of antidepressant and anti-schizophrenic drugs have reduced the number of long-term residents so that the mental hospital population declined. The goal now is to supply short-term care until the patient can return home. Community mental health centers and halfway houses have become alternatives to large state hospitals. These types of care are effective, but many people who would have been in large hospitals are now in nursing homes, prisons, or they are homeless. (p. 584)

10. Some people with psychological disturbances fail to recognize that there is anything wrong with them. One argument is that such people should be treated. The arguments against such treatment are that families often put unwanted relatives in institutions and psychiatrists may overuse ECT and drugs. With "preventive detention," psychologically disturbed people who are considered dangerous to society can be put in mental hospitals against their will. This raises the question of how responsible a therapist is for a client who warned her or him about intended violence. (p. 585)

POSTTEST

Take this test with all of your books and notes out of sight. This should give you a good idea of how well you understand the material. The answers are on p. 242.

Matching

Put the letter of the psychotherapy in the blank beside the description.

Psychotherapy

1. _____ sets explicit goals for changing behavior and emphasizes people's interpretations of situations

2. _____ attempts to change people's inappropriate beliefs

3. _____ uses free association and dream analysis

4. _____ doesn't rely on talking as main method

5. _____ frees client from inhibiting social influences so client can solve own problems

6. _____ may use any type of therapy, but treats several family members

7. _____ involves no therapist

A. person-centered therapy

B. self-help group

C. cognitive-behavior therapy

D. family systems therapy

E. psychoanalysis

F. rational-emotive therapy

G. behavior therapy

Multiple-choice
Circle the best alternative

Overview of Abnormal Behavior

1. Multiple personality:
   a. is another term for schizophrenia
   b. means that the person has a single, seriously disordered personality
   c. is one of the most common mental disorders
   d. is diagnosed less often now than in the past
   e. means that one has several distinct personalities

2. What is the problem with statistics about the frequencies of mental disorders?
   a. they may be misleading because psychological disorders are a matter of degree
   b. it is impossible to give differential diagnoses to psychological disorders
   c. too many people show no symptoms at all
   d. there are no accepted guidelines for diagnosis
   e. both b and d

3. Which of the following is not an axis of DSM-IV?
   a. list of disorders that involve use of addictive substances
   b. list of disorders that last throughout life
   c. list of physical disorders
   d. evaluation of how much stress a person must endure
   e. evaluation of person's overall level of functioning

Psychotherapy

4. A therapist asks you to describe your dream and he then interprets it for you. The therapist is probably using which therapy?
   a. humanistic
   b. person-centered
   c. psychoanalysis
   d. nondirective
   e. behavioral

5. A client is angry that the therapy doesn't seem to be helping and he tells the therapist, "I'm going to stop coming if things don't get better soon". A therapist using person-centered therapy is likely to respond:
   a. you are angry with me because you are treating me like your father
   b. thinking that everything must work quickly is irrational
   c. you must not let such thoughts enter your mind or the therapy will never work
   d. think about what you can do to make me happy
   e. so you don't think this is helping; tell me more

6. How does aversion therapy differ from most behavior therapy programs?
   a. it is based on operant conditioning; most behavior therapy programs are based on classical conditioning
   b. aversion therapy deals more with thoughts; behavior therapy programs deal with specific behaviors
   c. aversion therapy is very similar to systematic desensitization; behavior therapy is similar to implosive therapy
   d. aversion therapy relies on punishment; behavior therapy usually relies on positive reinforcement

7. Which type of therapy focuses more on changing what people do than what they think?
   a. behavior therapy
   b. rational-emotive therapy
   c. cognitive therapy
   d. psychoanalysis
   e. person-centered therapy.

8. Cognitive therapists differ from rational-emotive therapists in that they:
   a. try to help people substitute more favorable beliefs; rational emotive therapists don't
   b. focus more on past experiences than rational-emotive therapists
   c. focus on behavior much more than rational-emotive therapists
   d. try to get clients to examine the evidence underlying their beliefs; rational emotive therapists often tell clients their thoughts are irrational
   e. cognitive therapists treat the family as a unit; rational emotive therapists treat individuals

9. Why might self-help groups be preferred over other types of group therapy?
   a. the treatment takes place over a strictly limited period of time
   b. people can work on how they relate to others
   c. all members are available to one another at any time, without charge
   d. self-help group leaders have greater education and experience
   e. self-help groups treat the entire family and not an individual alone

10 Brief therapy:
   a. is less effective than long-term therapy, although it is cheaper
   b. is ineffective, but so are most therapies
   c. usually lasts less than 1 month
   d. usually makes a client begin dealing with main problems promptly
   e. involves a time limit set by the therapist, but that is unknown to the client

11. All psychotherapists:
   a. only treat people with identifiable psychological disorders
   b. try to get clients to commit to making changes
   c. concentrate on getting clients to understand the reasons behind their behaviors
   d. try to change clients' irrational thoughts
   e. allow therapy to go on as long as is necessary

12. State mental hospitals:
    a. have shifted from having a goal of short-term care to long-term custody
    b. usually provide therapy by psychologists and psychiatrists
    c. provide much better care than community health centers
    d. are often prisonlike even today
    e. have received large increases in funding as their goals have changed

13. Deinstitutionalization has:
    a. successfully moved most patients from mental institutions to community-based care
    b. may have helped to increase the number of homeless people
    c. forced states to plan adequate alternatives for care and housing
    d. resulted in more cost to states because alternative care is more expensive than hospitals
    e. has been unsuccessful because populations in mental institutions have actually increased rather than decreased

14. Which of the following is true?
    a. psychiatrists say that patients who refuse treatment show hostility, emotional withdrawal, and disordered thinking
    b. more people would be judged insane by the M'Naghten Rule than by the Model Penal Code
    c. according to the Durham rule, a person is insane if he did not know the nature and quality or the act he was doing, or if he didn't know it was wrong
    d. the laws concerning involuntary commitment are the same from state to state
    e. psychiatrists usually agree on whether a defendant is sane or insane

15. A community psychologist practicing secondary prevention might do which of the following?
    a. start an afternoon recreation program for teenagers
    b. conduct an education program for older women returning to the workforce
    c. open a halfway house for homeless people with borderline mental disorders
    d. work to ban toxins that can cause brain damage
    e. open high quality day care centers

ANSWERS TO POSTTEST

Correct Answer	Questions Testing a Similar Concept	
	Comprehension Check	Short-Answer

Matching

1. C (p. 573)	8	--
2. F (p. 573)	6,8a	--
3. E (pp. 569-570)	3,4b	3,4
4. G (pp. 571-572)	4,5	4
5. A (p. 574)	7,8d	4
6. D (p. 575)	10	6
7. B (p. 577)	10d	6

Multiple-Choice

1. e (pp. 562-563)	--	--
2. a (p. 561)	1	2
3. a (p. 565)	2	--
4. c (p. 570)	4	3,4
5. e (p. 574)	7,8d	4
6. d (p. 572)	5c	--
7. a (p. 571)	4,5	5
8. d (p. 573)	6	--
9. c (p. 577)	10d	6
10. d (p. 575)	9e	--
11. b (p. 581)	12	8
12. d (p. 584)	13	9
13. b (pp. 584-585)	14d	--
14. a (p. 585)	14,15	9,10
15. c (p. 588)	16	--

CHAPTER 16 ABNORMALITIES AND THERAPIES II: EXPLORATIONS OF SPECIFIC DISORDERS

OBJECTIVES

Anxiety and Avoidance Disorders

I. Many psychological disorders are marked by fear, anxiety and attempts to avoid anxiety (p. 593)
   A. Generalized anxiety disorder involves exaggerated worries (p. 593)
   B. Panic disorders involve a fairly constant state of anxiety plus occasional panic attacks and overresponse to mild stressors (pp. 593-594, Figs. 16.1, 16.2)
      1. Social phobia involves an avoidance of other people (p. 594)
      2. Agoraphobia is an excessive fear of open places (p. 594)
II. Some disorders involve exaggerated avoidance (p. 595)
   A. Avoidance behaviors are resistant to extinction (p. 595)
      1. Avoidance behaviors persist long after the response is unnecessary (p. 595)
   B. Phobias are strong fears that interfere with everyday living (pp. 595-596)
      1. 11% of the population suffers from a phobia at some time (p. 596)
      2. Phobias may be learned from classical conditioning (p. 596)
      3. Phobias may also develop by observing fearful others (pp. 597-598)
         a. Observers need to know what the fearful other is frightened of to develop a fear (p. 598, Fig. 16.6)
      4. People may be prepared to develop some phobias (pp. 598-599)
         a. People develop phobias most easily to unpredictable and uncontrollable objects (p. 599)
      5. Phobias may persist because exposure to the objects doesn't occur (p. 599)
      6. Systematic desensitization and flooding are effective therapies for phobias (pp. 599-600)
   C. Phobias and other anxieties may be treated with drugs (p. 600)
      1. Benzodiazepines relieve anxiety, relax muscles, and induce sleep (p. 600)
         a. They facilitate transmission at synapses using GABA (p. 600, Fig. 16.9)
   D. Obsessive-compulsive disorder involves unwelcome thoughts and repetitive behaviors (pp. 600-601)
      1. Obsessions may stem from trying not to think of something (p. 601)
      2. One type of compulsion is cleaning excessively (p. 601)
      3. Another type of compulsion is checking excessively (pp. 601-602)
      4. There is some evidence for a genetic basis (p. 603)
      5. Psychotherapy and drugs may help (p. 603)
         a. Exposure therapy exposes people to the situation and prevents the rituals from being performed (p. 603)
         b. Clomipramine which prolongs the neurotransmitter serotonin seems to help some people (p. 603)

The message: Emotions, cognitions, and the link between them are important in excessive anxieties (p. 603).

Substance-Related Disorders

III. Substance dependence (addiction) occurs when a person cannot quit a self-destructive habit (p. 605)
   A. Most addictive drugs stimulates dopamine receptors in the brain (p. 606)
   B. The more rapidly a substance enters the brain, the more likely it is to be addictive (p. 606)
IV. Some people may be predisposed to become addicted to drugs (pp. 606-607)
   A. Genetics plays some role in alcoholism (p. 607)

B. Sons of alcoholics respond differently to alcohol than others (pp. 608-609)
   1. Alcohol provides more stress reduction for sons of alcoholics than for others (p. 608)
   2. Sons of alcoholics underestimate how much they have drunk (p. 608)
   3. Young men who underestimate how intoxicated they are more likely to become alcoholics later than young men who report more intoxication (p. 608)
V. Treatments for addictions are only moderately successful (pp. 609-610)
  A. Alcoholics Anonymous uses self-help groups (p. 609)
  B. Antabuse makes people ill if they drink (pp. 609-610)
  C. It is not clear that substance abuse is a disease (pp. 610-611)
  D. Whether alcoholics can learn to drink in moderation is controversial (p. 611)
  E. Methadone is the most common treatment for opiate addiction (pp. 611-612)

The message: Substance abuse is costly to society as well as to individuals (p. 612).

Mood Disorders

VI. Major depression lasts most of each day for months and involves little interest, little pleasure, and little reason for productive activity (p. 614)
  A. Some people may be genetically predisposed to depression (p. 615)
  B. Depression is more common in women than in men (pp. 615-616)
   1. Postpartum depression occurs after childbirth (p. 615)
   2. Women may ruminate more about depression than men (p. 616)
  C. Unpleasant events often cause depression (p. 616)
   1. Some people are more vulnerable than others (p. 616)
VII. Depressed people may focus on the unpleasant side of life (p. 616)
  A. Learned helplessness may be a cause of depression (pp. 616-617)
   1. Animals don't learn to escape if they had earlier learned that there was no escape (p. 616)
  B. People may become depressed because of their attributions for failure (pp. 617-618)
   1. People who make internal attributions for failure have a pessimistic explanatory style (p. 617)
VIII. Depression can be treated with psychotherapy or drugs (pp. 618-619)
  A. Aaron Beck pioneered cognitive therapy for depression (p. 618)
   1. Clients are invited to examine evidence for their beliefs (p. 618)
  B. There are three main classes of drugs (pp. 618-619, Fig. 16.17)
   1. Tricyclics block reabsorption of neurotransmitters (p. 619)
   2. Monoamine oxidase inhibitors (MAOIs) block metabolic breakdown of released neurotransmitters (p. 619)
   3. Second-generation antidepressants block serotonin reabsorption (p. 619)
  C. Cognitive therapy is slightly more effective than drugs, but drugs are faster and cheaper than therapy (pp. 619-620)
   1. Drugs work better than placebos (p. 619)
   2. Drugs have side-effects (p. 619)
  D. Electroconvulsive therapy (ECT) produces a convulsion, which alleviates depression (p. 620)
   1. Why this works is unclear (p. 620)
   2. It is controversial because its effects may only be temporary and it has a history of being misused (p. 620)
IX. People with seasonal affective disorder are depressed in winter (pp. 620-621)
X. People with bipolar disorder alternate between mania and depression (pp. 621-622)
  A. In the depression phase, people may wish they were dead (p. 621)
  B. In the manic phase, people follow impulses and are very active (pp. 621-622
  C. Longer periods of depression usually alternate with shorter periods of mania (p. 622)
  D. Lithium is an effective treatment for bipolar disorder (p. 622)

1. It isn't a cure because symptoms return after the drug is stopped (p. 622)

XI. Suicide frequently accompanies depression (p. 622)

    A. Women attempt suicide more often than men, but more men die by suicide (p. 623, Fig. 16.21)

    B. People who are thinking about suicide need professional help (p. 623)

The message: *Depression is more than sadness; it is an inability to feel happy, no matter what good events occur (p. 624).*

Schizophrenia

XII. In schizophrenia, the emotions and the intellect seem to be separated (p. 626, Fig. 16.22)

    A. Schizophrenia afflicts about 1% of people at some point in their lives (p. 626)

    B. Hallucinations occur when sensory experiences don't correspond to the outside world (pp. 626-627)

    C. Delusions are unfounded beliefs (p. 627)

    D. People with schizophrenia may show little sign of emotion (p. 627)

    E. People with schizophrenia show loose and idiosyncratic associations (pp. 627-628)

    F. Symptoms of schizophrenia are positive and negative (p. 628)

        1. Positive symptoms, such as hallucinations, delusions, and thought disorder, are present (p. 628)

            a. Positive psychotic symptoms are hallucinations and delusions (p. 628)

            b. Positive disorganized symptoms are thought disorder, bizarre behavior, and inappropriate emotions (p. 628)

        2. Negative symptoms, such as lack of emotional expression, lack of social interaction, are absent (p. 628)

XIII. There are several types of schizophrenia (pp. 628-629)

    A. Undifferentiated has basic symptoms (p. 628)

    B. Catatonic includes movement disorders (p. 628, Fig. 16.24)

    C. Disorganized is characterized by incoherent speech, lack of social relationships, and odd behavior (p. 628)

    D. Paranoid includes hallucinations and delusions (p. 629)

XIV Schizophrenia has multiple causes (p. 629)

    A. Minor, widespread brain damage accompanies schizophrenia (pp. 629-630, Fig. 16.25)

    B. Genetics and prenatal environment may predispose people to schizophrenia (pp. 630-631, Fig. 16.26)

        1. A marker for schizophrenia is a failure to filter out irrelevant information (p. 630)

        2. Another marker is an inability to move the eyes smoothly while tracking an object (p. 630)

    C. Mothers may catch viruses that result in prenatal brain damage (pp. 631-632)

    D. Experience plays a role in schizophrenia (p. 632)

        1. The "bad mother" theory has been discounted (p. 632)

        2. Stress may aggravate a predisposition to schizophrenia (p. 632)

XV. Neuroleptic drugs are effective in treating schizophrenia (p. 632)

    A. They work by blocking dopamine receptors (p. 632)

        1. Excessive dopamine may be the underlying cause of schizophrenia (p. 632)

        2. The underlying cause may be deficient stimulation of glutamate synapses (p. 632)

    B. Tardive dyskinesia (a movement disorder) is a side effect (pp. 632-633)

    C. Psychotherapy can be a valuable adjunct to drug therapy (p. 633)

The message: *People who are diagnosed with schizophrenia may be very different so researchers wonder whether schizophrenia may be several disorders (p. 633).*

COMPREHENSION CHECK

Answer these questions soon after reading the chapter. Circle the *best* alternative. Check your answers, pp. 250-252. If you gave a wrong answer, try to write why it was wrong. Check your reasons, pp. .250-252.

Anxiety and Avoidance Disorders

1. Mary occasionally experiences severe chest pains, sweating, faintness and shaking. At first she thought she was having heart attacks but her doctor says she is fine. Mary likely suffers from:
   a. phobia
   b. obsessive-compulsive disorder
   c. panic disorder
   d. dissociative disorder
   e. a lack of generalized anxiety

Correct _____ If wrong, why? _____

2. Which of the following is a phobia?
   a. Jean looks the other way when the cobra bites the hero in the movie
   b. Mary tries to squash the spiders in her hotel room in a slum area so they don't bite her
   c. Gladys looks around fearfully as she goes to the bank in a "bad" area with a large sum of money
   d. Susan has stopped gardening because there might be a snake outside
   e. all of the above are phobias

Correct _____ If wrong, why? _____

3. Watson and Rayner made a loud sound at the same time that Little Albert saw a white rat. Albert came to fear white rats. Which of the following is true?
   a. the sound is the CS; the rat is the UCS
   b. fear to the sound is the CR; fear to the rat is the UCR
   c. the sound is the UCS; fear to it is the CR
   d. the rat is the CS; fear to it is the CR

Correct _____ If wrong, why? _____

4. Lab monkeys show a fear of snakes:
   a. from birth; apparently the fear is genetic
   b. after watching a wild-born monkey show fear, even though the snake is out of sight
   c. after watching a wild-born monkey show fear, with the snake in sight
   d. only if they have been specifically conditioned to fear snakes with something like a shock as the UCS

Correct _____ If wrong, why? _____

5. The therapist is treating Susan's phobia of snakes by asking her to imagine herself at the bottom of a pit of 1,000 snakes. She cannot escape as they crawl all around on her and some bite her. The type of therapy is:
   a. implosion
   b. systematic desensitization
   c. similar to Skinner's shaping procedure
   d. b and c
   e. gradual exposure to the feared object via virtual reality

Correct _____ If wrong, why? _____

6. A person who constantly thinks about dying has:
   a. a compulsion
   b. an obsession
   c. a preparedness reaction
   d. a checker reaction
   e. a cleaner reaction

Correct _____ If wrong, why? ___Stick with most—the aversions are not as hard as you think.___

Substance-Related Disorders

7. Addictive substances:
   a. usually stimulate dopamine synapses in the brain
   b. enter the brain more slowly than non-addictive substances
   c. are addictive because of their characteristics, independent of the circumstances of use
   d. are more likely to cause addiction if they are eaten than if they are smoked

Correct _____ If wrong, why? _____

8. Sons of alcoholics:
   a. show less of a decline in stress when they drink alcohol than sons of nonalcoholics
   b. who sway more after drinking are more likely to become alcoholics later than those who sway less
   c. underestimate the amount of alcohol they have drunk
   d. who reported feeling intoxicated after drinking were more likely to become alcoholics than those who didn't feel intoxicated

Correct _____ If wrong, why? _____

9. Alcoholism:
   a. must be treated with total abstinence to prevent relapse
   b. may be treated with disulfiram, which produces a threat of sickness
   c. is clearly a progressive disease, because alcoholics always grow worse with time if they do not abstain
   d. is little affected by environmental factors, giving good evidence for the disease concept
   e. is best treated by controlled drinking

Correct _____ If wrong, why? _____

Mood Disorders

10. Joe suffers from major depression; it is severe and has lasted for several months. Joe has always blamed himself for failure. Joe's depression is probably:
    a. a postpartum depression
    b. bipolar
    c. due to learned helplessness
    d. related to a pessimistic explanatory style

Correct _____ If wrong, why? _____

11. A type of evidence that there is a genetic predisposition to depression is that:
    a. some women show postpartum depression following childbirth
    b. some types of depression respond better to drugs than to psychotherapy
    c. adopted children usually have more adoptive than biological relatives who are depressed
    d. relatives of depressed people are more likely to be depressed than other people

Correct _____ If wrong, why? _____

12. Dogs are held in place in a shuttle box while a tone precedes a shock. Later, the dogs can jump to escape the shock. What happens?
    a. the dogs learn the escape response faster than animals who aren't shocked first, because they learn that a tone predicts shock
    b. the dogs show many symptoms of schizophrenia
    c. the dogs develop learned helplessness
    d. the dogs show seasonal affective disorder

Correct _____ If wrong, why? _____

13. Each of the people below has just failed two tests. Given the explanatory styles below, which person is most likely to become depressed?
    a. Greg, who thinks he failed because the tests were bad
    b. Sally, who thinks she failed because she is stupid
    c. Mary, who thinks she failed because she didn't study hard
    d. John, who thinks he failed because he partied all night

Correct _____ If wrong, why? _____

14. Cognitive therapy for depression:
    a. involves telling clients what to think
    b. was pioneered by Aaron Beck
    c. stresses interpretation of dreams
    d. uses bright lights to reduce depression
    e. is much less effective than drug therapy

Correct _____ If wrong, why? _____

15. The class of drugs called monoamine oxidase inhibitors:
    a. work by preventing the reuptake of serotonin
    b. block the reabsorption of serotonin, norepinephrine, and dopamine
    c. are made from natural substances that can't be patented
    d. cause tardive dyskinesia as a side effect
    e. block the metabolic breakdown of serotonin, norepinephrine, and dopamine

Correct _____ If wrong, why? _____

16. Why would ECT be used rather than antidepressant drugs?
    a. antidepressant drugs decrease certain neurotransmitter molecules, but ECT increases them; an increase is helpful to some patients
    b. it has much more permanent effects than drugs
    c. drugs only help 20-30% of all depressed people
    d. ECT takes effect faster than drugs
    e. drugs produce side effects, such as nausea and blurred vision, even if the dose is only slightly greater than the recommended level

Correct _____ If wrong, why? _____

17. Rob recently quit his job and sold his house, and is building a sports shop in Aruba that will specialize in snow skiing. This is a great idea because there are no such shops on the tropical island of Aruba. Rob probably has:
    a. severe unipolar depression
    b. schizophrenia
    c. seasonal affective disorder
    d. mania

Correct _____ If wrong, why? _____

Schizophrenia

18. The term <u>schizophrenia</u> refers to:
    a. bipolar as compared with unipolar disorder
    b. split personality--a person who alternates between two or more personalities
    c. a split between emotional and intellectual aspects of personality
    d. a person who alternates between extreme happiness and extreme sadness

Correct _____ If wrong, why? _____

19. A patient who has been diagnosed as schizophrenic thinks that "they" are trying to control his mind. This person has what type of schizophrenia?
    a. undifferentiated
    b. paranoid
    c. catatonic
    d. disorganized
    e. delusion of grandeur

Correct _____ If wrong, why? _____

20. Schizophrenia is:
    a. more likely to be diagnosed in younger than older adults
    b. more common in women than men
    c. usually characterized by sudden onset
    d. develops in adults who had many friends as children
    e. probably caused by a bad mother

Correct _____ If wrong, why? _____

21. According to the dopamine theory of schizophrenia, drugs that are effective for schizophrenia:
    a. reverse the impaired development of the nervous system
    b. reduce symptoms by blocking dopamine synapses
    c. reduce symptoms by increasing activity at dopamine synapses
    d. work by shrinking the ventricles in the brain
    e. work by directly stimulating glutamate synapses

Correct _____ If wrong, why? _____

ANSWERS AND EXPLANATIONS FOR COMPREHENSION CHECK

Correct Answer	Other Alternatives Are Wrong Because:

1. c (p. 593)
   Obj. I-B

   a. her anxiety is not attached to a specific object
   b. doesn't have repetitive thoughts or actions
   d. hasn't separated one set of memories from others
   e. too much anxiety; persists when there is nothing to be anxious about

2. d (pp. 595-596)
   Obj. II-B

   a. normal; doesn't interfere with her life
   b. her fear is not irrational; she's doing something about it
   c. her fear is rational and limited to one situation
   e. see a, b, and c

3. d (p. 597, Fig. 16.5)
   Obj. II-B-2

   a. children naturally fear loud sounds, so that is the UCS; the rat is the CS
   b. Albert showed no natural fear of the rat, so fear to it is the CR; fear to sound is UCR
   c. fear to sound is UCR

4. c (pp. 597-598)
   Obj. II-B-3-a

   a. lab-reared monkeys show no fear of snakes
   b. lab-reared monkey has to see the snake also to develop the fear
   d. can be learned via observational learning; direct conditioning is not necessary

5. a (p. 599)
   Obj. II-B-6

   b. the feared stimulus would be exposed gradually and the person would remain relaxed while imagining
   c. b is similar to shaping, which involves gradual increases in mastery of the response
   d. see b
   e. exposure here isn't gradual; it's sudden

6. b (p. 601)
   Obj. II-D-1

a. not unless repetitive behavior also occurs
c. means that some things are easily learned because of evolutionary influences; not relevant
d. not unless he constantly checks his body for physical symptoms
e. not unless he constantly washes and bathes

7. a (p. 605)
   Obj. III-A

b. addictive substances enter it faster
c. depending upon how a substance is used, it may or may not be addictive; addiction is in the user
d. smoking is more likely to be addictive because the substance enters the brain faster

8. c (p. 608)
   Obj. IV-B-2

a. they showed more decline in stress after alcohol
b. it's the opposite; those who become alcoholic sway less
d. it's the opposite; those who didn't feel intoxicated were more likely to become alcoholics

9. b (pp. 609-610)
   Obj. V-B

a. alcoholics treated with abstinence also relapse
c. some don't grow worse
d. environmental factors, such as an improved family life and new interests, can help
e. controversial; such treatment may not work for many alcoholics

10. d (p. 614)
    Obj. VII-B-1

a. women sometimes develop this after giving birth
b. must have manic phases also
c. no specific evidence that he has learned to fail; not considered a viable explanation anymore

11. d (p. 615)
    Obj. VI-A

a. may show a relation between depression and hormones, not genetics
b. true, but not evidence for a genetic component
c. it's the opposite; more depression among biological relatives

12. c (p. 616)
    Obj. VII-A-1

a. instead, they learn that they are helpless and don't try to escape later
b. show signs of depression
d. occurs in humans, not dogs; becoming depressed during a specific season, usually winter

13. b (p. 617)
    Obj. VII-B

a. external; his attribution is outside of himself
c. internal, but unstable; she can study more next time
d. can attribute failure to partying

14. b (pp. 618)
    Obj. VIII-A

a. no, this is more likely in rational-emotive therapy
c. this would occur in psychoanalysis
d. treatment for seasonal affective disorder
e. cognitive therapy is slightly more effective than drug therapy

15. e (p. 619, Fig. 16.17)
     Obj. VIII-B-2

a. second-generation antidepressants do this
b. tricyclics for depression do this
c. lithium for bipolar disorder is a natural substance
d. side effect of neuroleptic drugs, used for schizophrenia

16. d (p. 620)
     Obj. VIII-B,D

a. drugs increase these neurotransmitters; ECT may do the same
b. the effects of ECT are temporary
c. drugs help 50-70%; placebos help 20-30%
e. side effects of lithium, used for bipolar disorder

17. d (pp. 620-621)
     Obj. X-B

a. is showing mania, so can't have unipolar depression
b. no evidence that social relations and self-care have deteriorated
c. he isn't depressed, he's manic

18. c (p. 626)
     Obj. XII

a. bipolar alternates between mania and depression; unipolar is
   depression only; neither is schizophrenia
b. multiple personality, a different disorder
d. manic-depressive disorder

19. b (pp. 628-629)
     Obj. XIII-D

a. basic symptoms, but not delusion of persecution
c. no movement disorders here
d. no evidence for incoherent speech or silly behavior
e. the patient may have delusions of grandeur, but that is not a type of
   schizophrenia

20. a (p. 629-630)
     Obj. XIV

b. equally common in men and women
c. usually gradual onset
d. opposite; schizophrenics had few friends as children
e. probably not; it develops after child is independent of mother and
   occurs even if child is adopted and raised by normal mother

21. b (p. 632)
     Obj. XV-A

a. neurodevelopmental hypothesis is a theory of schizophrenia; drugs
   can't change development that occurred before or at birth
c. drugs for depression may do this
d. ventricles are enlarged, but drugs don't do anything to this
   condition
e. drugs may stimulate glutamate synapses but it's because they block
   dopamine synapses; this is the glutamate hypothesis

LECTURE MATERIAL

Don't forget to review your lecture material. Process each topic meaningfully. First, be sure that you understand the material in each lecture--if you don't, ask your instructor or teaching assistant. Associate the material with things that you already know and with your personal experiences. If you can make up mental images of any of the material, do so. Try to think of real-life applications of the concepts. Write comments on each day's lecture notes. Then write questions to cover each concept.

SHORT-ANSWER ESSAY QUESTIONS

Write brief answers to each of the following. The answers are on pp. 255-257, but do try to write the answers yourself before looking at them.

Anxiety and Avoidance Disorders

1. Explain how superstitions are related to phobias.

2. Describe the experiment with monkeys in which they learned fear by watching other monkeys who were afraid.

3. Describe how systematic desensitization might be used to treat someone who fears elevators. How might this be modified to use virtual reality technology?

4. Describe an experiment that shows how memory in obsessive-compulsive "checkers" may differ from that of normal people.

Substance-Related Disorders

5. Discuss the things that make a substance addictive.

6. What are two ways in which the sons of alcoholic parents differ from the sons of non-alcoholic parents?

7. Describe the view of alcoholism taken by Alcoholics Anonymous. What is the alternative view?

8. Describe how methadone has been used to help people who are addicted to opiates.

Mood Disorders

9. Discuss the risk factors involved in depression.

10. Describe the learned-helplessness theory. How has it been modified to help to explain depression?

11. Explain how antidepressant drugs work.

12. Describe ECT and the conditions under which it is used today.

13. Describe seasonal affective disorder.

14. Describe the bipolar cycles in people with bipolar disorder.

Schizophrenia

15. What symptoms must a person show to be diagnosed as schizophrenic?

16. Discuss three characteristics of disordered thought in schizophrenia.

17. Discuss the evidence for a genetic predisposition to schizophrenia.

****

Find the questions that you wrote over lecture material and write answers to them.

****

ANSWERS TO SHORT-ANSWER ESSAY QUESTIONS

1. Superstitions are behaviors that cannot be expected to be effective. People persist in them because nothing goes wrong if they do them and, if something does go wrong, they assume that they did not try hard enough. Phobias are similar in that if people avoid the feared object, they never get hurt by it. Because they don't get close to it, they never learn that it really is harmless. (p. 595)

2. Lab-reared monkeys have no fear of snakes, but wild-reared monkeys show a strong fear of snakes. A lab-reared and a wild-reared monkey both saw a snake. Later, when the lab-reared monkey saw a snake, it showed fear. The lab-reared monkey had to see that it was a snake that the wild-reared monkey was afraid of; simply seeing the wild-reared monkey show fear was   not enough for the lab-reared monkey to develop a fear. (pp. 597-598)

3. The person would first be taught to relax. Then, while in a relaxed state, she would be asked to imagine something that is not very frightening, such as looking at an elevator across the room. Then she would be asked to imagine gradually more frightening things until she is finally able to imagine being in an elevator that is stuck between floors. If the distress becomes too severe at some point, she would go back to imagining an easier scene. In the high-tech version, the client is given a helmet that displays a virtual-reality scene, so that the client can feel as if he or she is actually present in the scene. The therapist can change the scene to gradually expose the client to progressively more frightening situations, and the display can be turned off if the client becomes too fearful. (p. 599)

4. Subjects read a word and thought of an associated word. Later, they were asked to identify which words they had read and which words they had only thought. The two groups were equally accurate in their identifications, but the obsessive-compulsive group was less confident in their answers. They may not trust their memories as much. (pp. 601-602)

5. Drugs that enter the bloodstream quickly are more likely to be addictive than drugs that enter more slowly. A given drug is more addictive if it is taken in a way that makes it enter the bloodstream more quickly; e.g., injected cocaine is more addictive than sniffed cocaine. One theory is that addictive substances all activate dopamine synapses and produce reinforcing effects. Actually, almost any substance can become addictive, but the addiction is in the user and not in the substance itself. (pp. 605-606)

6. Young men whose fathers were and were not alcoholics were placed in stressful situations. Half of the men were given alcohol to drink before the stressful situation. Drinking alcohol reduced heart rate and resulted in less reported anxiety. However, these effects were larger in the sons of alcoholics than in the other men. In a second study, sons of alcoholics and nonalcoholics drank varying amounts of vodka. They then estimated how much they had drunk and how intoxicated they were. The sons of alcoholics underestimated how much they had drunk and how intoxicated they were. Later, men who had underestimated the most were the most likely to develop into alcoholics (p. 608)

7. AA believes that alcoholism is a disease that will grow worse with time and that can only be helped by total abstinence. A single drink can cause a complete collapse in control. The disease view downplays the importance of environmental factors. An alternative view is that drinking is a habit that can be controlled. Whether or not controlled drinking works is still controversial. (pp. 609-610)

8. Many addicts continue to have recurring urges to take opiates even after the withdrawal symptoms have subsided. Methadone can be taken in pill form, which does not produce the "rush" associated with opiates, but it does satisfy the craving. People using methadone are still addicted to opiates; but many can hold a job, and they commit fewer crimes than when they were using heroin or morphine. (pp. 611-612)

9. There is a genetic component, in that depressed people are more likely to have biological relatives who are depressed than are nondepressed people. Depression is more common in women than men. Hormones may influence the timing of depression in women, because postpartum depression sometimes occurs after the birth of a child when hormonal changes are great. However, the hormonal changes may not cause depression but they may trigger an episode. Severe losses early in life may make people more vulnerable to depression and people with little social support may be more vulnerable. (pp. 615-616)

10. Animals who have learned that they cannot escape some bad event, such as shock, do not learn later that shocks are escapable. They learn that they are helpless. In humans, it isn't failing itself that results in depression, but why people think they've failed. People who make internal (the cause is within me), stable (it's a permanent characteristic), and global (it applies to many situations) attributions have a pessimistic explanatory style that is related to depression. (pp. 616-617)

11. Tricyclic drugs block the reabsorption of dopamine, norepinephrine, and serotonin by the axon's terminal button. MAOIs block the conversion of these neurotransmitters into nonactive molecules. Second-generation antidepressants are also known as serotonin reuptake blockers. They block the reuptake of serotonin. Thus, each type of drug increases the time period in which these neurotransmitters can activate surrounding neurons. (p. 619, Fig. 16.17)

12. Electroconvulsive therapy consists of a brief electric shock across the head. People are usually given muscle relaxants and anesthetics. It is used when antidepressant drugs have been ineffective, for people with serious thinking disorders, and for people who are suicidal. It works faster than drugs, so it is effective in suicidal patients. (p. 620)

13. Most people with this disorder become depressed in the winter and are normal or slightly manic in the summer. They seem to respond to the amount of sunlight they see each day. The disorder can be helped by having people sit in front of lights to artificially lengthen the day. Annual summer depressions also occur in some people. (pp. 620-621)

14. Mood alternates between mania, being constantly active and uninhibited, and depression, feeling helpless, guilt ridden, and sad. In the depressive phase, people have trouble sleeping and often contemplate suicide. In the manic phase, people may either be angry or happy. They have trouble inhibiting their impulses. They may show rambling speech, jumping from one topic to another. Each mood may last for months or just a few days. (p. 622)

15. The person must show a deterioration in daily activities for at least 6 months. This includes work activities, social relations, and self-care. In addition, a person must show at least two of the following: hallucinations, delusions, incoherent speech, grossly disorganized behavior, thought disorders, or a loss of normal emotional responses and social behaviors. However, if a person shows severe hallucinations or delusions, no other symptoms are necessary. (p. 626)

16. Use of loose associations and idiosyncratic associations: Illogical leaps and misuse of words.
Difficulties in using abstract concepts: Tendency to interpret everything literally.
Vague, roundabout ways of saying things: Saying things in complex rather than simple ways.
(pp. 627-628)

17. Adopted children who develop schizophrenia often have biological relatives who are schizophrenic. If one identical twin has schizophrenia, there is a 50% chance that the other one will, and both have an equal probability of having schizophrenic children whether or not both are schizophrenic. Environmental factors determine if the genes will show up, so the term genetic predisposition is used. Markers for whether or not schizophrenia will develop include a failure to filter out irrelevant information and rapid jerky eye movements instead of smooth movements when following a target. (pp. 630-631)

POSTTEST

Take this test with all of your books and notes out of sight. This should give you a good idea of how well you understand the material. The answers are on p. 262.

Matching

Put the letter of the disorder in the blank beside the description.

Mood Disorders and Schizophrenia

1. _____ includes silly behavior and incoherent speech

2. _____ People become depressed in winter and somewhat manic in summer

3. _____ deterioration of daily activities plus hallucinations, delusions, or thought disorder

4. _____ constantly suspicious in addition to basic symptoms

5. _____ alternate between being slow, inactive, and inhibited and very active and uninhibited

6. _____ includes movement disorders

7. _____ great sadness that lasts for months

A. undifferentiated schizophrenia

B. depression

C. paranoid schizophrenia

D. bipolar disorder

E. seasonal affective disorder

F. catatonic schizophrenia

G. disorganized schizophrenia

Multiple-choice

Circle the best alternative.

Anxiety and Avoidance Disorders

1. In panic disorder:
   a. people feel a strong state of anxiety in response to mild stress or exercise
   b. generalized anxiety attaches itself to a specific object
   c. people don't breath deeply enough
   d. people don't show a physiological response to stressful situations
   e. the panic attack usually lasts several hours

2. Which of the following is true about phobias?
   a. systematic desensitization is an effective therapy
   b. they are easily treated by explaining that there is no reason to be afraid
   c. "irrational fears" is the best definition
   d. people rarely show any physical symptoms when they confront the object
   e. they are more common for objects that are part of technological societies (guns, cars) than for natural objects (animals, lightning)

3. Watson and Rayner's study with Little Albert showed that phobias:
   a. represent unconscious desires
   b. are only developed to objects that have caused injury
   c. develop any time one animal observes another animal showing fear
   d. are genetic in that people are born with a few intense fears
   e. can develop through learning

4. What was the conditioned stimulus in the Little Albert study?
   a. the loud sound
   b. the white rat
   c. trembling to the loud sound
   d. trembling to the white rat
   e. the sight of Watson

5. What would a therapist using implosion do to treat a phobia of snakes?
   a. first try to discover the origin of the phobia
   b. have the client imagine being in a place with many snakes
   c. attempt to identify which type of snake was the UCS
   d. have the client begin by imaging a small picture of a snake and gradually work up to a large realistic image or to an actual snake
   e. have the client try to understand what snakes represent so that the real problem can be discussed

6. Which of the following is <u>not</u> characteristic of both obsessive-compulsive checkers and cleaners?
   a. drugs that inhibit the reuptake of serotonin usually help
   b. realize that their rituals are inappropriate
   c. are usually average or above average in intelligence
   d. feel better after their rituals
   e. tend to be hard-working, perfectionist people

7. How do the memories of obsessive-compulsive people differ from those of normal people?
   a. Obsessive-compulsive people are less able to remember what they did and what they thought
   b. Obsessive-compulsive people are much slower to learn in avoidance learning
   c. Obsessive-compulsive people are less confident in their judgments of what they did and what they thought
   d. Obsessive-compulsive people show very fast extinction in avoidance learning
   e. Obsessive-compulsive people are overconfident in the accuracy of their memories

<u>Substance-Related Disorders</u>

8. Alcohol addiction:
   a. may be more likely for sons of alcoholics because alcohol reduces stress more for them than for sons of nonalcoholics
   b. always gets worse and worse
   c. is best treated using the AA approach according to the research
   d. can easily be turned into controlled social drinking
   e. is independent of culture

9. Which of the following is true about the statement "alcoholism is a disease"?
   a. it is true because it fits all of the medical criteria for the term disease
   b. it is a bad definition because if makes alcoholics feel too guilty about their own role in their disorder
   c. it is true because alcoholism always gets progressively worse
   d. it is misleading because it downplays the role of environmental factors
   e. it is true because "controlled drinking" programs are unsuccessful

10. Why is methadone better as a morphine substitute than heroin?
    a. methadone does not produce the rush that heroin does and it does not produce rapid withdrawal symptoms
    b. methadone, when taken as a pill, is so fast-acting that it doesn't produce any rush, so addicts quickly stop using it
    c. methadone enters the brain faster than heroin
    d. methadone actually cures the addiction, heroin doesn't
    e. heroin is addictive, methadone is not

Mood Disorders

11. Why do women develop depression more often than men?
    a. hormonal changes in the menstrual cycle cause depression
    b. they have lower status and power
    c. women are likely to be diagnosed as depressed but men are likely to be diagnosed as alcoholic
    d. women ruminate more about depression whereas men distract themselves
    e. all of the above may contribute to depression, but none of the alternatives explain why there is a sex difference

12. Most antidepressant drugs work by:
    a. altering the pattern of blood flow in the brain
    b. making people forget that they are depressed
    c. affecting the chemical pathways within neurons
    d. prolonging the stimulation of dopamine, norepinephrine, or serotonin synapses in the brain
    e. increasing the body's ability to use vitamins, such as B-1

13. ECT probably works by:
    a. making the depressed person forget why he or she was depressed
    b. increasing stimulation of dopamine and norepinephrine synapses
    c. causing the patient to become ecstatic just before the seizure
    d. threatening the patient; he or she had better stop being depressed or more shocks will be given
    e. blocking dopamine receptors

14. A hospital removes all of the fire alarms from a floor because the patients continually pull them. The patients on this floor probably have:
    a. mania
    b. major depression
    c. learned helplessness
    d. an internal, stable, and global explanatory style
    e. seasonal affective disorder

15. John seems like two different people. One week he is extremely happy and uninhibited. The next month he is very depressed and can only think of suicide. John's disorder is:
    a. major depression
    b. learned helplessness
    c. suicidal tendencies
    d. multiple personality
    e. bipolar disorder

16. Lithium salts:
    a. are used to cure manic-depressive disorder
    b. produce side effects including nausea and blurred vision
    c. have been aggressively marketed by drug companies in the U.S.
    d. are especially effective for undifferentiated schizophrenia
    e. decrease the amount of dopamine in the brain

17. Suicide:
    a. is the most common cause of death among people over age 50
    b. attempts are more common among men than among women
    c. is not usually committed by people who talk about it
    d. is often committed by people who are depressed
    e. will not be committed by someone who has tried and failed

Schizophrenia

18 The term schizophrenia:
    a. means split personality, another name for multiple personality
    b. is Latin for premature senility
    c. comes from the Greek terms meaning disordered thought
    d. refers to a split between emotional and intellectual parts of personality
    e. refers to a split between the situation and a person's reactions to it

19. A person who believes that she has been selected to receive messages from outer space that will ultimately save the world has:
    a. delusions of persecution
    b. catatonic schizophrenia
    c. manic-depressive disorder
    d. undifferentiated schizophrenia
    e. delusions of grandeur

20. Which of the following is not a characteristic of the thought disorder of schizophrenia?
    a. highly limited vocabularies
    b. roundabout ways of saying simple things
    c. difficulty with abstract concepts
    d. use of loose and idiosyncratic associations
    e. literal interpretations of words

21. Which of the following is true about the cause of schizophrenia?
    a. there is some brain damage in that cerebral ventricles are too small
    b. since effective drugs work by blocking dopamine receptors, schizophrenics may have too little dopamine in their brain
    c. confusing signals from the mother may cause schizophrenia
    d. schizophrenia has no genetic component
    e. prenatal infections may result in brain damage that leads to schizophrenia

ANSWERS TO POSTTEST

Correct Answer	Questions Testing a Similar Concept	
	Comprehension Check	Short-Answer

Matching

1. G (p. 628)	19d	15
2. E (p. 620)	14d,17c	13
3. A (p. 628)	19d	15
4. C (p. 629)	19b	15
5. D (p. 621)	17	14
6. F (p. 628)	19c	15
7. B (p. 614)	10	--

Multiple-Choice

1. a (pp. 593-694)	3	--
2. a (pp. 595-596)	4	3
3. e (pp. 596-597)	5	--
4. b (p. 597)	5	--
5. b (p. 599)	7	--
6. d (pp. 601-602)	8	4
7. c (p. 602)	--	4
8. a (pp. 608)	7,9	6,7
9. d (pp. 610-611)	9	7
10. a (p. 611-612)	--	8
11. e (pp. 615-616)	11a	--
12. d (pp. 618-619, Fig. 16.17)	15	11
13. b (p. 620)	16	12
14. a (pp. 621-622)	17	14
15. e (pp. 612-622)	17	14
16. b (p. 622)	15c,16e	--
17. d (pp. 622-623)	--	--
18. d (p. 626)	18	15,16
19. e (p. 627)	19e	16
20. a (p. 628)	--	16
21. e (pp. 629-630)	20	17

GUIDE FOR NONNATIVE SPEAKERS

by Sally Gearhart

The purpose of *this* **guide for Nonnative Speakers of English** is to provide still another resource for you as you move through the Maki *Study Guide* that precedes this section and, of course, the course text, Kalat's **Introduction to Psychology.**

This particular section is broken down both in terms of lesson concepts and in terms of language to help you better comprehend the text material which may not be familiar to you.   It includes the following features:

<u>Prereading aids which give a sense of the direction or focus of each chapter:</u>

Key verbs: Verbs taken from the text which can help the reader predict chapter concepts.

Chapter organization exercises focusing on headings, chapter divisions, and cues such as bold print and italics.

Key Idea: A focus point or central idea taken from the chapter, usually including important quotes from the author.

Paraphrasing and summarizing practice to help you, the student, analyze concepts and put the author's ideas into your own words.

Outlining exercises: Practice in outlining sections of text to get a clearer understanding of how concepts fit together.

Structural Clues: Exercises to help you understand signals the writer uses to indicate cause and effect, contrast, example, emphasis, etc.

Scanning activities: Exercises that help you focus on a specific kind of information and locate it quickly. *Skimming activities* help you get general overviews.

Vocabulary Exercises: Word attack practice and rephrasing of idioms to help you build the vocabulary comprehension you need.

Recommended procedure for using this guide with <u>**Introduction to Psychology**</u>:

1. <u>Without</u> referring to a dictionary, get a general idea of the assigned chapter of the text by *skimming* through its content, including introduction, module headings, illustrations, concept checks, and ***The Message***.

2. **Refer to this guide section for nonnative speakers to get an idea of how to approach the assigned chapter,** that is, what to focus on first.

3. Start reading the assigned text chapter more slowly, **referring to this guide to help you as you move through the various sections.**

4. **Review the chapter material by referring to the regular *Study Guide*,** which precedes this section for Nonnative Speakers.

5. **Complete the exercises in <u>both sections of the *Study Guide*</u>** to help you understand and remember material in Kalat's <u>**Introduction to Psychology**</u>.

CHAPTER 1: WHAT IS PSYCHOLOGY?

<u>**Before you begin Chapter 1**</u>: *Pay attention to the organization of this chapter* to predict what is coming.

Key Verbs:	predict	assume	demonstrate	determine	influence	imply

Predicting: Seeing and Describing What is Coming Next:

A good way to understand a new topic is to *focus on what we already know about the topic.* Usually we have heard or seen words related to it before, and we have already formed some idea of what the subject covers.

Brainstorm the topic of **"psychology."** List your ideas below---in any order, using just simple words or phrases, not sentences. Note as many terms as you can in the space provided. Next, if possible, check with others to see if they agree. The list is started for you:

Ideas related to psychology:

Human behavior
Experiments

>>>>>**KEY IDEA:**
Now look at P.4 of the text, and underline the author's words, *" You have just encountered the theme of this book: Ask for the evidence. "* How do the terms you wrote relate to this idea of getting "evidence"? How closely do your terms relate to the definition of psychology the author provides on page 5, *"the systematic study of behavior and experience"?*

Creating questions about content:
Asking questions is another way to help us think about a topic. The description of *determinism* tells us that scientists *"made an assumption.... that everything that happens has a cause...."* <u>Make that into a question about what scientists believed, but couldn't prove:</u>
Example:
What did scientists who believe in "determinism" assume?

Now look for the author's answer again. When you find it, <u>underline</u> it; then copy it here.

_____

Go on in the chapter, paying special attention to questions the author is asking. Try to form an idea of the author's points of emphasis on the *relationship between the mind and the brain.*

Summarize the author's questions on the mind/brain connection here: *The author asks:*

_____

Can you find the answer to the question you wrote on the mind/brain relationship? Is there a definite answer?

*The answer I found seems to say......*_____

_____

Nature-Nurture: Look over this section and copy the question that best <u>covers</u> <u>its points</u> here: (Note: If you think the focus is only on sex differences, look again.)

_____

_____?

Write an answer for your question here:

_____

<u>Do the same question/answer pattern with the rest of the chapter</u>, which discusses different types of psychologists and their objectives. For each section, find a question that you can use, or, better, *form your own question by rewording, restating the questions in the text*. Then supply an answer based on your reading.

<u>Asking questions about text organization</u>:
Up to now we have been looking closely at ideas in the reading and asking questions about information within the example paragraphs. *Another kind of question to ask is about text organization*.

Ask yourself the following question: **"Is there any change in the focus of this section of the chapter as it moves from discussing research fields in psychology to another focus?"** What new, but related, focus did you find? Where?

<u>Practice making questions with the summary terms</u>. <u>Then answer them</u> without looking at the answers in the text.

Practice your new skills to aid your understanding of new material: *Predict chapter content* within **"Psychology Then and Now." (See Module 1.2.) Use brainstorming to come up with ideas that might be discussed in this section.**

<u>Psychology Then and Now</u>:

Read the section and <u>underline</u> ideas that connect to your predicted terms. **Then list below some key questions that you could create about important persons and concepts discussed.** Try to form your own questions.

Example: **What were Wilhelm Wundt's most important contributions to psychology?**
(Of course when you find the answer(s), underline them.)

Now look again at *text organization.* **What questions might you ask about the last part of the chapter after finishing the section on famous psychologists?   Circle below some concepts that fit:**
The Current (Present) Era in Psychology:

What are changes in the field?   What were common beliefs of the mid 1700's?

What did Darwin say?   What did Titchener believe about the structure of the mind?

What is important today about human diversity?

Word Attack:
Word endings, suffixes, help us understand the form of a word.   **Fill in the blanks for the suffix that fits the correct word category (part of speech) shown**. The first one is done for you:

Noun form +adjective suffix	Adjective Suffix: (-al; -cal)	Adverb Suffix: (-ally; -cally)
Biologist (-**cal**)	Biologi**cal**	Biologi**cally**
Psychologist (-cal)		
Development (-al)		
Environment (-al)		
Behaviorist (-al)		
Experiment (-al)		

Extending Your Vocabulary Knowledge
In addition to knowledge of word parts, knowledge of idioms and phrasal verbs is helpful.   The phrases below **express relationships.**

> --Write **R** next to those which express *result (effect).*
> --Write **C** next to those which express only a *connection.*

___derive from   ___ stem from   ___ associated with

___ to be due to   ___ depend on   ___ relate to

CHAPTER 2: SCIENTIFIC METHODS IN PSYCHOLOGY

Note: Before you begin Chapter 2:

1. Review Ch. 1 of both the Kalat text and the Maki Study Guide to be sure you have covered all key concepts and terms.
2. Next, pay attention to the organization of this section of the guide for <u>non native speakers</u> <u>of English</u>. It will give additional support as you move from chapter to chapter.

| Key Verbs: | claim | investigate | evaluate | measure | calculate | interpret |

Predict what is coming in Chapter 2 by focusing on what you already know about the topic.
<u>Using the key words above to get you started, list a few phrases about</u> *scientific methods*:

<u>Ideas related to</u> *scientific methods*:

claim =state unproven theory that needs careful *investigation*

procedures with statistics that systematically *measure*

>>>>>**KEY IDEA:**
Now look at the section of Ch.2 with the heading, "Steps for Gathering and Evaluating Evidence." Underline the author's words, *"We also gain scientific knowledge by testing hypotheses, which are testable predictions of what will happen under certain conditions."* How do the ideas you wrote relate to this idea of "testable predictions?" How do your ideas connect with the author's points on **falsifiable** theories, p.31?

<u>Creating questions about content</u>: As in Ch.1 of this nonnative speakers' guide, one strategy presented to help you think about a topic is to form your own questions.
<u>Create questions to fit the answers</u> provided below:

<u>Answer</u>: The examples of perpetual motion machines, Clever Hans, the horse, and the example of ESP all show this principle.
Question:_____?

Try forming another question about chapter content, this time for the following answer :
<u>Answer:</u> "One kind of evidence consists of…people's reports of isolated events."
Question: _____?

Another answer: Hypothesis, methods, results, and interpretation are part of these procedures.
Your question:

_____

_____ ?

Asking questions about text organization also helps you use text resources better:

The Kalat text, <u>Introduction to Psychology</u>:

As in Ch. 1, you will notice that chapters are divided into different sections. **Ask yourself what the specific purposes of the subsections are** starting with "Summary" at the end of the first section of Ch.2. (In other words, ask yourself _why these sections are included._)

<u>Utilizing the Maki Study Guide</u> for the Kalat text:

1. **<u>Create a question</u>** for each of the first 3 subdivisions of Ch. 2 in the Maki guide, which are taken from the Kalat text. The first one is started for you:
    a. _How do scientists evaluate theories?_
    b.
    c.
 2. **<u>List the headings</u>** of the major sections of the Study Guide, Ch. 2, to guide you.
Include a paraphrase, your own words for the same idea. The first one is provided.

    a. **Objectives** (outline of content)
    b. **Comprehension Check** (self-test of your understanding of chapter content)
    c.
    d.
    e.
    f.
    g.
    h.

Predict chapter content within the next section, "Methods of Investigation in Psychology," this time by previewing, that is, looking ahead, at the <u>Study Guide</u> outline for that section.

<u>Paraphrasing the Study Guide</u>: Focus on Module 2.2.
The Study Guide lists some key phrases about "Methods of Investigation..."**Another way of saying the same thing (a paraphrase) is also given for underlined phrases and terms:**

II. Research follows some <u>general principles</u>:
    Research follows some <u>basic steps.</u>

A. <u>Variables</u> should be operationally <u>defined</u>:
   Things that vary results should be <u>identified</u> and <u>described.</u>

B. Samples should be <u>representative and random</u>.
   Samples should <u>be chosen in specific ways to fairly represent the target group.</u>

C. Observers and subjects should be "<u>blind</u>".
   <u>Participants shouldn't know what results are expected</u>.

Now *You* **try to paraphrase** some of the following. (Hint: You can also use the minor points and examples to help you understand major points. **In addition, you do <u>not</u> need to write every word, only key ideas. When you finish, reread Chapter 2 in the Kalat text.)**

III. Observational research designs don't show cause and effect relationships.

> **Observational research=** *research involving watching, observing, seeing*
> A. Naturalistic: *natural conditions*
> B. Case Histories: _____
> C. Surveys: _____
> D. Correlational Study: *research that studies relationship, not cause/effect*

IV. Experiments involve the manipulation of variables:
   Experiments: involve controlling and influencing things that vary results:
   A. Independent variables:_____ Dependent variables:_____
   B. Experimental groups:_____Control groups: _____
   C. Example of an experiment: *study of influence of TV violence on behavior*

V. Demand characteristics may produce self-fulfilling prophecies : *Messages that show what behavior is expected can influence the behavior that results.*
VI. Ethical issues:_____

Now see the section, "Measuring and Reporting Results" in the <u>Study Guide</u>. **You will see that Section VII A and B do not need paraphrasing. Move on to VIII**, and <u>underline the author's paraphrase of "statistically significant."</u> **(Do you understand more than you thought?)**

<u>Word Attack</u>:

Note the suffix, *-ate*, for the first verb below; then fill in the same suffix to <u>change each of the following nouns to a verb</u>.

Replication: evaluation calculation indication investigation   correlation
Replic<u>ate</u>: evalu____ calcul____ indic____ investig____   correl____

Note the suffix *–able* for the first adjective below; then fill in missing suffixes to <u>change verbs to adjectives</u>.

Vary:	observe	falsify	conceive	compare	measure	depend
Vari**able**	observ___	falsifi___	conceiv___	compar___	measur___	depend___

Write the *verb suffix* you practiced : _____

Write the *adjective suffix* you practiced: _____

Sentence examples:

CHAPTER 3: BIOLOGICAL PSYCHOLOGY

Before you begin Chapter 3:

1. *Review Ch. 2 of both the Kalat text and the Maki guide* to be sure you have covered all key concepts and terms.

2. *Next, pay attention to the organization of Chapter 3* <u>to predict</u> what is coming:

Key Verbs:	control	interact	transmit	combine	activate	release

Add these nouns:	behavior	environment	chemicals	message	system

Predict chapter content:

Using the key words above, (both verbs and nouns), **and the following 3 terms, write phrases in notes and questions** <u>to make connections.</u> Do so in the following order:

> *a. genes (p.63)*   *b. neurons (p.75)*   *c. nervous system (p.85)*

Example of questions:
Do <u>genes</u> <u>control</u> <u>behavior</u> ?   Example of notes: *neurons > transmit messages*
Do <u>neurons</u> <u>interact</u> with <u>chemicals</u>?

>>>>>**KEY IDEA:**
Find the author's statement on p.63: *...*"*Ideally, we would like to know exactly how certain genes influence development, which aspects of environment are most crucial, and how genes and environment combine and interact.*"
Find, also, the following statement, p. 93, under *Conclusions about Brain Organization*:
"...the main point is that the brain is full of separate systems with separate tasks...If part of the brain is lost, part of behavior and experience is lost as well." **Look now at** *The Message,*
p. 100, to see how the author describes the relationship of these separate systems.

Asking Questions About Text Organization : Text Cues: **Bold Print** and *Italics*:
In addition to headings, authors use **bold** print and *italics* to cue the reader something is important.   Often these are found together in the Kalat text to signal important concepts and terms. Many of those appear again in the review activities at the end of each chapter.

<u>Below, **write the meaning in italics for the bold terms on the pages listed**</u>: **Examples:**
...chromosomes (p.63) : strands of hereditary material   **...genes (63):**
...mutations (p.70)   **...natural selection (70)**
...species-typical behaviors (p.71)   **...heritability (p.66)**

<u>**Now try listing the bold term for the meanings in italics:**</u>
<u>**Example:**</u>
...nerve cells: <u>neurons</u> (p. 75)

...widely branching structures that receive transmissions from other (p. 75):_____

...a single, long, thin, straight fiber with branches near its tip (p. 75):_____

<u>**Refer to the Study Guide for Ch. 3 to predict key concepts for this unit, using these strategies:**</u>

      l. Circle or highlight key terms, being careful **not to include all the words, <u>only key words</u>.**
      2. Look for these highlighted terms in the Kalat text. See the example below:

<u>**Practice:**</u> <u>**Highlight the key terms in this item**</u> **from the Maki Study Guide, Ch.3:**

      B. Nerve impulses are called action potentials.
         l. Inflow of sodium ions makes inside of axon positive.

(**Hint**: Key terms to circle, underline or highlight might be <u>action potentials</u>, <u>sodium</u>, and <u>axon positive</u>.) If you refer back to the Kalat text, you will see that the Guide is summarizing and paraphrasing the information in the text, Ch.3):

"Certain kinds of stimulation can disrupt this stable resting potential. The **action potential** occurs when *the membrane briefly opens little gates (called sodium gates) along its surface to allow sodium ions to enter the axon...***As those sodium ions cross the membrane, they <u>eliminate the negative potential</u> that is usually present inside the cell.**

(Notice that the Guide takes this idea about elimination of negative potential and phrases it as "makes inside of axon positive." However, <u>the idea is the same</u>.)

Study Strategy: Create your own textual cues: <u>Highlight key concepts as shown in the examples above:</u>

l. Find and highlight key terms in the Guide.
2.Find and highlight corresponding terms and ideas in the text.

After using the Kalat text chapter and the ***Study Guide***, check the review section at the end of the chapter in both texts.   For example, reinforce your understanding through *Concept Check* and *Summary* sections. See the following from the *Summary* section of the text, Ch.3:

The action potential: Information is conveyed along an axon by an action potential, <u>which is regenerated without loss of strength</u> at each point along the axon. (Again, the focus is on the positive force=”without loss of strength.”)

Use all of your resources, <u>text, Study Guide, and this section for nonnative speakers</u> to help you understand and retain what you learn.

Other Study Strategies:
In addition to highlighting important words and concepts, another way to understand and remember that you might find useful is to illustrate the concepts you read in some way:

      1. Draw a picture of a process
      2. Draw a graphic representation, such as a chart or diagram

<u>**Practice:**</u>
Refer to the section of Ch. 3, “Explanations of Behavior at the Level of the Nervous System,” page 85-87. On another paper make an illustration and label it for :

1. Central Nervous System
2. The Spinal Cord
3. The Autonomic Nervous System

<u>Compare your illustration to the illustrations in the text to see if you understood the general ideas.</u>

<u>**Use the strategies you have practiced to help yourself continue in Chapter 3:**</u>

1. Focus on **bold** print and *italics.*
2. Use both the Kalat text and the <u>Study Guide</u> to get key concepts.
      a.   Highlight only key terms
      b.   Look for the same ideas in all resources, including review sections.
3. Draw your own illustrations of concepts discussed and label them.

4. Compare your illustration to those in the text and make adjustments.
    ALSO: Don’t forget to take chapter post tests in the Guide and check your answers.

<u>**Word Attack: Idioms:**</u>

To an extent: to a certain point; to a certain degree

To do so: to do things that specific/stated way

So far, so good: Up to this point, no problem.

CHAPTER 4: SENSATION AND PERCEPTION

Before you begin Ch. 4:

l. Review Ch. 3 of both the Kalat text and the Maki guide to be sure you have covered all key concepts and terms.

2. Next, pay attention to the organization of Chapter 4 to predict what is coming:

Key Verbs:	convert	respond	adapt	perceive	stimulate	inhibit	detect

Look for Chapter Themes or Main Ideas: Use chapter subheadings:

What can you predict about the contents of the following 3 major sections of Chapter 4, "Sensation and Perception"? Write your ideas next to the subtitle:

  Example: **Vision:**   sight   about seeing   about eyes   how we see

   *Nonvisual Senses:

   The Interpretation of Sensory Information:

Note: If you looked at all three subheadings before starting the first one, you probably noticed they all deal with one general topic, covered in the chapter title.

Write that general topic here, using other words than those of the title itself.
In other words, paraphrase the chapter title. "Sensation and Perception" covers information on:_____
_____

> **>>>>>KEY IDEA: Notice the author's words at the top of page 105 in Ch. 4: "Our experiences *translate* the stimuli of the outside world into a very different representation."** What can you conclude from this comment?

Skimming: Although we have been practicing strategies that focus on specific ideas, we can do the opposite: get a general idea, without concentrating on specifics.
Practice:
Look over the Table of Contents of Kalat's text, Introduction to Psychology. **Get a general idea of chapter subjects without focusing on any particular one.   Do that as quickly as you can; that is skimming.**

* Note: Compare your terms with terms the author uses to describe the senses.

<u>**Now do the following**</u>: **Skim the captions,** *the written explanation under illustrations throughout the chapter.* These are found with each numbered "figure" showing a diagram or drawing of some kind. <u>Notice that these captions support key ideas connected to each heading.</u>

l. Skim the first section of the chapter, Module 4.1, "Vision," and circle or underline the item below that best fits its general content in your opinion:

a. cones and rods
b. accommodation of the lens
c. how we focus in various situations
d. how brains construct the images we see

2. Skim the second section of the chapter, " Nonvisual Senses," Module 4.2, and circle the item below that best fits its general content in your opinion:

a. different kinds of sounds the ear hears
b. definitions of sensory systems
c. how non visual sensory systems function
d. touch, taste, and smell

3. Skim the subheadings only for last section of the chapter, Module 4.3, "The Interpretation of Sensory Information," many of which are listed below.

Circle a <u>KEY WORD</u> (1 only) that best fits its general content:

I. Perception of Minimal Stimuli
     A. Sensory Thresholds and Signal Detection
     B. Subliminal Perception
     C. What Subliminal Perception Cannot Do
     D. What Subliminal Perception Can Do

II. Perception and the Recognition of Patterns
     A. The Feature-Detector Approach
     B. Do Feature Detectors Explain Perception?
     C. The Gestalt Psychology Approach
     D. Gestalt Principles in Hearing
     E. Feature Detectors and Gestalt Psychology

III. Perception of Movement and Depth
     (subcategories)

Note: If you circled the word **"perception,"** for I-III, you made a good guess. The last section's "Message,"(p. 150), says, "Everything we have experienced in the past, everything that we know (or think that we know) influences what we perceive."

Looking Back:
Answers from the beginning of this section: (#1:d; #2:c.)

Paraphrasing Practice:
Now that you have a general idea of the chapter content, write your own paraphrase, your own words for the chapter title, without looking back at what you wrote at the beginning of this chapter:

The chapter **"Sensation and Perception" discusses**:_____

_____

Word Attack:

Change the nouns below to adjectives, based on the suffix in the following example:

Verb	Noun	Adjective
respond	response	respons-*ive*
sense	sense	sensit
interpret	interpretation	interpret
conclude	conclusion	conclus
perceive	perception	percept
receive	reception	recept
deduct	deduction	deduct
adapt	adaptation	adapt
elude	elusion	elus

Idioms:

To draw a distinction: to distinguish one thing from another; differentiate

To be led astray: to be misled; to be deceived

To happen to deal with: to be about; to refer to

Even so: Even though this is true; nevertheless

To get locked into: To become convinced of something

CHAPTER 5: ALTERED STATES

1. *Review Ch. 4 of both the Kalat text and the Maki guide* to be sure you have covered all key terms and concepts.
2. *Look over the organization of Chapter 5* to predict what is coming next.

| Key Verbs: alter induce impair deprive restore tolerate distinguish abuse |

Predict chapter content:

Chapter 4 has information that you have probably thought about or discussed with someone several times in your life. You will quickly recognize some topics from your own life experiences and those of other people you know.

| Below, **check the terms and concepts that are already familiar to you,** even though only partially: |

____ hallucinate
____ circadian rhythms ("morning people" and "evening people")
____ meditation
____ stages of sleep
____ withdrawal
____ stimulants
____ tranquilizers
____ sleep walking
____ hypnosis
____ repair and restoration
____ alcohol
____ sleep talking
____ insomnia
____ consciousness and unconsciousness
____ physical and/or psychological dependence
____ nightmares
____ energy conservation

Now organize the above terms into the 3 categories used by the author; some terms may fit in more than one category. Try to group them without using the text. See if you understand relationships of major topics and examples.

Sleep and Dreams:

Hypnosis:

Drugs and Their Effects:

Review:
<u>Key Verbs:</u> *alter   impair   deprive   restore   tolerate   distinguish   induce   abuse*

<u>Vocabulary Practice:</u> **Using the "Key Verbs" listed above, <u>fill in the correct verb for each blank based on information drawn from the chapter topics:</u>**

Many people have experienced some condition in which they were not aware of things in the same way as they normally would be. The author discusses various ways people change or _____ their sense of reality either consciously or unconsciously. During sleep, for example, the body works to _____ its functions. For most people, less than the typical amount of sleep can _____ the body of the rest it needs.   Not all sleep is satisfying, however, since interruptions such as nightmares or insomnia can _____ the individual's ability to move through the various sleep stages that are considered necessary for adequate rest.

Other "states" of altered consciousness described by the author are artificially created. One example is hypnosis, which can _____ a condition in which the individual follows suggestions more readily than otherwise might occur.   However, the author cautions us to _____ between valid claims about hypnosis and hearsay, things people tell you that may not be based in fact.   Another example of altered states of consciousness occurs with drug and alcohol use.   The author describes how different types of drugs affect users who may _____ more than normal amounts and therefore _____ the drug, suffering physical and/or psychological consequences.

>>>>>**KEY IDEA:**
The author's words on the first page of Chapter 5 summarize the message of the chapter:
"Evidently the distinction between consciousness and unconsciousness is not a yes-or-no question: There are various degrees of consciousness."   He reinforces, that is, strengthens this argument by adding on the same page, *" The main problem is that one's consciousness, being an internal experience, can be observed by oneself, but not by others. The best we can do scientifically is to examine procedures that seem to alter consciousness…."*

What is your paraphrase, your own words that explain the above comments?

_____

_____

<u>Word Attack:</u>

I. In each example below <u>choose the correct form of the word: noun, verb, or adjective</u>:

l. East-coast people adjust to West-coast time more easily than West coast people adjust to East-coast time.   Time _____are difficult for people to make.
          (adjusted/adjustments)

2.Sleep deprivation leads to _____concentration and irritability; prolonged
          (impaired/impairment)
deprivation can impair the function of the immune system and increase the risk of becoming ill.

3.We cannot draw cause-and-effect conclusions from correlational studies. We cannot say that just because one thing _____with another that it therefore leads to or is
          (correlates/correlation)
 a result of the other.

 4.Although people assume that hypnosis is somehow related to sleep, the connection is only superficial. In other words, that _____ is not completely accurate.
          (assumed/assumption)

 5.Research studies _____ changes that occur during experiments.
          (document/documentation)

III. <u>Compare and fill in the missing word forms</u>:

<u>Noun:</u>	<u>Adjective:</u>	<u>Adverb:</u>
Hypnosis:	**hypnotic**	**hypnotically**
psychosis:		
neurosis:		

Answer key:
Vocabulary practice: alter; restore; deprive; impair; induce; distinguish; tolerate; abuse
Word Attack: adjustment; impaired; correlates; assumption; document

CHAPTER 6: LEARNING

Before you begin Chapter 6:

1. *Review Chapter 5 of both the Kalat text and the Maki guide* to be sure you have covered all key concepts and terms.
2. *Next, pay attention to the organization of Chapter 6* to predict what is coming:

Key Verbs:	elicit	evoke	excite	provoke	acquire	reinforce
extinguish						

What general idea is communicated by the following verbs:

                elicit   *evoke*   *excite*   *provoke*

elicit= to draw out, get
evoke=produce or call out
excite=raise strong feelings; cause to happen
provoke=to cause a feeling or action
The *general idea expressed by these verbs* is:_____

_____

Which **key verb** in the box above might express the *opposite* meaning?_____

Predict Chapter Content: Summarize Themes or Main Ideas

In each chapter of the text, the author begins with an introduction, which usually has some analogies or examples to help the reader understand the central idea of the chapter.

Read pages 190 and 191 in Ch. 6, "Learning."   Pay special attention to the paragraph on p.190 that begins, **" Psychologists have spent an enormous amount of time studying learning. One of their main discoveries is......"**   Underline the key idea there. What can you predict about ideas coming in this chapter?
In the space below, briefly summarize the author's message from these first 2 pages:
_____

_____

>>>>>**KEY IDEA:**
      Use "The Message" in Ch. 6 on p. 224 to find the author's central idea about
      conditioning and/or learning. **Then summarize it by doing the following:**

        a.Underline 1 or 2 key points.
        b.Paraphrase them.
        c.Write a one-sentence summary statement of your paraphrased idea:

Ask questions about text organization: What terms or phrases show relationship between ideas? How do we know when the author is pointing out that one action affects another or is the opposite of another?

Practice seeing relationships between ideas in order to understand main ideas better.

Below is a list of terms that show relationships. Match the purpose of the term (indicated by #1 or #2) to the appropriate phrase or word:

Terms Showing Relationships

l. **Cause and effect**

2. **Contrast or <u>un</u>expected result**

_____ influence	_____ produce	_____ still	_____ subject to
_____ therefore	_____ based on	_____ lead to	_____ except
_____ consequently	_____ instead	_____ although	_____ evidently
_____ depending on	_____ despite	_____ rather	_____ by contrast

With the following <u>excerpts</u> from the chapter, tell which shows #1 and which shows #2. In other words, decide what the relationship of the ideas is:

_____ l. The rats that had received shocks while drinking avoided only the tube that produced lights and noises. **Evidently**, rats...have a built-in predisposition to associate illness mostly with what they have eaten or drunk.

_____ 2. You do not automatically imitate the behavior of someone else, even someone you admire. **Rather**, you imitate behavior that has proved reinforcing for that person.

_____ 3. **Despite** widespread publicity about the consequences of driving drunk, using addictive drugs, or engaging in unsafe sex, many people ignore the dangers.

_____ 4. Certain behavior can lead to certain rewards **while** other behavior can result in lack of reward as a reinforcement.

_____ 5. **Instead**, reinforcement gradually increased the probability of one behavior.

Other words that show relationships:

The following words show *probable or possible relationships*, (although perhaps not cause and effect):

Noun:	Verb:	General Meaning:
1. tendency	to tend to	to tend/ be likely to/ predisposed to: expected to
2. likelihood	to be likely to	to be associated /correlate with= connected with
3. predisposition	to be predisposed to	
4. association	to be associated with	
5. correlation	to correlate with	

Idioms: Make note of the following idioms, which are used in Chapter 6:

In the long run: after enough time; in the end

(" ...but in the long run they made as many presses as did rats that never received any punishments" (p. 211).

To **sound straight-forward:** To seem to be self evident; to appear to reflect reality

("That definition may sound pretty straight-forward, but in fact psychologists find it difficult to specify exactly..." (p 199).

ANSWERS TO "WORDS SHOWING RELATIONSHIPS:"

Influence: l; therefore:1; consequently:1: depending on: 1 produce:1 based on: 1; instead:2 ; despite:2; still: 2; lead to: 1; although: 2: rather: 2: subject 2: 1: except: 2: evidently: 1: by contrast: 2

Answers to "excerpts:": l: 1; 2: 2; 3: 2; 4: 1; 5: 2

CHAPTER 7: MEMORY

<u>**Before you begin Chapter 7:**</u>

1. *Review Chapter 6 of both the Kalat text and the Maki guide* to be sure you have covered all key concepts and terms.
2. *Next, pay attention to the organization of Ch.7* to predict what is coming.

Key Verbs: memorize   interfere   store   retrieve   process   recall   decay   reconstruct

---

I. <u>Chapter Organization</u>: Turn to the initial page of Ch.7. Write your own prediction, your guess, about the focus of each section based on the subtitles.

<u>Look at both the **title** in bold print and the other **subtitles** that are not indented.</u>
<u>**Example:**</u>

1. Types of Memory. (Note the key words: experiment; view; theory: other distinctions)
                                                                                      different kinds of memory
The focus of this section is probably a discussion of _____

<u>**Now you try:**</u>
2. Memory Improvement.   (Note the key words:)

           emotions   storage and processing   self monitoring   spacing   strategies

Note: "monitoring"= watching something carefully to gain understanding; therefore, self-monitoring is a way of watching or studying yourself.

The focus of this section is probably: _____

---

3. Memory Loss: (Note the key words for the two main emphases:)

           ---forgetting   ---amnesia: brain damage, infant, old age

The focus of this section is probably: _____

A sample summary sentence that explains the theme or central focus of this chapter:
Chapter 7 explains different kinds of memory and what affects how well we remember.

4. The Reconstruction of Memory: <u>Record below both key words and a summary sentence for the expected content of this chapter:</u> (Hint: Reconstruction=rebuilding)

II. Using Illustrations to help you understand chapter content:

In addition to headings and subheadings, (and text organizers shown previously), <u>illustrations and captions help us focus on key ideas.</u>

Look over the illustrations and read the captions below each illustration in the first section, **Module 7.1**, of the chapter, **"Types of Memory." Then list the key terms and ideas from these textual aids below. (One is already provided for you.)**

Key terms: **Key ideas:**

Ebbinghaus

Note: Use the "Concept Check" section, p. 231, to see how much you already understood.

<u>Related examples:</u>

Now look again specifically at pages 230-231. Why are Fig. 7.1, 7.2, 7.3, and 7.4 grouped together on these 2 pages? Can you summarize their main idea?

Now go back and read about Ebbinghaus, pages 229-231 to see if you were right. Ask yourself which of the illustrations (7.1-7.4) best summarizes the key idea presented.
Answer:
(If you chose Fig. 7.4, you were right. Did you see anything in the text that connected to the key idea in 7.4? Mark it. How did you remember where to find it quickly? Did you use any memory strategy? *Read on in Module 7.1 of Ch. 7 to find out how you yourself remember*.)

Use your skills with illustrations on the other sections of the chapter now.

C. Other Textual Cues: Bold print and italics.

Often, key terms related to important concepts are in <u>bold print</u> to focus our attention. <u>List below the bold print terms</u> you find <u>in the first section of the</u> **Memory** chapter. The example ones, found on p. 231, are shown here:

P. 231: proactive interference and **retroactive interference**. (Definition in italics).
Note: *Interference* seems to be the key concept here, part of both terms. Look ahead in the chapter to find which testing method would be helpful for remembering the distinction between these two terms.

Other bold print examples:

Italics: In addition to bold print, *italics* are another way to focus reader attention. For example, italics are used for the term *"retrieval cue"* on p. 234.

Can *italics* help you review? **Try "cued recall" with italics to remember key ideas.** Copy only the italicized terms in the Summary Section, p. 239-240. Then try to recall what they refer to after reading the chapter more carefully.

<u>**Review ways just shown to quickly locate chapter themes and key ideas:**</u>
--titles and subtitles with key words
--illustrations and captions
--bold print and italics

<u>**Use the ways you have learned in the first section of this chapter to remember main ideas:**</u>

In retrospect, that is, looking back, what do you recall the major points of the <u>first</u> section of Chapter 7 are ? **(Review by writing two or three summary sentences based on key words in headings:)**

_____
_____
_____

Part II: Memory Improvement: Preview

Using illustrations and captions in Module 7.2, see if you can **find relationships to the key ideas expressed in the headings or subtitles.** (Find an illustration that is "meaningful" for you.)

Using **bold** print and *italics*, try to identify key terms of this section of the chapter. Then look again at the illustrations to find connections between them and the bold print or italicized terms, reinforcing main ideas.

Can you recall the **SPAR** method of memory improvement for understanding and remembering a text lesson? (See p. 244.)

Part III: Memory Loss: Follow the same procedure you did for the previous sections of the chapter, making sure to carefully read the whole chapter when you finish to fully understand major themes and relationships. **Hint**: Notice that this section begins with "normal"forgetting. Therefore, logically, the second section on "amnesia" explains "*ab*normal" forgetting.

Part IV: The Reconstruction of Memory:

You will recall that "reconstruction" means rebuilding; however, the dictionary definition says:

"To rebuild after destruction or damage." After reading the author's comments in Module 7.4, <u>you may see why this definition fits.</u> Notice the author's use of terms that indicate that some memories are changed later, that is altered from their original form:

Note such key words as the following:

        expectation   *bias*   *false memories*   *repression*

<u>**Word Attack**</u>: What relationship do you see between the following words based on their prefix, *re*: **recall; recognition; reconstruction; relearn; reinforcement; review: The prefix "re" is usually used to indicate:**_____

CHAPTER 8: COGNITION AND LANGUAGE

Before you begin Chapter 8:

l. *Review Ch. 7 of both the Kalat text and the Maki guide* to be sure you have covered all key concepts and terms.
2. *Next, pay attention to the organization of Chapter 8* to predict what is coming:

Key Verbs:	categorize	link	imagine	recognize	rely	estimate

Section I: Thinking and Mental Processes:

Note the introductory sentence on p. 269 in Module 8.1: Cognition is psychologists' word for *thinking, gaining knowledge, and dealing with knowledge.* Now answer this question based on the next sentence in the text: **What do cognitive psychologists study?**
Cognitive psychologists study _____
_____
_____

One of the key verbs in the box above, *imagine*, is found in many related forms in this unit, particularly in the first section, "Thinking and Mental Processes"(Module 8.1).

Note the different word forms related to the verb "imagine":

image   imagery   imagination   imaginative   imaginary

Can you predict some of the content of the initial section of Chapter 8 based on these words ?
Write your prediction here:
Chapter 8 deals, at least partly, with _____
_____

>>>>>**KEY IDEA**:
Now look at the following statements from pages 268-269 of the chapter and <u>consider how the author</u> might connect *imagination* to these points:
...."In this chapter, you will be asked to think about thinking..."
...."psychological researchers focus as much as possible on results from carefully controlled experiments, not just on what people say they think ....."   and
...."in many cases people are not fully aware of their own thought processes."

A question to ask yourself :
If "people are not fully aware of their own thought processes,"how does this relate, also, to"attention?"(See pages 274-276, Ch. 8, on "preattentive and attentive processes.")

Section II, Ch. 8: Problem Solving, Expertise, and Error.

Another key verb, *estimate,* is found in this second section of Ch. 8.
Note the different forms related to the verb "estimate:"

estimate   estimation   estimable   esteem

For these words, the dictionary refers to judgment or calculation of value given to something or someone. **When problem solving, people tend to *estimate* the value of ideas and specific information.**

> *"Psychologists study problem-solving behavior partly to understand the thought processes behind it and partly to look for ways to help people reason more effectively (p. 279).*

...and....
"Most of the difference between experts and the merely average-to-good performers depends on effort and practice." (p. 280)
…and…
"Generally, we go through four phases when we set about solving a problem."(p. 281)
Note: generating (producing) a *hypothesis* and testing it are among the phases.

The author seems to be saying that problem solving requires _____

_____

_____

Section III: Language:
Using the theory of "spreading activation," Ch. 8, p. 271, look again at **"Key Verbs,"** and *predict connections* between the remaining terms and *language:*

Recognize: to know someone or something that you have seen before; to accept and admit that something is true or real
Categorize: to put into groups according to type; classify
Link: to connect
Rely: to trust or depend on someone or something

Ch. 8, Section III "Language" probably discusses:_____

_____

Using available resources: Connecting with the Study Guide :

Using the Maki *Study Guide*, focus on the outline form that is used to categorize concepts from the text, Introduction to Psychology.

Study the first section of the Maki outline for Ch. 8, p. 113, "Thinking and Mental Processes," taken from the Kalat text. Then close the *Study Guide* and fill in the missing parts of that outline for the second section, "Problem Solving, Expertise, and Error" shown here. Parts of the outline are provided for you. **Refer to the text for other parts, using short sentences or phrases. In other words, paraphrase where possible.   Start with VI:**

> VI. **Problem solving involves four phases:**
>   A.**Problems need to be made simple and understandable**
>   B.**Hypotheses should be generated (produced**
>   l. **Algorithms**
>   2. **Heuristics:**
>   C.
>   D.**Solutions should cover all similar cases**
>
> VII. **Characteristics of Insightful Problem Solving**
>   A. **Progress**
>   B.
>   C. **Creative people ....**
>
> VIII. **Approaches that lead to illogical conclusions:**
>   A. **Overconfidence**
>   B.
>   C.
>   D.
>   E. **People are influenced by questions that imply losses**
>
> IX. **Gambling as an example of learning, memory, and thinking:**
>   A. **People overestimate....**
>   B. **People don't understand long shot (low likelihood)**
>   C.
>   D. **Vicarious (indirect) reinforcement comes from seeing others win.**
>   E. **Availability and representativeness heuristic**
>   F.

Afterward try to outline the final section, "Language"on your own. Refer to the example.

Word Attack:

Prefixes can be whole words such as **over** (more than necessary) or **under** (less than necessary):In this chapter, we see several examples of words to which the prefix *over* is attached. **Complete the examples below**:

  Overestimate _____use: _____confident

Idioms:

Look at the definitions of the following idioms; find them in context in Chapter 8:

Take for granted: p.269 : expect that someone will always support you or something will always be available

Address the question: p.285: to focus on answering a specific question or solving a specific problem

Lead us astray: p.289: persuade someone to believe something that isn't true or do something wrong

NOTE: Most of these idioms refer to interactions between people engaged in problem solving of some kind.

CHAPTER 9: INTELLIGENCE AND ITS MEASUREMENT

Before you begin Chapter 9:

1. *Review Ch. 8 of both the Kalat text and the Maki guide* to be sure you have covered all key concepts and terms.
2. *Next, pay attention to the organization of Ch. 8* to predict what is coming:

Key Verbs: (**You** provide some below this time…before you even begin the chapter.)

___

Read the paragraph that begins in the second column of p. 315, giving a summary of definitions of intelligence. **Next list the verbs that psychologists use to define intelligence (315):**

adapt   judge   _____   _____   _____   _____

Read the rest of the paragraph and review the strategy you practiced for Ch. 2, for example:
Ask questions about content by changing some part of the following statement to a question:
"…Just as all the objects in the world are composed of compounds of 92 elements, most psychologists expect to find that all the kinds of intelligence are compounds of a few basic abilities. They have proposed several models of how intelligence is organized."

My question:
_____
_____?

Now answer your own question by outlining the information that follows on various views of intelligence. Remember to list major points and related subpoints (examples, etc.)
Summarize each theory in one sentence or phrase. *Then check yourself by referring to the text and the Study Guide.*

I. **Spearman's Psychometric Approach**: all mental tasks share general ability
    A. General ability, called "g" factor, "rules" lesser abilities
    B. Suggested specific lesser abilities connect to "g"

II. Cattel Theory:

III. Gardner's Theory:

IV. _____'s Theory:

Review *textual cues* as signals to relate ideas: Using the following, complete the sentences below to compare the theories and summarize them:

---

1. **Although** Spearman believed_____

Gardner suggested _____

2. Cattell suggested two kinds of ability; **however,** Gardner_____
_____

3. Sternberg's theory deals with three kinds of intelligence; **for example**, *the individual's own internal mental process,* _____
_____, and _____
_____

Continue making similar statements about relationships between IQ tests, the next section of the chapter:

1. The Weschsler test is helpful for measuring strengths and weaknesses; **in contrast**, the Stanford Binet test_____
_____

2. The Stanford-Binet and Wechsler tests are not suitable for testing persons of non English speaking cultures; Raven's Progressive Matrices do not require verbal responses. **Therefore,**
_____

3. The Progressive Matrices Test is fairer than the Stanford-Binet and Wechsler tests for nonnative speakers of English if they can take paper and pencil tests; **however,**
_____

4. The SAT, Scholastic Assessment Test predicts performance in college; **moreover,** it includes both a _____
_____.

5. **Despite the fact** that existing IQ tests are one way to measure intelligence,
_____

—

Notice the author's words on page 327, *"One of the major tasks for researchers is to determine whether the tests measure what their designers claim they measure and whether they apply fairly to all groups."*

Paraphrase the author's perspective of IQ tests in the preceding statement:

_____

_____

Read the section **"Distribution of IQ Scores,"** and <u>list the 2 math terms</u> that you notice are key to the discussion of how people score across a range.

1._____ score: middle score

2._____ measurement of how much scores vary from the middle.

What is the *Flynn effect* **(p. 328)** and what does it demonstrate?

<u>**Fill in the appropriate math terms through the next section,** *Evaluation of Tests*</u>:

_____ : shows **correlation between scores on first test and on retest (repeatability of scores).**

4. _____ : demonstrates that **test items correctly measure what they are intended to measure.**

5._____ : refers to **usefulness and practicality** of test.

(Note: Which of the above is more likely to reflect changes in results (fluctuations in scores) from one test to the next?)

Read further in"Group Differences." **Summarize in one sentence what the author says about differences in scores among ethnic groups.**

_____

_____

Find the message of the section on *family intelligence* factors; follow the same procedure:
  1. Read and underline key points.
  2. Summarize the main message, the central idea.

Does the author draw a definite conclusion about the influence of heredity (genetic background of an individual) and environmental influences in determining level of intelligence? **Find and underline the author's opinion,** which repeats several places in this section.

What question might your instructor ask about *heredity* vs *environmental* influences? How would you answer it? Find several examples to support your answer.

Word Attack:

Idioms :

To account for the fact (p.316): to explain

In short (p.323): Briefly, In summary

In a way (p.325): somewhat

Lose sight of the fact (p.331): to forget

Bear in mind (p.332): to remember

CHAPTER 10: DEVELOPMENT

Before you begin Chapter 10:

1. *Review Ch. 9 of both the Kalat text and the Maki guide* to be sure you have covered all key concepts and terms.
2. *Next, pay attention to the organization of Ch. 9* to predict what is coming:

Key Verbs:	mature	infer	reason	assimilate	accomodate	fluctuate

Predicting chapter content: Headings and key terms that "explain" chapter themes:

Hypothesis (p.350): suggested explanation for something not yet proven
Interpretation: (p.351): one explanation for an event or action
Implications: (p.362): suggestion of possible effects or results

Note that the author often indicates his interpretation of key concepts
by the following headings:
   --Concept Check
   --The Message
   -- Summary

>>>>>**KEY IDEA**:
What might you expect Chapter 10 to cover, based on the author's introduction to this chapter where he says, **"The goal of developmental psychology is to understand everything that influences human behavior "from womb to tomb."** (What is the "womb"? What is the "tomb"?) ....And what kinds of development might be included within that range of growth and experience?

Using textual cues to understand chapter content: **punctuation**

To distinguish various theories or their elements from one another, as in this chapter on "Development," the author often uses specific punctuation to signal some form of classification.

The colon (:) a punctuation signal that prepares the reader for important information, often in list form, *moving from general to specific.*   Note the following examples:

The Development of Thought and Knowledge: Piaget's Contributions

Piaget's stages of intellectual development

"Piaget contended that children progress through four major stages of intellectual development:" (See the four stages listed, p.355.)

The Sensorimotor Stage: Infancy (p.355)

The Preoperational Stage: Early Childhood (p.355).

What might come next in the stages of development of an individual moving from infancy (baby years) to adulthood? Notice that the author has covered only the early stages so far; the reader must continue looking for the next stages and their specific characteristics. *Punctuation is one way to see that a list has begun.*

(Note: A colon also is used to introduce a definition. See reference to Gilligan's *caring orientation* on p. 365.)

<u>the dash</u> (--) is another punctuation signal that prepares the reader for important information that is coming, ...moving, as with the colon, from general to specific.

<u>Example:</u>
Kohlberg devised a series of moral dilemmas--problems that pit one moral value against another. (p.363)

....or moving from essential to non essential information.

<u>Example:</u>

<u>Using textual clues to understand chapter content</u>: **transitions that signal conclusions**:

The important point about research **is this**: (P.351): "Especially when we are dealing with infants…

That is: (p. 355): "That is, they show a sense of self ..."

In other words---(p. 354): "In other words—and this is one of Piaget's central insights—children's thought processes are ..."

In general (p. 361): "In general, the progression from one stage of thinking to another appear to be gradual and not sudden."

Therefore: (p. 362) "Therefore, it is inefficient to expect children to rediscover the accumulated wisdom of humanity..."

In short: (p. 377) "In short, contrary to Kohlberg's views..."

Word Attack:

Fill in the noun suffixes -*ance* or – *ence* = a state or quality

Verb	Noun	
		maintenance
maintain	mainten(a)	_____
infer	infer(e)	_____
prefer	prefer(e)	_____

Fill in the verb ending : *ate*

habitu**ate**	habituation
assimil _____	assimilation
accommo _____	accommodation
fluctu _____	fluctuation
accultur _____	acculturation
associ _____	association

Idioms:

To tell the difference between: to know/recognize how 2 or more things are different

To have something going on: to have something happening

To point out: to emphasize some fact or stress some piece of information

To state something in terms of: to say how a particular fact or piece of information is related to something.

CHAPTER 11: MOTIVATION

Before you begin Chapter 11:

1. *Review Chapter 10 of both the Kalat text and the Maki guide* to be sure you have covered all key concepts and terms.
2. *Next, pay attention to the organization of Ch. 10* to predict what is coming.

Note : Chapter 11 <u>organization</u> is announced on p. 391 in the chapter headings: To focus on the author's categories for this chapter, **fill in the missing words below**:

> *We begin this chapter with an overview of*_____
> _____
>
> *Then we will study **3 different aspects of motivation**:*_____ ,
> _____ , *and* _____ .

Key Verbs: achieve   activate   direct   inhibit   reduce   maintain   arouse

How do the above verbs relate to *motivation? (Motivate=provide with strong reason for doing something.)*

Use the following comparison/contrast relationship to paraphrase the author's message about the 3 motivations discussed in this chapter:

Although_____**and** _____**serve a biological need,**_____**is based first on social needs related to competition.**

<u>Chart below the different categories of motivation discussed early in Chapter 11</u>:

<u>**Contrasting Motivational forms:**</u>

Drive (from biological force)   *<u>incentive (from external stimuli)</u>*

Extrinsic (based on rewards or punishments)   _____

Primary (automatic, built-in process)

_____
Summarize in 1 sentence Maslow's "heirarchy of needs" as discussed here:

_____

What is the author's view of this theory? (P. 398): **"Depending on the circumstances...."**

_____
_____

_____
_____

>>>>>**KEY IDEA:** The author asks and answers many questions about *motivation*. Notice the verb "depends" appears repeatedly. The author seems to say that most motivation, either biologically induced or socially induced, depends on the interaction of various factors and represents a basic human response, the need to attain. Notice this comment from *The Message* in the *Summary*, p. 398: *"Motivated behaviors persist until the individual reaches the goal. They are controlled by internal and external forces and by biological and social forces"...and "vary from time to time, situation to situation, and person to person."*

Asking questions about content:

Since most readers feel the subject matter of biological and social drives is a familiar topic, it is useful to test yourself to see how much, in fact, you do or do not already know.

Preread the *Concept Check* and *Summary* section of Chapter 11, "Motivation." Underline statements or questions for which *you* need answers. Record them here, or create your own related questions.

l. List below key questions you need to answer about hunger motivation:

Example: *What is the relationship between insulin levels and hunger?*

Example: *What are some causes of being overweight?*

2. List below key questions you need to answer about sexual motivation:

Example: *How does testosterone affect the development of sexual orientation?*

3. List below key questions you need to answer about achievement motivation:

Example: *What difference is there, if any, between men and women in achievement needs?*

Now : Make notes on answers to your questions from the information given.

Using available resources: The *Study Guide*:

Check your understanding of the lessons in Chapter 11 by doing each of the following in the *Study Guide:*

Comprehension Check

Short-Answer Essay Questions

Post-Test

Follow up each test with a review of answer keys provided to be sure you have understood.

<u>Word Attack</u>: Follow the suffix form shown, changing from adjective to noun :

<u>Adjective</u> form:	**<u>Noun</u> form** *(-ity)*	
Obese	obes	<u>obes**ity**</u>
Variable	variabil	_____
Homosexual	homosexual	_____
Heterosexual	heterosexual	_____

CHAPTER 12: EMOTIONS, HEALTH PSYCHOLOGY, AND COPING

WITH STRESS

Before you begin Chapter 12:

l. *Review Chapter 11 of both the Kalat text and the Maki guide* to be sure you have covered all key concepts and terms.

2. *Next, pay attention to the organization of Ch.12* to predict what is coming.

| Key Verbs: | perceive | function | produce | threaten | cope | contribute | control |

Using various "Key Verbs" above and the chapter title to help you, write a sentence that uses many of the terms and concepts expressed.   Such a sentence is provided for you:

Example:
How people <u>perceive</u> their emotions <u>contributes</u> to or <u>threatens</u> their health and how well they <u>function</u> and <u>cope</u> with events that they may or may not <u>control.</u>

Your Example:

_____
_____
_____

Previewing Chapter Organization:

Using the paragraph on the first page of Ch.12, starting with "In this chapter, we shall consider...." **list below the two main focuses of this chapter.** The third is supplied for you:

l. .

2. **ways people cope with emotions associated with stress**

>>>>>**KEY IDEA**:

The author establishes a connection between emotion and decision making ability (emotional intelligence) on p. 436 and suggests that emotions control our actions. He further suggests that emotions are **"*related to the activity of the autonomic nervous system and....the body in general"* (p. 442)** and adds that how people monitor and cope with stress is a factor in managing health and well being.   However, the author's clear message is that psychologists have not been able to establish the range of emotions or agree on basic emotions that have been identified; furthermore, psychologists feel that health is affected by *both* emotions and genes.

<u>Using Textual Cues</u>:   More practice with **transitions**: Work with the following signals.

> **Readers need to follow supporting points that relate to a central idea. Sometimes these points list *examples*, sometimes *contrasts* or *similarities*, sometimes *results*, and sometimes only *emphasis*.**

<u>Below fill in the purpose of the transition</u> for each example from the chapter:

a. add an idea   ___ also; furthermore; moreover; in addition
b. result or reason   ___ therefore; thus; consequently, in view of
c. contrast or unexpected result   ___ however; nevertheless; still; yet; nonetheless
d. similarity   ___similarly; likewise; just as; in the same way
e. emphasis   ___in fact; indeed; certainly; of course
f. example or illustration   ___that is; in other words
g. summarize or generalization   ___in short; in general; overall; in summary

1.___ **Therefore**, critics argue, the epinephrine injections may have ...(p.444)

2.___ **Furthermore**, the fact that people of all cultures can recognize...(p.449)

3.___ **Nevertheless,** whatever it is that these happiness reports measure...(p.451)

4.___ **Still**, even if certain disorders are associated with an increased risk...(p.456)

5.___ **Just as** they do with other kinds of criminals, psychologists...(p.457)

6.___ **In short**, people tell themselves, "I'm in control; my life is ...(p.471)

<u>Note:</u> In dependent (subordinate) clauses:
   ***Contrast between ideas* is expressed with these :** *although; even though; despite the fact that; no matter*...
These expressions have the same purpose, though not the same grammar, as contrast transitions such as ***however, nevertheless, in contrast, yet,*** etc.

<u>Example</u>: (Dependent clause): *Although* any kind of frustration or disappointment can...
<u>Example</u>: (Transition): Any kind of frustration or disappointment can.....; **however,**.....

Introductory phrase with acknowledgment or recognition of an idea: *granted that; given that; in view of the fact that*

<u>Example</u>: *Given this view*, the proper measure of stress would ...(p.462)

Word Attack:

Much of Chapter 12 focuses on *how* people behave as a result of emotions, in other words the *manner* in which actions happen. Adverbs are used to express the manner in which actions occur:

Change the adjective to the adverb form, (in most cases, the suffix -ly) based on the example provided:

<table>
<tr><td align="center">Adjectives:</td></tr>
<tr><td align="center">calm   rational   emotional   logical   intelligent   active   violent</td></tr>
</table>

calm<u>ly</u> rational___ emotional___ logical___ intelligent___ active___ violent___

Notice the change in spelling with adjectives that end in "y:" (add –i)

voluntary---voluntar*ily*   unhappy---unhapp*ily*

Idioms with "**draw**":

To **draw a distinction**: to show a difference between two things

To **draw a conclusion**: to decide something is true after some consideration

To **draw on**: to use past experience to assist your present decision or action

CHAPTER 13: PERSONALITY

Before you begin Chapter 13:

*l. Review Chapter 12 of both the Kalat text and the Maki guid*e to be sure you have covered all key concepts and terms.

2. Next, pay attention to the organization of Chapter 13 to predict what is coming.

Key Verbs: imitate strive transform represent repress modify standardize

Predict the chapter content: Scanning:

Scanning allows the reader to look over a reading passage for only l specific kind of information. **Practice now locating only the following. Then list the answers:**

l. Names of prominent theorists (famous persons who developed theories) covered in the chapter:

a. **Sigmund Freud**= focused on sexual motivation

b.

c.

Hint: Check "The Message, p. 483 to see if you were right.

2. Terms for key approaches to study of personality: (The first is supplied for you)

a. Psychodynamic Approach =personality related to interplay of conflicting inner forces, some unconscious

b.

c.

d.

3. Freud's "stages of pyschosexual development:"

a. Oral stage= stimulation of mouth during infancy

b.

c.

d.

4. Freud's "defense mechanisms" (defense=a mental process of self protection)
a.
b.
c.
d.
e.
f.
g.
h.
Author's opinion of Freud's theories:

>>>>>**KEY IDEA:**
The author seems to state that, as with most areas of psychology, personality is full of variables. In the "Message," p.483, he states, **"...*a full description of personality emerges from a combination of research approaches.*" (Can you find evidence for that statement throughout this chapter?)**

Using textual cues to understand chapter content: Comparison and Contrast terms and expressions used like transitions*: Subordinate clauses signals.*

Important: *The author often uses terms and expressions showing comparison to signal the reader that specific theories and theorists differ from one another.*

Scan for examples using the following terms to establish a contrast:

Unlike (p.477)

Whereas (p.479)

Rather than (p. 508)

Scan for key definitions:

In the section "Personality Traits," scan for the following:

1. The definition of the word **"trait;"** write it below:

Trait: _____

2. Five general personality traits:
a.

b.

c.

d.

e.

3. The author's conclusion on the results of studies of monozygotic and dizygotic twins :

4. The author's advice about personality tests in general: (Hint: See pages 511-513.)

<u>Word Attack</u>:

Circle the words from the chapter that seem to describe your own personality traits.
Group the words by listing them in their appropriate category, *noun* or *adjective*. Refer to
the following pages for ideas: p. 498-499 and p. 489. Also look back to previous chapters.

neurotic   neurotics   agreeableness   agreeable   extroversion   extrovert

open   openness   conscientious   conscientiousness

sociability   ambition   sociable   ambitious   anxiety   anxious

<u>Nouns:</u>   <u>Adjectives:</u>

CHAPTER 14: SOCIAL PSYCHOLOGY

Before you begin Chapter 14:

l. *Review Chapter 13 of both the Kalat text and the Maki guide* to be sure you have covered all key concepts and terms.

2. *Next, pay attention to the organization of Ch. 14* to predict what is coming.

Key Verbs: attribute   reject   share   conform   lean   pressure   defeat   cooperate

---

Circle the verb **"attribute"** in the *Key Verbs* above. **Notice its definition**:
Attribute:
To believe something to be the result of ; to say something is responsible for a specific action or quality.

Now read the author's definition of the term, **"social psychology:"** Social psychology is "the study of social behavior and influence…to include such matters as attitudes, persuasion, and certain aspects of self understanding."

Why might the key verb "attribute" be important in this chapter as we examine influences on behavior?

What kinds of connections can you find among the other key verbs? Consider the following:

share   conform   pressure   cooperate

What happens when people share information and experiences? What happens to attitudes and behavior? Are the consequences positive or negative or possibly both? Can attitudes change over time? Why?

>>>>> **KEY IDEA: The author summarizes the components of "attitudes" on p. 524. Complete his statement below as you find it in the chapter by filling in the missing phrases:**
Your attitudes include an emotional component (…._____),
a cognitive component (_____), and a behavioral component
(_____).

Using textual cues to understand chapter content: **Reference:**

Often a writer makes a statement which refers back to a previous statement without repeating the previous statement. Notice the following examples:

Example:

Other things being equal, the first information we learn about someone influences us more than later information does...This tendency.... (*This tendency* refers back to the concept just explained, that is, being influenced by first information most (P.517).

Example:

In contrast, when people listen to a message on a topic of little importance to them, they pay more attention to such factors as the speaker's appearance and reputation or the sheer number of arguments presented, regardless of their quality. This superficial approach...
(*This superficial approach* refers back to the concept just explained, that is, people's tendency to pay more attention to appearance and reputation of the speaker if the topic is not important to them.)

Now you try to identify the core, or essential, idea to which the underlined reference applies. Underline *the key part* of that original idea to indicate the relationship.

---

1. On certain topics, however, many people form strong, unshakeable attitudes based on almost no information at all. <u>One such topic</u> is the death penalty.

2.Beginning in the 1930's the party's membership and support began to dwindle, until eventually the party stopped nominating candidates. Was <u>that</u> because the Socialists had failed?

3. We like people who resemble ourselves—in any way. In one striking illustration of <u>this tendency</u>, students were asked to read a very unflattering description of Grigori Rasputin, the "mad monk of Russia," and then rate Rasputin's personality on several scales such as.....

4. You can probably think of examples in which a speaker began by stressing his or her resemblance to the audience. "I remember when I was a student like you." "I grew up in a town similar to this one." " I believe in family values, and I'm sure you do too." <u>This technique</u> ....

5. The general principle is that if you get people to do something they would not otherwise do by means of a minimum reward or a tiny threat, so that they are acting voluntarily or almost voluntarily, they will change their attitudes to defend what they are doing in order to reduce cognitive dissonance. <u>This procedure</u> is a particularly powerful way of changing people's attitudes because people are actively participating, not just quietly listening to someone....

6. According to this approach, men prefer young women because women reach menopause and therefore stop being fertile at about age 40-50. Men have therefore

evolved a tendency to find younger (probably fertile) women more attractive than older women. <u>This theory</u> sounds rather persuasive, although it is difficult to test.

Other textual cues: *Italics* and bold **print**:
Review the sections with italics and/or bold print. Most of them contain key chapter concepts.

Questions about chapter content: Review Pre reading questions **in each section of the chapter** as well as questions in *Concept Check* and *Summary* sections. **Create your own also.**

<u>**Word Attack: The prefix "self"+**</u>
You already, no doubt, know words like *self*-confident or *self*-interest. **Using the prefix *self* to form words from this chapter, fill in the appropriate choice for each blank.** Choose from the list provided:

self-defeating   self-monitoring   self-handicapping   self-serving   self-esteem

---

Self-defeating: preventing your own success
Self-monitoring: watching or checking on yourself to control behavior
Self-handicapping: creating a disadvantage for yourself
Self-serving: serving your own interests first
Self-esteem: valuing your own worth

1. Attributions that we adopt in an effort to maximize our credit for success and minimize our blame for failure are called _____ biases (p.522).

2. People can also protect their image by adopting _____ when they intentionally put themselves at a disadvantage to provide an excuse for an expected failure (p. 522).

3. When you enter an unfamiliar situation, do you immediately look around to determine what other people are doing and what is expected of you? Some do. They are known as high _____ ... (p. 525).
Note: In #3, above, use the plural noun rather than the gerund (-in) form.

4. Cognitive dissonance is a state of unpleasant tension that people experience when they hold contradictory attitudes or when they behave in a way that is inconsistent with their attitudes, especially if they perceive that inconsistency as a threat to their _____ (p.531).

Which two choices above are basically synonymous (have the same meaning)?
_____ and _____ .

CHAPTER 15: ABNORMALITIES AND THERAPIES I: GENERAL PRINCIPLES

Note: Before you begin Chapter 15:

1. *Review Ch. 1 of both the Kalat text and the Maki Study Guide* to be sure you have covered all key concepts and terms.
2. *Next, pay attention to the organization of Chapter 15* to predict what is coming.

Key Verbs: define   observe   regard   classify   diagnose   function   represent

Circle all the terms above that deal with *putting something into a clear category*.

Are clear categories of human behavior always easy to establish? Why not?   Keep that concept in mind as you move through Chapter 15, a presentation on abnormal human behavior and types of therapy.

>>>>>**KEY IDEA:**
Look for ways the author *signals distinctions*, differences between specific types of behavior and forms of therapy ; pay attention to the view point, stated in the following quote taken from the Chapter 15 *Summary*, **"Although psychologists and psychiatrists try to be objective and scientific in identifying abnormal behavior, some judgments are necessarily difficult and *dependent on value judgments*."**

Paraphrase, that is explain in your own words, what the author wants us to understand in this quote about categorizing people's behavior.
_____

_____

The author emphasizes another factor that affects how we evaluate people's behavior.
"Each time and place has interpreted abnormal behavior according to its own world view."
(p. 563)

Explain the author's comments from the second quote below:

_____

_____.

The author uses many expressions to differentiate/contrast theories, personality disorders, **etc.**
Knowing how such contrasts are introduced can help the reader.
Look at the following; then write the number for type of contrast that could follow:

---

l. names /lists different examples
2.compares thinking/methods of different psychologists
3. contrasts thinking /methods of different time periods.
4. contrasts acceptable and unacceptable interpretations according to author's view

___at one time.../by the early 1990's...

___abnormal behavior has three major aspects:

___classify each patient along five separate axes (lists)

___In some types of psychotherapy.../in others.../still others

___At first, Freud.../He soon abandoned that approach...

___ Resistance can take many forms...

___ ...but unlike psychoanalysts...

___ That ruling may sound reasonable, but

___ The problem is not ...but...

___ What distinguishes family therapists is...

___ Table 15.3 contrasts five major types of psychotherapy...

___ Instead, they practice...

___ The advantage of this system is.../The disadvantage is...

___ Here we are not interested in...To draw a conclusion, we need...

___ And yet you know...

___ Until the 1950's.../With the advent of ...

___ Several studies have compared...

___ Here we shall consider three examples...

Be an attentive reader: Be familiar with these ways of signaling a contrast coming.

<u>**Categorizing with charts:**</u>

The author uses illustrations of various kinds to contrast different information also. Take a moment to survey Chapter 15 to find what ways graphics are used to compare and contrast various behavior forms, related causes and therapies.

Keep these graphic aids in mind while making your own chart of contrasts you want to remember. See example for one type of categorizing activity below. Complete with the information from Ch.15. (Then try charting DSM-IV categories **discussed in the chapter.**)

<u>Example: General Trends in Psychotherapy (pp. 575-577)</u>
<u>Brief Therapy:</u> limited therapy --client +therapist agree on length (eg., 2 mo.)
advantage= less cost; disadvantage= not enough for those w/more problems
<u>Group Therapy:</u>
<u>Self-Help Groups:</u>

<u>Note:</u> If you are working with a classmate, be sure to share your charts to increase your understanding of the contrasts covered in this chapter.

Hint: **When charting information from a reading, list major categories in capital letters and supporting examples and details in smaller print, indented to catch your eye.** Later you can highlight, underline, asterisk (*star), check, circle, etc., the points you forget.

Word Attack:

Compound words derived from prefixes: **Two separate words combined to express a concept:**

Under+lying= underlying (adjective)= being the real explanation for some behavior whose cause is not obvious.

> Underlying **drives**
> Underlying **sexual motives**
> Underlying **power and superiority motives**

Used to describe unconscious behavior, *underlying* characteristics or behavior help explain the real reason why people act in specific ways.

Hyphenated words: two separate words joined by a hyphen (-) to express a concept in which one characteristic or concept is influenced by another.

Examples:
Anxiety + provoke =anxiety-provoking (adjective)
Self + help= self help (adjective or noun)
Life + threaten= life-threatening (adjective)
Person + center = person-centered (adjective)

Idioms:

To give a damn: to care about something (colloquial)
"But psychotherapy does little good unless a client gives the proverbial damn."

Other things being equal: Assuming that other factors do not change the situation…

To use a trial-and-error approach: To try to solve a problem or accomplish something without any specific plan.

CHAPTER 16: ANXIETY AND AVOIDANCE DISORDERS

Note: **Before you begin Chapter 16**:

1. *Review Ch.15 of both the Kalat text and the Maki Study Guide* to be sure you have covered all key concepts and terms.
2. **Next, pay attention to the organization of this section of the guide for non native speakers of English.** It will give additional support as you move from chapter to chapter.

Key Verbs: avoid   cope   react   fear   embarrass   extinguish   reinforce   characterize

---

Chapter Organization: Categorization –a way to organize and remember

We have seen how key ideas are introduced through everything from headings to topic sentences to illustrations. Often main ideas are also repeated several times within a passage. Help yourself cope with the many descriptions and terms in this text. Summarize what you read. As in Ch. 15, *creating charts to contain short, specific notes is one way to cope with many categories of information.*

>>>>>**KEY IDEA:**

In the introduction to Chapter 16, the author stresses the importance of understanding the differences between psychological disorders. He states, " *Medical progress ...has been marked by increasing ability to distinguish one disorder from another...and* "*much of the progress in abnormal psychology has come from making appropriate distinctions between one disorder and another and developing treatments aimed at specific disorders.*"

Brainstorm ways to categorize numerous psychological disorders using graphic illustrations **that contain adequate room for notes on the specific characteristics of each disorder.**

An example follows:

PHOBIAS

	(+) Present in Anxiety Disorder	(-) Absent in Anxiety Disoder
Features:		
Learned behavior	+	
Avoidance behavior	+	
Cyclic (series of) occurrence:		---
Interferes with normal living	+	
Causes physical reaction	+	
Unpredictable/non specific fear		

You try: Add just 1-2 more features to the list shown. (Limit the number to recall .)
Hint: Try including something on successful experiments or therapies.

Now practice writing a short description of *phobias,* **based on the information in the grid (chart shown above).**

Now: Refer back to the section of Ch. 16 to check your description of this disorder.
On a paper, create other such organizing tools to help you remember characteristic features of the many disorders described in this chapter. **For example, chart and compare *phobias* with *panic disorders* or compare *obsessive compulsive disorders*.**

The Message: **Throughout the Kalat text, the author has summarized central points for each section of the chapter in *"The Message."*** Paraphrase the central point of the section on *anxieties and avoidances* from reading comments in *The Message* on the relationship between specific disorders and an individual's cognitions (conscious thought) and emotions:

_____

_____

<u>Other Organizational Aids: Outlining</u>

In an earlier chapter, we practiced <u>outlining</u>, *that is ordering and categorizing major and minor points* **of information, putting *main points first* and *examples and details next*. Look over the following outline from the section on** "Mood Disorders." **Fill in the missing information, paying attention to** *the order of the ideas.*

MOOD DISORDERS

I. <u>Depression</u>
  A. Characteristics of depressed persons
    1. Lack of normal interest in life, which persists for several months or more
    2.
    3. Sleeping and eating abnormalities
  B. Types of depression disorders:
    1. Bipolar disorder
            a. periods of depression
            b.
    2. Seasonal Affective Disorder

  C. Factors influencing depression
        1. Female problem solving patterns
        2.

    D. Feelings of Failure: Self blame
    E. Therapies for depression
        1. Cognitive therapy: helping patients discover errors in their thinking patterns

2.
3. Electric shock
II. Suicide
    A. Gender differences
    B. Associated factors from Table in Ch.16 of Text:

Now: Try to create your own outline for the section on *Substance Related Disorders* or *Schizophrenia*.

Word Attack:

Literal vs Figurative language:

In this chapter, the author discusses the communication problems that occur with schizophrenic individuals who cannot understand proverbs, for example, because they "take things literally." (Review the following illustrations from Ch. 16, pages 627-628, which show an example of such thinking.)

    Proverb: People who live in glass houses shouldn't throw stones.
    Interpretation: *It would break the glass.* (Actual meaning: *Don't criticize others.*)

    Proverb: All that glitters is not gold.
    Interpretation: *It might be brass.* (Actual meaning: *Some things are not what they appear.*)

In each case here, the person interpreting the proverb never thought of how the proverb was not being used to describe what the words actually said but rather as an example with deeper meaning. Native speakers understand proverbs need to be interpreted as analogies, comparisons.

Look over the following *idioms*, also used in this chapter. Note that their meaning is different than what the actual words mean individually but they do not represent a "life lesson" as do proverbs.

To run in families: to pass from one generation to the next through heredity
To address the question: to answer a specific question

Review: Now use these special strategies for understanding and remembering this material, not only when you read your texts but also when reviewing for examinations.

Take the guesswork out of succeeding in college with . . .

College Survival Guide:
Hints and References to Aid College Students,
Fourth Edition
by Bruce Rowe, Los Angeles Pierce College

How can I finance my college education?
Can I get credit through examination?
What can I do to get better grades on my exams?

You'll find the answers to these questions and more in Bruce Rowe's 77-page paperback. If you're like many students just starting out at college, the whole experience can be somewhat overwhelming. By the time you've figured out what you need to know to succeed, you've already wasted a lot of time and money going in wrong directions!

Now, for just $5.95*, you can get a concise guide that will give you practical information on such topics as:

- How to manage your time
- How to study for and take exams
- How to use the Internet to do research for assigned papers
- How to finance your education
- How to maintain your concentration
- How to get credit through examination
- How and when to use the credit/no credit option
- And much more!

*Download the College Survival Guide from the Internet for just $5.95!
Visit us at http://www.brookscole.com. If you do NOT have Internet access or would prefer to order by phone or mail, you can purchase the manual for $11.95 by calling toll free (800) 354-9706, or by filling out and returning the coupon provided.

ORDER FORM

Yes, I want to purchase: *College Survival Guide: Hints and References to Aid College Students, Fourth Edition* (ISBN: 0-534-35569-2)

Residents of: AL, AZ, CA, CT, CO, FL, GA, IL, IN, KS   _____ **Copies x $11.95** _____
                KY, LA, MA, MD, MI, MN, MO, NC, NJ,   **Subtotal**   _____
                NY, OH, PA, RI, SC, TN, TX, UT, VA, WA,   **Tax**   _____
                WI must add appropriate state sales tax.   **Handling**   **$4.00**
                                                                     Total Due _____

Payment Options

_____ Check or money order enclosed *or*

Bill my _____ VISA _____ MasterCard _____ American Express

Card Number: _____

Expiration Date:_____

Signature: _____

Please ship my order to:

Name _____

Institution _____

Street Address _____

City _____ State _____ Zip+4 _____ + _____

Telephone (   ) _____

Your credit card will not be billed until your order is shipped. Prices subject to change without notice. We will refund payment for unshipped out-of-stock titles after 120 days and for not-yet-published titles after 180 days unless an earlier date is requested in writing from you.

Mail to: Wadsworth Publishing Company

Source Code 9BCPY175
Ten Davis Drive
Belmont, California 94002-3098
Phone: (800) 354-9706
Fax: (800) 522-4923

Photocopy, fold, close, and return with payment